Shojo Beat

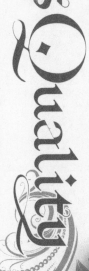

Queen's Quality

1

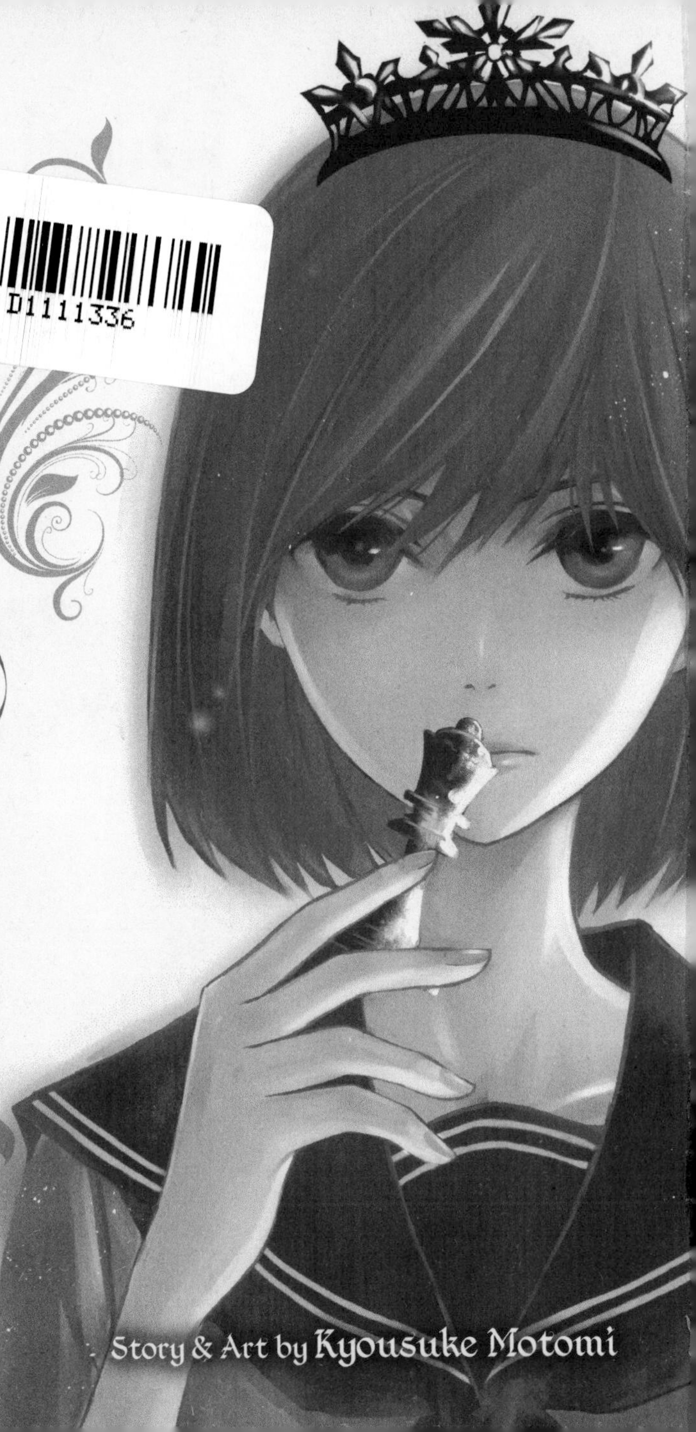

Story & Art by Kyousuke Motomi

Queen's Quality

CONTENTS

1

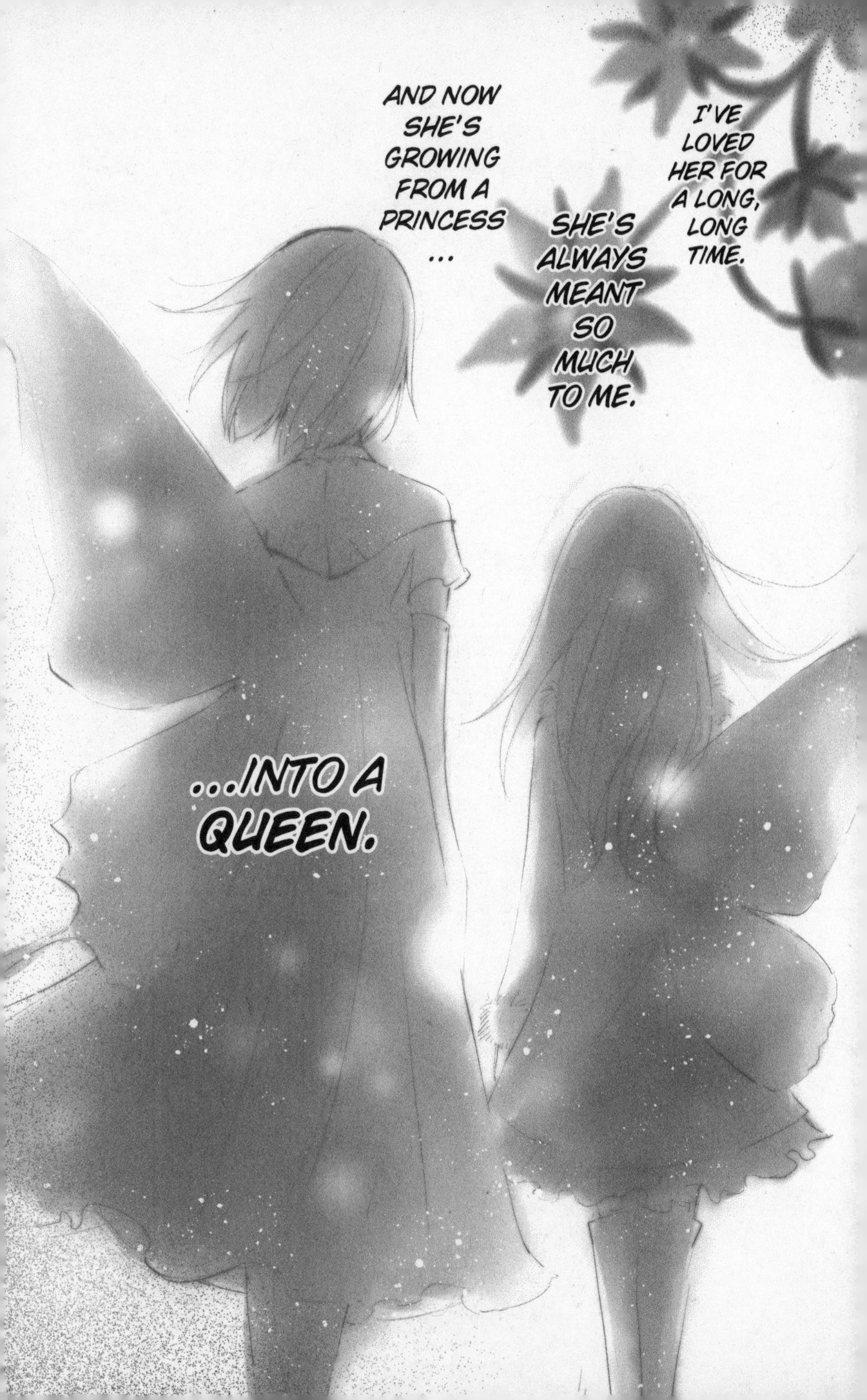
I'VE LOVED HER FOR A LONG, LONG TIME.
SHE'S ALWAYS MEANT SO MUCH TO ME.
AND NOW SHE'S GROWING FROM A PRINCESS...
...INTO A QUEEN.

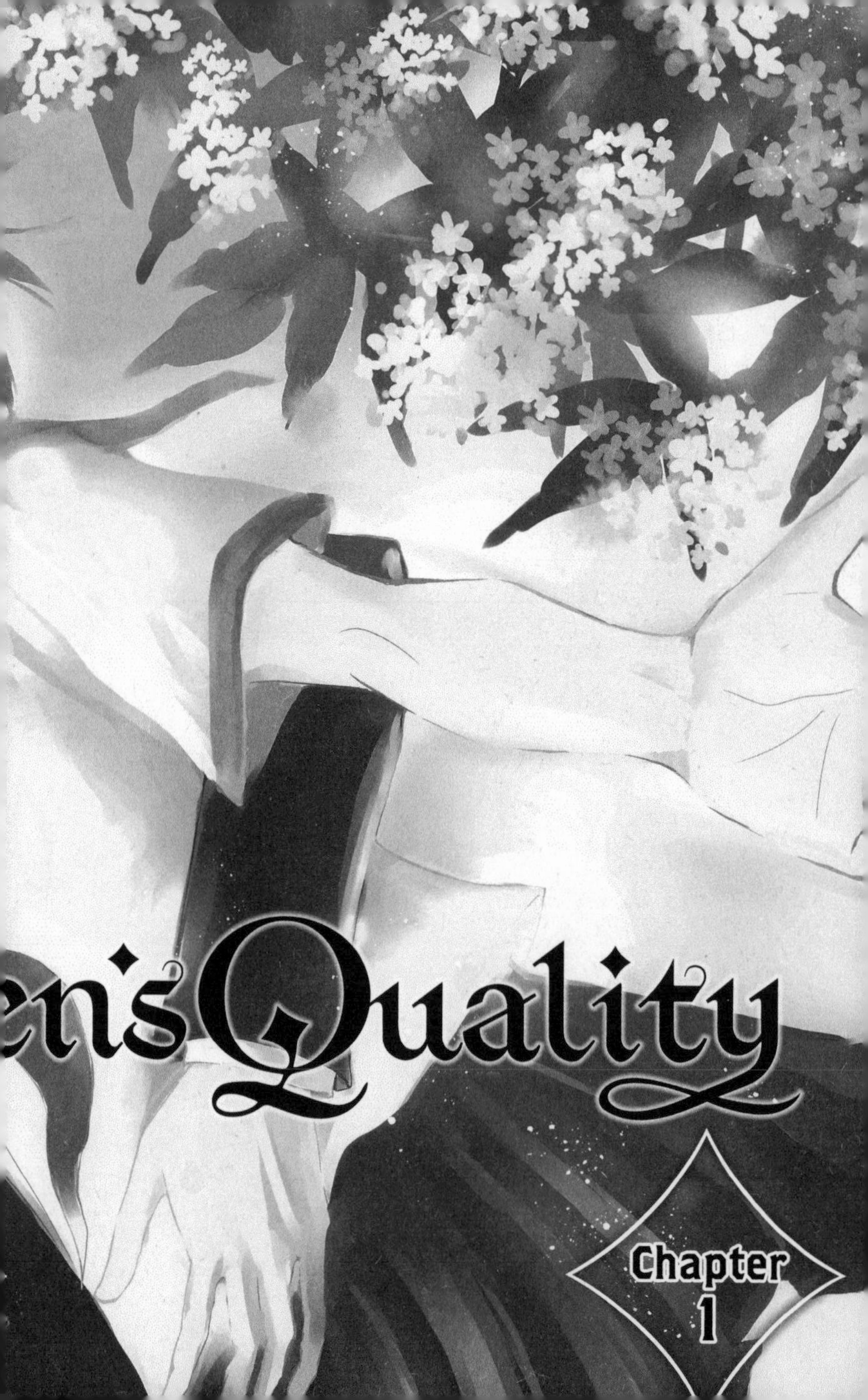
ens Quality
Chapter
1

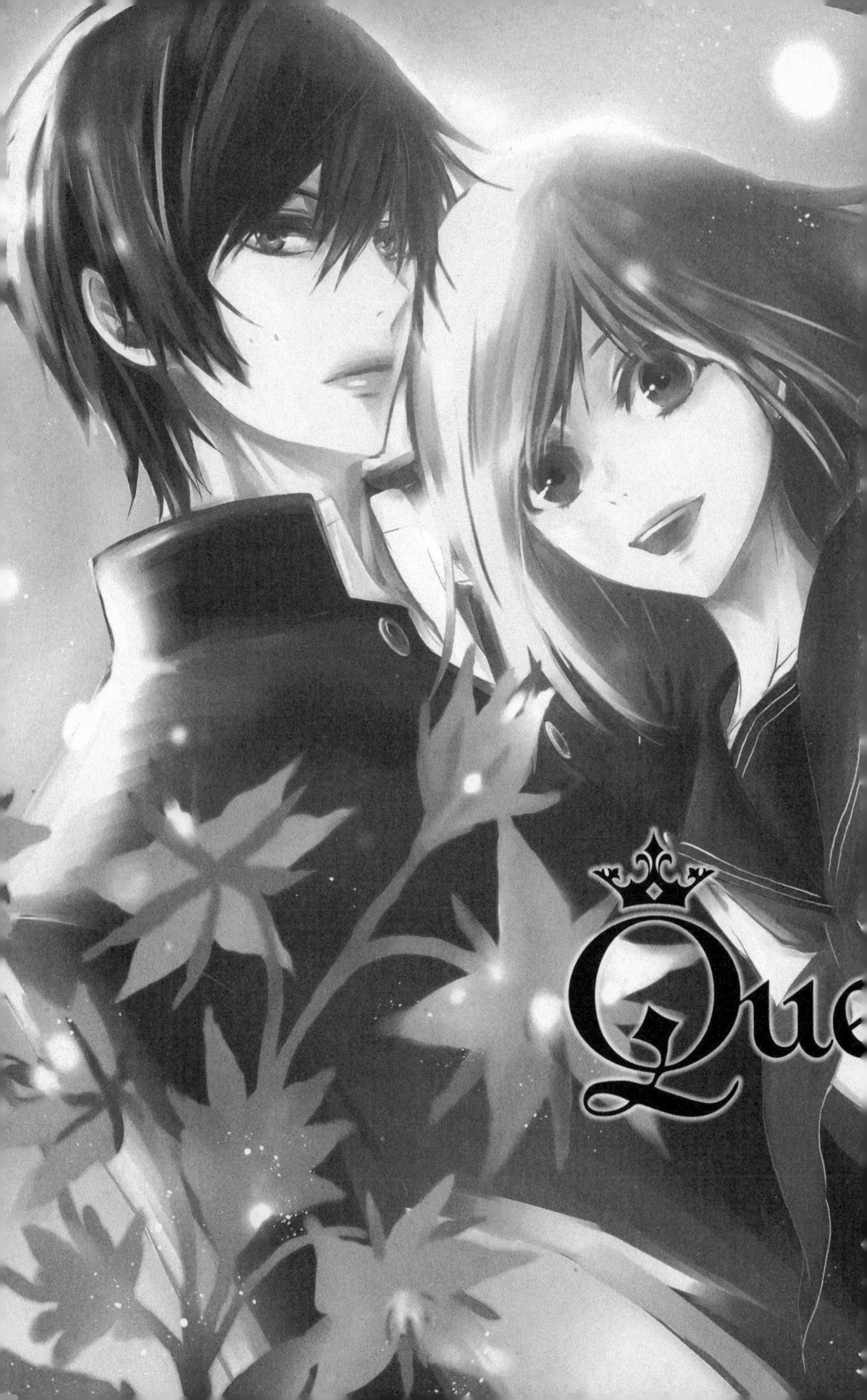
Que

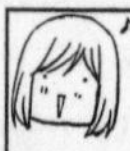

Hi, everyone!
This is Kyousuke Motomi.
Thank you for picking up
volume 1 of *Queen's Quality.*

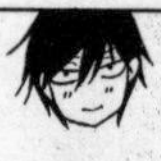

The story has a new title now, but it's actually a continuation of the three-volume series *QQ Sweeper.* I hope you'll enjoy it just as much under its new name! And if you're a reader who isn't familiar with *QQ Sweeper,* I hope you'll still enjoy *Queen's Quality!*

Queen's Quality is a story of love and grime—a tale of mental cleansing! It's a love story that occasionally includes bloodshed and bug squishing.

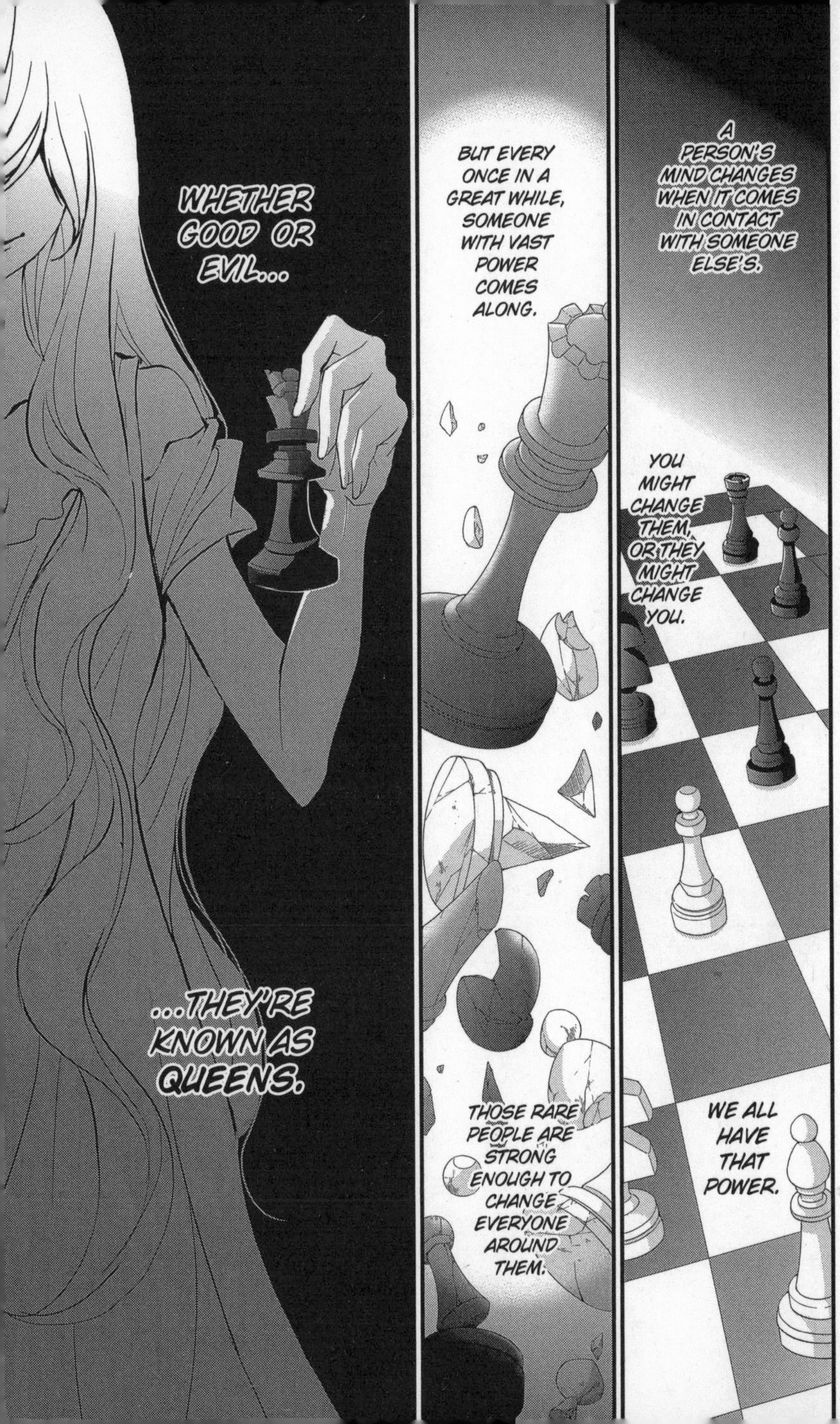

A PERSON'S MIND CHANGES WHEN IT COMES IN CONTACT WITH SOMEONE ELSE'S.
YOU MIGHT CHANGE THEM, OR THEY MIGHT CHANGE YOU.
WE ALL HAVE THAT POWER.
BUT EVERY ONCE IN A GREAT WHILE, SOMEONE WITH VAST POWER COMES ALONG.
THOSE RARE PEOPLE ARE STRONG ENOUGH TO CHANGE EVERYONE AROUND THEM.
WHETHER GOOD OR EVIL...
...THEY'RE KNOWN AS QUEENS.

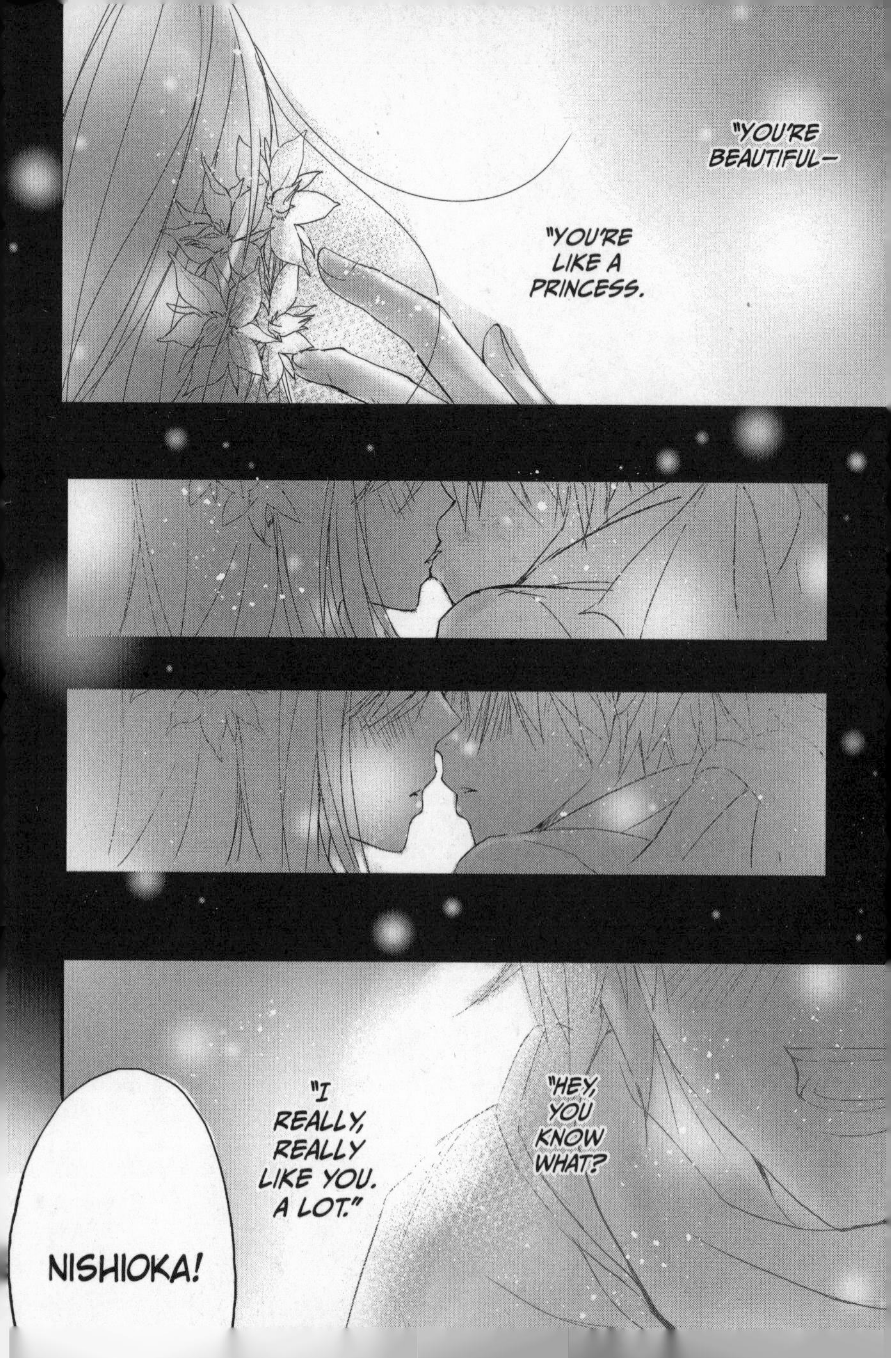
"YOU'RE BEAUTIFUL—
"YOU'RE LIKE A PRINCESS.
"HEY, YOU KNOW WHAT?
"I REALLY, REALLY LIKE YOU. A LOT."
NISHIOKA!

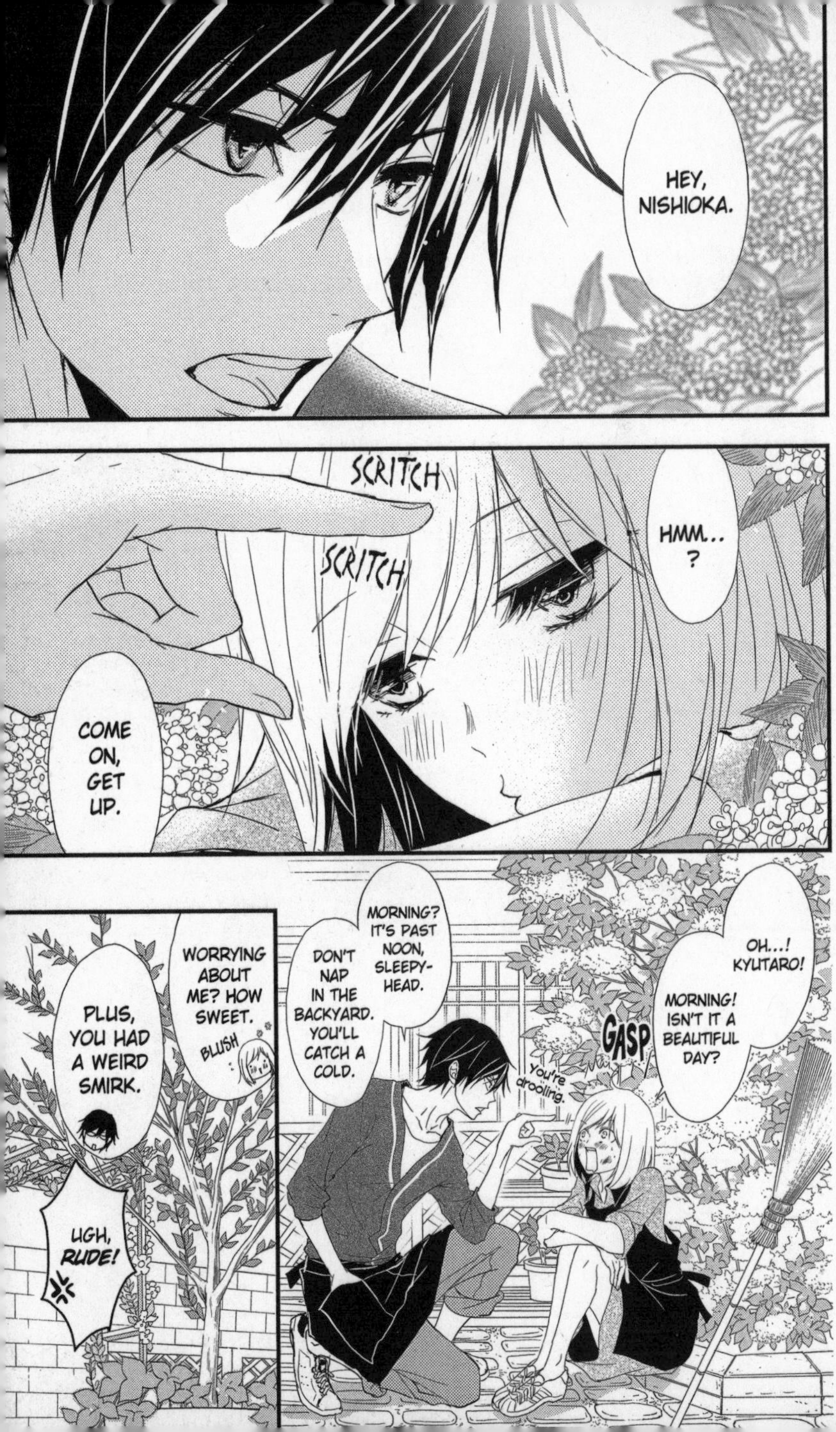
HEY, NISHIOKA.
HMM...?
SCRITCH
SCRITCH
COME ON, GET UP.
OH...! KYUTARO!
MORNING! ISN'T IT A BEAUTIFUL DAY?
GASP
You're drooling.
MORNING? IT'S PAST NOON, SLEEPY-HEAD.
DON'T NAP IN THE BACKYARD. YOU'LL CATCH A COLD.
WORRYING ABOUT ME? HOW SWEET.
BLUSH
PLUS, YOU HAD A WEIRD SMIRK.
UGH, RUDE!

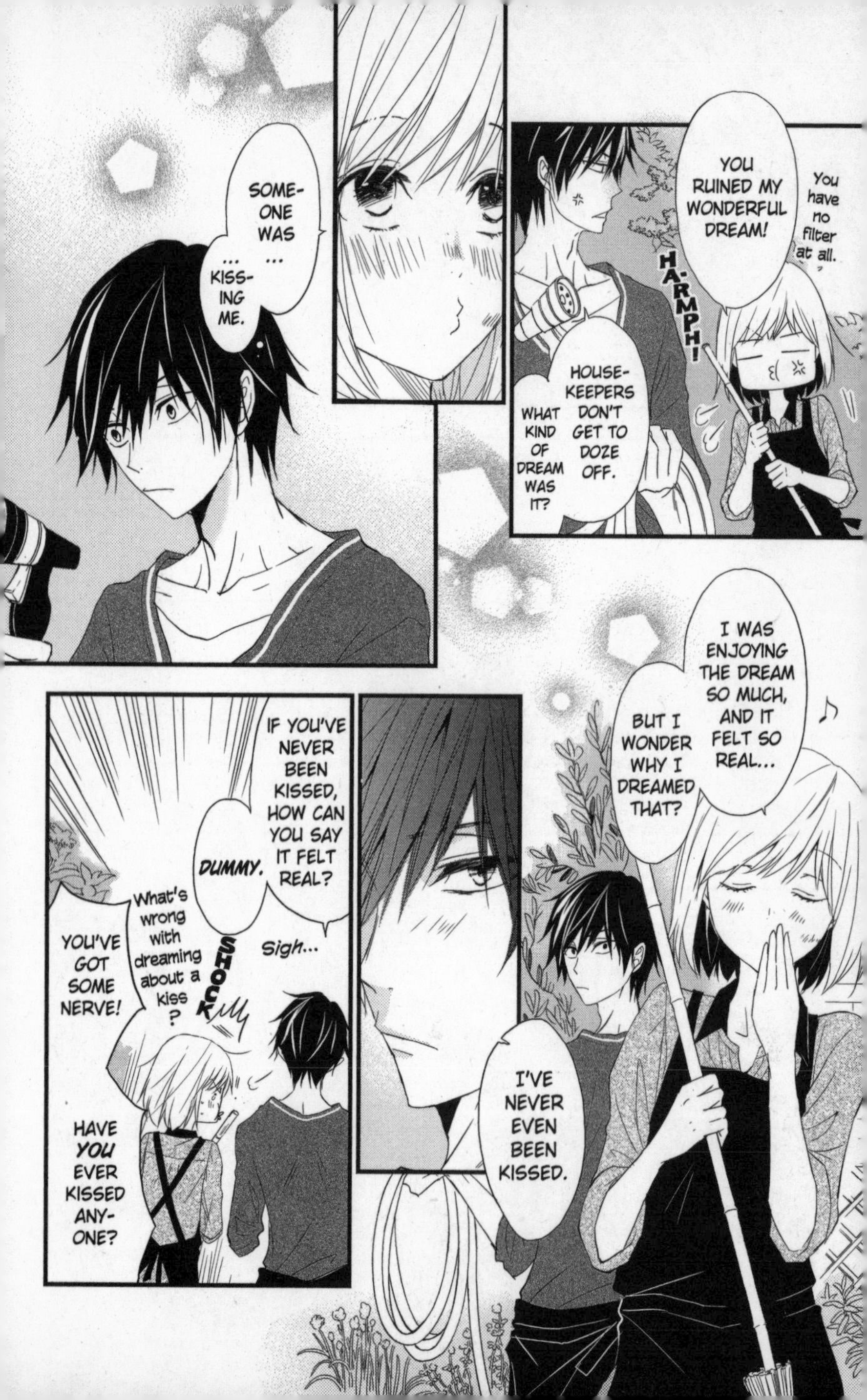
YOU RUINED MY WONDERFUL DREAM!
You have no filter at all.
HARMPH!
HOUSE-KEEPERS DON'T GET TO DOZE OFF.
WHAT KIND OF DREAM WAS IT?
SOME-ONE WAS ... ... KISS-ING ME.
I WAS ENJOYING THE DREAM SO MUCH, AND IT FELT SO REAL...
BUT I WONDER WHY I DREAMED THAT?
I'VE NEVER EVEN BEEN KISSED.
IF YOU'VE NEVER BEEN KISSED, HOW CAN YOU SAY IT FELT REAL?
DUMMY.
Sigh...
SHOCK
What's wrong with dreaming about a kiss?
YOU'VE GOT SOME NERVE!
HAVE YOU EVER KISSED ANY-ONE?

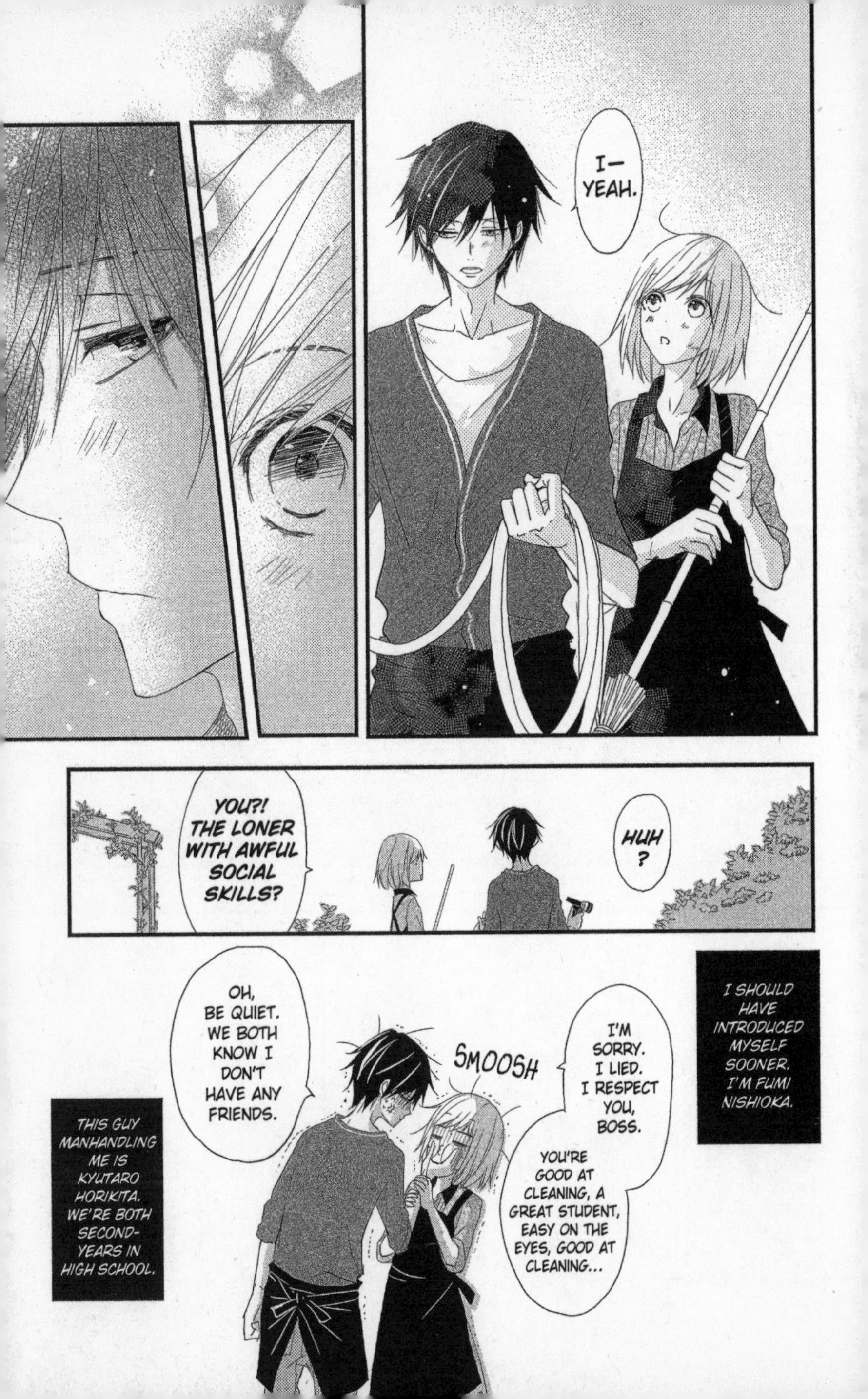
I— YEAH.
HUH ?
YOU?! THE LONER WITH AWFUL SOCIAL SKILLS?
I SHOULD HAVE INTRODUCED MYSELF SOONER. I'M FUMI NISHIOKA.
I'M SORRY. I LIED. I RESPECT YOU, BOSS.
YOU'RE GOOD AT CLEANING, A GREAT STUDENT, EASY ON THE EYES, GOOD AT CLEANING...
SMOOSH
OH, BE QUIET. WE BOTH KNOW I DON'T HAVE ANY FRIENDS.
THIS GUY MANHANDLING ME IS KYUTARO HORIKITA. WE'RE BOTH SECOND-YEARS IN HIGH SCHOOL.

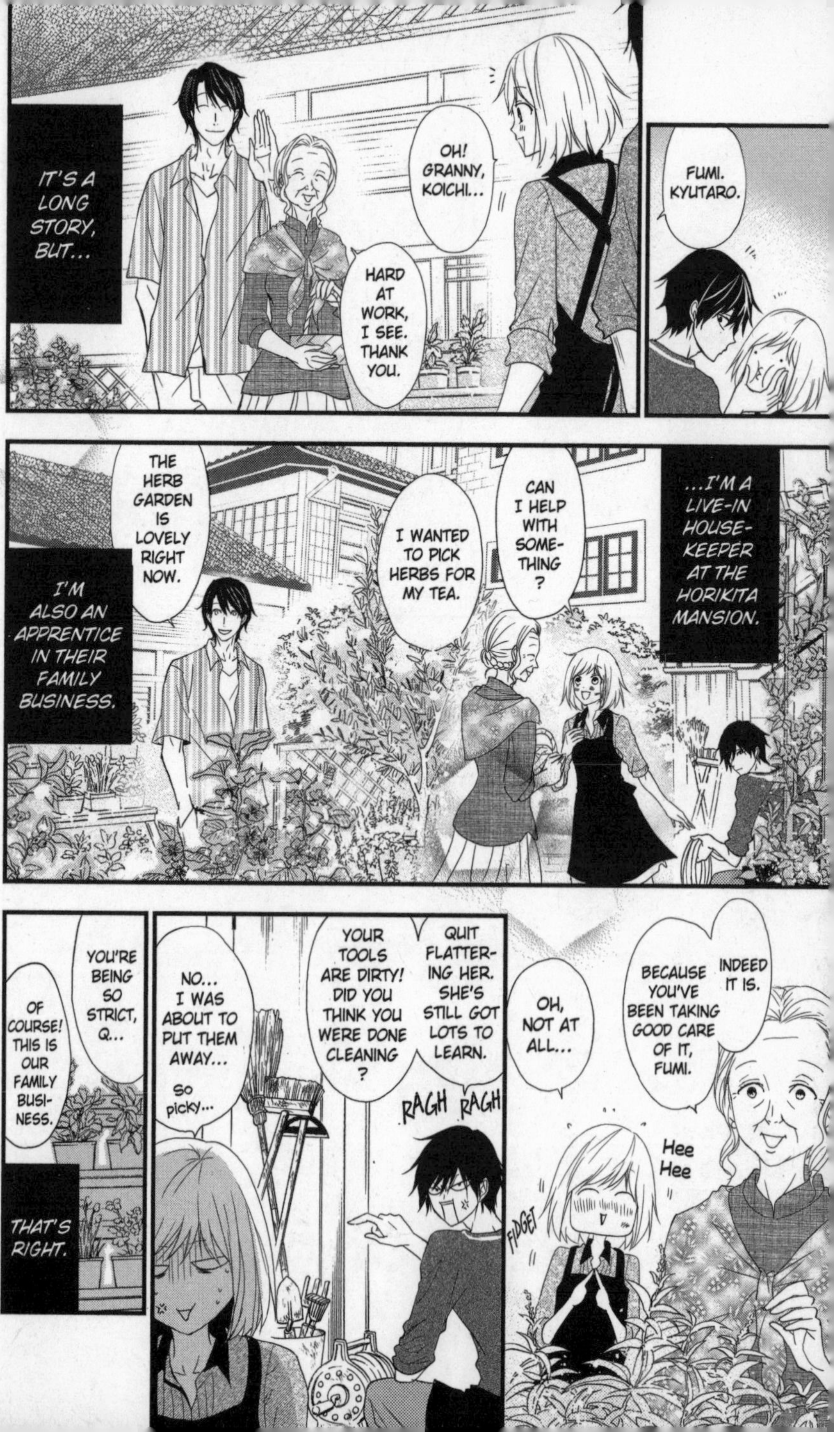
FUMI. KYUTARO.
OH! GRANNY, KOICHI...
HARD AT WORK, I SEE. THANK YOU.
IT'S A LONG STORY, BUT...
...I'M A LIVE-IN HOUSEKEEPER AT THE HORIKITA MANSION.
CAN I HELP WITH SOMETHING?
I WANTED TO PICK HERBS FOR MY TEA.
THE HERB GARDEN IS LOVELY RIGHT NOW.
I'M ALSO AN APPRENTICE IN THEIR FAMILY BUSINESS.
INDEED IT IS.
BECAUSE YOU'VE BEEN TAKING GOOD CARE OF IT, FUMI.
Hee Hee
OH, NOT AT ALL...
FIDGET
QUIT FLATTERING HER. SHE'S STILL GOT LOTS TO LEARN.
YOUR TOOLS ARE DIRTY! DID YOU THINK YOU WERE DONE CLEANING?
RAGH RAGH
NO... I WAS ABOUT TO PUT THEM AWAY...
So picky...
YOU'RE BEING SO STRICT, Q...
OF COURSE! THIS IS OUR FAMILY BUSINESS.
THAT'S RIGHT.

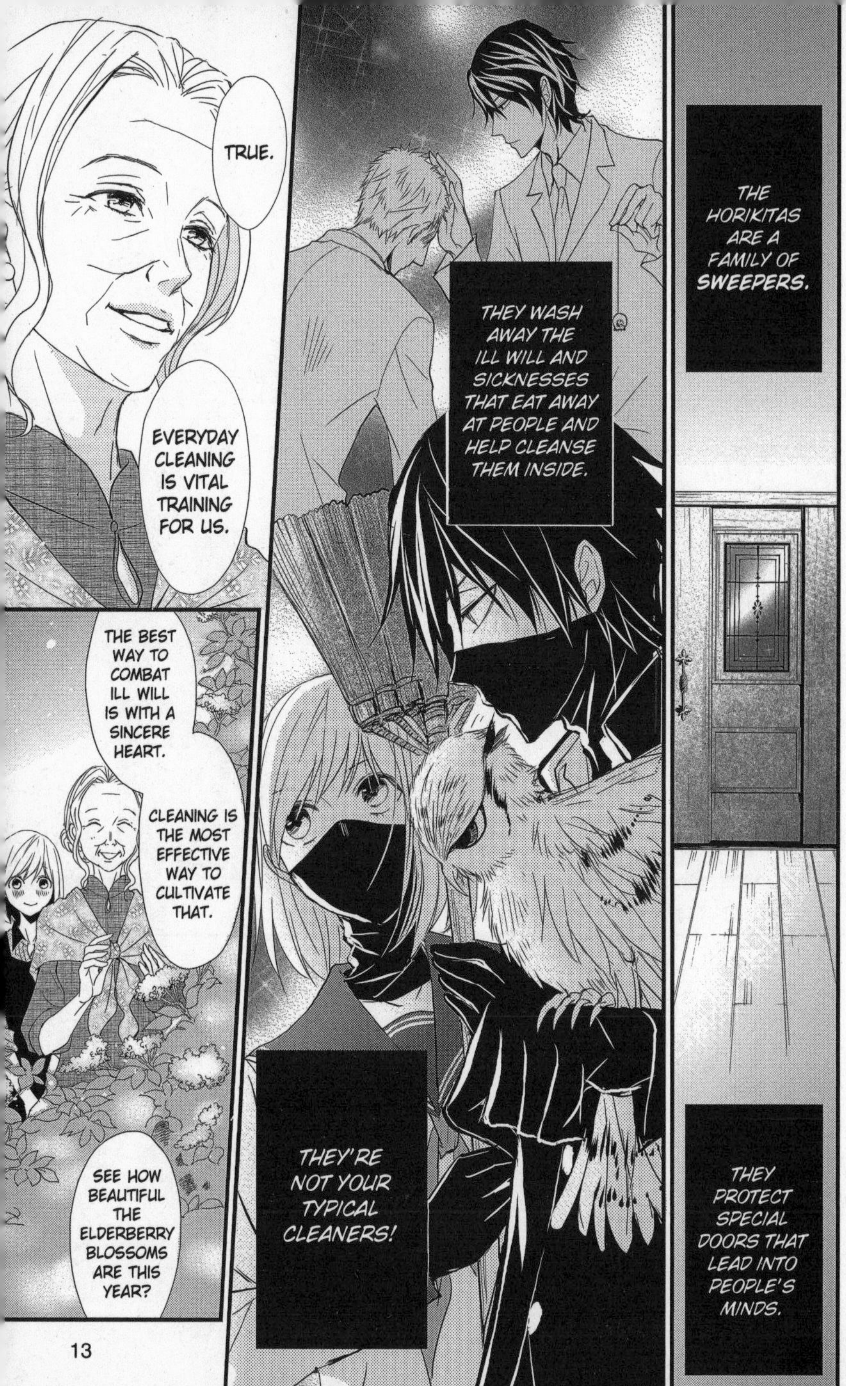
THE HORIKITAS ARE A FAMILY OF SWEEPERS.
THEY PROTECT SPECIAL DOORS THAT LEAD INTO PEOPLE'S MINDS.
THEY WASH AWAY THE ILL WILL AND SICKNESSES THAT EAT AWAY AT PEOPLE AND HELP CLEANSE THEM INSIDE.
THEY'RE NOT YOUR TYPICAL CLEANERS!
TRUE.
EVERYDAY CLEANING IS VITAL TRAINING FOR US.
THE BEST WAY TO COMBAT ILL WILL IS WITH A SINCERE HEART.
CLEANING IS THE MOST EFFECTIVE WAY TO CULTIVATE THAT.
SEE HOW BEAUTIFUL THE ELDERBERRY BLOSSOMS ARE THIS YEAR?

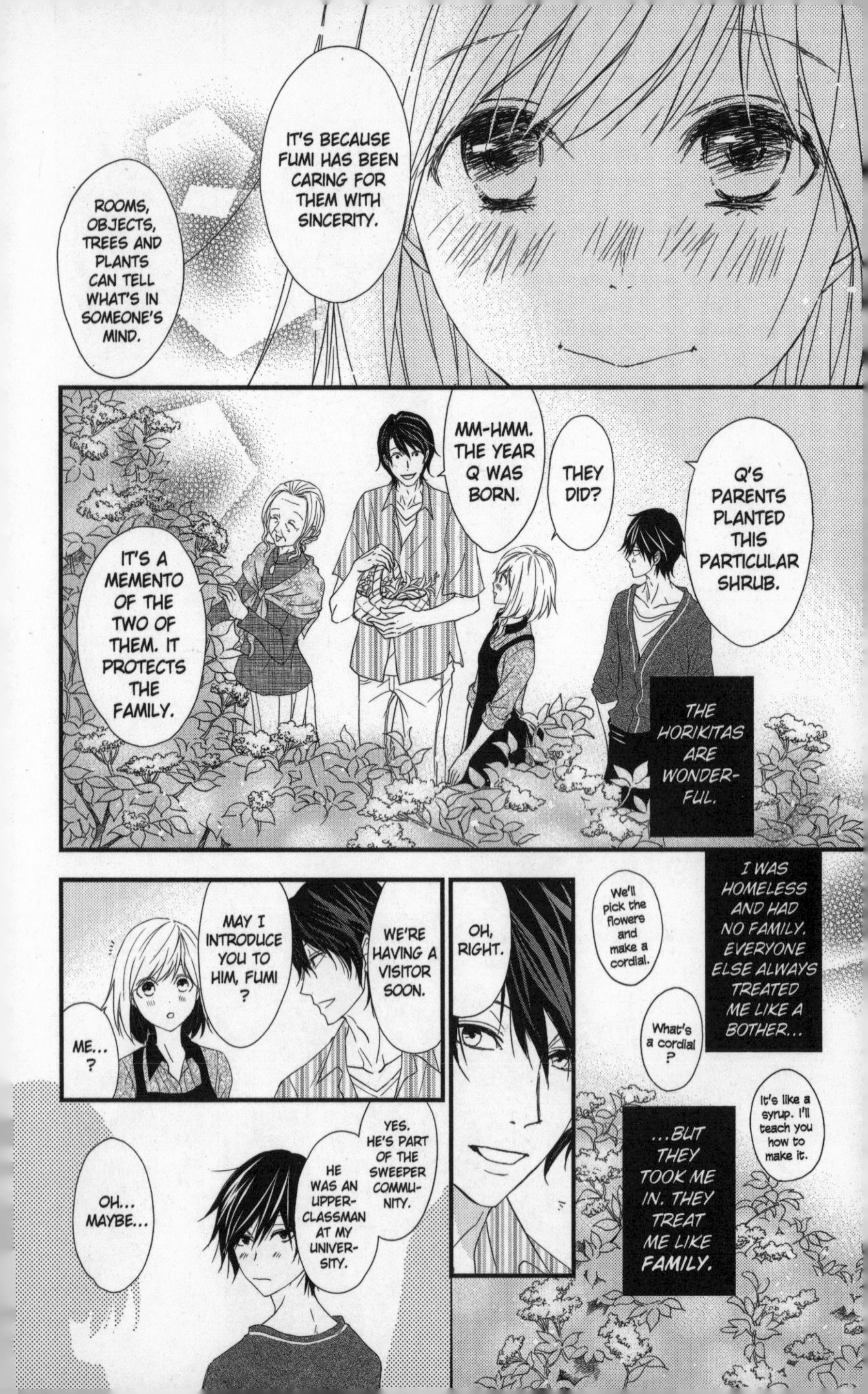
IT'S BECAUSE FUMI HAS BEEN CARING FOR THEM WITH SINCERITY.
ROOMS, OBJECTS, TREES AND PLANTS CAN TELL WHAT'S IN SOMEONE'S MIND.
Q'S PARENTS PLANTED THIS PARTICULAR SHRUB.
THEY DID?
MM-HMM. THE YEAR Q WAS BORN.
IT'S A MEMENTO OF THE TWO OF THEM. IT PROTECTS THE FAMILY.
THE HORIKITAS ARE WONDERFUL.
I WAS HOMELESS AND HAD NO FAMILY. EVERYONE ELSE ALWAYS TREATED ME LIKE A BOTHER...
We'll pick the flowers and make a cordial.
What's a cordial?
It's like a syrup. I'll teach you how to make it.
...BUT THEY TOOK ME IN. THEY TREAT ME LIKE FAMILY.
OH, RIGHT.
WE'RE HAVING A VISITOR SOON.
MAY I INTRODUCE YOU TO HIM, FUMI?
ME...?
YES. HE'S PART OF THE SWEEPER COMMUNITY.
HE WAS AN UPPERCLASSMAN AT MY UNIVERSITY.
OH... MAYBE...

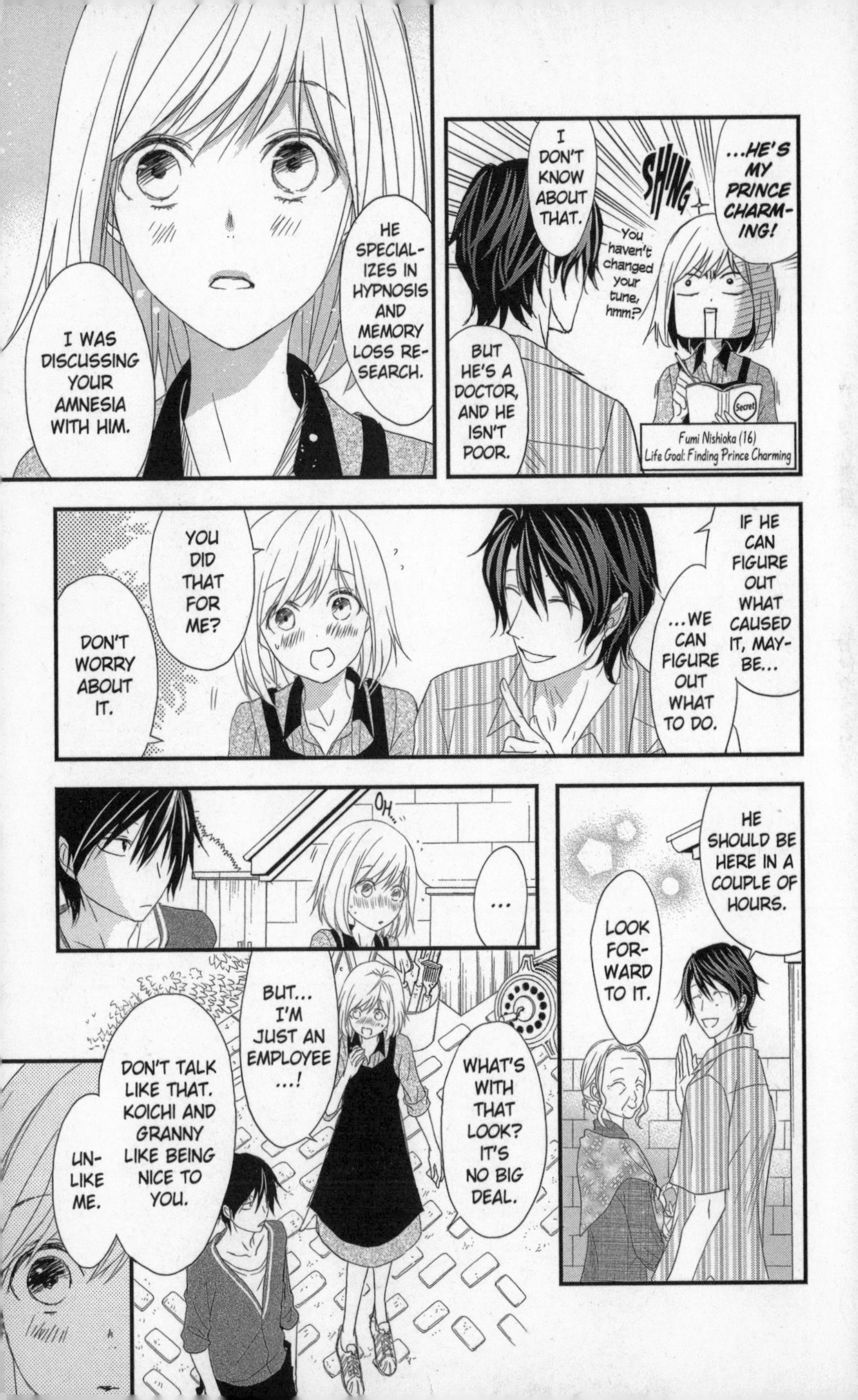
...HE'S MY PRINCE CHARMING!
SHING
I DON'T KNOW ABOUT THAT.
You haven't changed your tune, hmm?
Secret
BUT HE'S A DOCTOR, AND HE ISN'T POOR.
Fumi Nishioka (16) Life Goal: Finding Prince Charming
HE SPECIALIZES IN HYPNOSIS AND MEMORY LOSS RESEARCH.
I WAS DISCUSSING YOUR AMNESIA WITH HIM.
IF HE CAN FIGURE OUT WHAT CAUSED IT, MAYBE...
...WE CAN FIGURE OUT WHAT TO DO.
YOU DID THAT FOR ME?
DON'T WORRY ABOUT IT.
HE SHOULD BE HERE IN A COUPLE OF HOURS.
LOOK FORWARD TO IT.
OH...
...
WHAT'S WITH THAT LOOK? IT'S NO BIG DEAL.
BUT... I'M JUST AN EMPLOYEE ...!
DON'T TALK LIKE THAT. KOICHI AND GRANNY LIKE BEING NICE TO YOU.
UNLIKE ME.

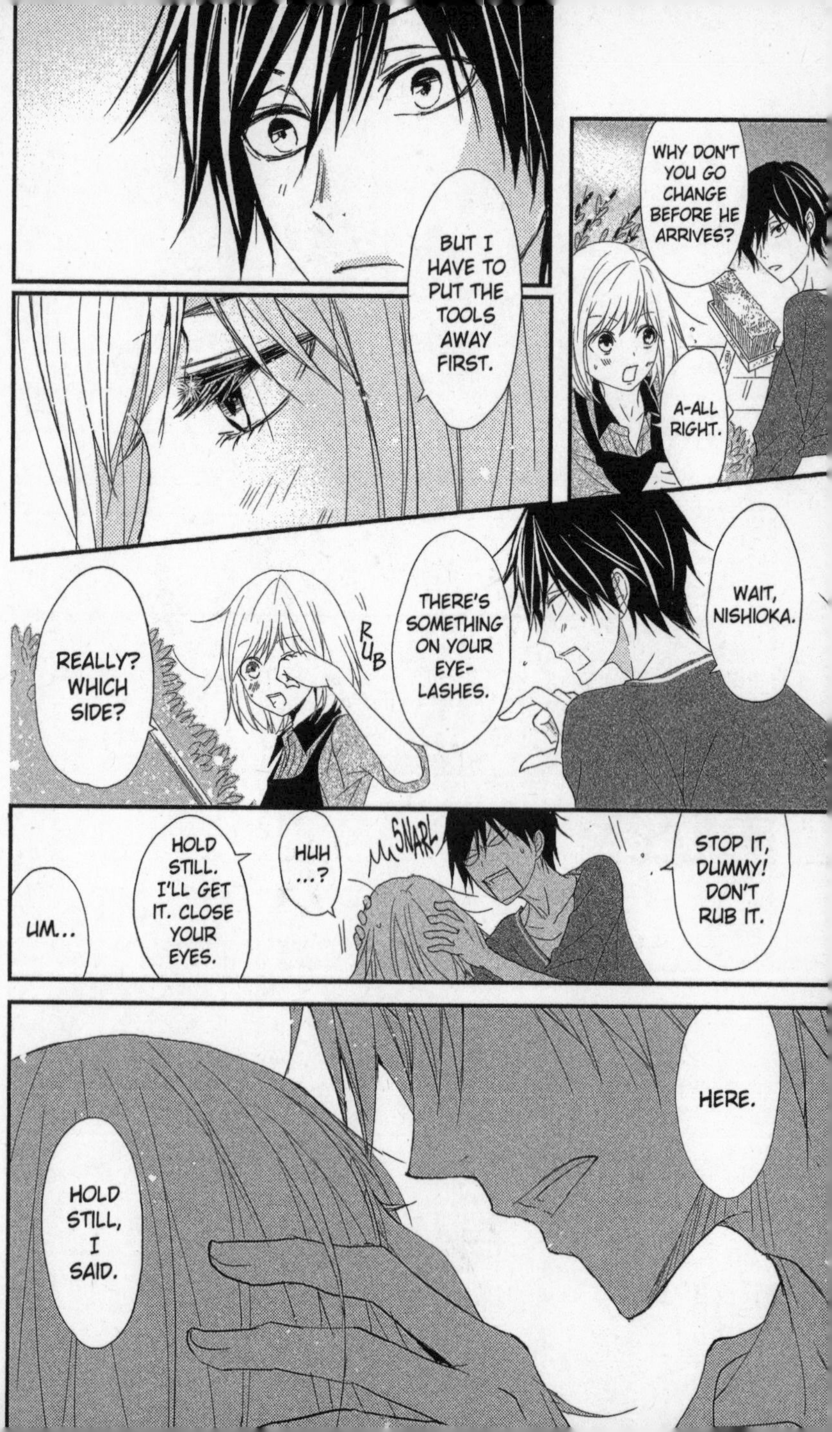
WHY DON'T YOU GO CHANGE BEFORE HE ARRIVES?
A-ALL RIGHT.
BUT I HAVE TO PUT THE TOOLS AWAY FIRST.
WAIT, NISHIOKA.
THERE'S SOMETHING ON YOUR EYE-LASHES.
RUB
REALLY? WHICH SIDE?
STOP IT, DUMMY! DON'T RUB IT.
SNARL
HUH ...?
HOLD STILL. I'LL GET IT. CLOSE YOUR EYES.
UM...
HERE.
HOLD STILL, I SAID.

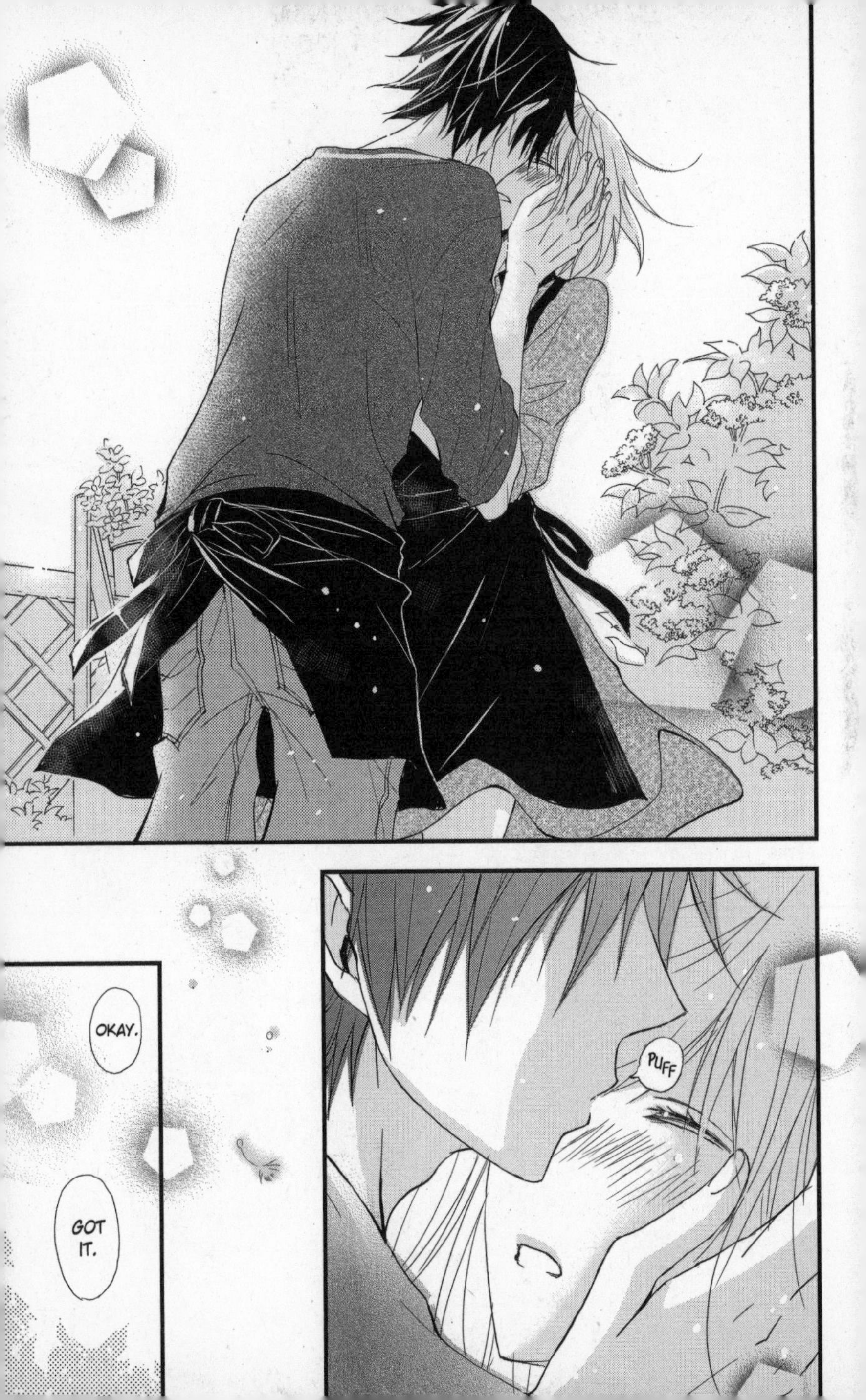
PUFF
OKAY.
GOT IT.

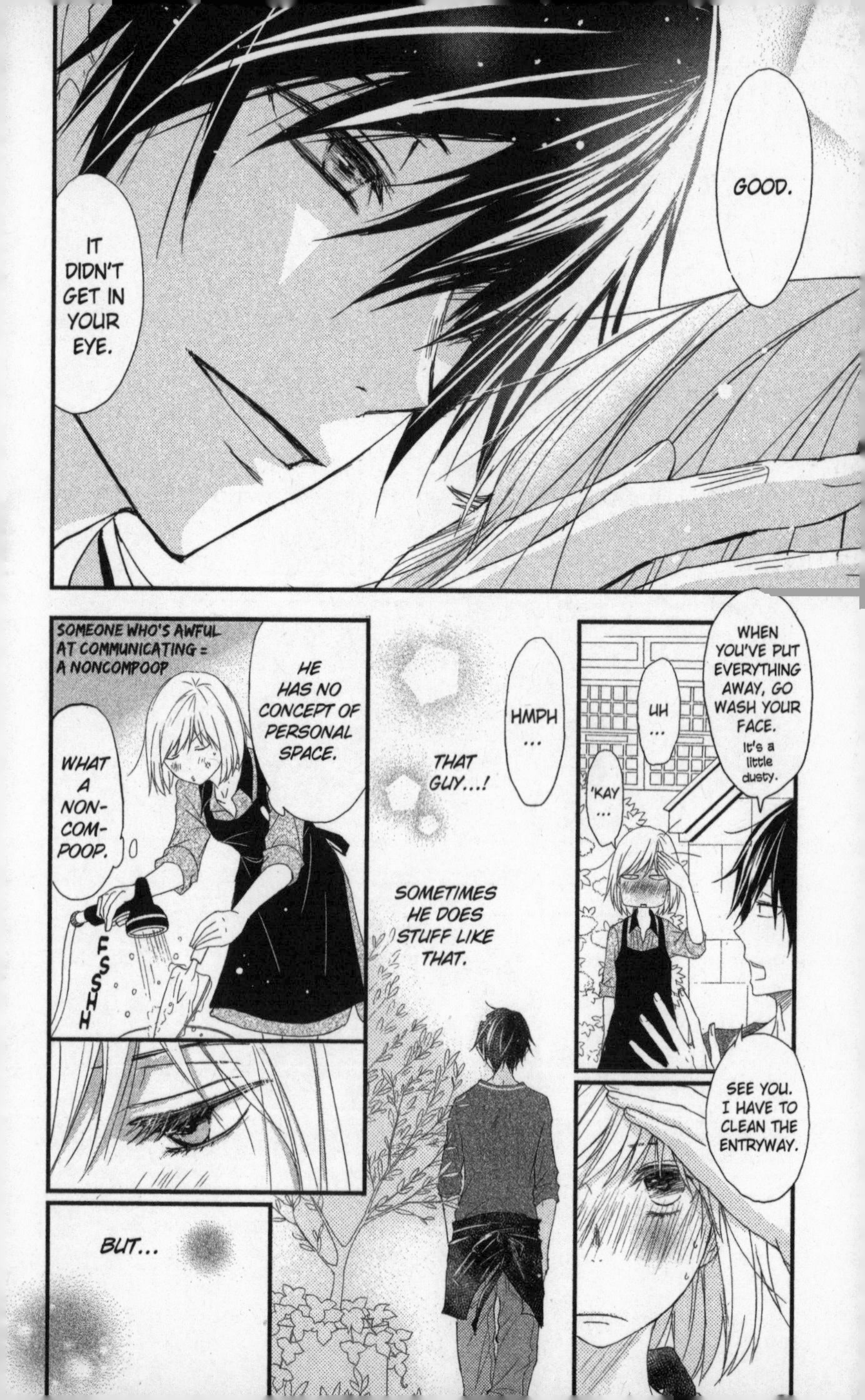
GOOD.
IT DIDN'T GET IN YOUR EYE.
WHEN YOU'VE PUT EVERYTHING AWAY, GO WASH YOUR FACE.
It's a little dusty.
UH ...
'KAY ...
HMPH ...
SEE YOU. I HAVE TO CLEAN THE ENTRYWAY.
THAT GUY...!
SOMETIMES HE DOES STUFF LIKE THAT.
SOMEONE WHO'S AWFUL AT COMMUNICATING = A NONCOMPOOP
HE HAS NO CONCEPT OF PERSONAL SPACE.
WHAT A NON-COM-POOP.
FSSHH
BUT...

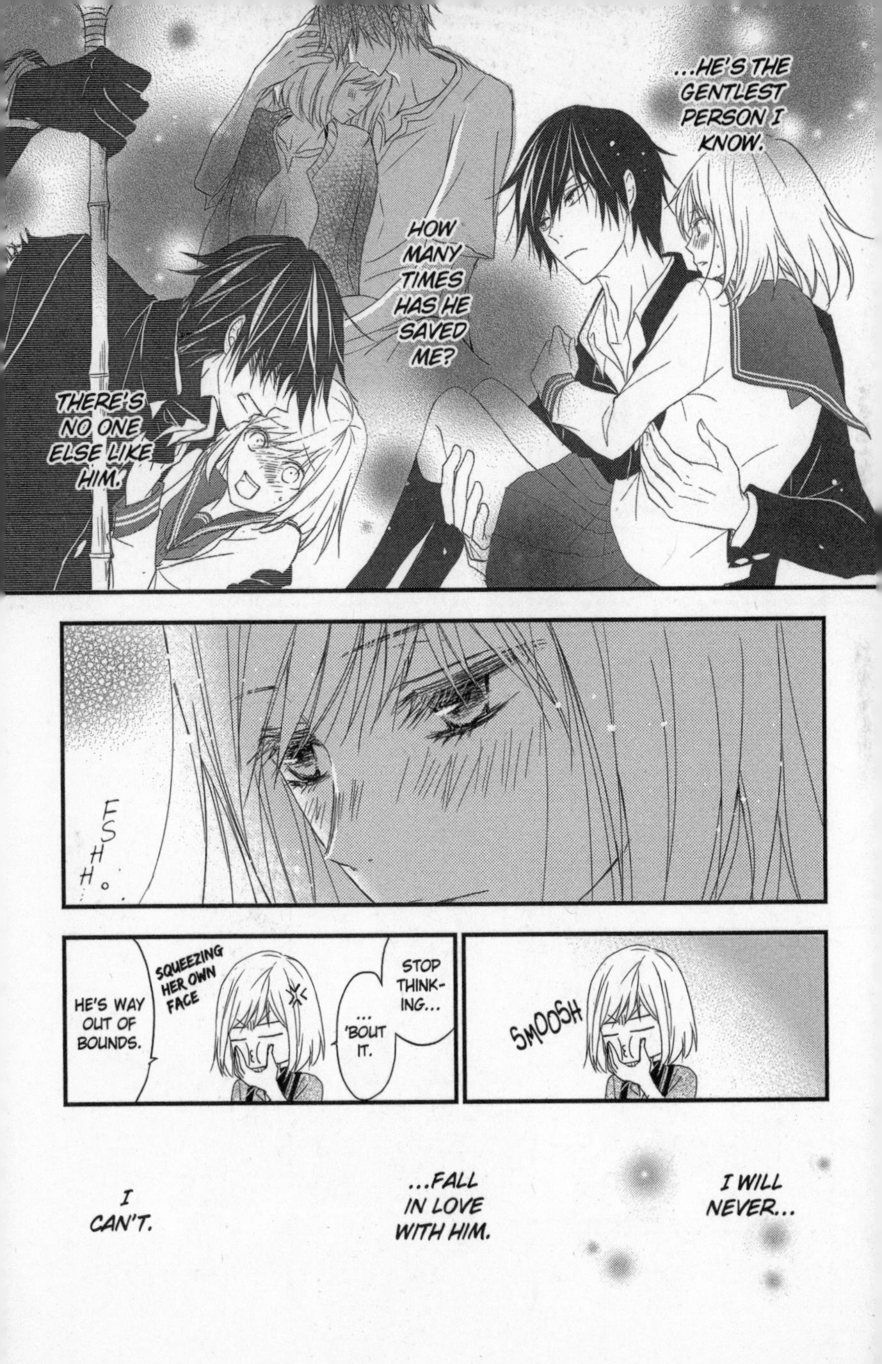
...HE'S THE GENTLEST PERSON I KNOW.
HOW MANY TIMES HAS HE SAVED ME?
THERE'S NO ONE ELSE LIKE HIM.
FSHH...
SMOOSH
STOP THINKING...
... 'BOUT IT.
HE'S WAY OUT OF BOUNDS.
SQUEEZING HER OWN FACE
I WILL NEVER...
...FALL IN LOVE WITH HIM.
I CAN'T.

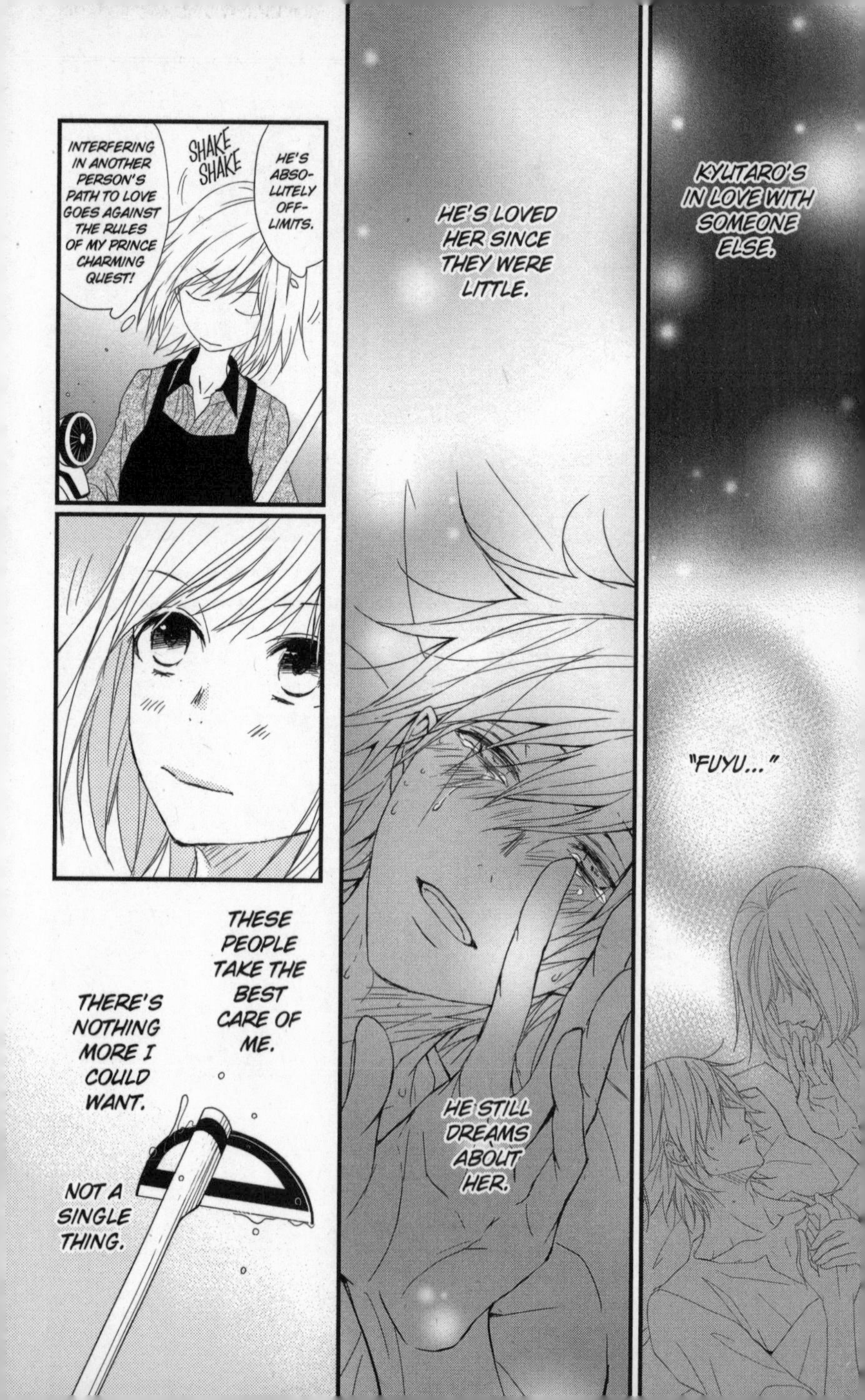
KYUTARO'S IN LOVE WITH SOMEONE ELSE.
"FUYU..."
HE'S LOVED HER SINCE THEY WERE LITTLE.
HE STILL DREAMS ABOUT HER.
HE'S ABSO-LUTELY OFF-LIMITS.
SHAKE SHAKE
INTERFERING IN ANOTHER PERSON'S PATH TO LOVE GOES AGAINST THE RULES OF MY PRINCE CHARMING QUEST!
THESE PEOPLE TAKE THE BEST CARE OF ME.
THERE'S NOTHING MORE I COULD WANT.
NOT A SINGLE THING.

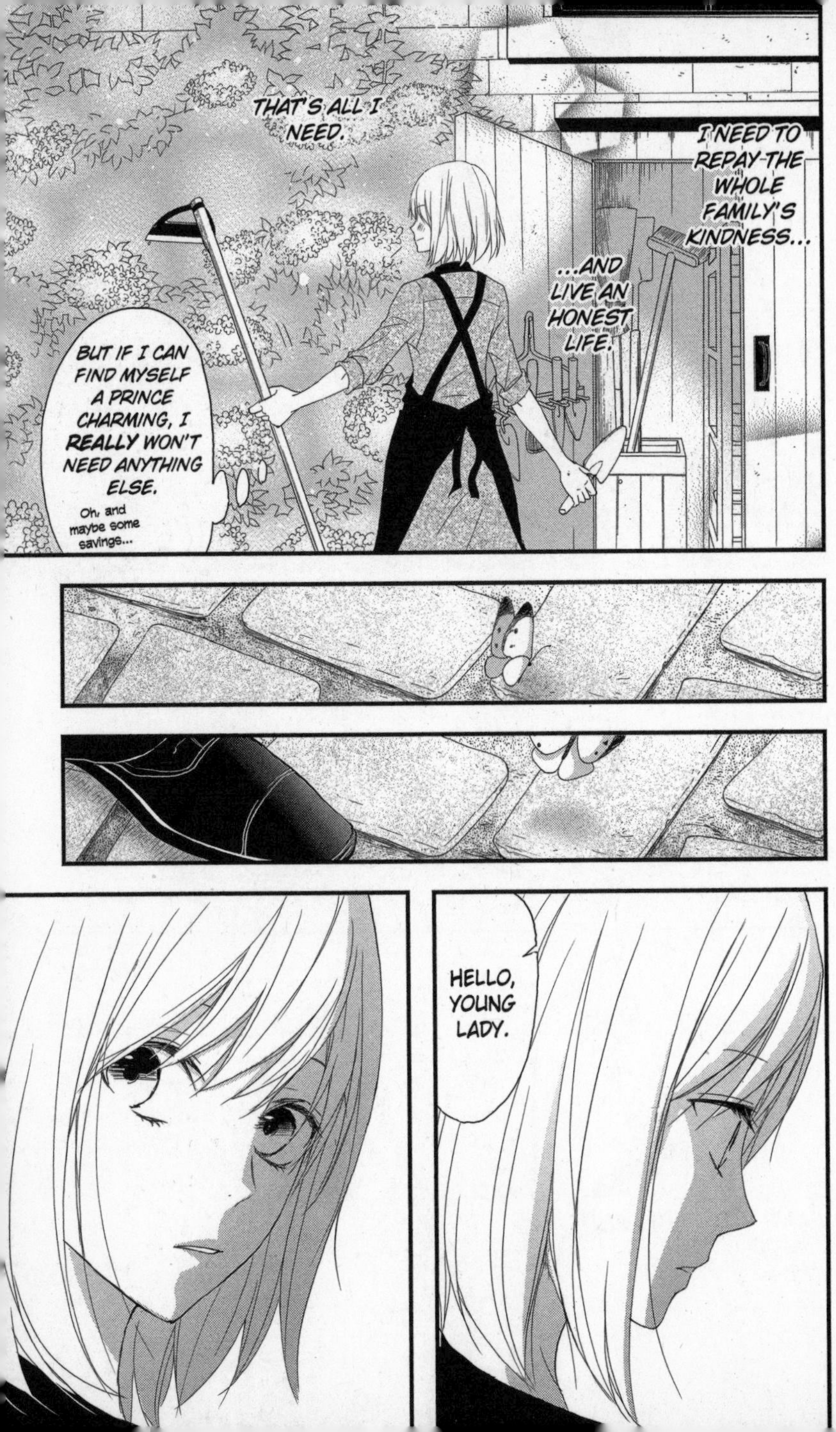
I NEED TO REPAY THE WHOLE FAMILY'S KINDNESS...
...AND LIVE AN HONEST LIFE.
THAT'S ALL I NEED.
BUT IF I CAN FIND MYSELF A PRINCE CHARMING, I REALLY WON'T NEED ANYTHING ELSE.
Oh, and maybe some savings...
HELLO, YOUNG LADY.

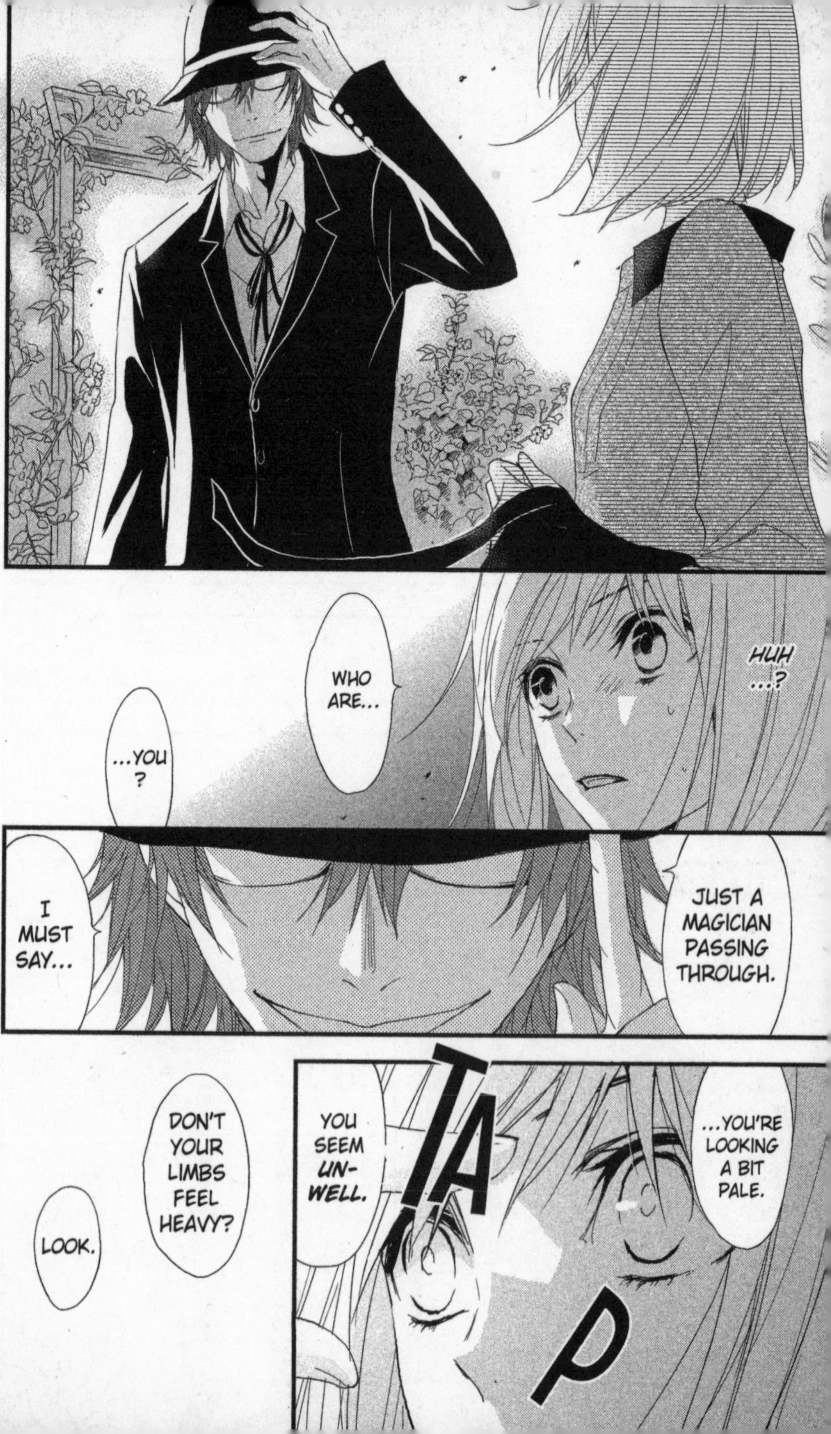
HUH ...?
WHO ARE...
...YOU ?
JUST A MAGICIAN PASSING THROUGH.
I MUST SAY...
...YOU'RE LOOKING A BIT PALE.
TAP
YOU SEEM *UN-WELL.*
DON'T YOUR LIMBS FEEL HEAVY?
LOOK.

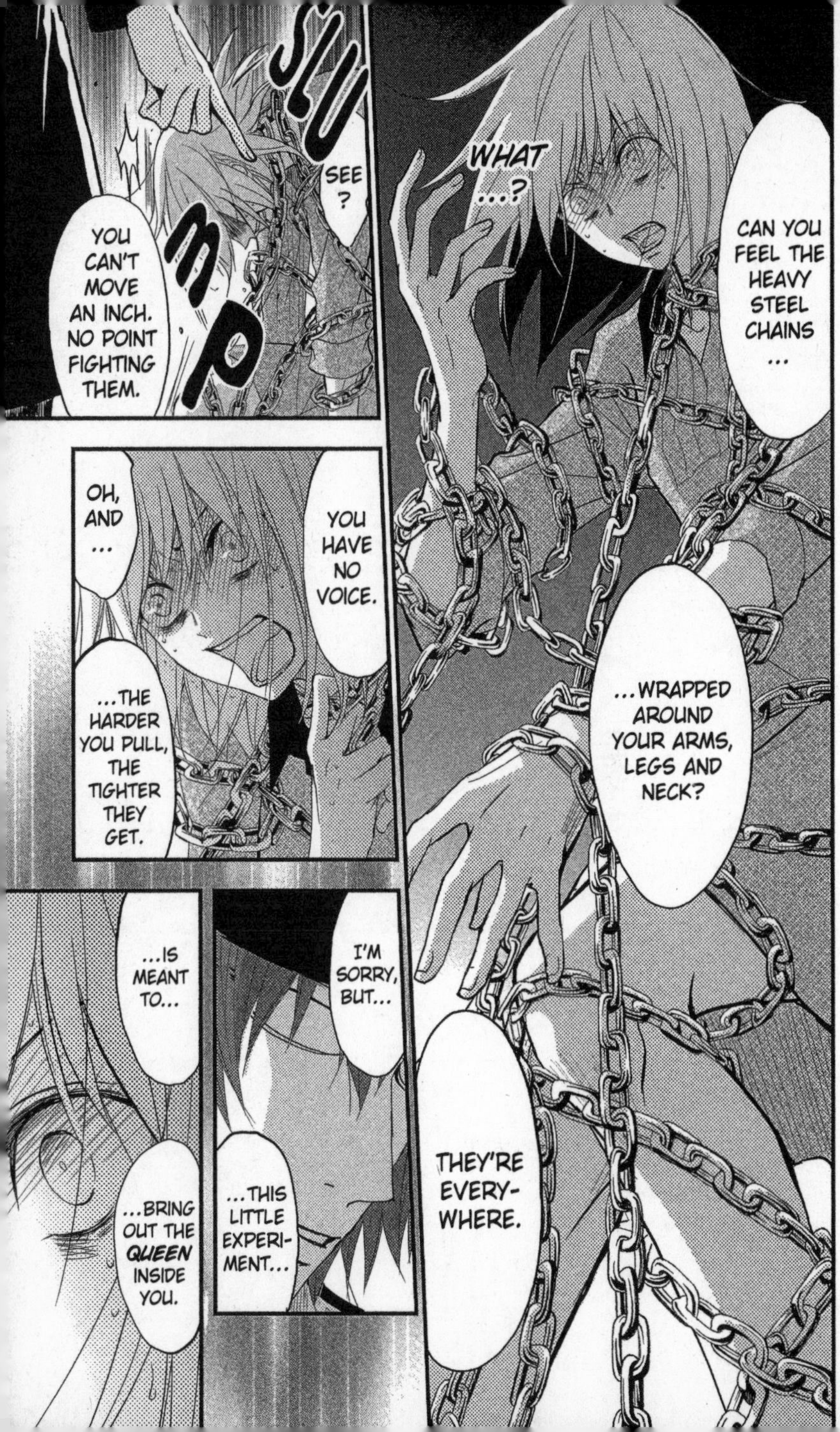
CAN YOU FEEL THE HEAVY STEEL CHAINS ...
WHAT ...?
...WRAPPED AROUND YOUR ARMS, LEGS AND NECK?
THEY'RE EVERY-WHERE.
SLUMP
SEE?
YOU CAN'T MOVE AN INCH. NO POINT FIGHTING THEM.
YOU HAVE NO VOICE.
OH, AND ...
...THE HARDER YOU PULL, THE TIGHTER THEY GET.
I'M SORRY, BUT...
...THIS LITTLE EXPERIMENT...
...IS MEANT TO...
...BRING OUT THE *QUEEN* INSIDE YOU.

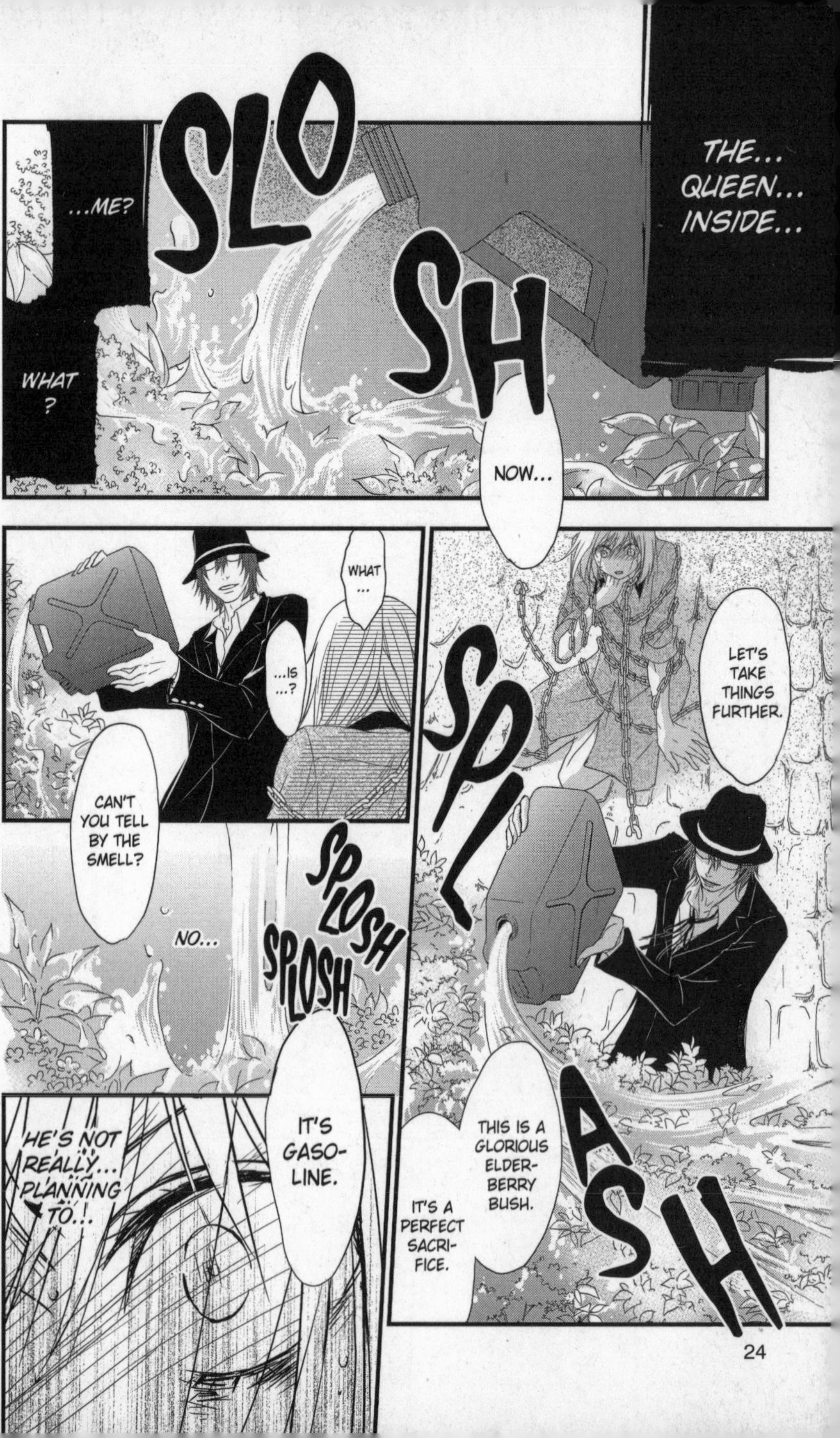
THE... QUEEN... INSIDE...
SLOSH
...ME?
WHAT ?
NOW...
LET'S TAKE THINGS FURTHER.
SPLASH
THIS IS A GLORIOUS ELDER-BERRY BUSH.
IT'S A PERFECT SACRI-FICE.
WHAT ...
...IS ...?
CAN'T YOU TELL BY THE SMELL?
SPLOSH
SPLOSH
NO...
IT'S GASO-LINE.
HE'S NOT REALLY... PLANNING TO..!

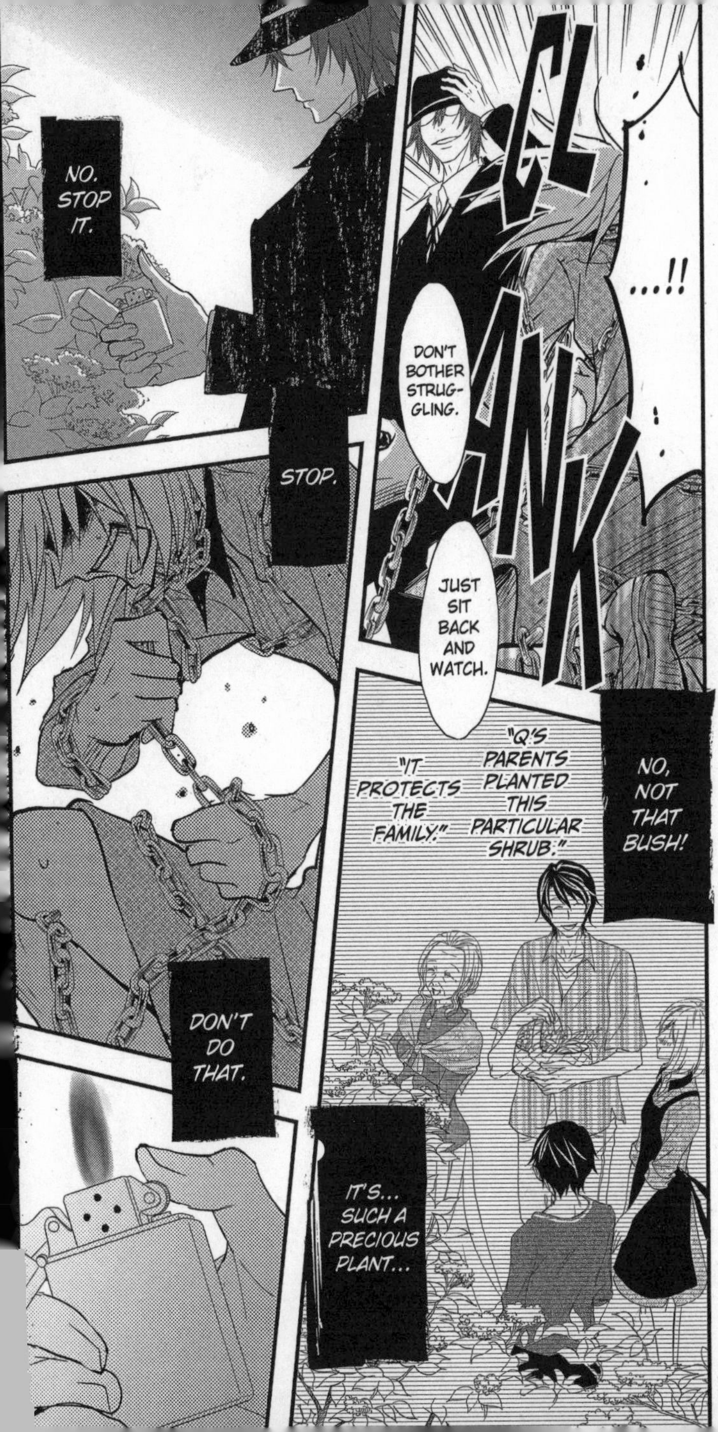
CLANK
...!!
DON'T BOTHER STRUG-GLING.
JUST SIT BACK AND WATCH.
NO. STOP IT.
STOP.
NO, NOT THAT BUSH!
"Q'S PARENTS PLANTED THIS PARTICULAR SHRUB."
"IT PROTECTS THE FAMILY."
DON'T DO THAT.
IT'S... SUCH A PRECIOUS PLANT...

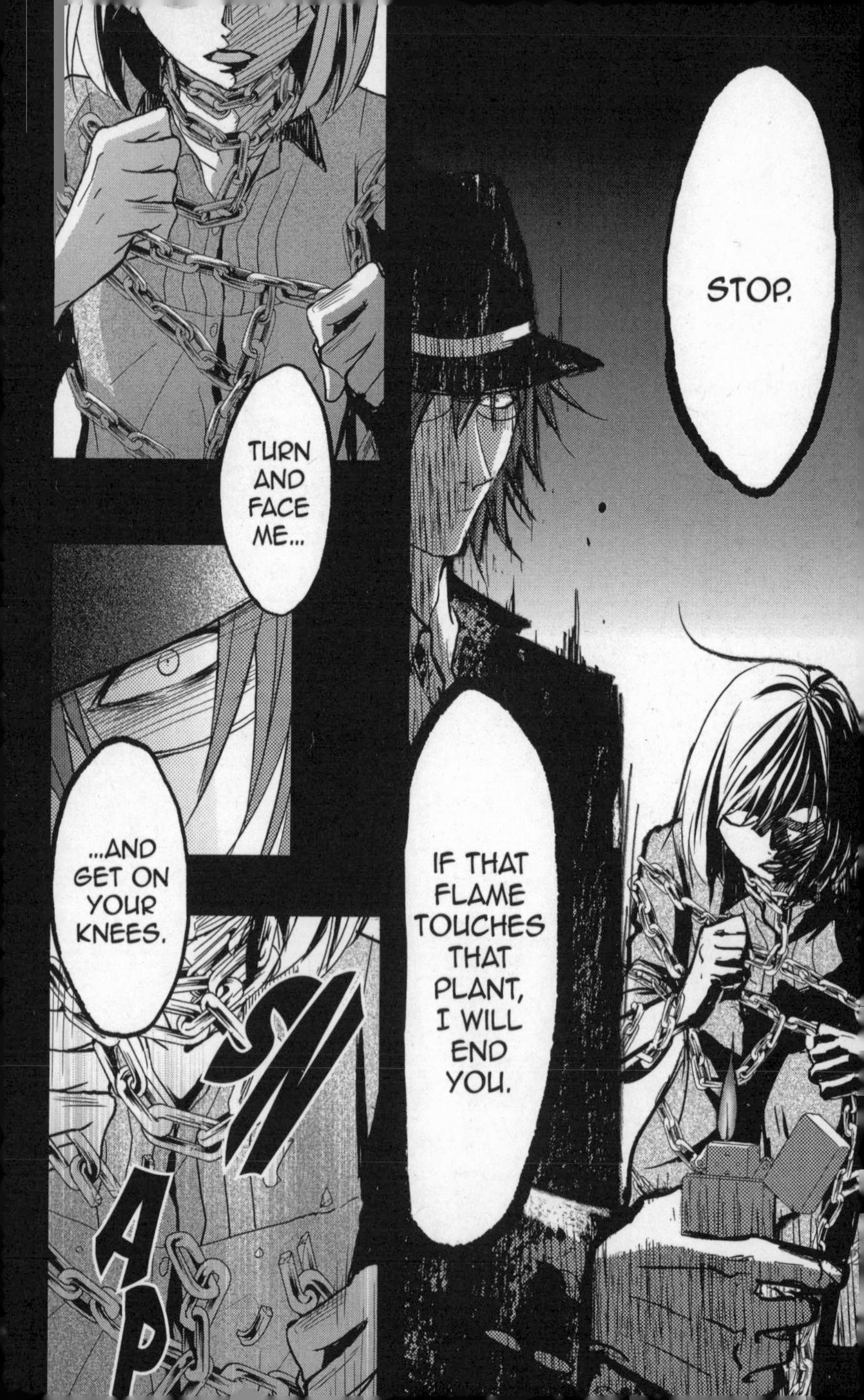
STOP.
IF THAT FLAME TOUCHES THAT PLANT, I WILL END YOU.
TURN AND FACE ME...
...AND GET ON YOUR KNEES.
SNAP

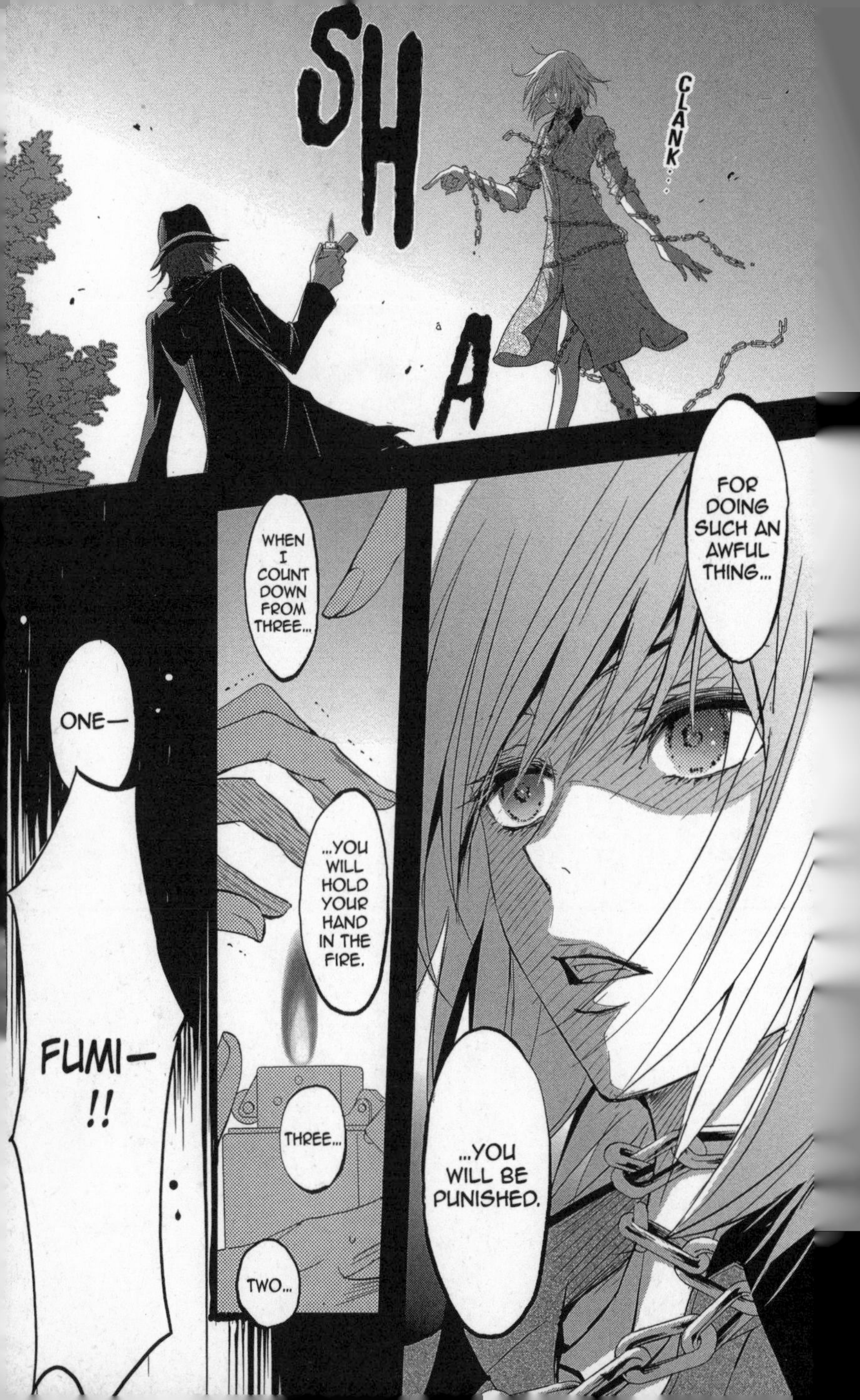
CLANK...
SHA
FOR DOING SUCH AN AWFUL THING...
...YOU WILL BE PUNISHED.
WHEN I COUNT DOWN FROM THREE...
...YOU WILL HOLD YOUR HAND IN THE FIRE.
THREE...
TWO...
ONE—
FUMI—!!

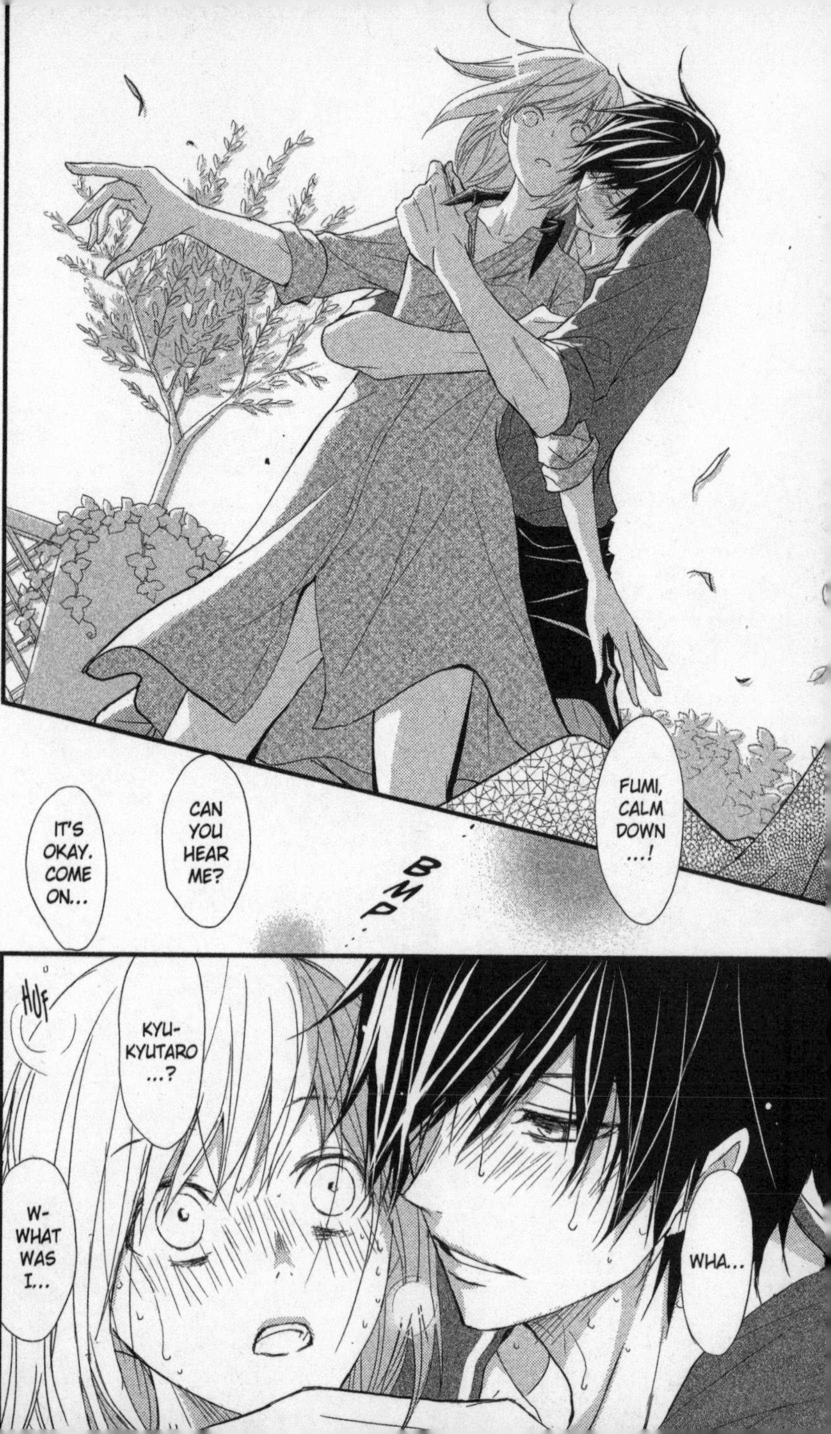
FUMI, CALM DOWN ...!
BMP...
CAN YOU HEAR ME?
IT'S OKAY. COME ON...
WHA...
KYU-KYUTARO ...?
HUF
W-WHAT WAS I...

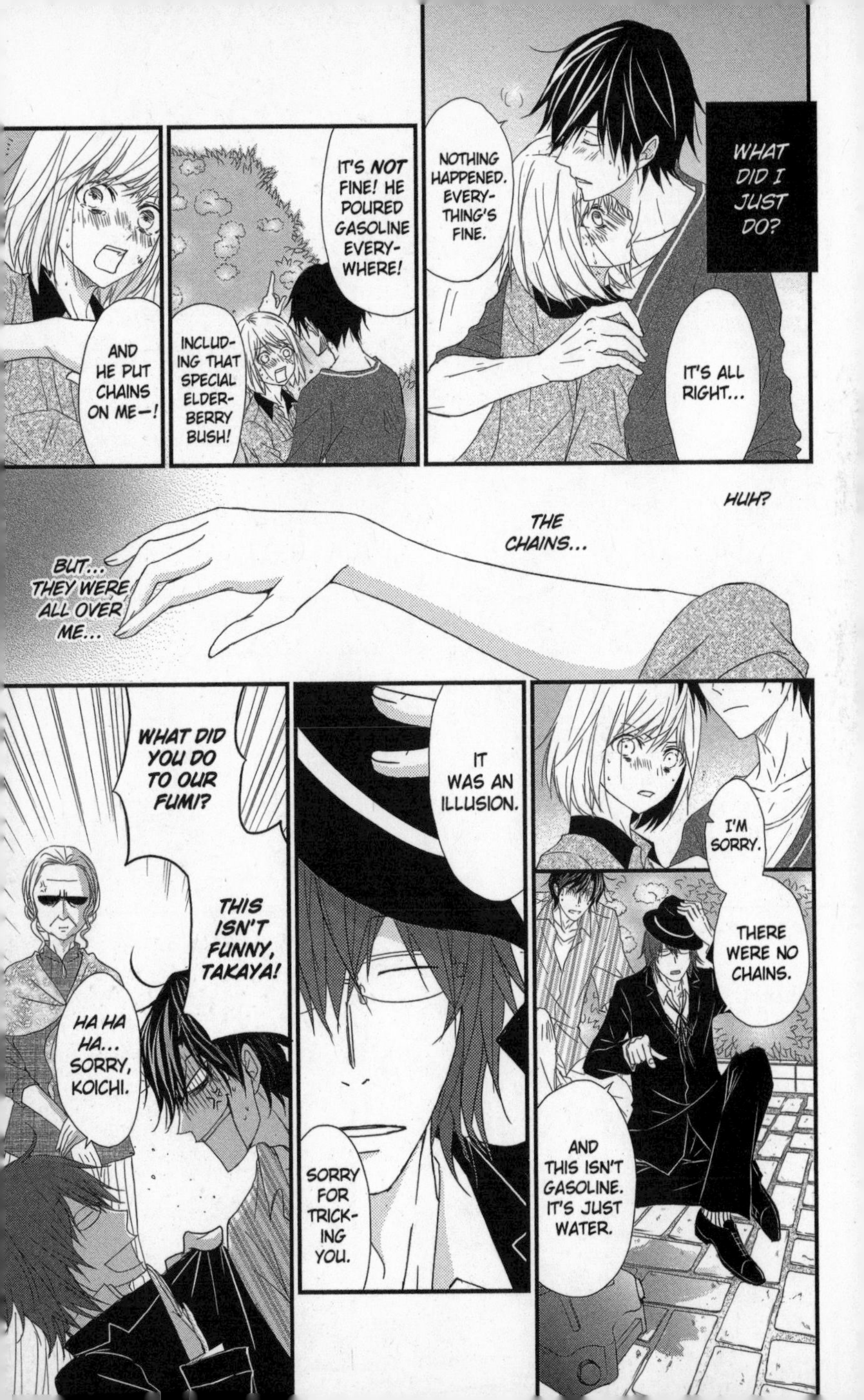
WHAT DID I JUST DO?
IT'S ALL RIGHT...
NOTHING HAPPENED. EVERYTHING'S FINE.
IT'S *NOT* FINE! HE POURED GASOLINE EVERYWHERE!
INCLUDING THAT SPECIAL ELDERBERRY BUSH!
AND HE PUT CHAINS ON ME—!
HUH?
THE CHAINS...
BUT... THEY WERE ALL OVER ME...
I'M SORRY.
THERE WERE NO CHAINS.
AND THIS ISN'T GASOLINE. IT'S JUST WATER.
IT WAS AN ILLUSION.
SORRY FOR TRICKING YOU.
WHAT DID YOU DO TO OUR FUMI?
THIS ISN'T FUNNY, TAKAYA!
HA HA HA... SORRY, KOICHI.

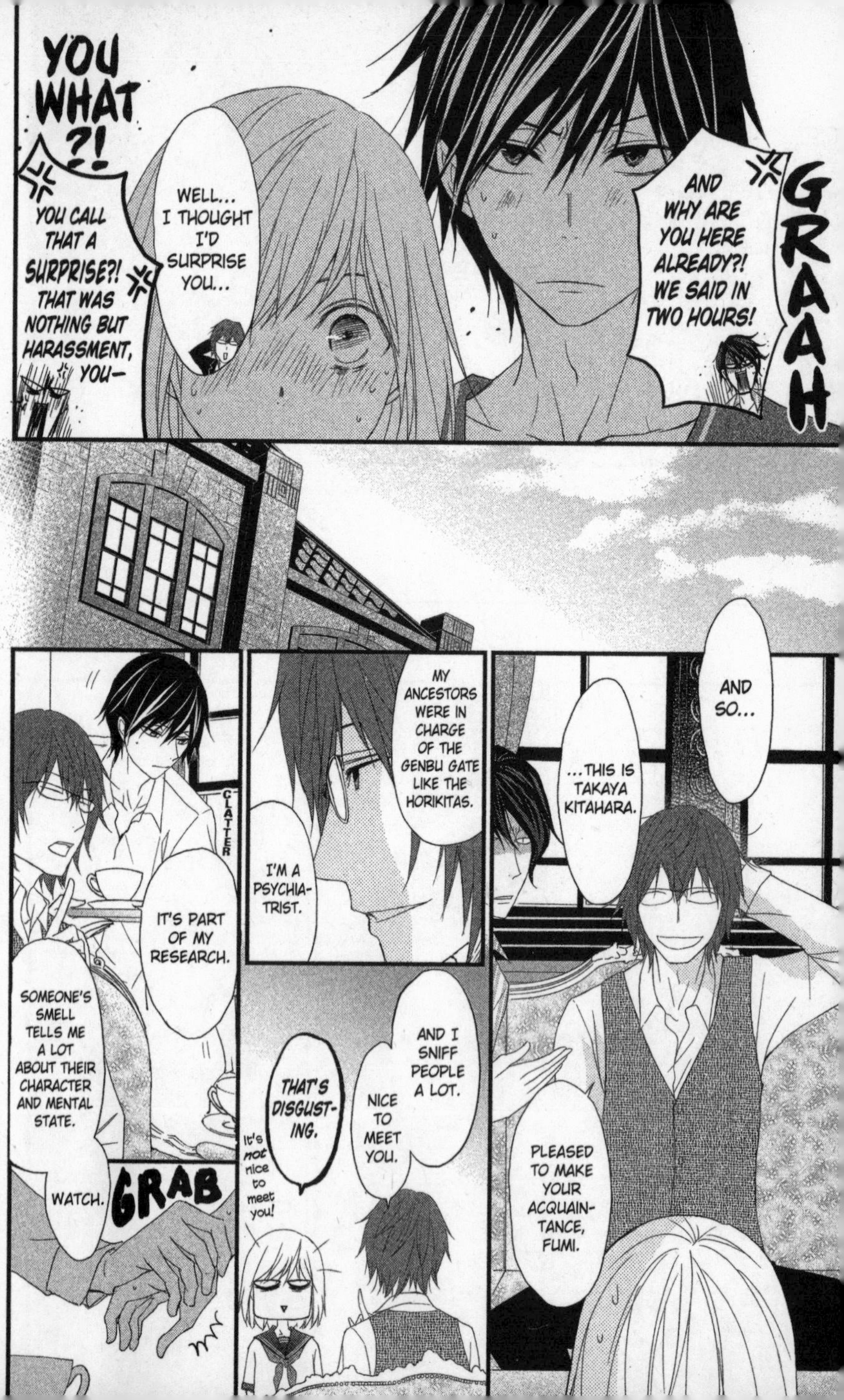
GRAAH
AND WHY ARE YOU HERE ALREADY?! WE SAID IN TWO HOURS!
WELL... I THOUGHT I'D SURPRISE YOU...
YOU WHAT?!
YOU CALL THAT A SURPRISE?! THAT WAS NOTHING BUT HARASSMENT, YOU—
AND SO...
...THIS IS TAKAYA KITAHARA.
PLEASED TO MAKE YOUR ACQUAINTANCE, FUMI.
MY ANCESTORS WERE IN CHARGE OF THE GENBU GATE LIKE THE HORIKITAS.
I'M A PSYCHIATRIST.
AND I SNIFF PEOPLE A LOT.
NICE TO MEET YOU.
THAT'S DISGUSTING.
It's *not* nice to meet you!
CLATTER
IT'S PART OF MY RESEARCH.
SOMEONE'S SMELL TELLS ME A LOT ABOUT THEIR CHARACTER AND MENTAL STATE.
WATCH.
GRAB

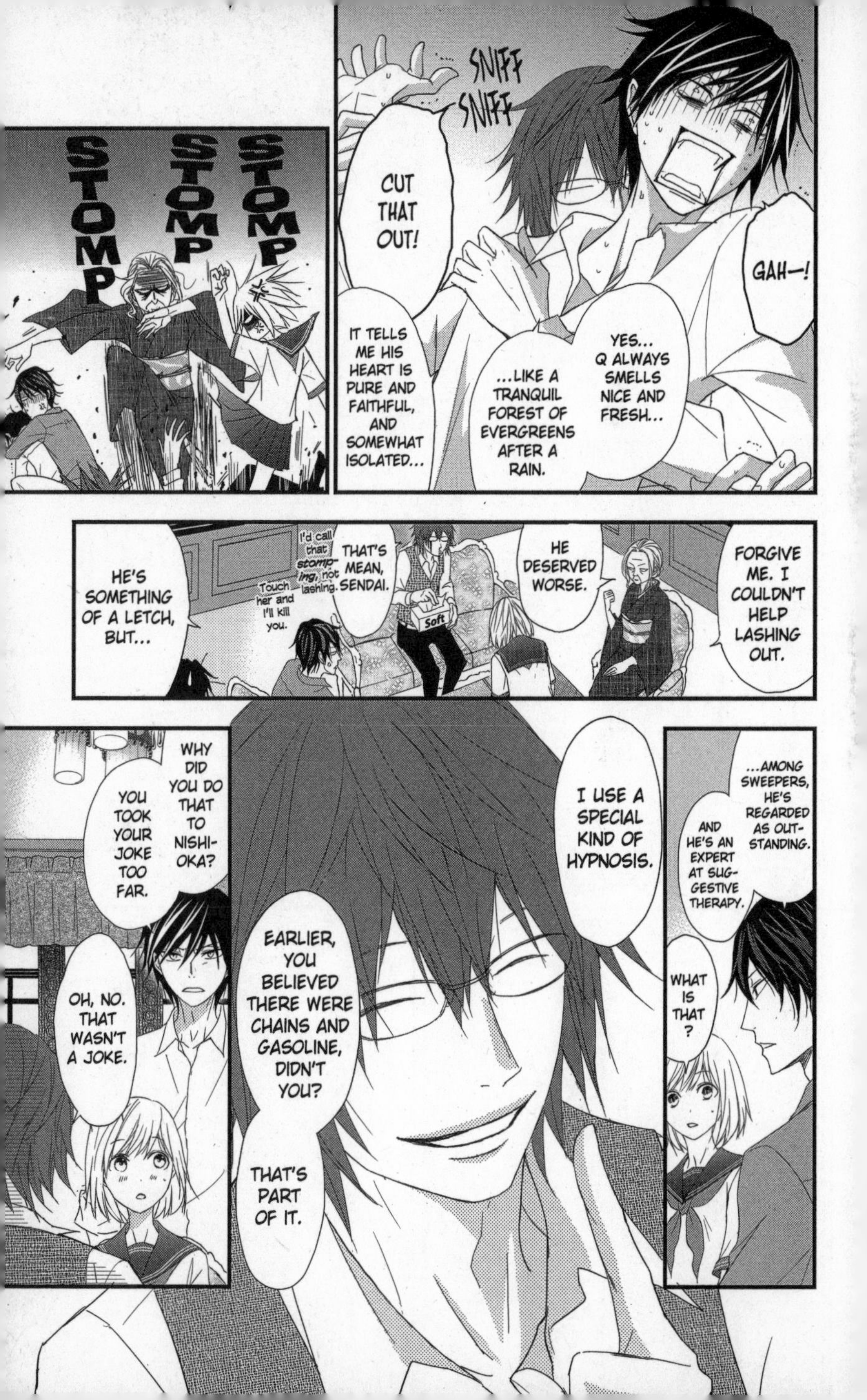
...SNIFF SNIFF
GAH—!
CUT THAT OUT!
YES... Q ALWAYS SMELLS NICE AND FRESH...
...LIKE A TRANQUIL FOREST OF EVERGREENS AFTER A RAIN.
IT TELLS ME HIS HEART IS PURE AND FAITHFUL, AND SOMEWHAT ISOLATED...
STOMP STOMP STOMP
FORGIVE ME. I COULDN'T HELP LASHING OUT.
HE DESERVED WORSE.
THAT'S MEAN, SENDAI.
I'd call that stomping, not lashing.
Touch her and I'll kill you.
Soft
HE'S SOMETHING OF A LETCH, BUT...
...AMONG SWEEPERS, HE'S REGARDED AS OUT-STANDING.
AND HE'S AN EXPERT AT SUG-GESTIVE THERAPY.
WHAT IS THAT?
I USE A SPECIAL KIND OF HYPNOSIS.
EARLIER, YOU BELIEVED THERE WERE CHAINS AND GASOLINE, DIDN'T YOU?
THAT'S PART OF IT.
WHY DID YOU DO THAT TO NISHI-OKA?
YOU TOOK YOUR JOKE TOO FAR.
OH, NO. THAT WASN'T A JOKE.

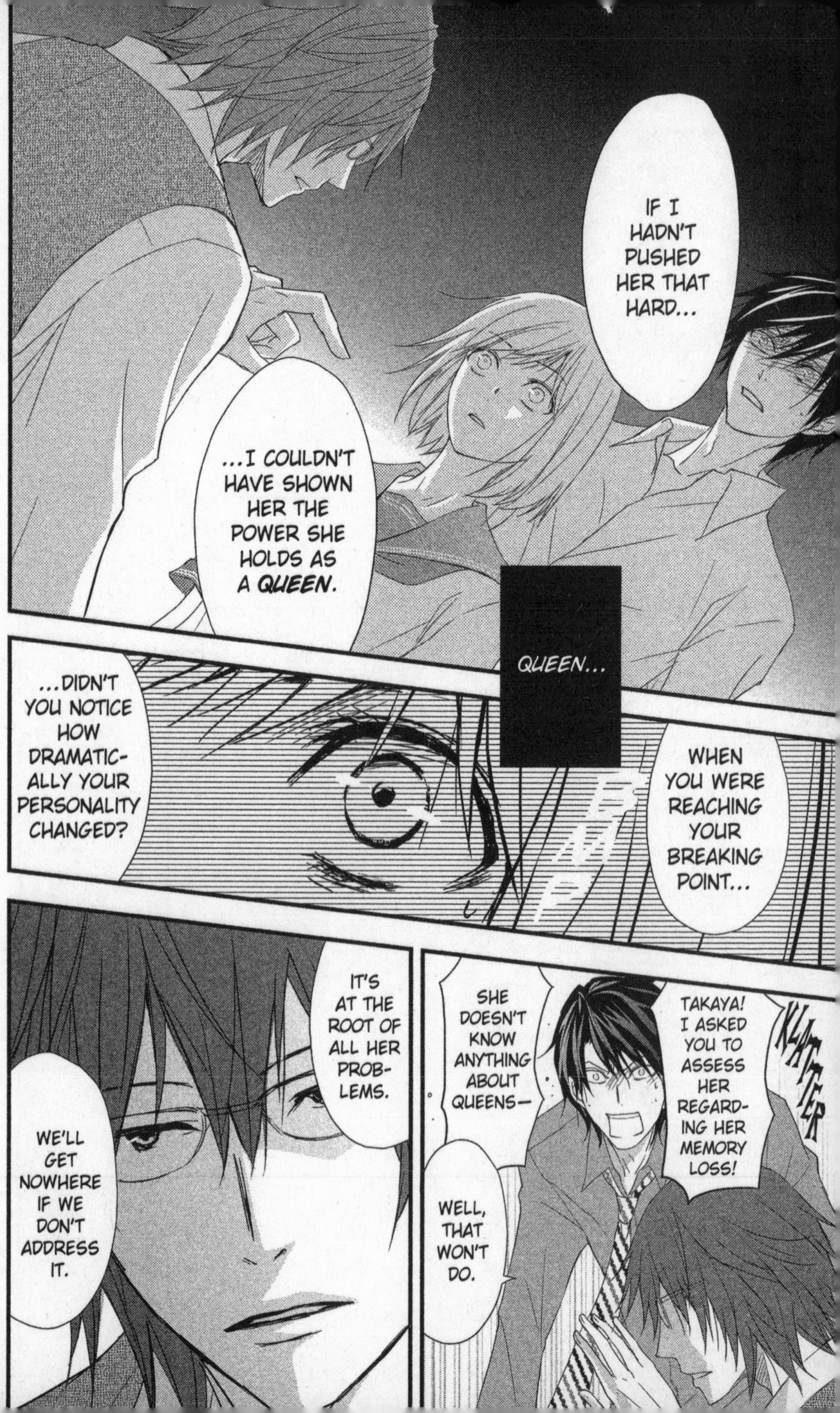
IF I HADN'T PUSHED HER THAT HARD...
...I COULDN'T HAVE SHOWN HER THE POWER SHE HOLDS AS A **QUEEN**.
QUEEN...
WHEN YOU WERE REACHING YOUR BREAKING POINT...
BMP
...DIDN'T YOU NOTICE HOW DRAMATIC-ALLY YOUR PERSONALITY CHANGED?
KLATTER
TAKAYA! I ASKED YOU TO ASSESS HER REGARDING HER MEMORY LOSS!
SHE DOESN'T KNOW ANYTHING ABOUT QUEENS—
WELL, THAT WON'T DO.
IT'S AT THE ROOT OF ALL HER PROB-LEMS.
WE'LL GET NOWHERE IF WE DON'T ADDRESS IT.

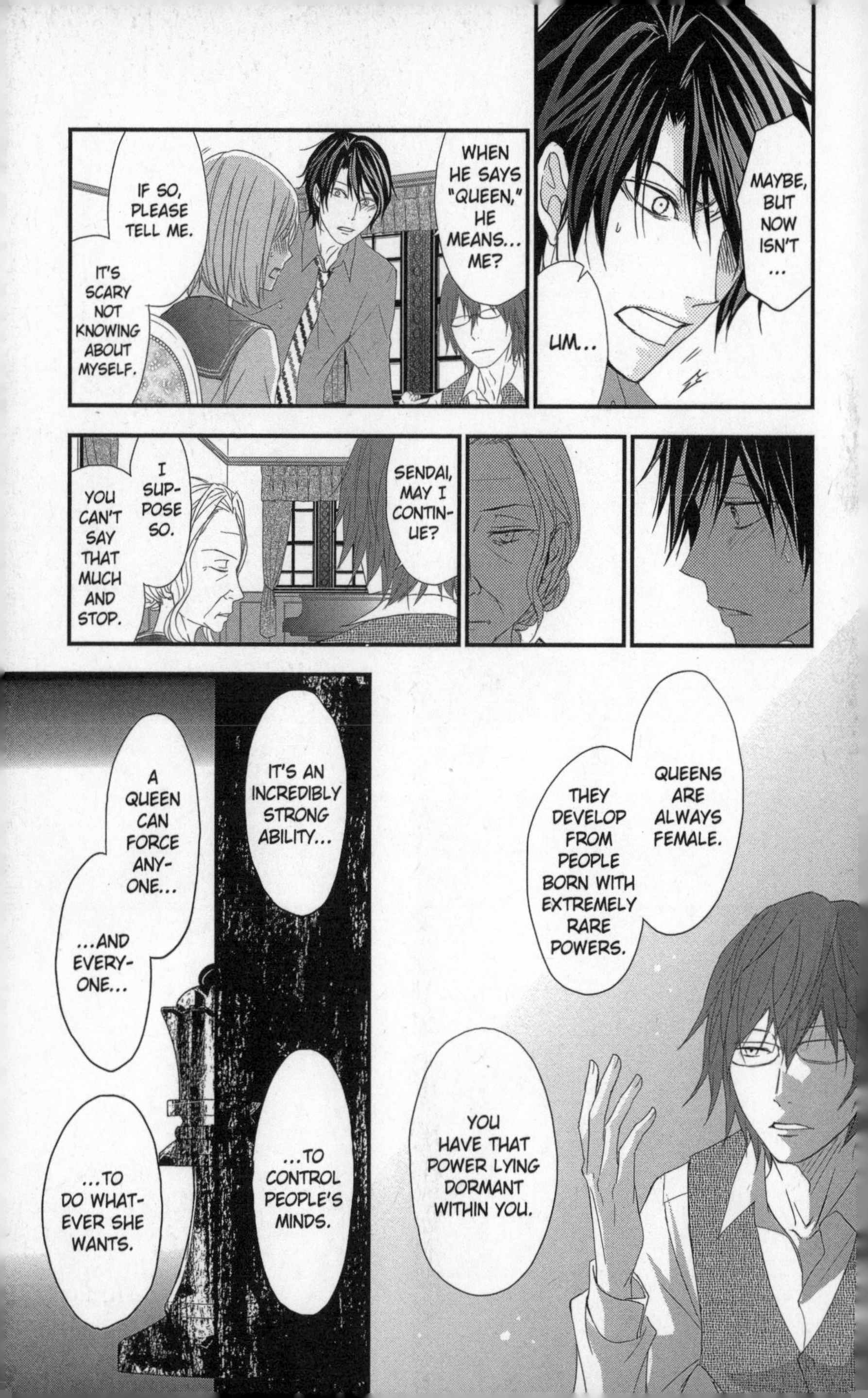
MAYBE, BUT NOW ISN'T ...
UM...
WHEN HE SAYS "QUEEN," HE MEANS... ME?
IF SO, PLEASE TELL ME.
IT'S SCARY NOT KNOWING ABOUT MYSELF.
SENDAI, MAY I CONTIN-UE?
I SUP-POSE SO.
YOU CAN'T SAY THAT MUCH AND STOP.
QUEENS ARE ALWAYS FEMALE.
THEY DEVELOP FROM PEOPLE BORN WITH EXTREMELY RARE POWERS.
YOU HAVE THAT POWER LYING DORMANT WITHIN YOU.
IT'S AN INCREDIBLY STRONG ABILITY...
...TO CONTROL PEOPLE'S MINDS.
A QUEEN CAN FORCE ANY-ONE...
...AND EVERY-ONE...
...TO DO WHAT-EVER SHE WANTS.

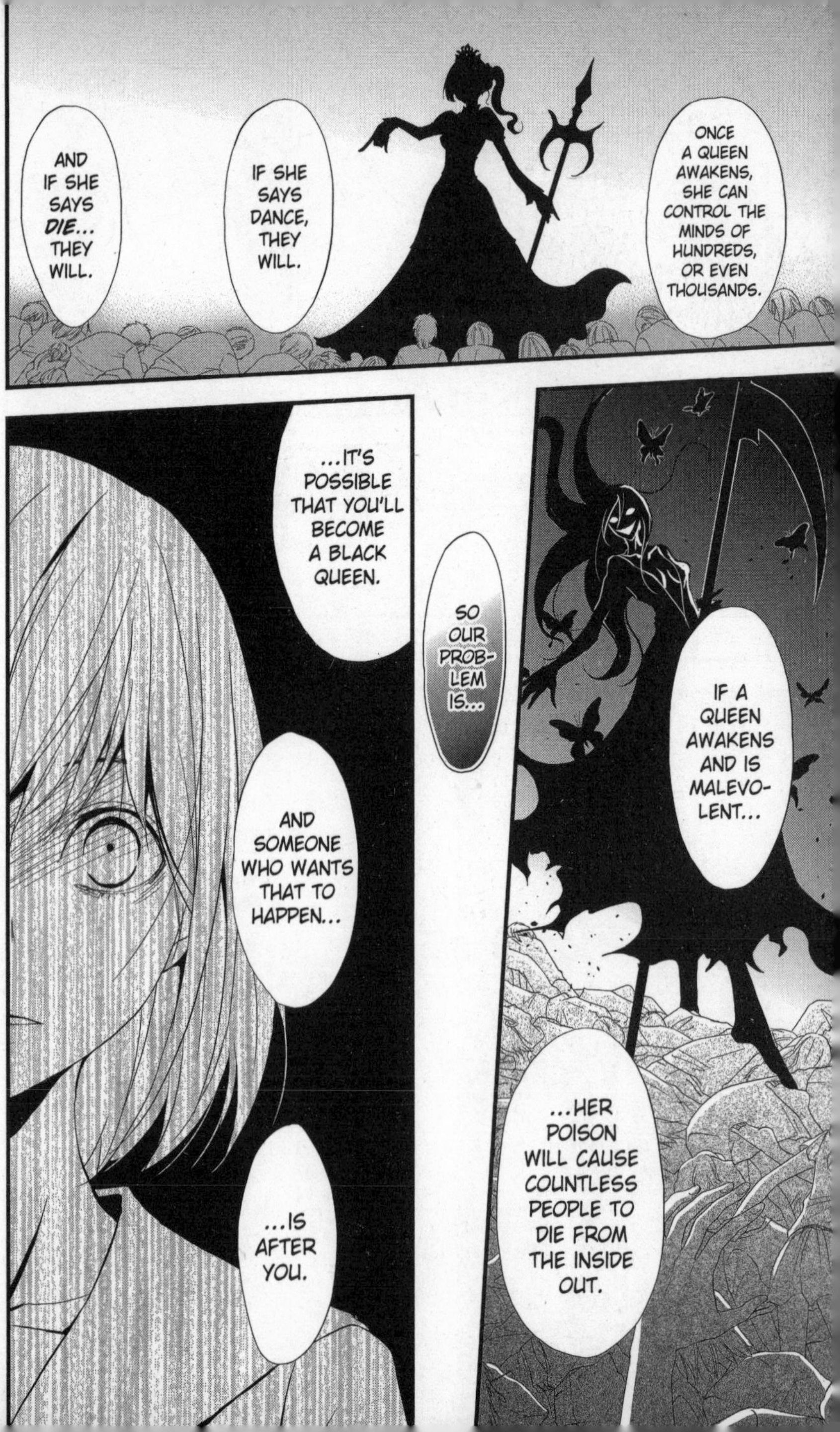
ONCE A QUEEN AWAKENS, SHE CAN CONTROL THE MINDS OF HUNDREDS, OR EVEN THOUSANDS.
IF SHE SAYS DANCE, THEY WILL.
AND IF SHE SAYS *DIE*... THEY WILL.
IF A QUEEN AWAKENS AND IS MALEVO-LENT...
...HER POISON WILL CAUSE COUNTLESS PEOPLE TO DIE FROM THE INSIDE OUT.
SO OUR PROB-LEM IS...
...IT'S POSSIBLE THAT YOU'LL BECOME A BLACK QUEEN.
AND SOMEONE WHO WANTS THAT TO HAPPEN...
...IS AFTER YOU.

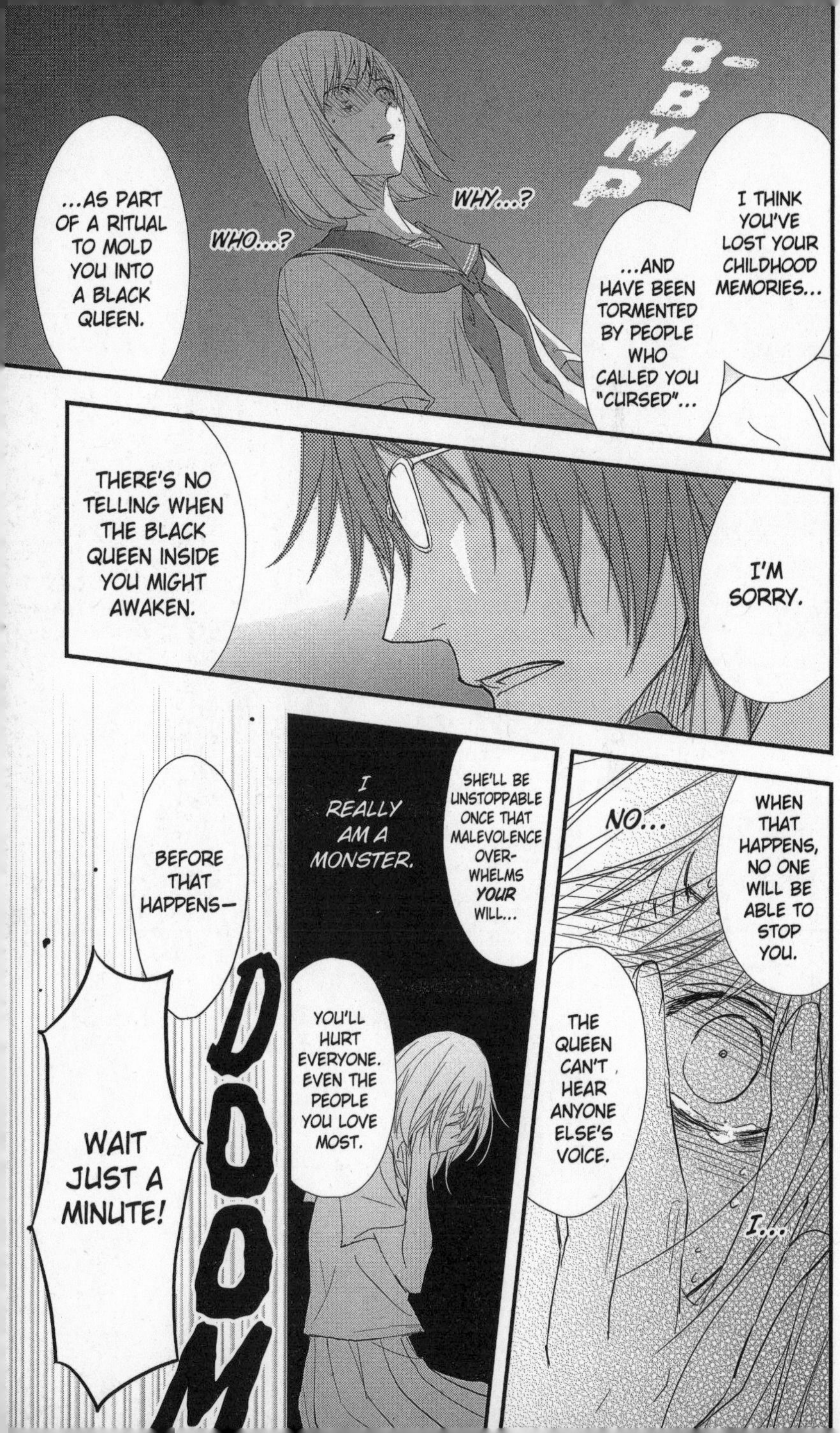
I THINK YOU'VE LOST YOUR CHILDHOOD MEMORIES...
B-B-BMP
...AND HAVE BEEN TORMENTED BY PEOPLE WHO CALLED YOU "CURSED"...
WHY...?
WHO...?
...AS PART OF A RITUAL TO MOLD YOU INTO A BLACK QUEEN.
I'M SORRY.
THERE'S NO TELLING WHEN THE BLACK QUEEN INSIDE YOU MIGHT AWAKEN.
WHEN THAT HAPPENS, NO ONE WILL BE ABLE TO STOP YOU.
NO...
THE QUEEN CAN'T HEAR ANYONE ELSE'S VOICE.
I...
SHE'LL BE UNSTOPPABLE ONCE THAT MALEVOLENCE OVER-WHELMS YOUR WILL...
I REALLY AM A MONSTER.
YOU'LL HURT EVERYONE. EVEN THE PEOPLE YOU LOVE MOST.
BEFORE THAT HAPPENS—
DOOM
WAIT JUST A MINUTE!

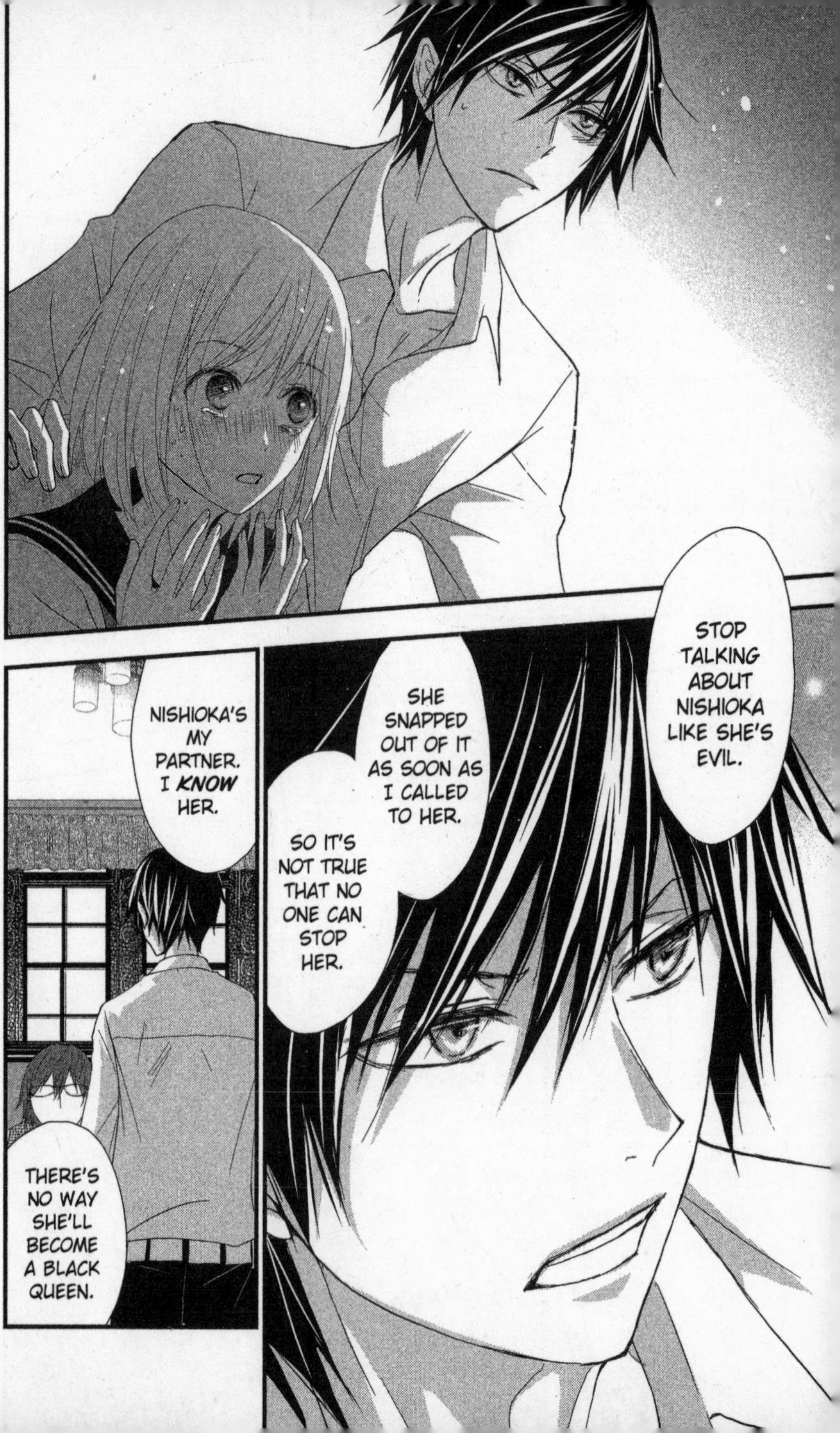
STOP TALKING ABOUT NISHIOKA LIKE SHE'S EVIL.
SHE SNAPPED OUT OF IT AS SOON AS I CALLED TO HER.
SO IT'S NOT TRUE THAT NO ONE CAN STOP HER.
NISHIOKA'S MY PARTNER. I *KNOW* HER.
THERE'S NO WAY SHE'LL BECOME A BLACK QUEEN.

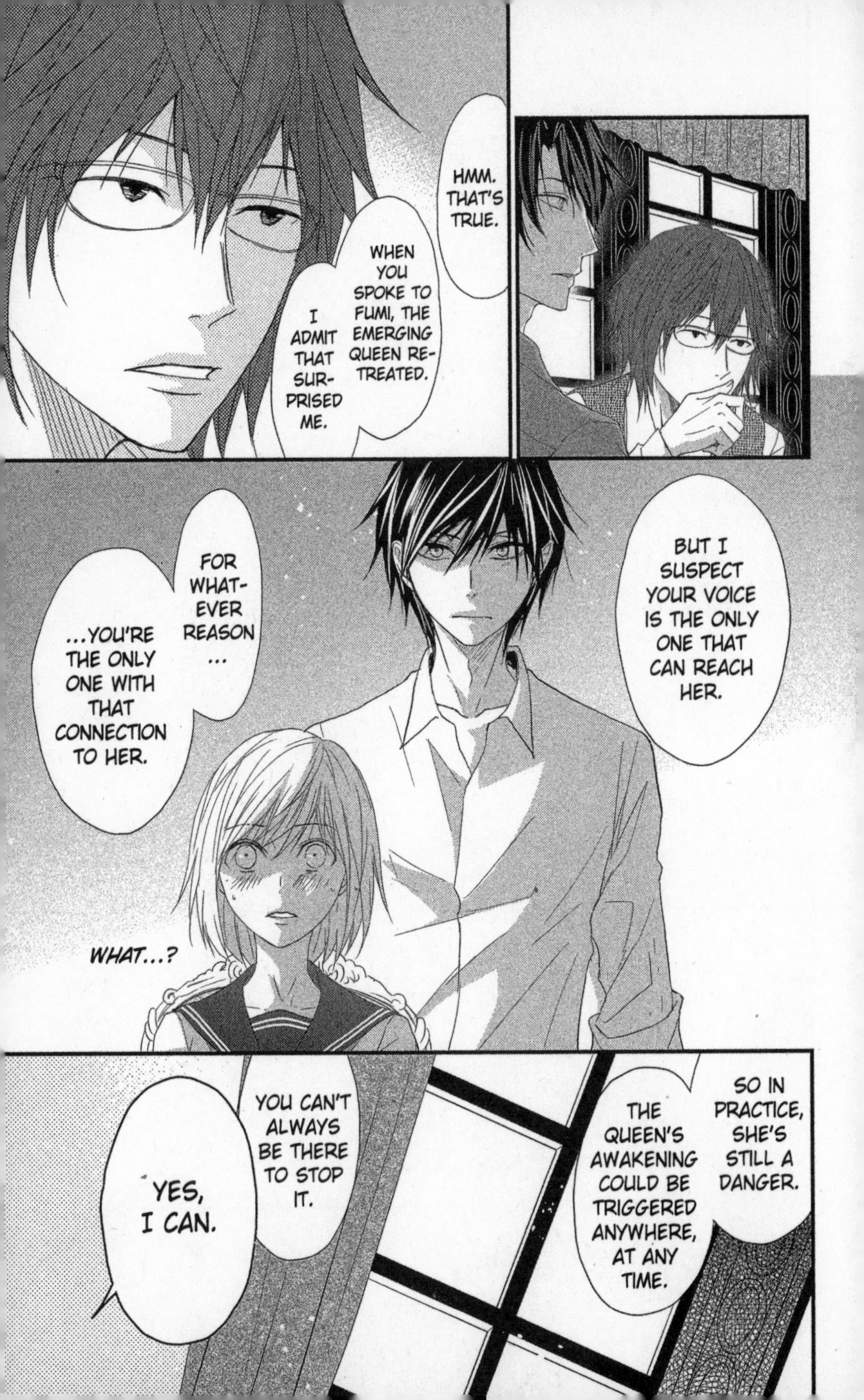
HMM. THAT'S TRUE.
WHEN YOU SPOKE TO FUMI, THE EMERGING QUEEN RE-TREATED.
I ADMIT THAT SUR-PRISED ME.
BUT I SUSPECT YOUR VOICE IS THE ONLY ONE THAT CAN REACH HER.
FOR WHAT-EVER REASON ...
...YOU'RE THE ONLY ONE WITH THAT CONNECTION TO HER.
WHAT...?
SO IN PRACTICE, SHE'S STILL A DANGER.
THE QUEEN'S AWAKENING COULD BE TRIGGERED ANYWHERE, AT ANY TIME.
YOU CAN'T ALWAYS BE THERE TO STOP IT.
YES, I CAN.

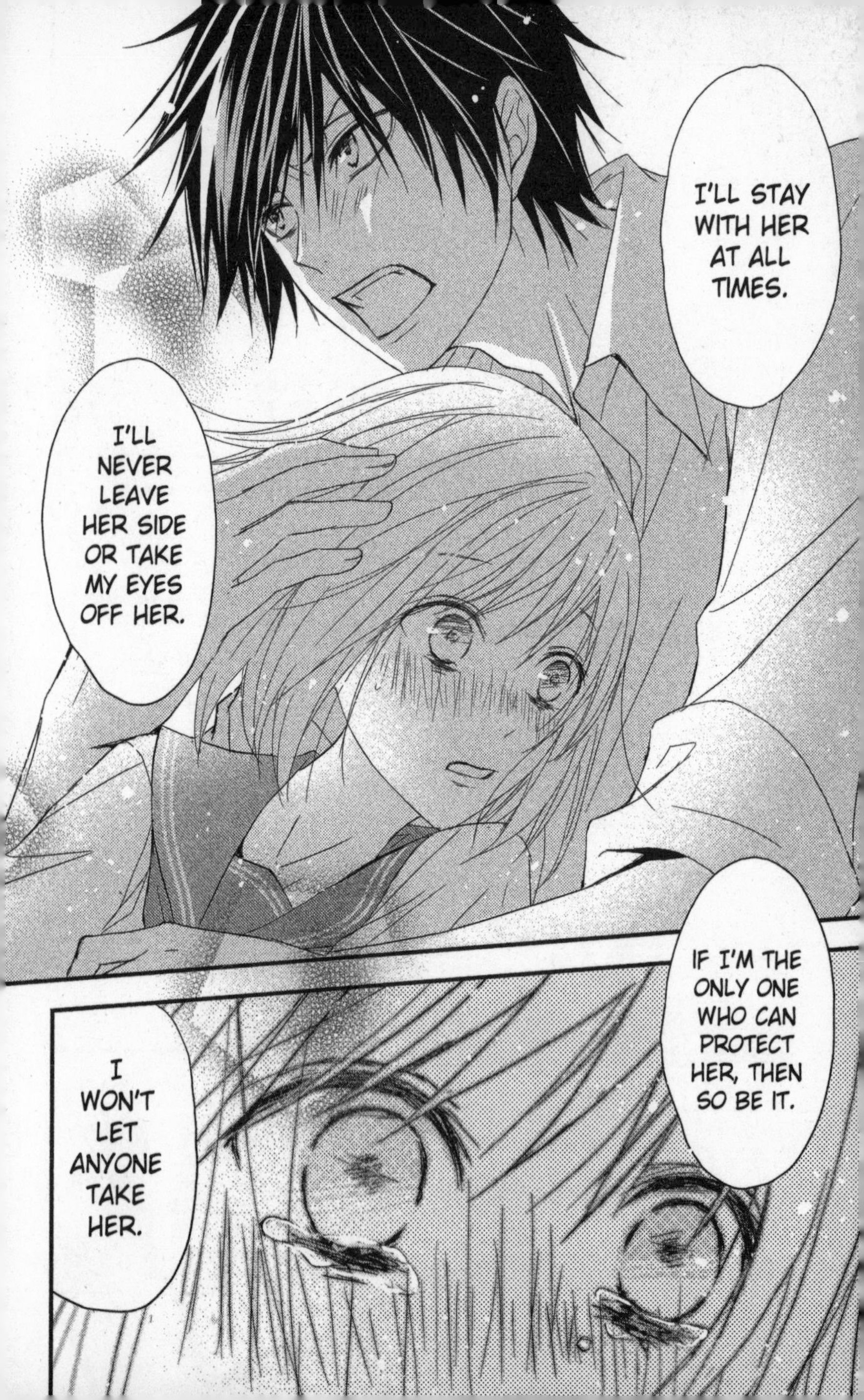
I'LL STAY WITH HER AT ALL TIMES.
I'LL NEVER LEAVE HER SIDE OR TAKE MY EYES OFF HER.
IF I'M THE ONLY ONE WHO CAN PROTECT HER, THEN SO BE IT.
I WON'T LET ANYONE TAKE HER.

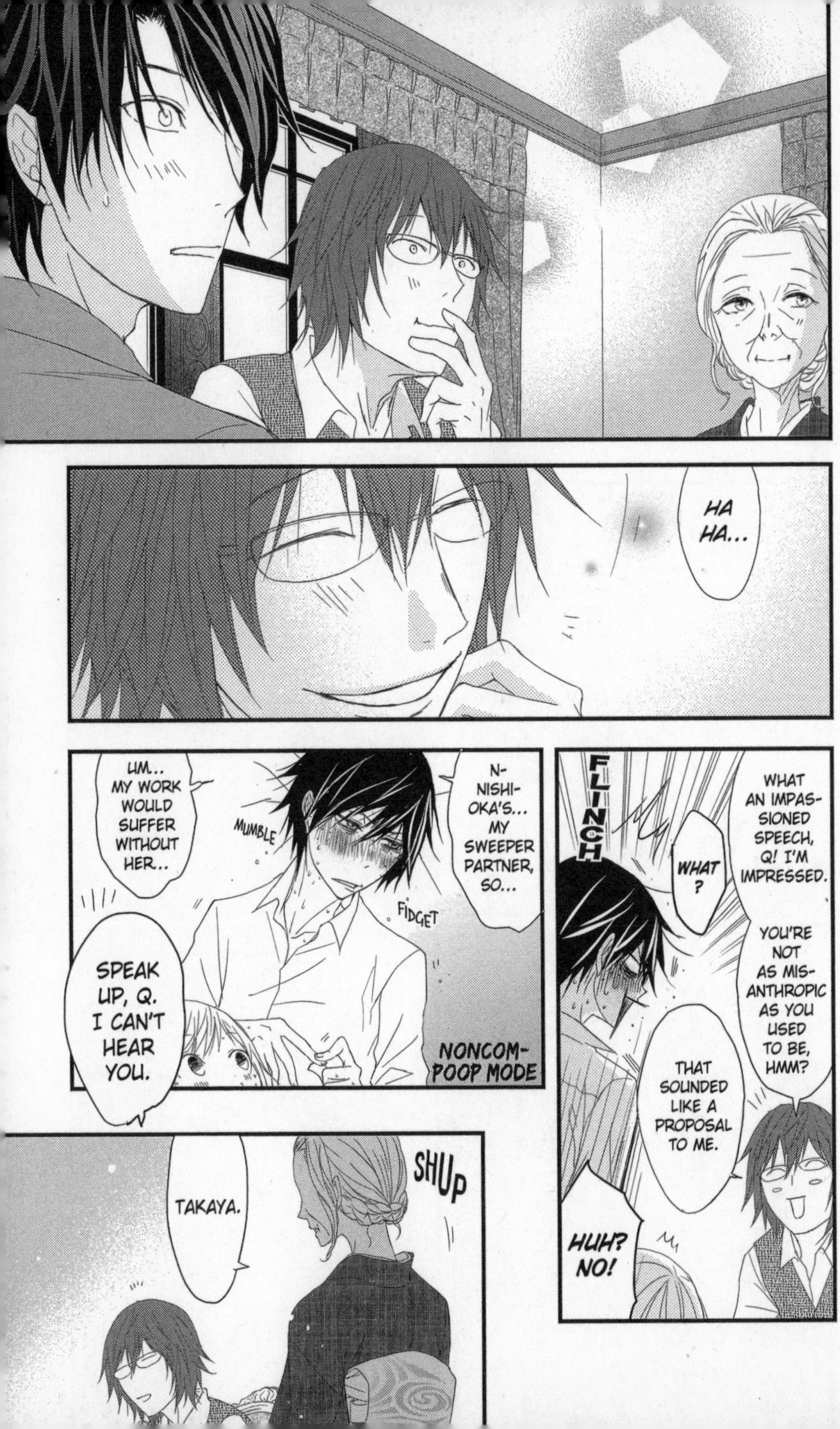
HA HA...
WHAT AN IMPASSIONED SPEECH, Q! I'M IMPRESSED.
FLINCH
WHAT?
YOU'RE NOT AS MISANTHROPIC AS YOU USED TO BE, HMM?
THAT SOUNDED LIKE A PROPOSAL TO ME.
HUH? NO!
N-NISHIOKA'S... MY SWEEPER PARTNER, SO...
UM... MY WORK WOULD SUFFER WITHOUT HER...
MUMBLE
FIDGET
NONCOMPOOP MODE
SPEAK UP, Q. I CAN'T HEAR YOU.
SHUP
TAKAYA.

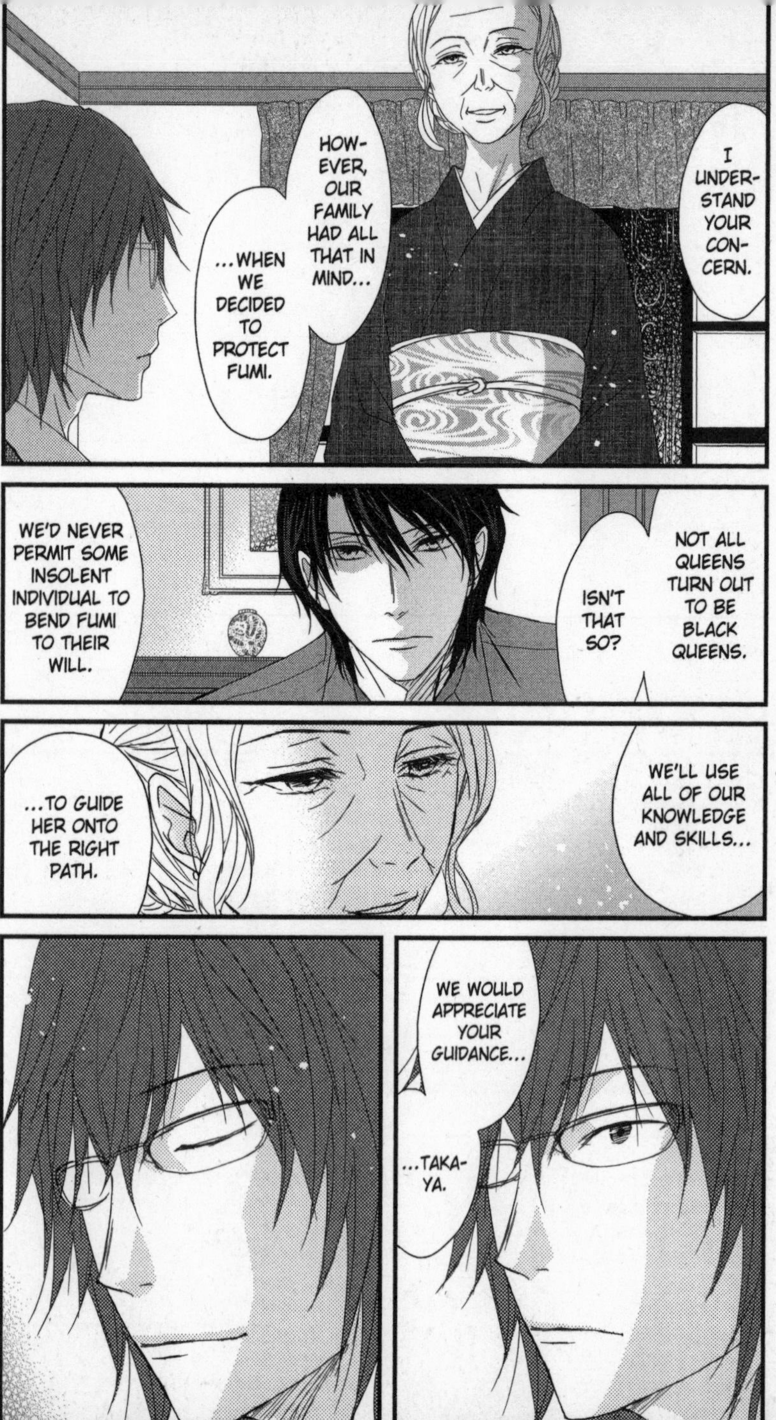
I UNDERSTAND YOUR CONCERN.
HOWEVER, OUR FAMILY HAD ALL THAT IN MIND...
...WHEN WE DECIDED TO PROTECT FUMI.
NOT ALL QUEENS TURN OUT TO BE BLACK QUEENS.
ISN'T THAT SO?
WE'D NEVER PERMIT SOME INSOLENT INDIVIDUAL TO BEND FUMI TO THEIR WILL.
WE'LL USE ALL OF OUR KNOWLEDGE AND SKILLS...
...TO GUIDE HER ONTO THE RIGHT PATH.
WE WOULD APPRECIATE YOUR GUIDANCE...
...TAKAYA.

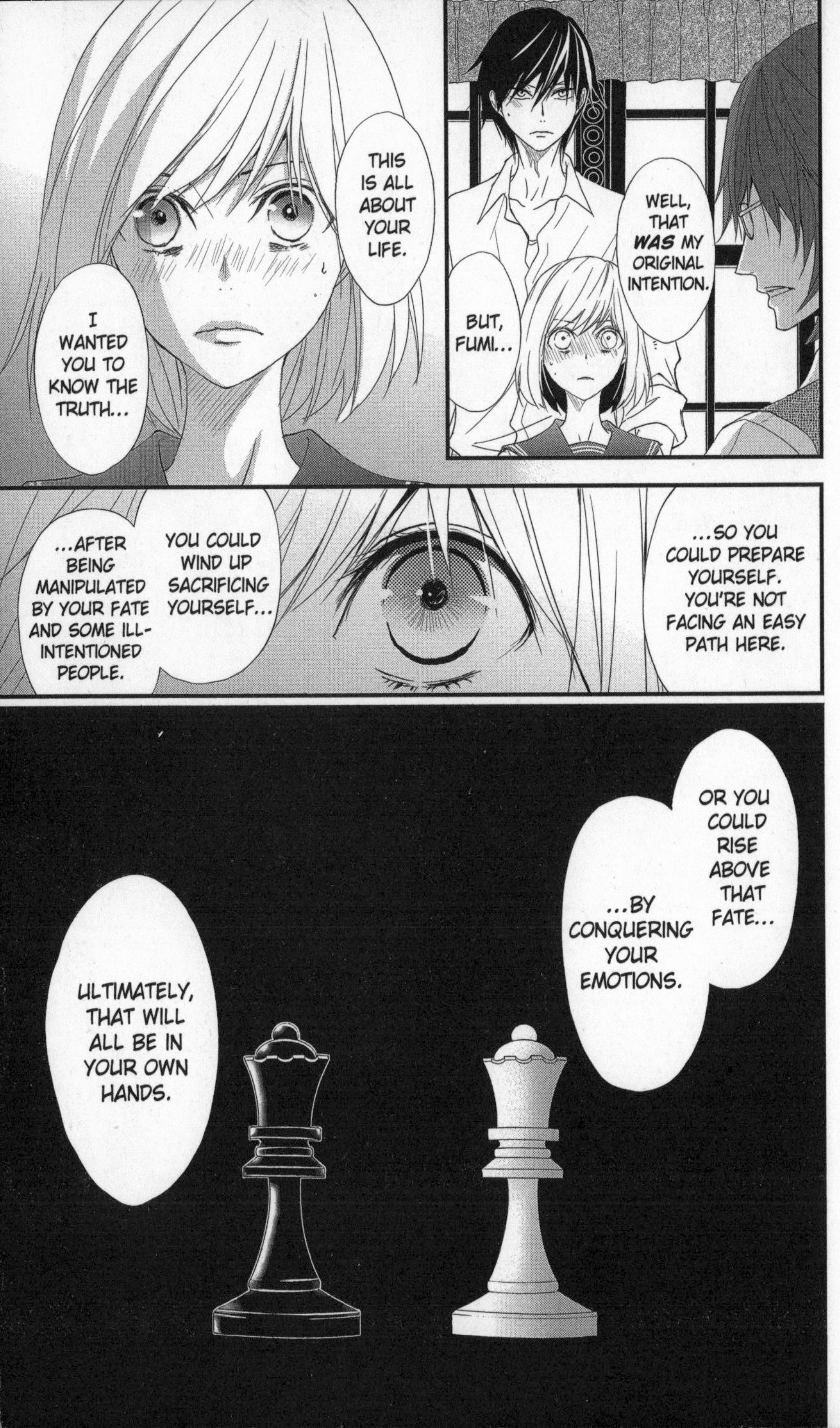
WELL, THAT WAS MY ORIGINAL INTENTION.
BUT, FUMI...
THIS IS ALL ABOUT YOUR LIFE.
I WANTED YOU TO KNOW THE TRUTH...
...SO YOU COULD PREPARE YOURSELF. YOU'RE NOT FACING AN EASY PATH HERE.
YOU COULD WIND UP SACRIFICING YOURSELF...
...AFTER BEING MANIPULATED BY YOUR FATE AND SOME ILL-INTENTIONED PEOPLE.
OR YOU COULD RISE ABOVE THAT FATE...
...BY CONQUERING YOUR EMOTIONS.
ULTIMATELY, THAT WILL ALL BE IN YOUR OWN HANDS.

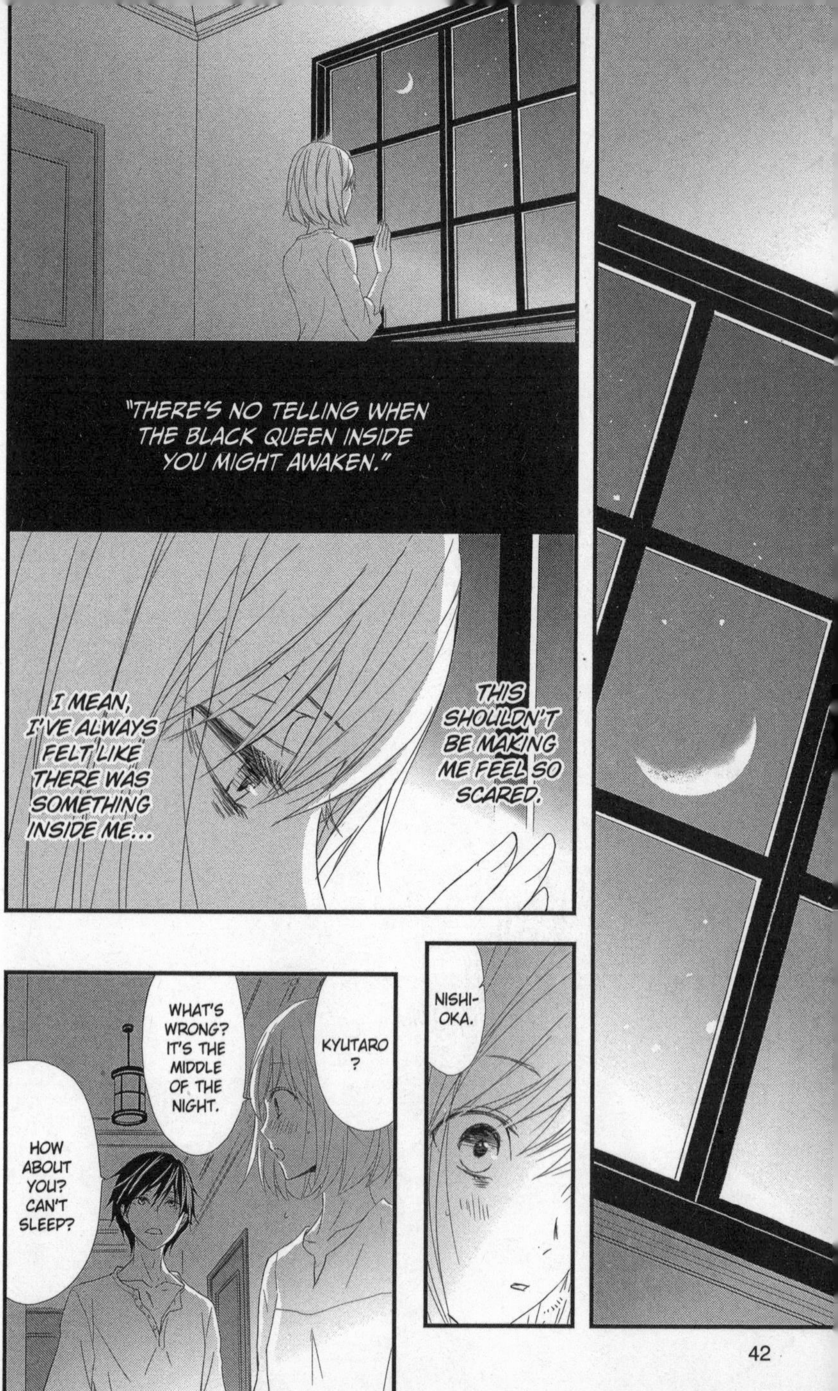
"THERE'S NO TELLING WHEN THE BLACK QUEEN INSIDE YOU MIGHT AWAKEN."
THIS SHOULDN'T BE MAKING ME FEEL SO SCARED.
I MEAN, I'VE ALWAYS FELT LIKE THERE WAS SOMETHING INSIDE ME...
NISHI-OKA.
KYUTARO?
WHAT'S WRONG? IT'S THE MIDDLE OF THE NIGHT.
HOW ABOUT YOU? CAN'T SLEEP?

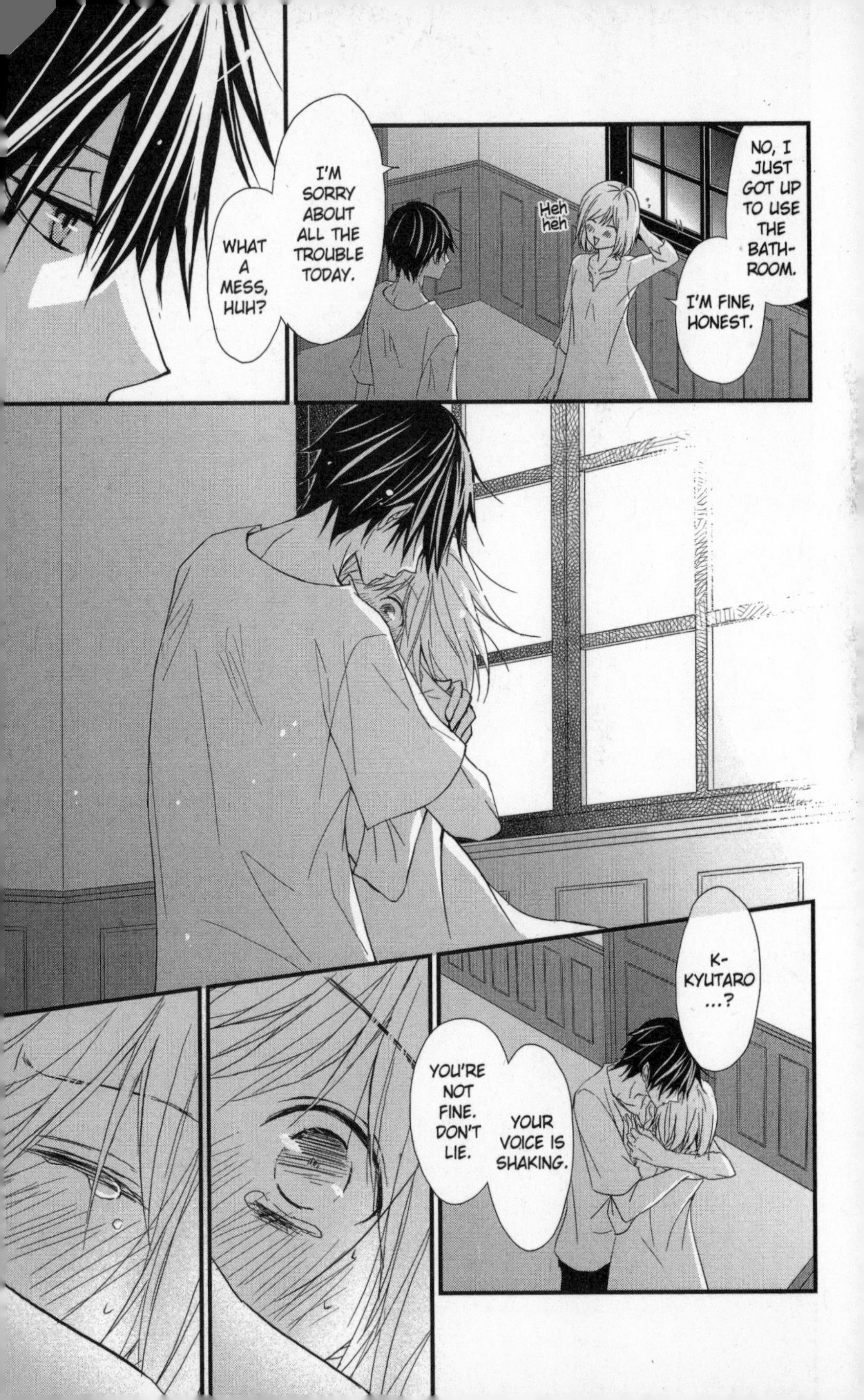
NO, I JUST GOT UP TO USE THE BATH-ROOM.
I'M FINE, HONEST.
Heh heh
I'M SORRY ABOUT ALL THE TROUBLE TODAY.
WHAT A MESS, HUH?
K-KYUTARO...?
YOUR VOICE IS SHAKING.
YOU'RE NOT FINE. DON'T LIE.

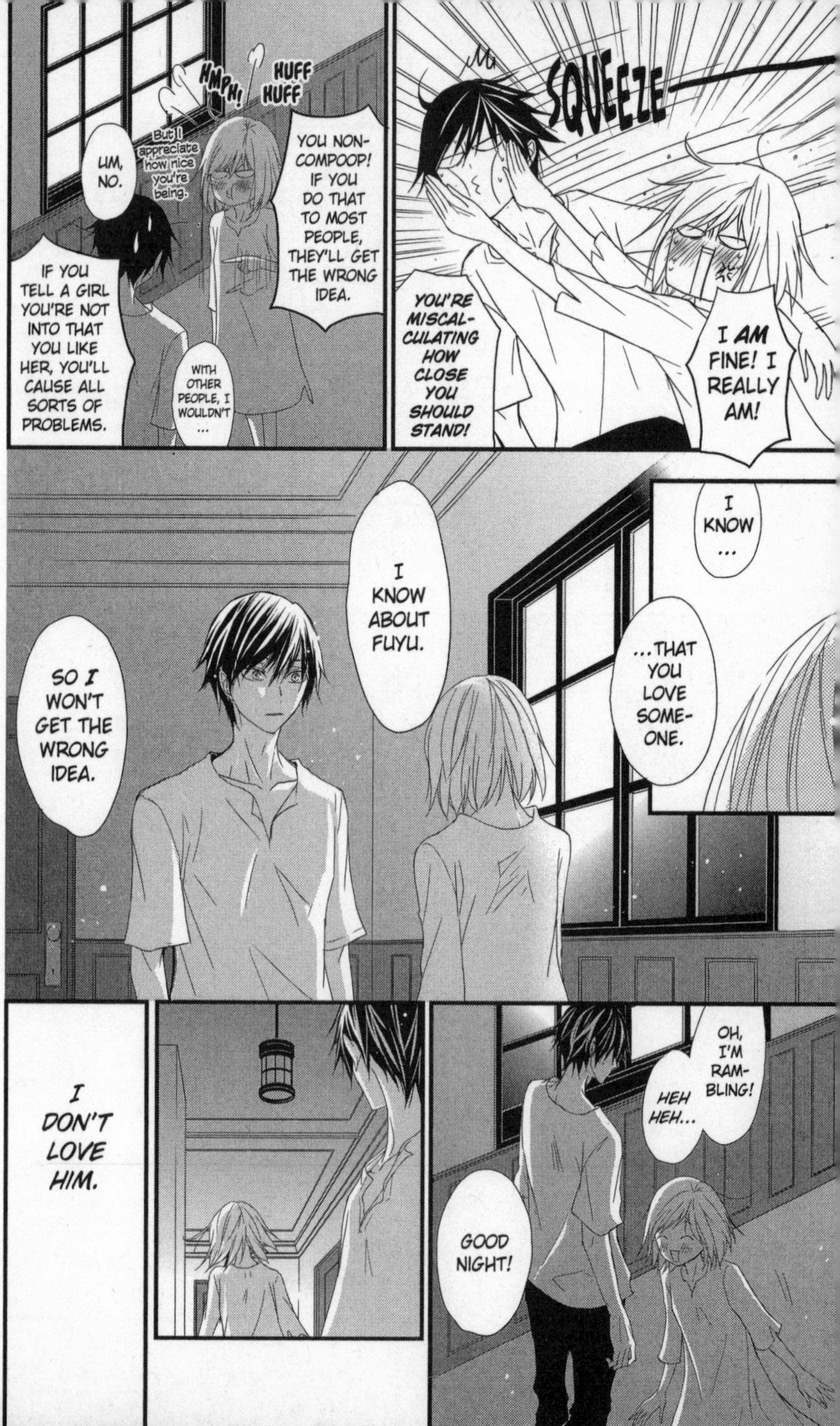
SQUEEZE
Mu
I AM FINE! I REALLY AM!
YOU'RE MISCALCULATING HOW CLOSE YOU SHOULD STAND!
HUFF HUFF
HMPH!
YOU NON-COMPOOP! IF YOU DO THAT TO MOST PEOPLE, THEY'LL GET THE WRONG IDEA.
But I appreciate how nice you're being.
UM, NO.
WITH OTHER PEOPLE, I WOULDN'T ...
IF YOU TELL A GIRL YOU'RE NOT INTO THAT YOU LIKE HER, YOU'LL CAUSE ALL SORTS OF PROBLEMS.
I KNOW ...
...THAT YOU LOVE SOME-ONE.
I KNOW ABOUT FUYU.
SO I WON'T GET THE WRONG IDEA.
OH, I'M RAM-BLING!
HEH HEH...
GOOD NIGHT!
I DON'T LOVE HIM.

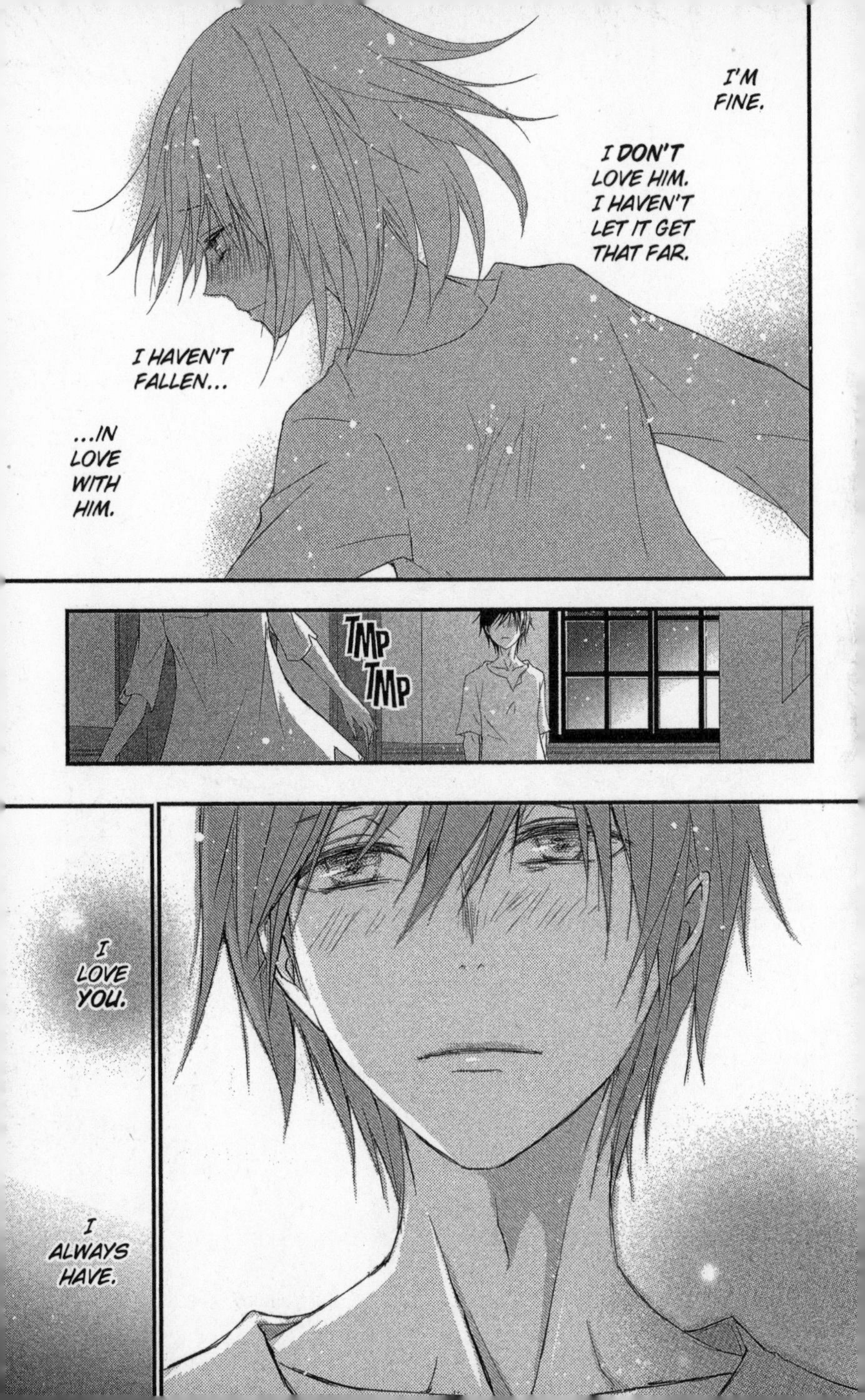
I'M FINE.
I DON'T LOVE HIM. I HAVEN'T LET IT GET THAT FAR.
I HAVEN'T FALLEN...
...IN LOVE WITH HIM.
TMP TMP
I LOVE YOU.
I ALWAYS HAVE.

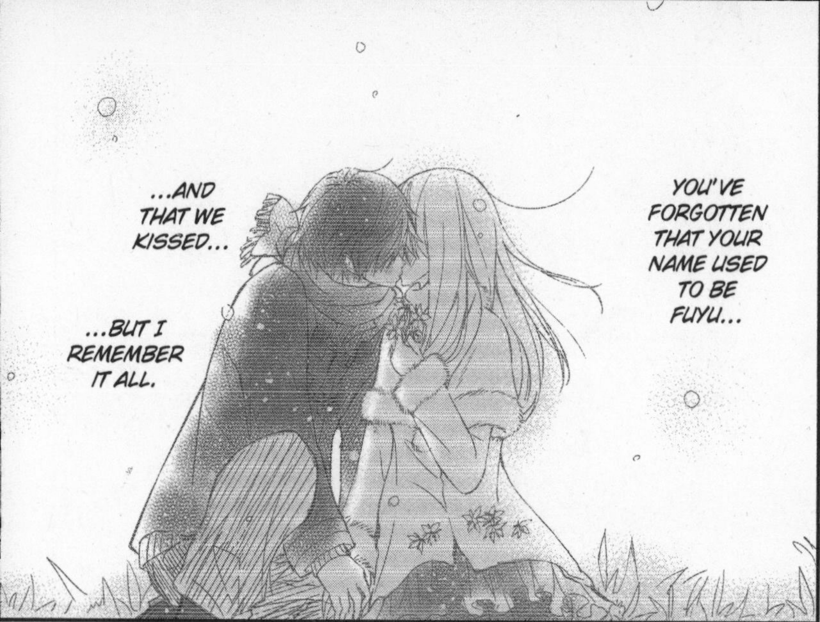
YOU'VE FORGOTTEN THAT YOUR NAME USED TO BE FUYU...
...AND THAT WE KISSED...
...BUT I REMEMBER IT ALL.

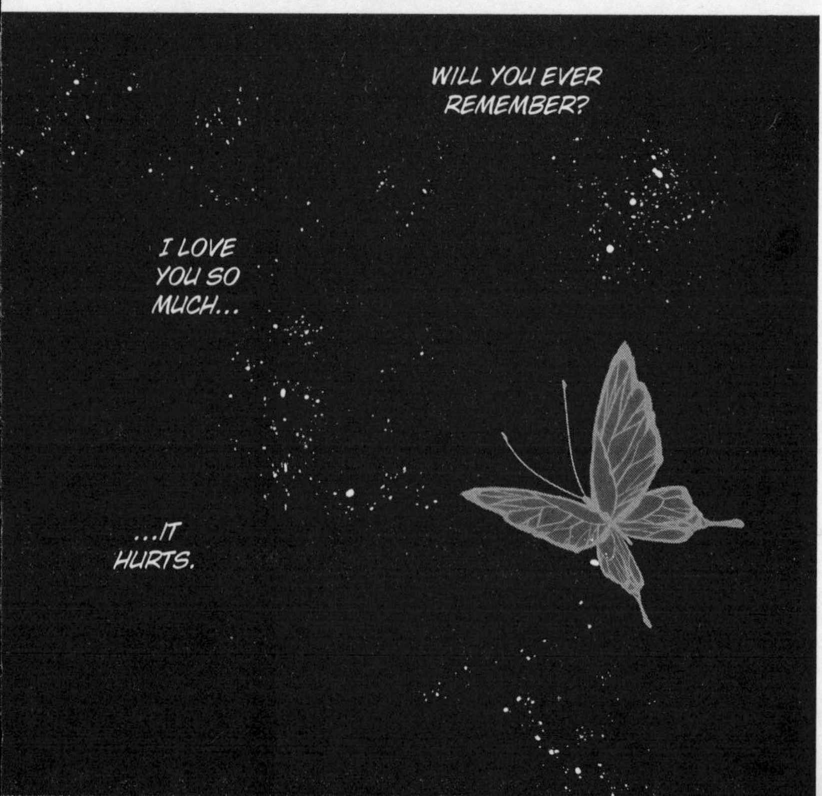
WILL YOU EVER REMEMBER?
I LOVE YOU SO MUCH...
...IT HURTS.

Chapter 2

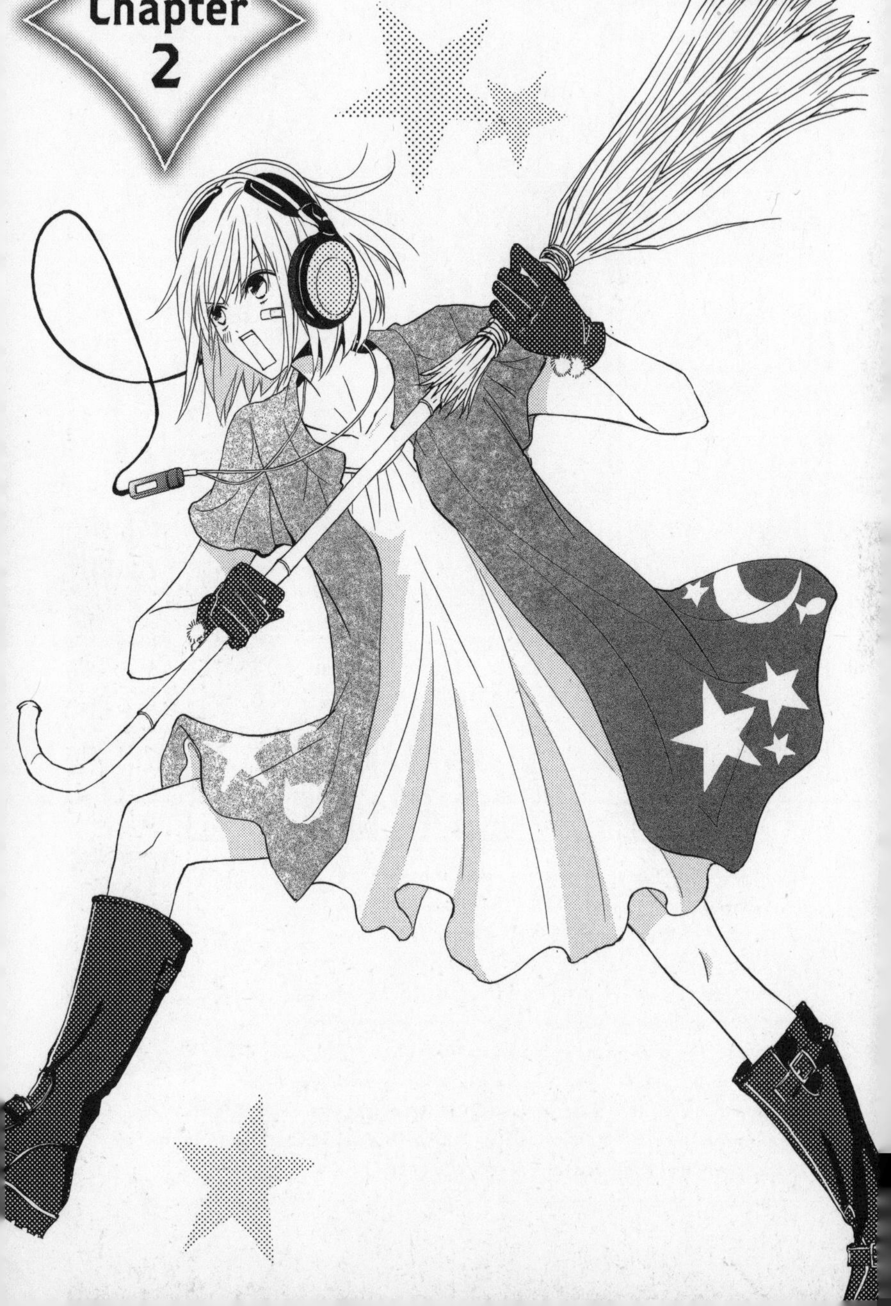

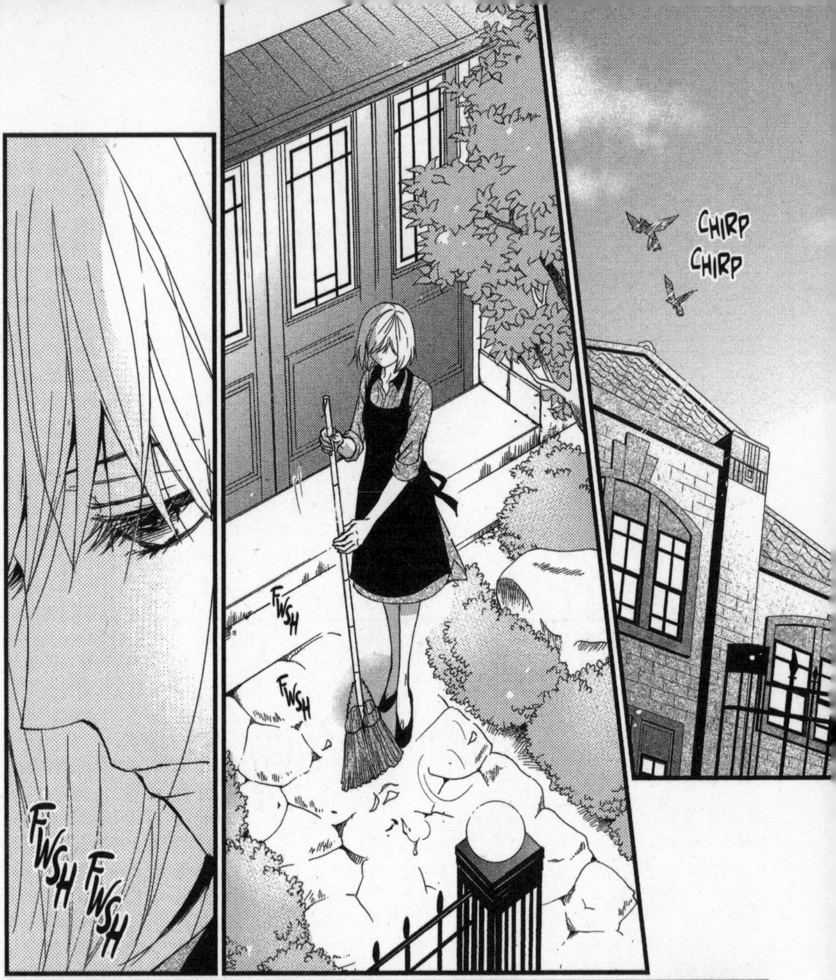
CHIRP
CHIRP
FWSH
FWSH
FWSH
FWSH

"Noncompoop" is one of the few new terms that are coming up in *Queen's Quality* (although there's also a new character). To be honest, I no longer felt comfortable with the term I was using before (it involved the word "disorder"), so I quickly came up with this new one. It's a bit vulgar—sorry about that! Of course, it's always possible that terms like this could hurt some people, but I need something to express the concept for this story. So I plan to use "noncompoop" with great care, and I'll try to always follow it up within 0.2 seconds with a line expressing love and respect for that person.

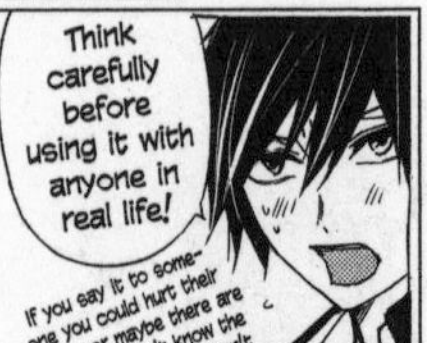
Think carefully before using it with anyone in real life!
If you say it to someone you could hurt their feelings, or maybe there are people who don't know the term because they haven't read previous volumes!
Noncompoop Spokesperson

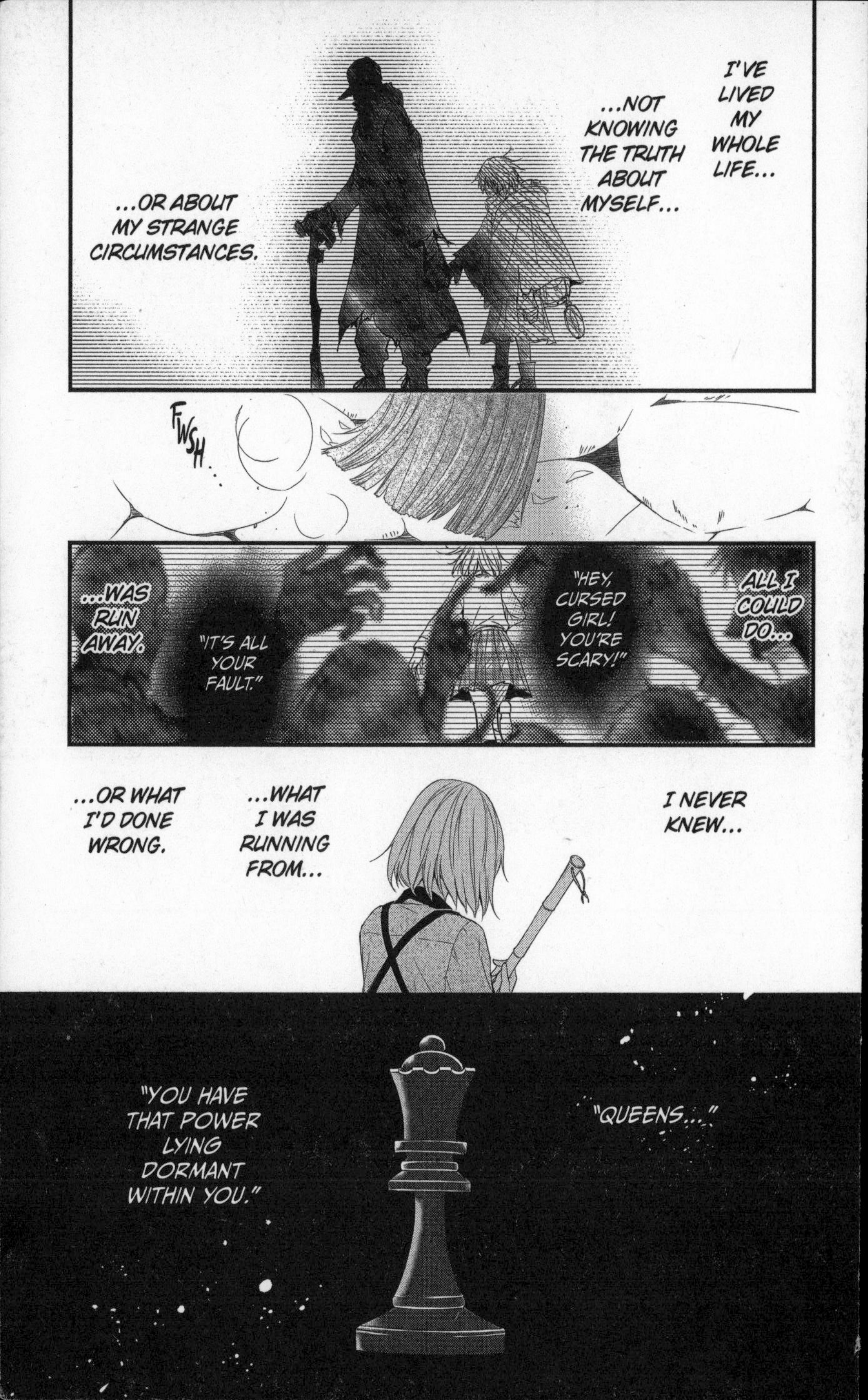
I'VE LIVED MY WHOLE LIFE...
...NOT KNOWING THE TRUTH ABOUT MYSELF...
...OR ABOUT MY STRANGE CIRCUMSTANCES.
FWSH...
ALL I COULD DO...
"HEY, CURSED GIRL! YOU'RE SCARY!"
"IT'S ALL YOUR FAULT."
...WAS RUN AWAY.
I NEVER KNEW...
...WHAT I WAS RUNNING FROM...
...OR WHAT I'D DONE WRONG.
"QUEENS..."
"YOU HAVE THAT POWER LYING DORMANT WITHIN YOU."

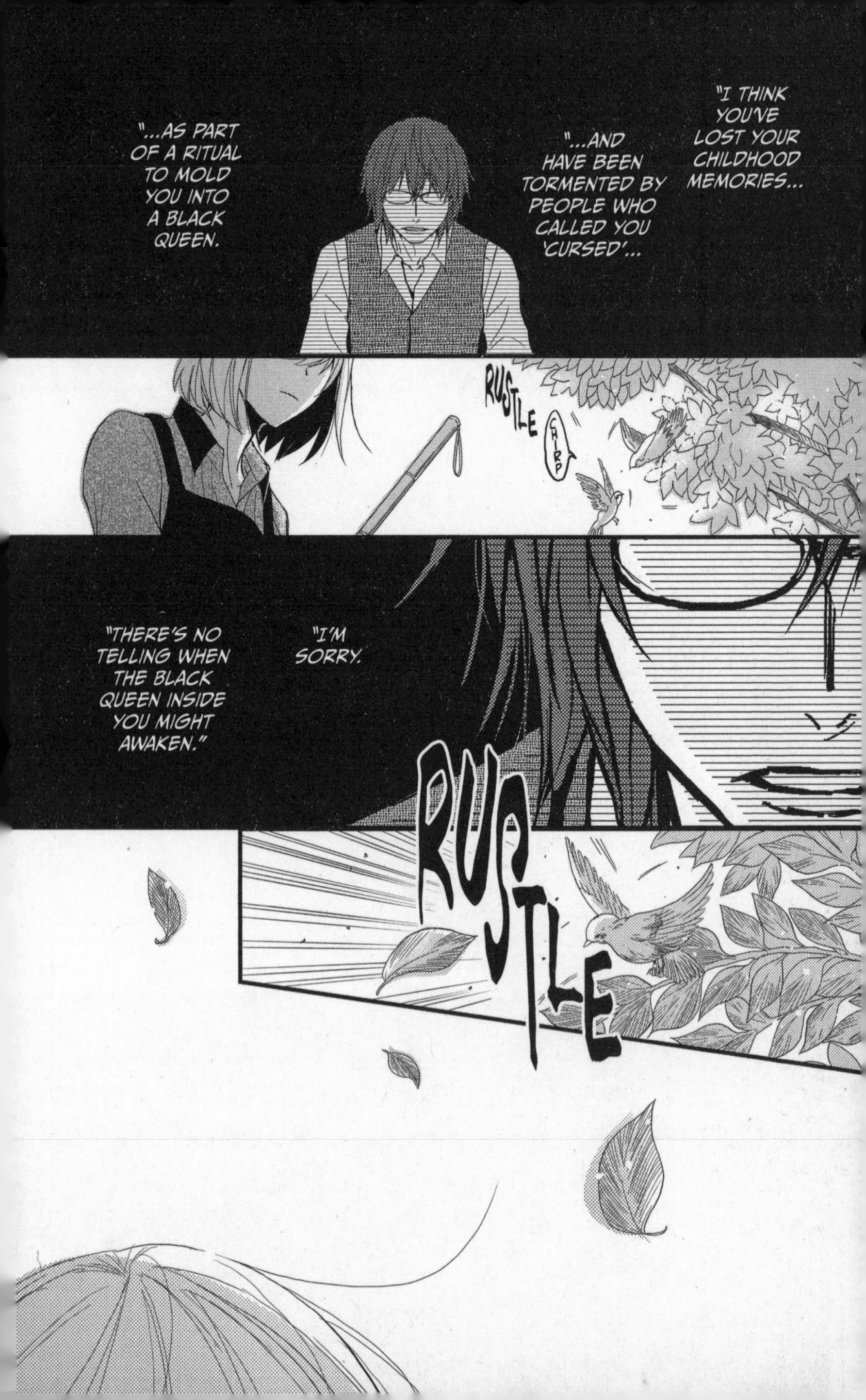
"I THINK YOU'VE LOST YOUR CHILDHOOD MEMORIES...
"...AND HAVE BEEN TORMENTED BY PEOPLE WHO CALLED YOU 'CURSED'...
"...AS PART OF A RITUAL TO MOLD YOU INTO A BLACK QUEEN.
RUSTLE
CHIRP
"I'M SORRY.
"THERE'S NO TELLING WHEN THE BLACK QUEEN INSIDE YOU MIGHT AWAKEN."
RUSTLE

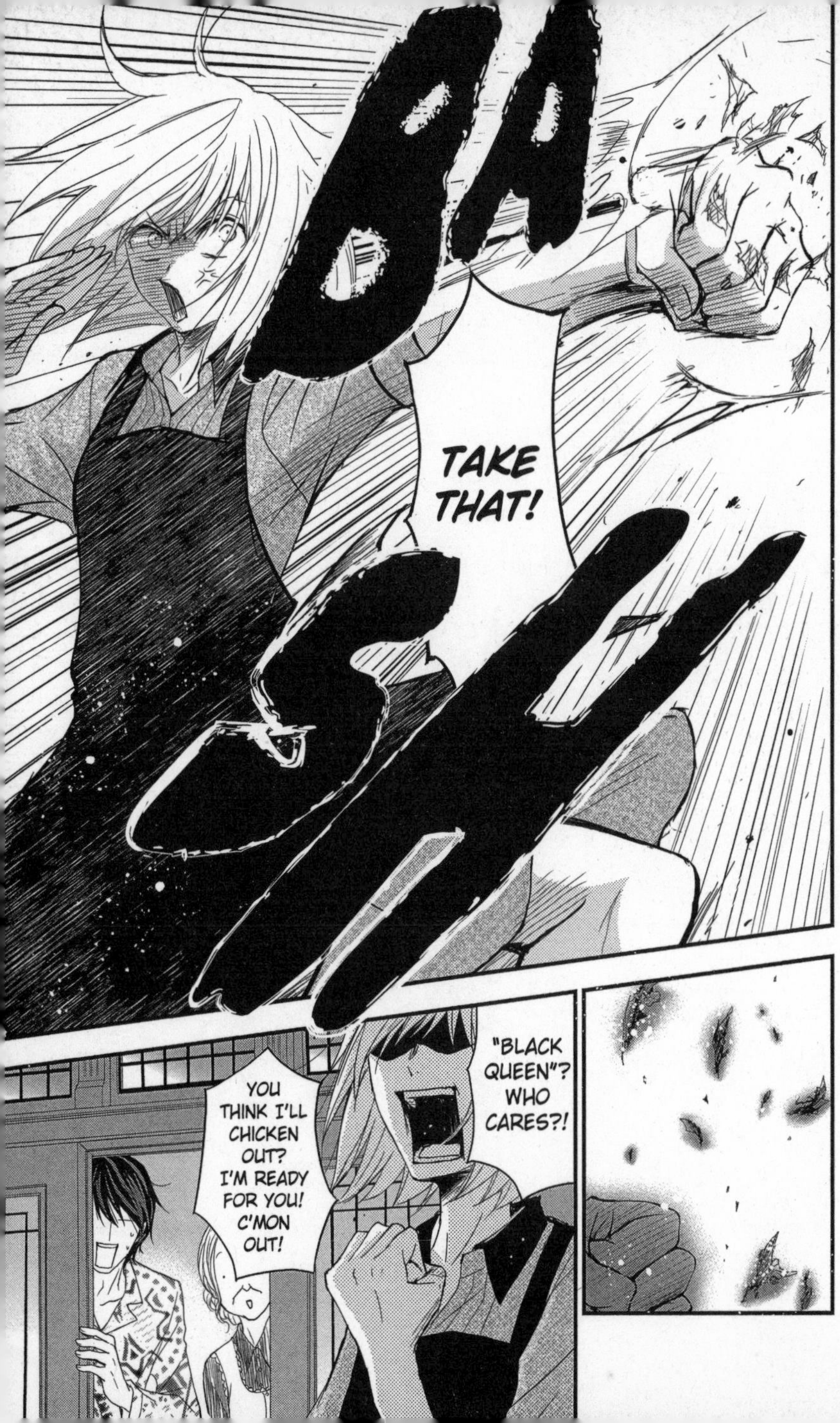
TAKE THAT!
"BLACK QUEEN"? WHO CARES?!
YOU THINK I'LL CHICKEN OUT? I'M READY FOR YOU! C'MON OUT!

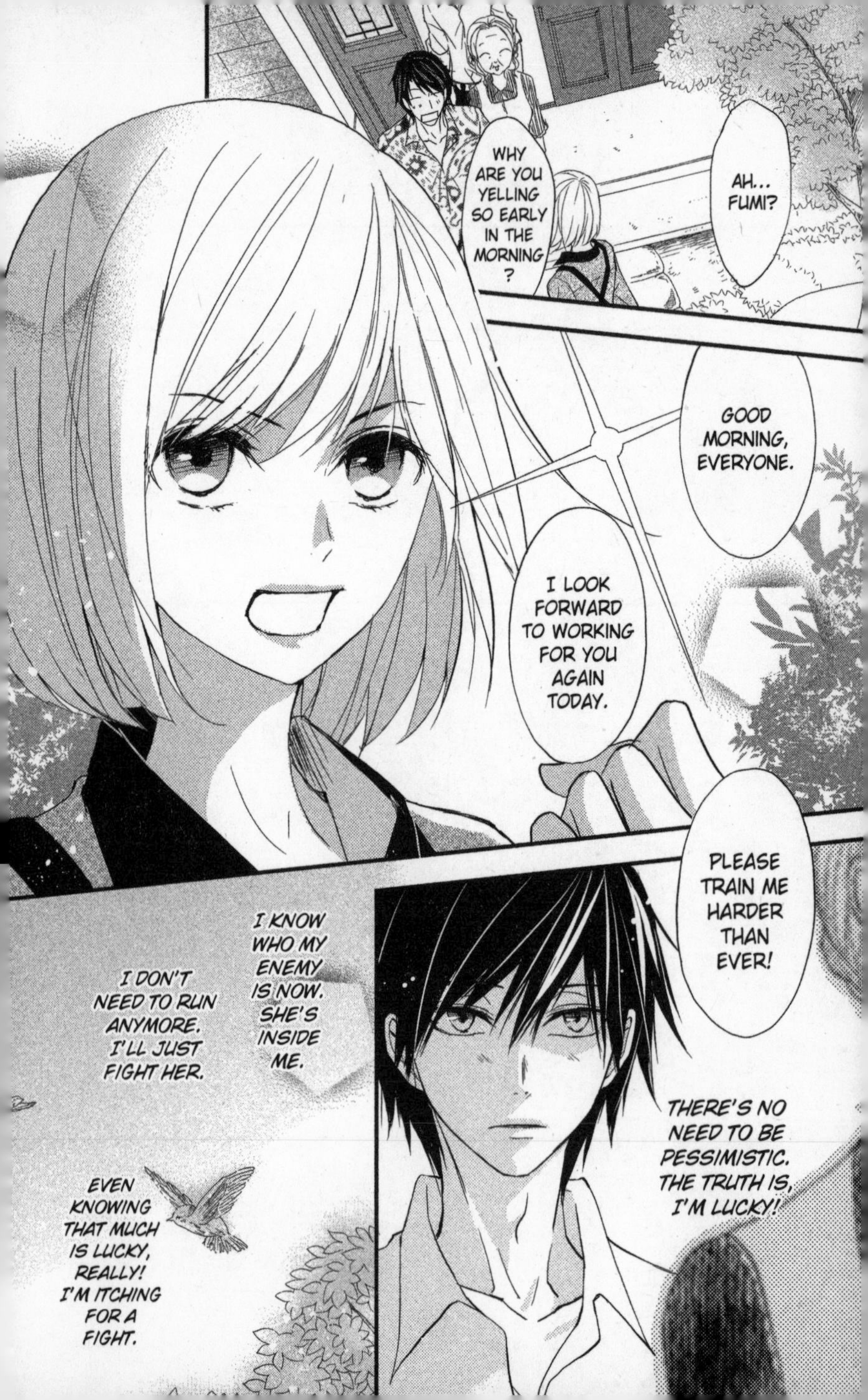
AH... FUMI?
WHY ARE YOU YELLING SO EARLY IN THE MORNING?
GOOD MORNING, EVERYONE.
I LOOK FORWARD TO WORKING FOR YOU AGAIN TODAY.
PLEASE TRAIN ME HARDER THAN EVER!
THERE'S NO NEED TO BE PESSIMISTIC. THE TRUTH IS, I'M LUCKY!
I KNOW WHO MY ENEMY IS NOW. SHE'S INSIDE ME.
I DON'T NEED TO RUN ANYMORE. I'LL JUST FIGHT HER.
EVEN KNOWING THAT MUCH IS LUCKY, REALLY! I'M ITCHING FOR A FIGHT.

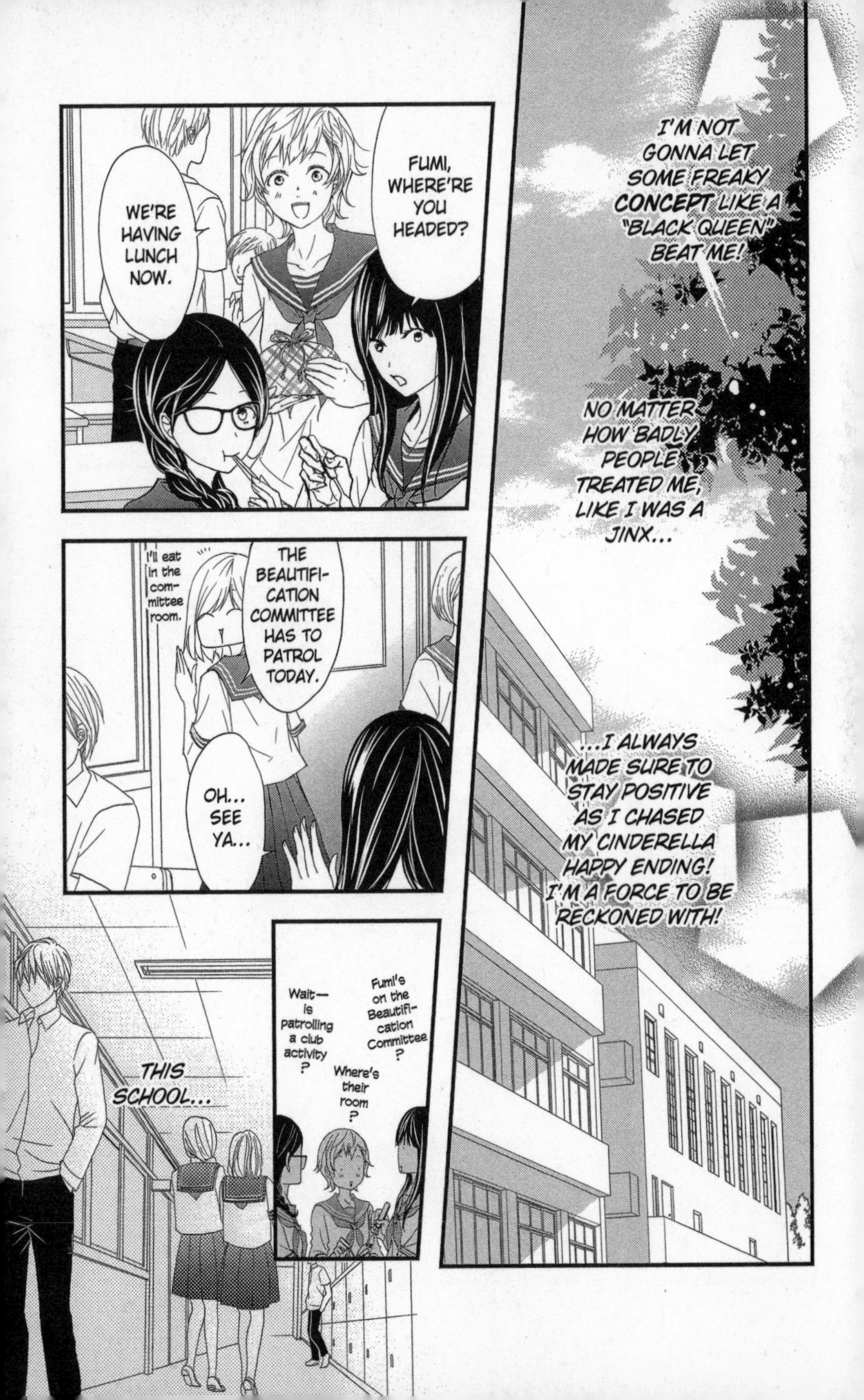
I'M NOT GONNA LET SOME FREAKY CONCEPT LIKE A "BLACK QUEEN" BEAT ME!
NO MATTER HOW BADLY PEOPLE TREATED ME, LIKE I WAS A JINX...
...I ALWAYS MADE SURE TO STAY POSITIVE AS I CHASED MY CINDERELLA HAPPY ENDING! I'M A FORCE TO BE RECKONED WITH!
FUMI, WHERE'RE YOU HEADED?
WE'RE HAVING LUNCH NOW.
THE BEAUTIFICATION COMMITTEE HAS TO PATROL TODAY.
I'll eat in the committee room.
OH... SEE YA...
Fumi's on the Beautification Committee?
Wait—is patrolling a club activity?
Where's their room?
THIS SCHOOL...

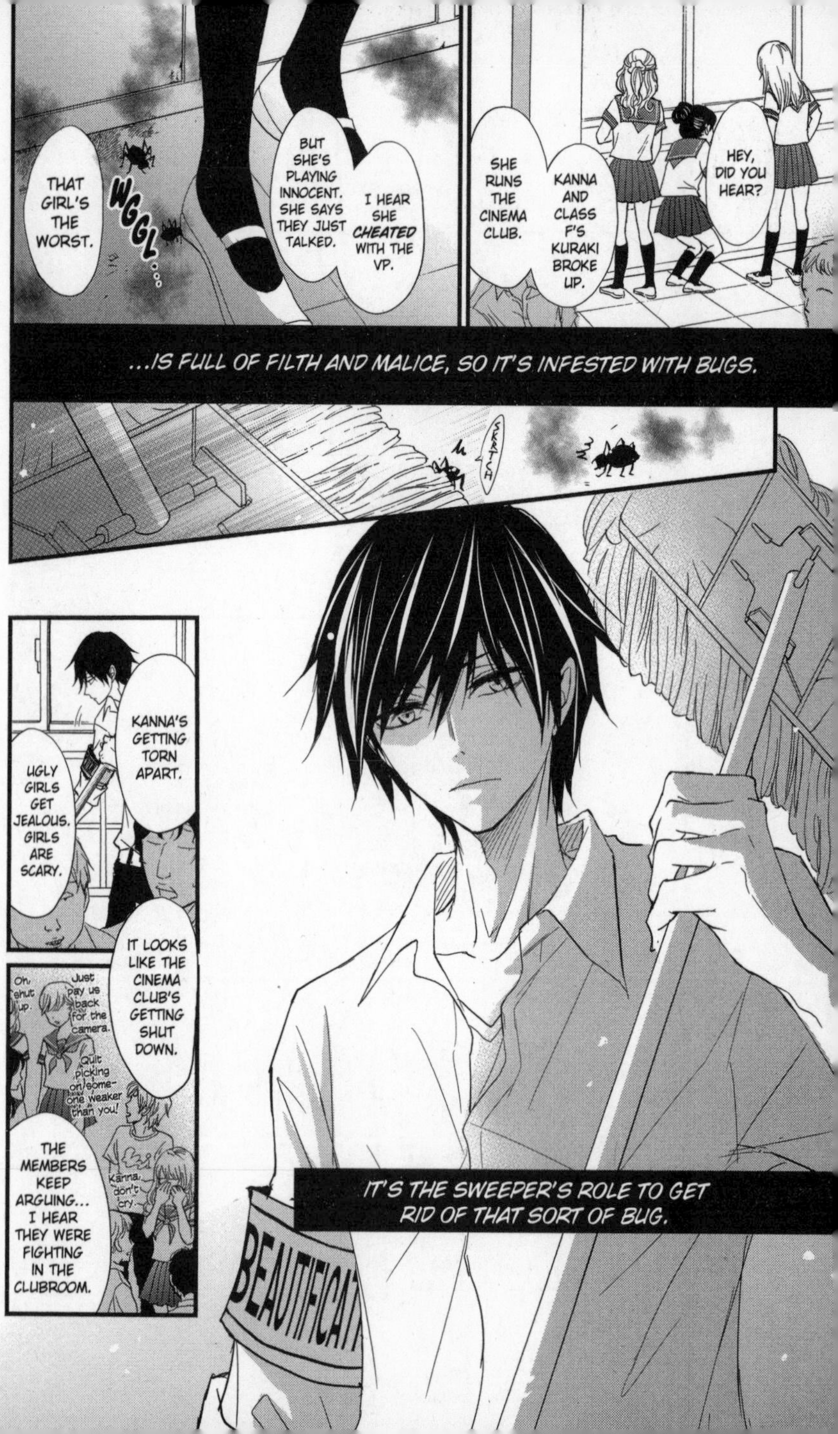
HEY, DID YOU HEAR?
KANNA AND CLASS F'S KURAKI BROKE UP.
SHE RUNS THE CINEMA CLUB.
I HEAR SHE *CHEATED* WITH THE VP.
BUT SHE'S PLAYING INNOCENT. SHE SAYS THEY JUST TALKED.
WGGL...
THAT GIRL'S THE WORST.
...IS FULL OF FILTH AND MALICE, SO IT'S INFESTED WITH BUGS.
SKRTCH
IT'S THE SWEEPER'S ROLE TO GET RID OF THAT SORT OF BUG.
BEAUTIFICAT
KANNA'S GETTING TORN APART.
UGLY GIRLS GET JEALOUS. GIRLS ARE SCARY.
IT LOOKS LIKE THE CINEMA CLUB'S GETTING SHUT DOWN.
Just pay us back for the camera.
Oh, shut up.
Quit picking on someone weaker than you!
Kanna, don't cry.
THE MEMBERS KEEP ARGUING... I HEAR THEY WERE FIGHTING IN THE CLUBROOM.

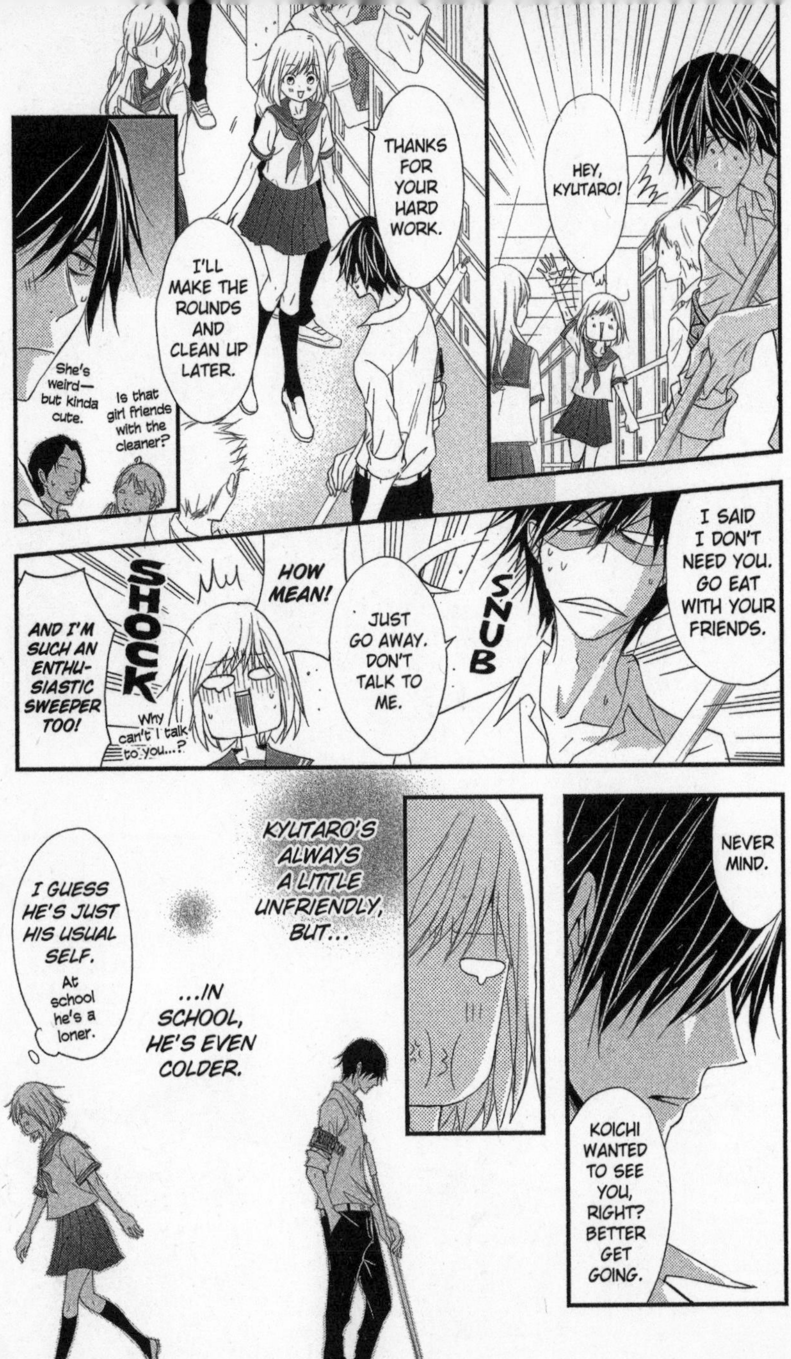
HEY, KYUTARO!
THANKS FOR YOUR HARD WORK.
I'LL MAKE THE ROUNDS AND CLEAN UP LATER.
Is that girl friends with the cleaner?
She's weird—but kinda cute.
I SAID I DON'T NEED YOU. GO EAT WITH YOUR FRIENDS.
SNUB
JUST GO AWAY. DON'T TALK TO ME.
HOW MEAN!
SHOCK
AND I'M SUCH AN ENTHU-SIASTIC SWEEPER TOO!
Why can't I talk to you...?
NEVER MIND.
KOICHI WANTED TO SEE YOU, RIGHT? BETTER GET GOING.
KYUTARO'S ALWAYS A LITTLE UNFRIENDLY, BUT...
...IN SCHOOL, HE'S EVEN COLDER.
I GUESS HE'S JUST HIS USUAL SELF.
At school he's a loner.

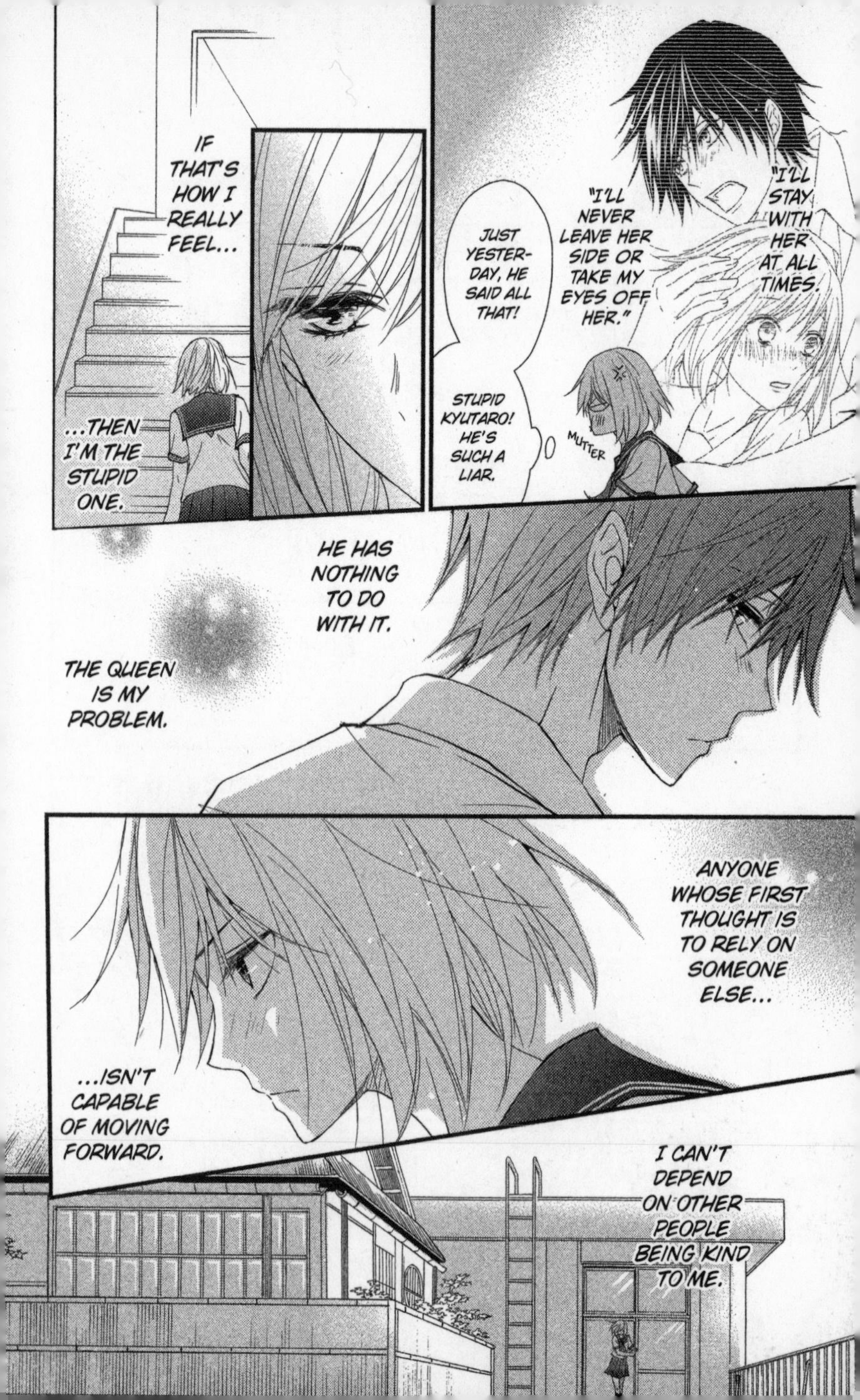
"I'LL STAY WITH HER AT ALL TIMES.
"I'LL NEVER LEAVE HER SIDE OR TAKE MY EYES OFF HER."
JUST YESTER-DAY, HE SAID ALL THAT!
MUTTER
STUPID KYUTARO! HE'S SUCH A LIAR.
IF THAT'S HOW I REALLY FEEL...
...THEN I'M THE STUPID ONE.
HE HAS NOTHING TO DO WITH IT.
THE QUEEN IS MY PROBLEM.
ANYONE WHOSE FIRST THOUGHT IS TO RELY ON SOMEONE ELSE...
...ISN'T CAPABLE OF MOVING FORWARD.
I CAN'T DEPEND ON OTHER PEOPLE BEING KIND TO ME.

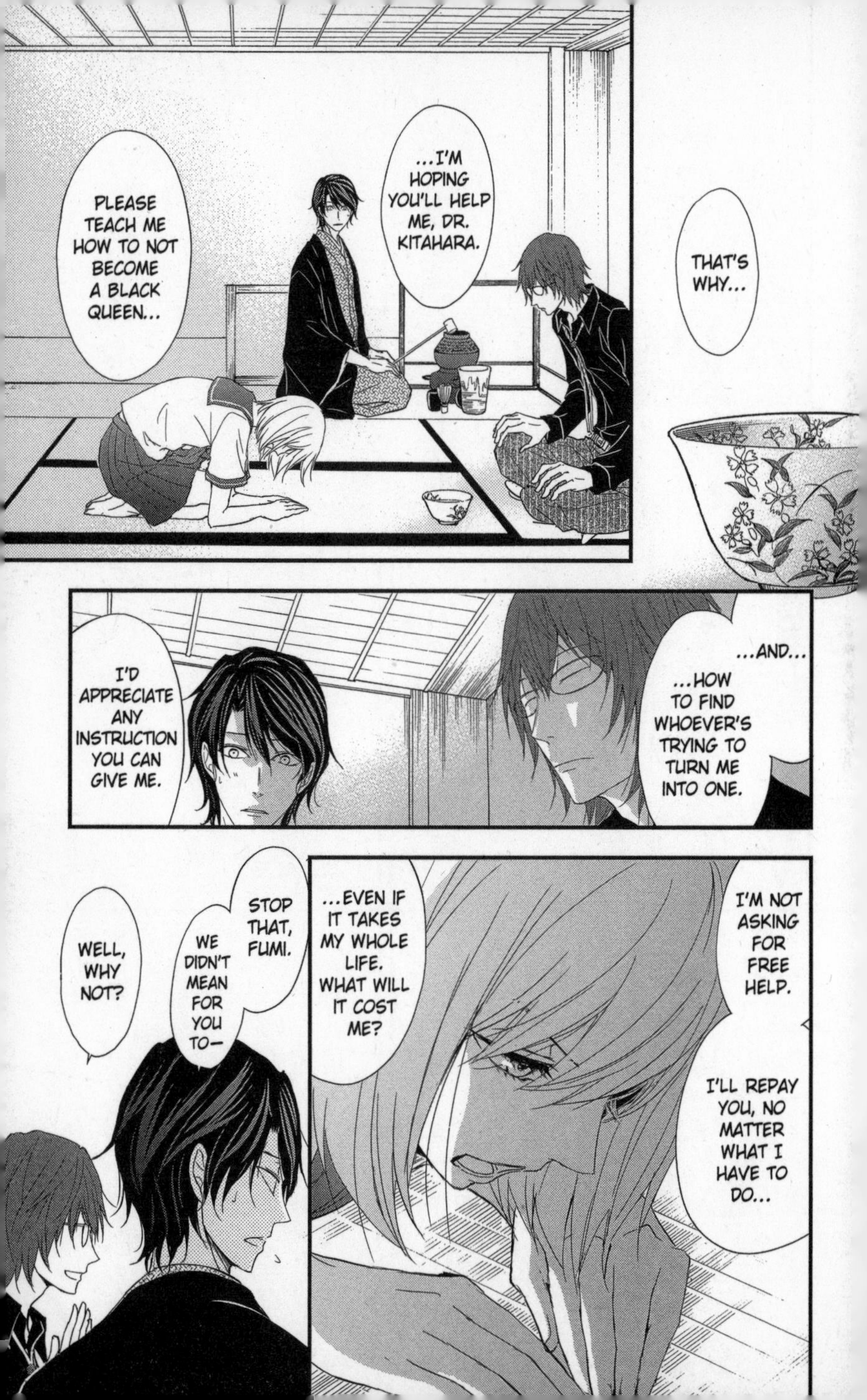
THAT'S WHY...
...I'M HOPING YOU'LL HELP ME, DR. KITAHARA.
PLEASE TEACH ME HOW TO NOT BECOME A BLACK QUEEN...
...AND...
...HOW TO FIND WHOEVER'S TRYING TO TURN ME INTO ONE.
I'D APPRECIATE ANY INSTRUCTION YOU CAN GIVE ME.
I'M NOT ASKING FOR FREE HELP.
I'LL REPAY YOU, NO MATTER WHAT I HAVE TO DO...
...EVEN IF IT TAKES MY WHOLE LIFE. WHAT WILL IT COST ME?
STOP THAT, FUMI.
WE DIDN'T MEAN FOR YOU TO—
WELL, WHY NOT?

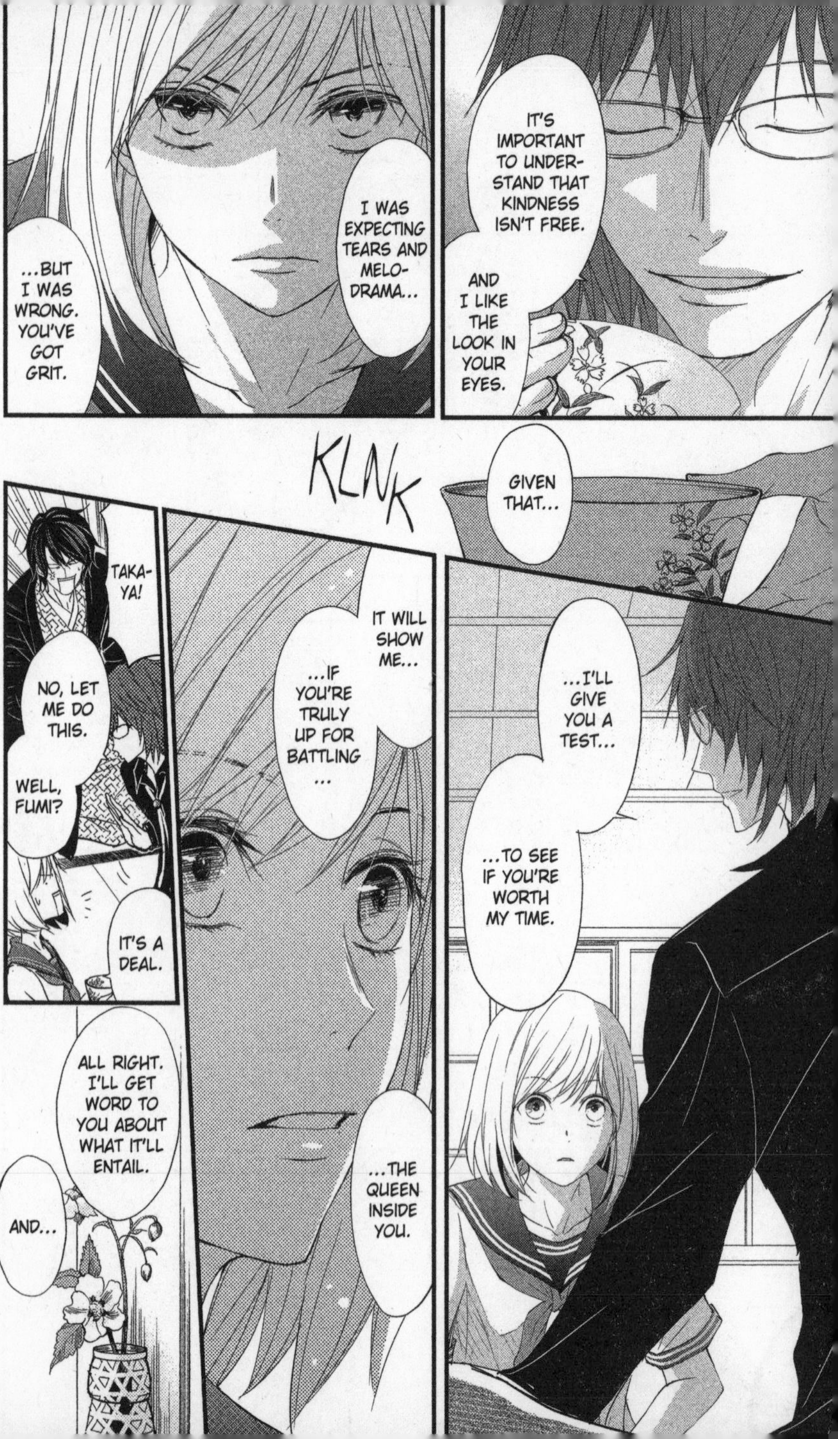
IT'S IMPORTANT TO UNDER-STAND THAT KINDNESS ISN'T FREE.
AND I LIKE THE LOOK IN YOUR EYES.
I WAS EXPECTING TEARS AND MELO-DRAMA...
...BUT I WAS WRONG. YOU'VE GOT GRIT.
KLNK
GIVEN THAT...
...I'LL GIVE YOU A TEST...
...TO SEE IF YOU'RE WORTH MY TIME.
IT WILL SHOW ME...
...IF YOU'RE TRULY UP FOR BATTLING...
...THE QUEEN INSIDE YOU.
TAKA-YA!
NO, LET ME DO THIS.
WELL, FUMI?
IT'S A DEAL.
ALL RIGHT. I'LL GET WORD TO YOU ABOUT WHAT IT'LL ENTAIL.
AND...

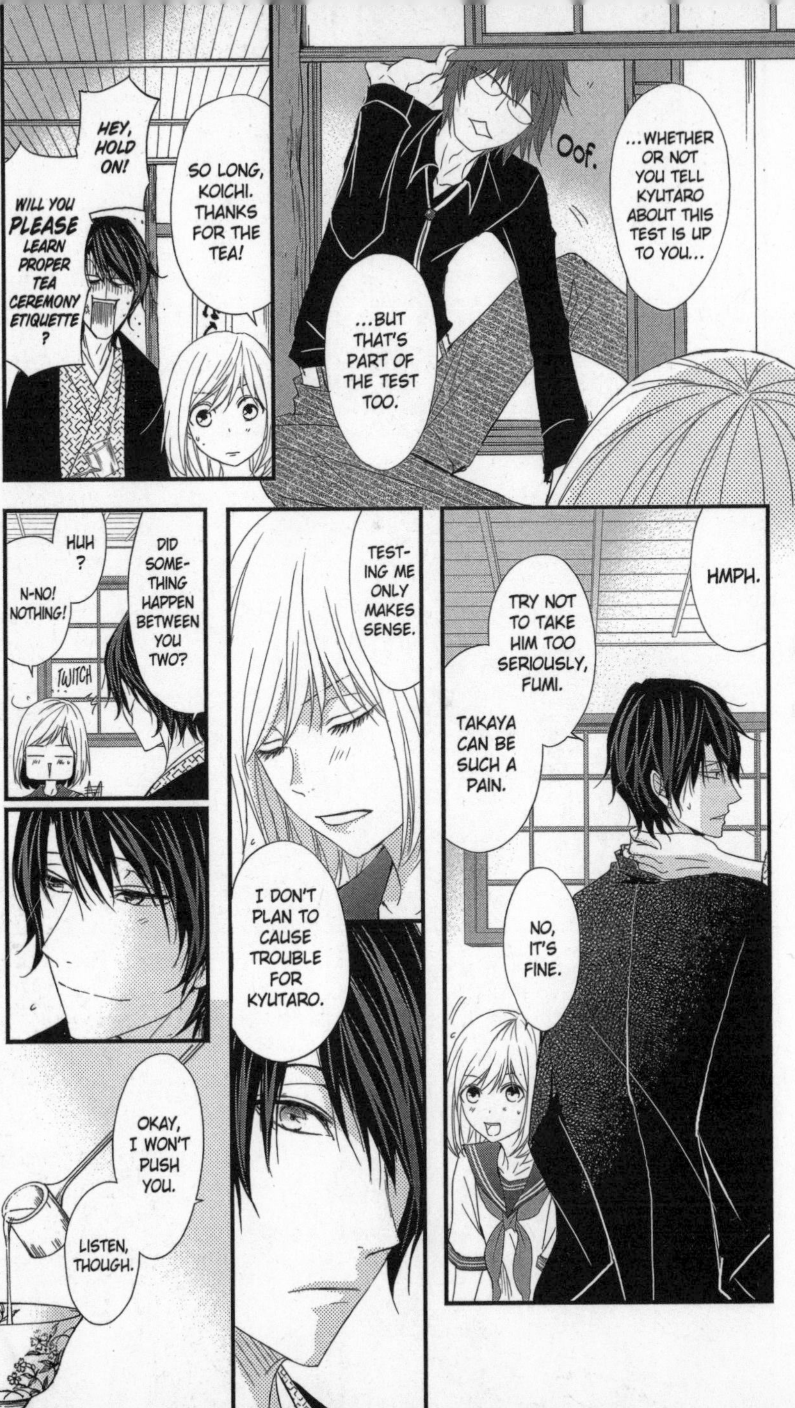
...WHETHER OR NOT YOU TELL KYUTARO ABOUT THIS TEST IS UP TO YOU...
Oof.
...BUT THAT'S PART OF THE TEST TOO.
SO LONG, KOICHI. THANKS FOR THE TEA!
HEY, HOLD ON!
WILL YOU PLEASE LEARN PROPER TEA CEREMONY ETIQUETTE?
HMPH.
TRY NOT TO TAKE HIM TOO SERIOUSLY, FUMI.
TAKAYA CAN BE SUCH A PAIN.
NO, IT'S FINE.
TESTING ME ONLY MAKES SENSE.
I DON'T PLAN TO CAUSE TROUBLE FOR KYUTARO.
DID SOMETHING HAPPEN BETWEEN YOU TWO?
HUH?
N-NO! NOTHING!
TWITCH
OKAY, I WON'T PUSH YOU.
LISTEN, THOUGH.

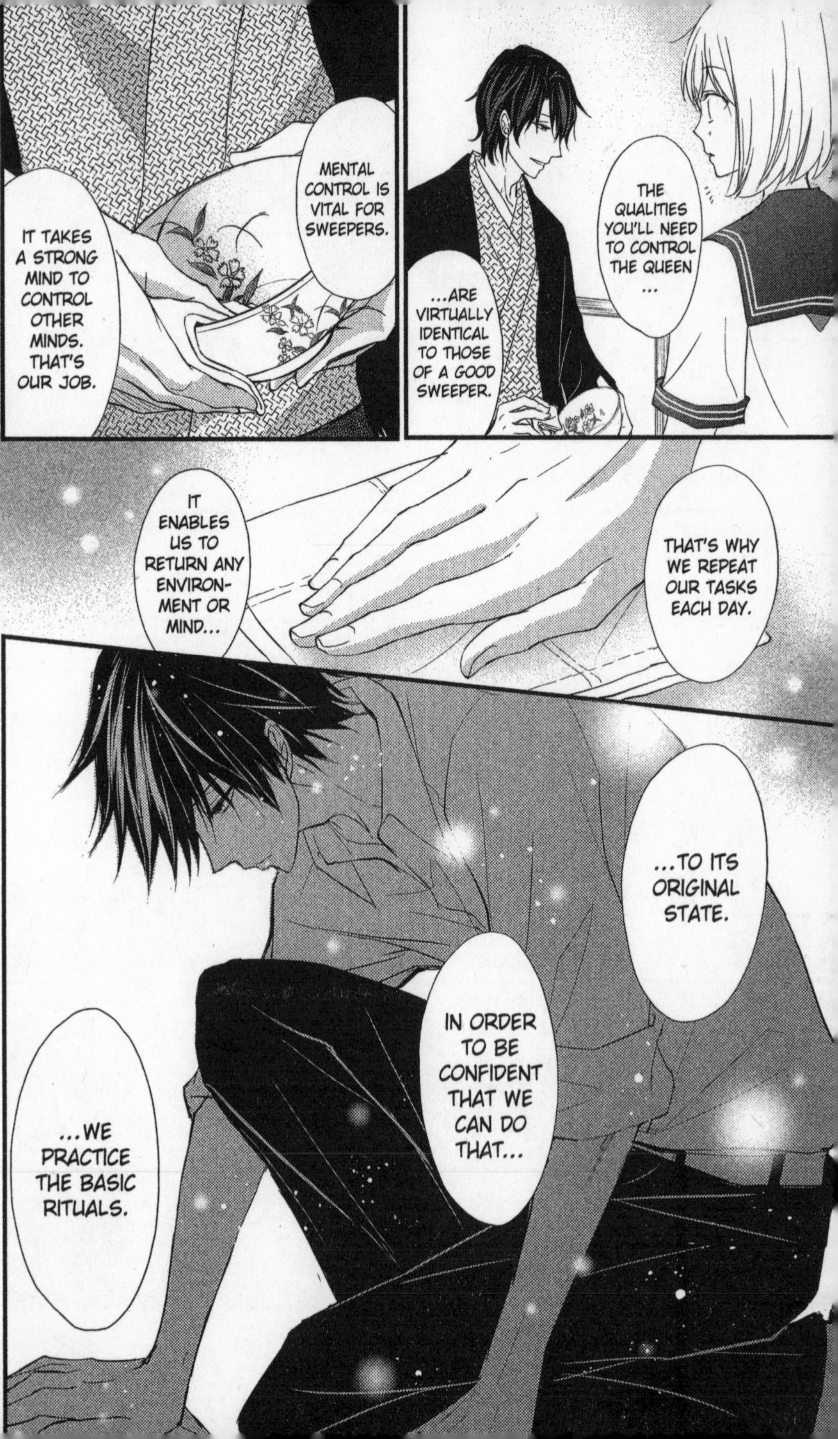
THE QUALITIES YOU'LL NEED TO CONTROL THE QUEEN ...
...ARE VIRTUALLY IDENTICAL TO THOSE OF A GOOD SWEEPER.
MENTAL CONTROL IS VITAL FOR SWEEPERS.
IT TAKES A STRONG MIND TO CONTROL OTHER MINDS. THAT'S OUR JOB.
THAT'S WHY WE REPEAT OUR TASKS EACH DAY.
IT ENABLES US TO RETURN ANY ENVIRON-MENT OR MIND...
...TO ITS ORIGINAL STATE.
IN ORDER TO BE CONFIDENT THAT WE CAN DO THAT...
...WE PRACTICE THE BASIC RITUALS.

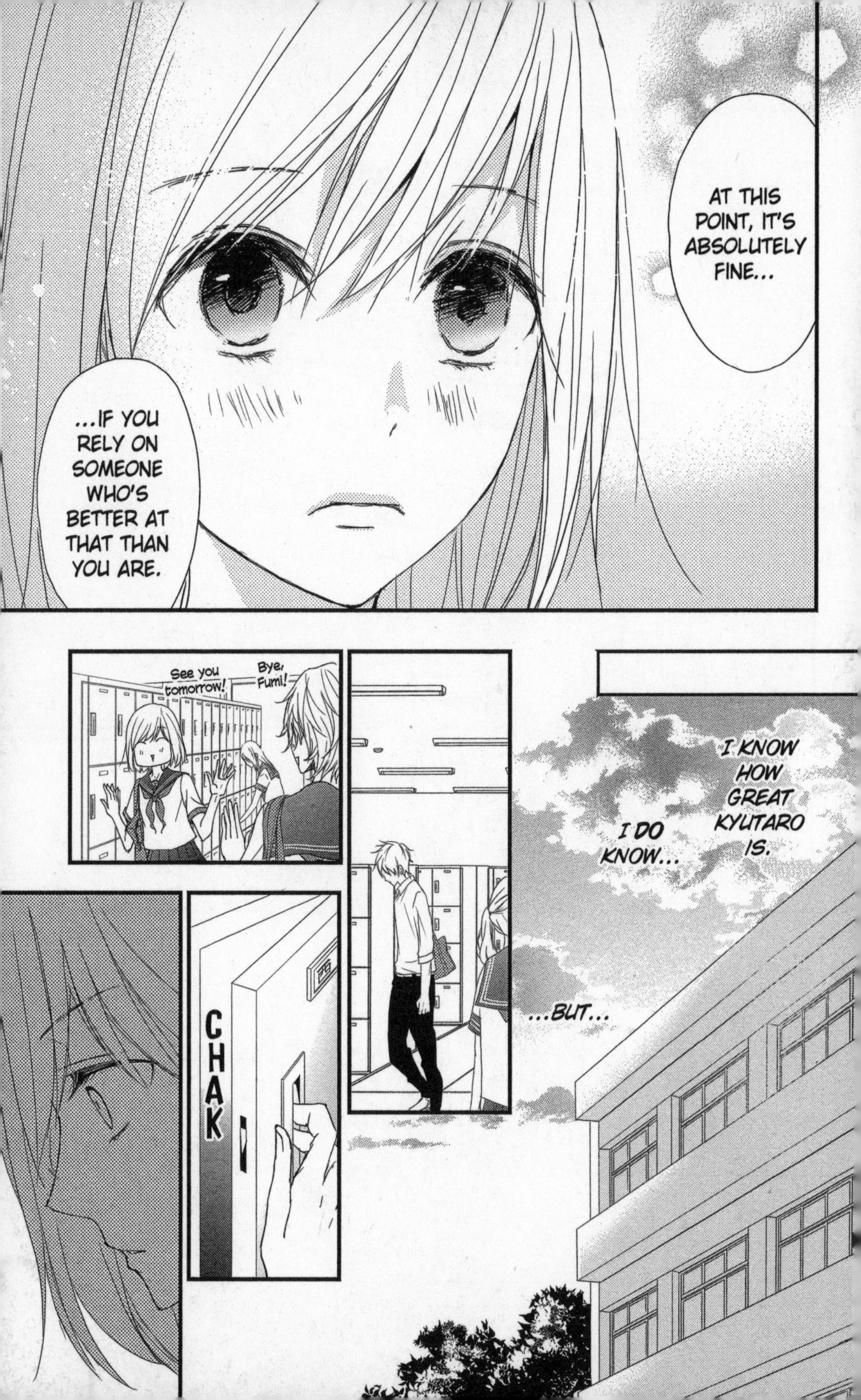
AT THIS POINT, IT'S ABSOLUTELY FINE...
...IF YOU RELY ON SOMEONE WHO'S BETTER AT THAT THAN YOU ARE.
I KNOW HOW GREAT KYUTARO IS.
I DO KNOW...
...BUT...
Bye, Fumi!
See you tomorrow!
CHAK

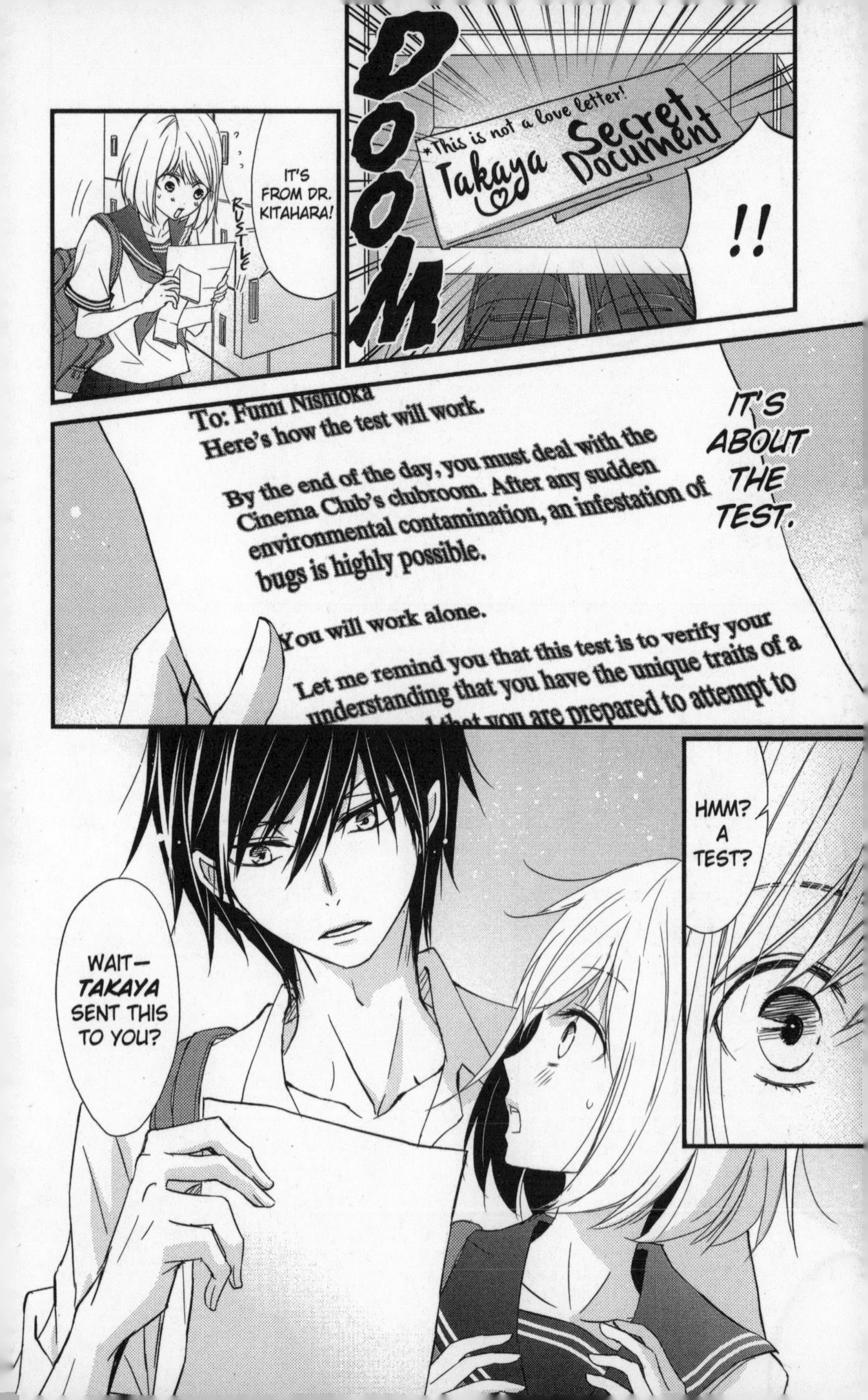
DOOM
*This is not a love letter!
Takaya Secret Document
!!
IT'S FROM DR. KITAHARA!
RUSTLE
IT'S ABOUT THE TEST.
To: Fumi Nishioka
Here's how the test will work.
By the end of the day, you must deal with the Cinema Club's clubroom. After any sudden environmental contamination, an infestation of bugs is highly possible.
You will work alone.
Let me remind you that this test is to verify your understanding that you have the unique traits of a
HMM? A TEST?
WAIT— TAKAYA SENT THIS TO YOU?

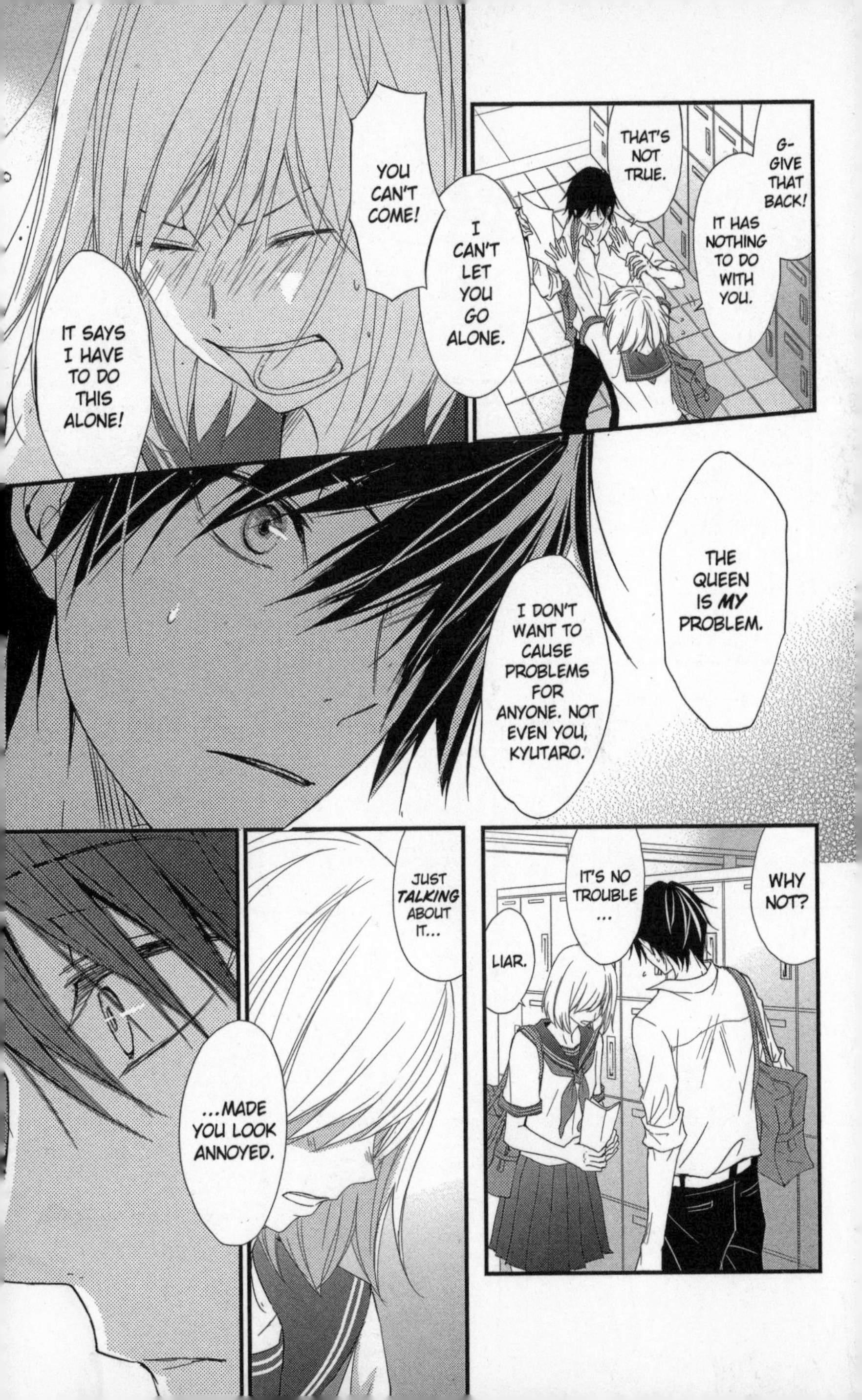
G- GIVE THAT BACK!
IT HAS NOTHING TO DO WITH YOU.
THAT'S NOT TRUE.
I CAN'T LET YOU GO ALONE.
YOU CAN'T COME!
IT SAYS I HAVE TO DO THIS ALONE!
THE QUEEN IS *MY* PROBLEM.
I DON'T WANT TO CAUSE PROBLEMS FOR ANYONE. NOT EVEN YOU, KYUTARO.
WHY NOT?
IT'S NO TROUBLE...
LIAR.
JUST *TALKING* ABOUT IT...
...MADE YOU LOOK ANNOYED.

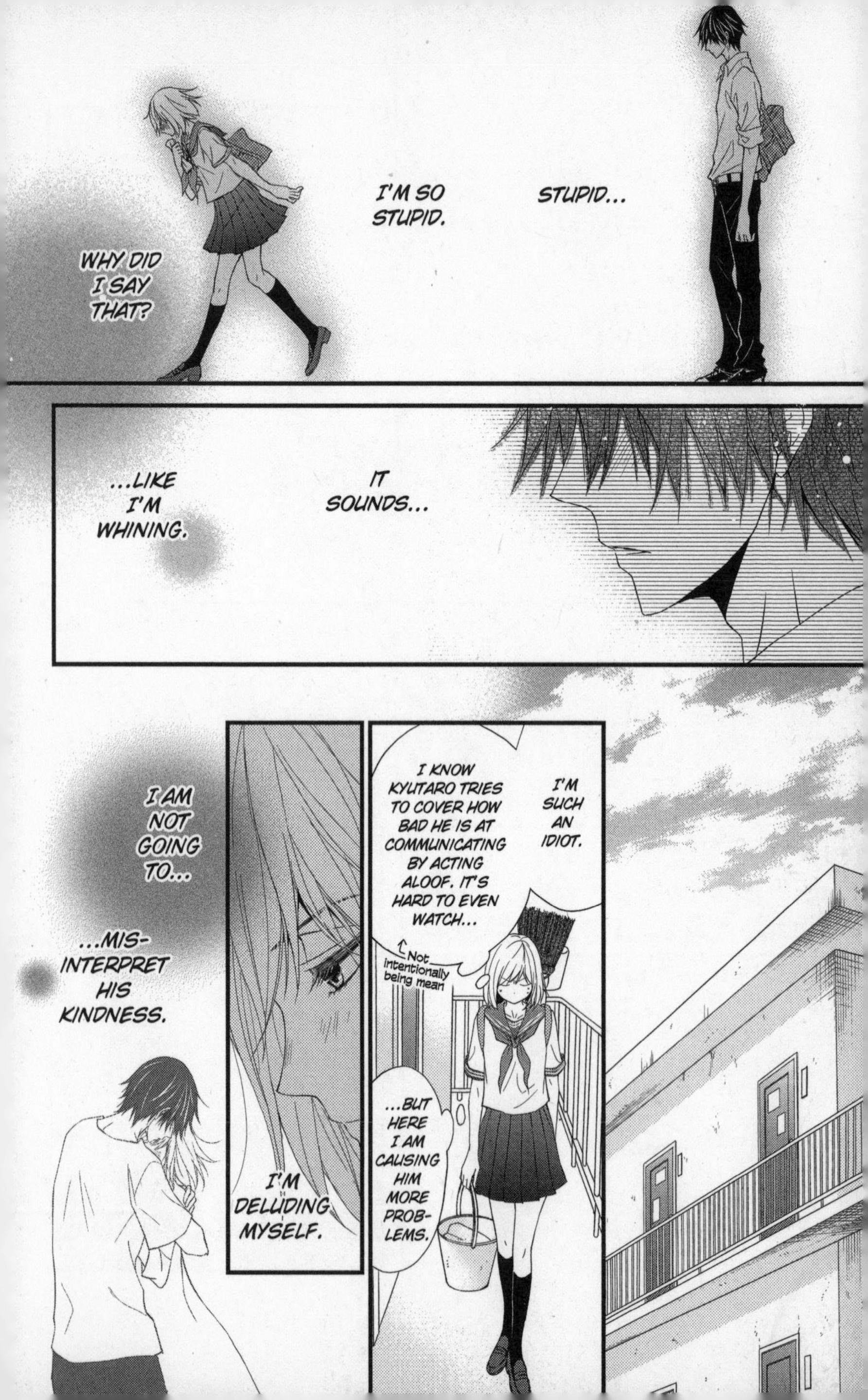
STUPID...
I'M SO STUPID.
WHY DID I SAY THAT?
IT SOUNDS...
...LIKE I'M WHINING.
I'M SUCH AN IDIOT.
I KNOW KYUTARO TRIES TO COVER HOW BAD HE IS AT COMMUNICATING BY ACTING ALOOF. IT'S HARD TO EVEN WATCH...
Not intentionally being mean
...BUT HERE I AM CAUSING HIM MORE PROBLEMS.
I'M DELUDING MYSELF.
I AM NOT GOING TO...
...MIS-INTERPRET HIS KINDNESS.

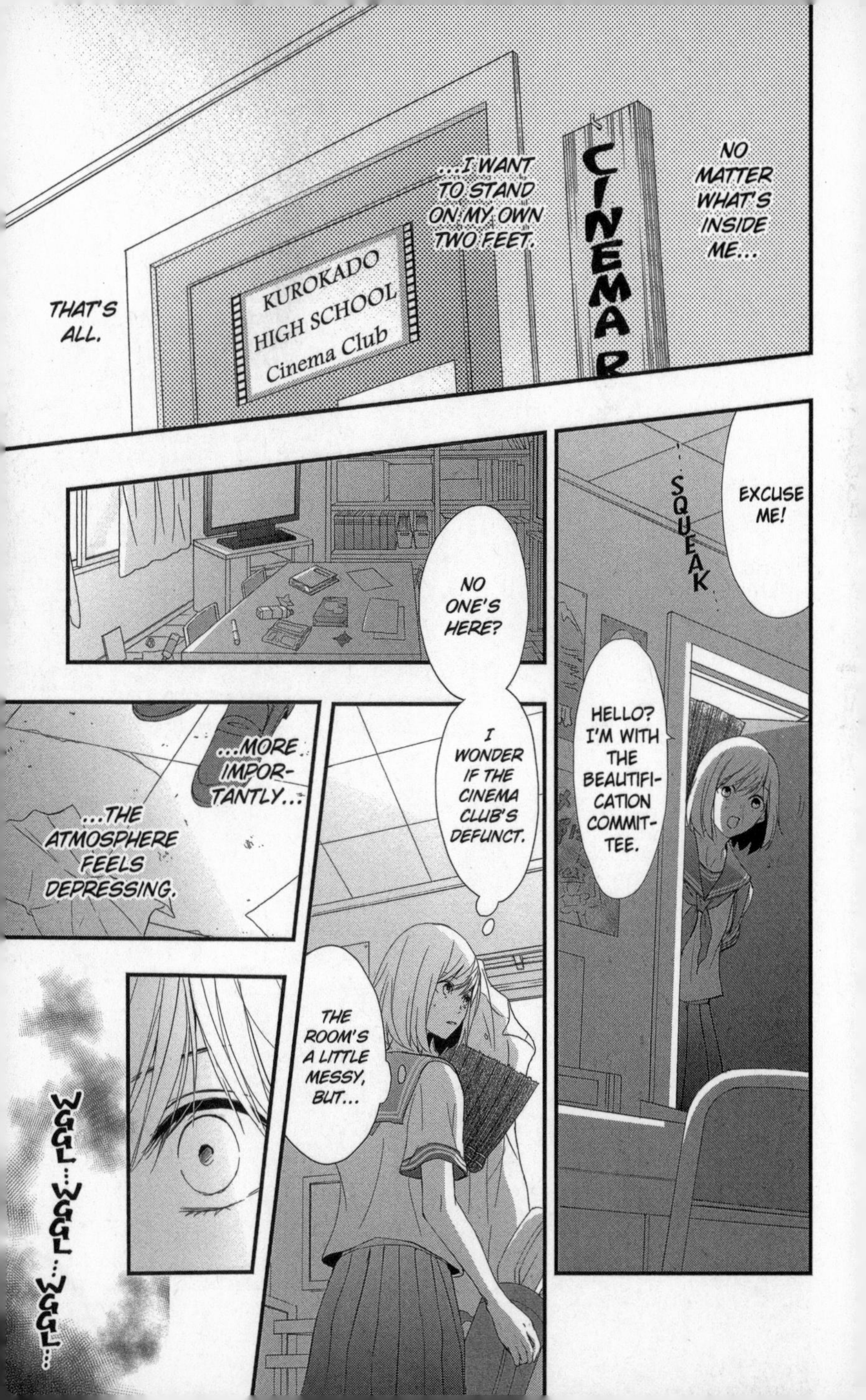
NO MATTER WHAT'S INSIDE ME...
...I WANT TO STAND ON MY OWN TWO FEET.
CINEMAR
KUROKADO HIGH SCHOOL Cinema Club
THAT'S ALL.
EXCUSE ME!
SQUEAK
HELLO? I'M WITH THE BEAUTIFICATION COMMITTEE.
NO ONE'S HERE?
I WONDER IF THE CINEMA CLUB'S DEFUNCT.
THE ROOM'S A LITTLE MESSY, BUT...
...MORE IMPORTANTLY...
...THE ATMOSPHERE FEELS DEPRESSING.
WGGL... WGGL... WGGL...

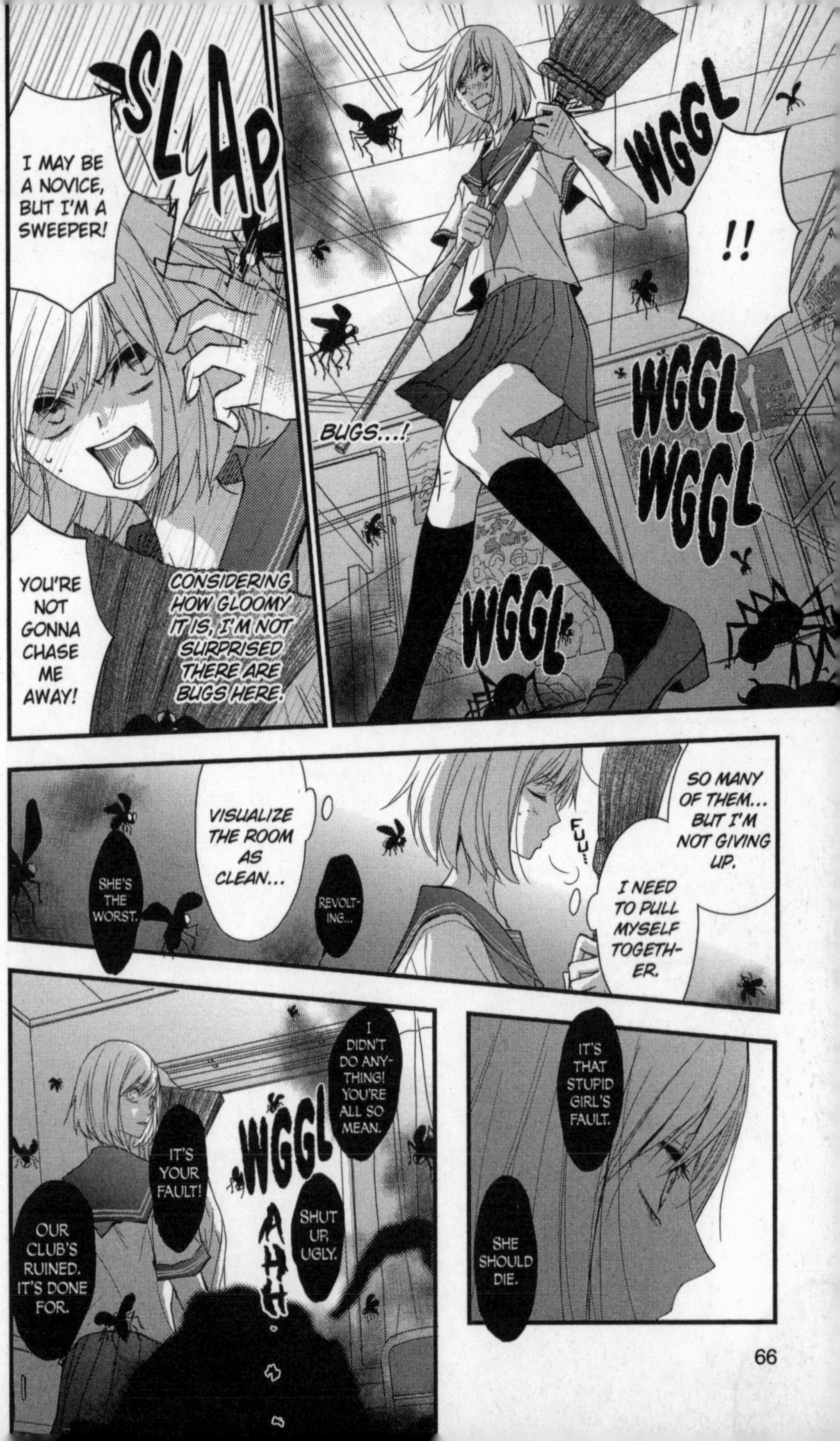
WGGL
!!
BUGS...!
WGGL WGGL
WGGL
CONSIDERING HOW GLOOMY IT IS, I'M NOT SURPRISED THERE ARE BUGS HERE.
SLAP
I MAY BE A NOVICE, BUT I'M A SWEEPER!
YOU'RE NOT GONNA CHASE ME AWAY!
SO MANY OF THEM... BUT I'M NOT GIVING UP.
I NEED TO PULL MYSELF TOGETH-ER.
FUU...
VISUALIZE THE ROOM AS CLEAN...
REVOLT-ING...
SHE'S THE WORST.
IT'S THAT STUPID GIRL'S FAULT.
SHE SHOULD DIE.
I DIDN'T DO ANY-THING! YOU'RE ALL SO MEAN.
WGGL
SHUT UP, UGLY.
IT'S YOUR FAULT!
AHH
OUR CLUB'S RUINED. IT'S DONE FOR.

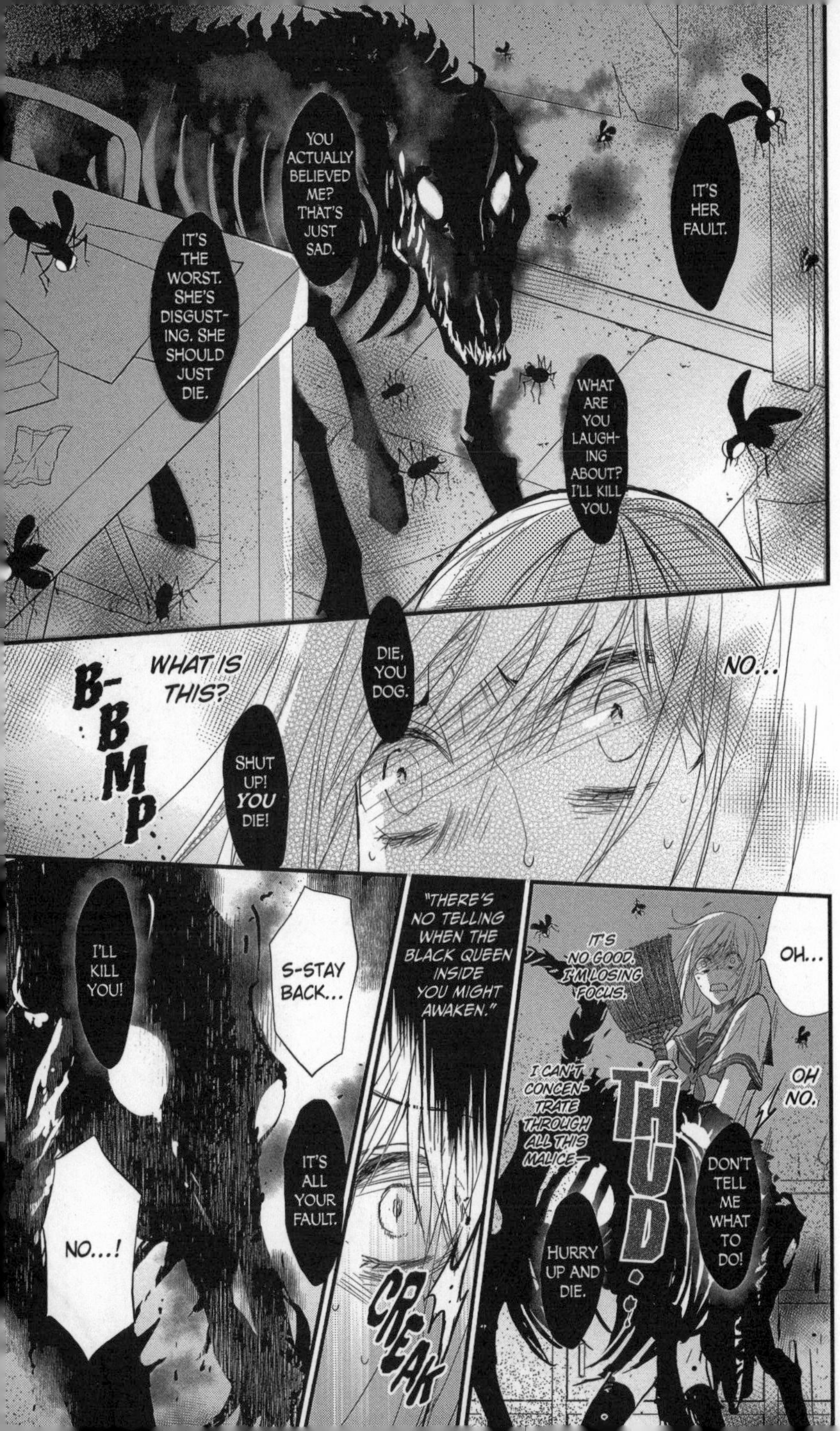
IT'S HER FAULT.
YOU ACTUALLY BELIEVED ME? THAT'S JUST SAD.
IT'S THE WORST. SHE'S DISGUST-ING. SHE SHOULD JUST DIE.
WHAT ARE YOU LAUGH-ING ABOUT? I'LL KILL YOU.
NO...
DIE, YOU DOG.
WHAT IS THIS?
B-BMP
SHUT UP! YOU DIE!
OH...
IT'S NO GOOD. I'M LOSING FOCUS.
OH NO.
I CAN'T CONCEN-TRATE THROUGH ALL THIS MALICE—
THUD
DON'T TELL ME WHAT TO DO!
HURRY UP AND DIE.
"THERE'S NO TELLING WHEN THE BLACK QUEEN INSIDE YOU MIGHT AWAKEN."
IT'S ALL YOUR FAULT.
CREAK
I'LL KILL YOU!
S-STAY BACK...
NO...!

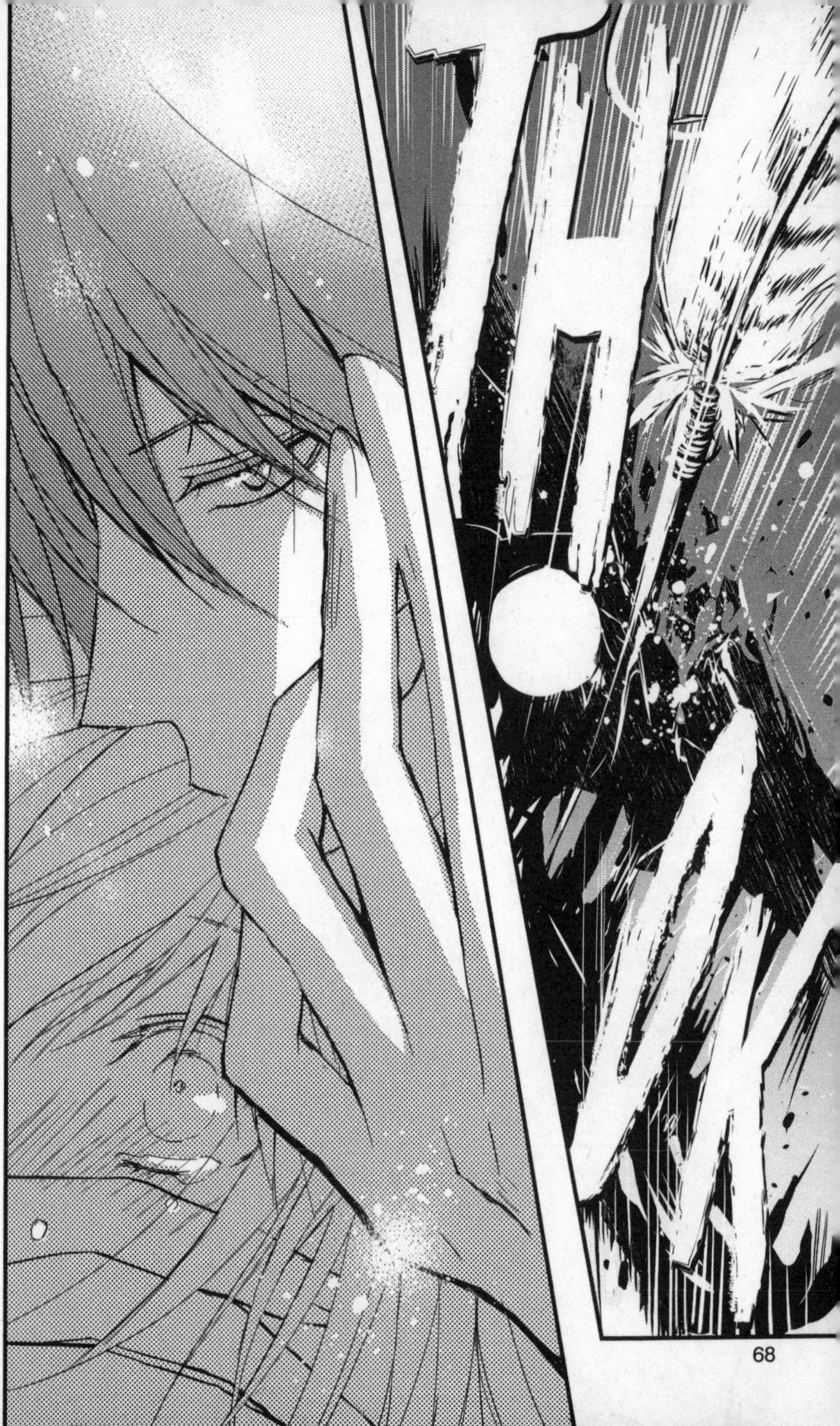

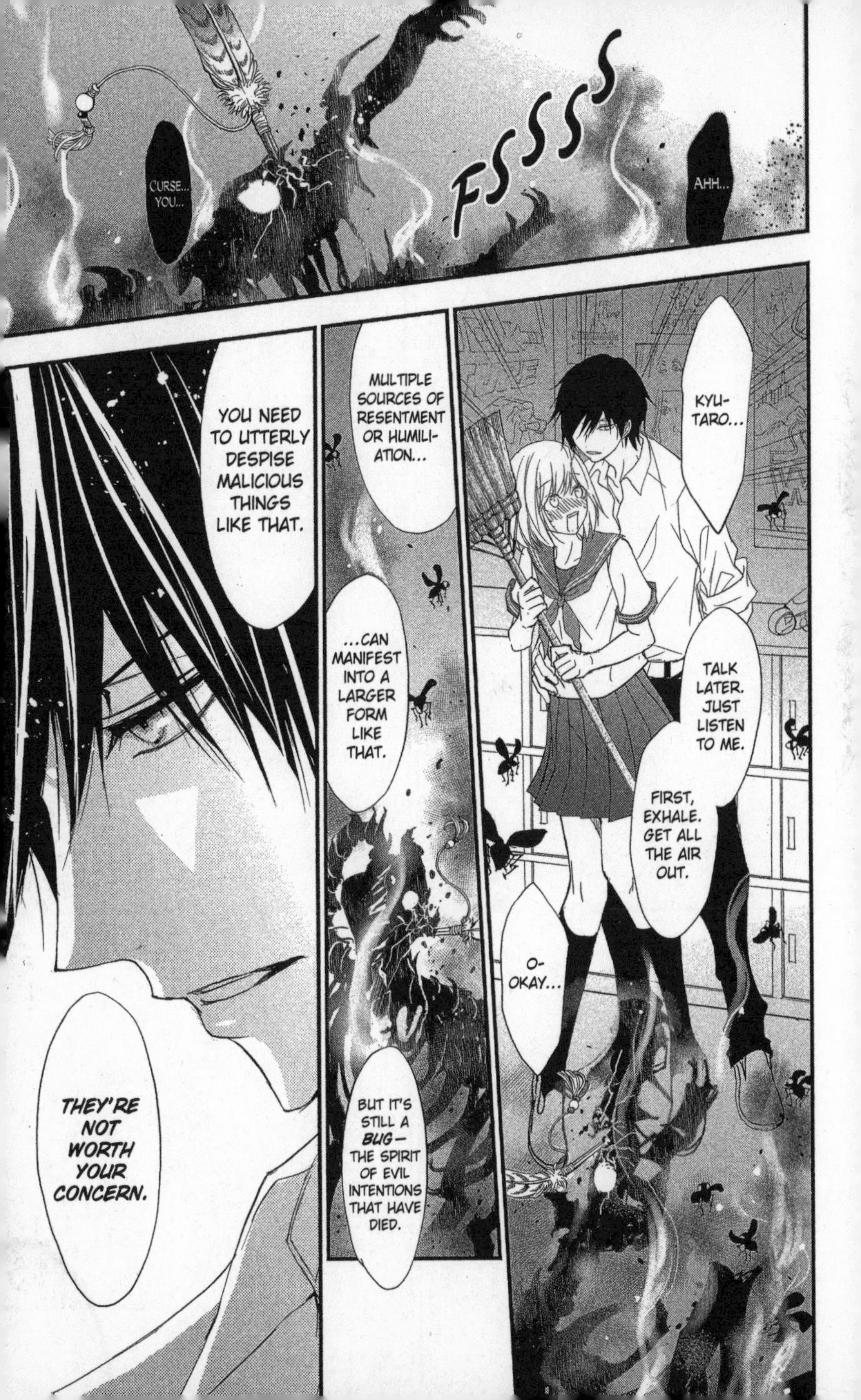
AHH...
FSSSS
CURSE... YOU...
KYU-TARO...
TALK LATER. JUST LISTEN TO ME.
FIRST, EXHALE. GET ALL THE AIR OUT.
O-OKAY...
MULTIPLE SOURCES OF RESENTMENT OR HUMILI-ATION...
...CAN MANIFEST INTO A LARGER FORM LIKE THAT.
BUT IT'S STILL A *BUG*—THE SPIRIT OF EVIL INTENTIONS THAT HAVE DIED.
YOU NEED TO UTTERLY DESPISE MALICIOUS THINGS LIKE THAT.
THEY'RE NOT WORTH YOUR CONCERN.

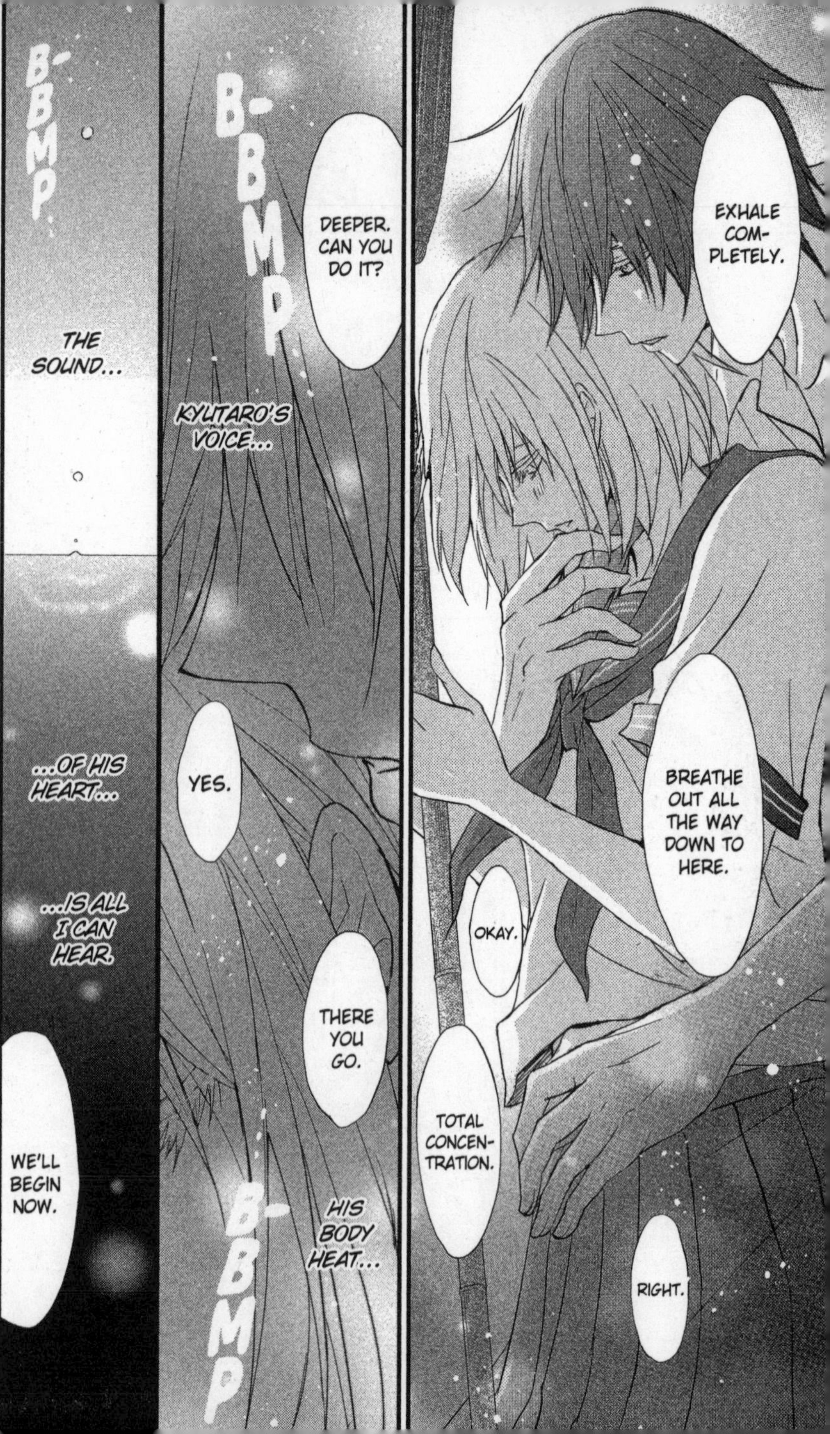
EXHALE COM-PLETELY.
BREATHE OUT ALL THE WAY DOWN TO HERE.
OKAY.
TOTAL CONCEN-TRATION.
RIGHT.
B-BMP
DEEPER. CAN YOU DO IT?
KYUTARO'S VOICE...
YES.
THERE YOU GO.
HIS BODY HEAT...
B-BMP
B-BMP
THE SOUND...
...OF HIS HEART...
...IS ALL I CAN HEAR.
WE'LL BEGIN NOW.

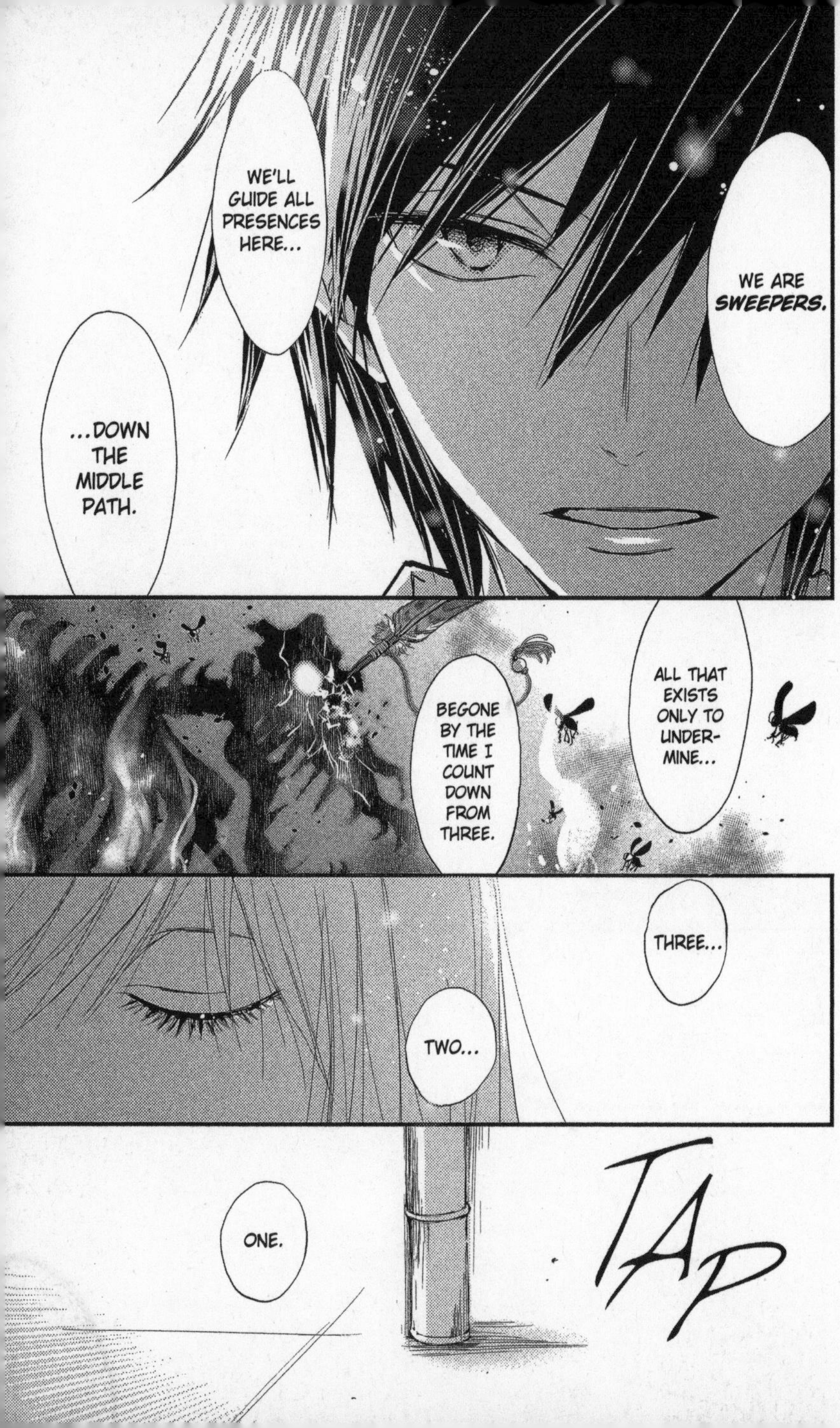
WE ARE SWEEPERS.
WE'LL GUIDE ALL PRESENCES HERE...
...DOWN THE MIDDLE PATH.
ALL THAT EXISTS ONLY TO UNDERMINE...
BEGONE BY THE TIME I COUNT DOWN FROM THREE.
THREE...
TWO...
TAP
ONE.

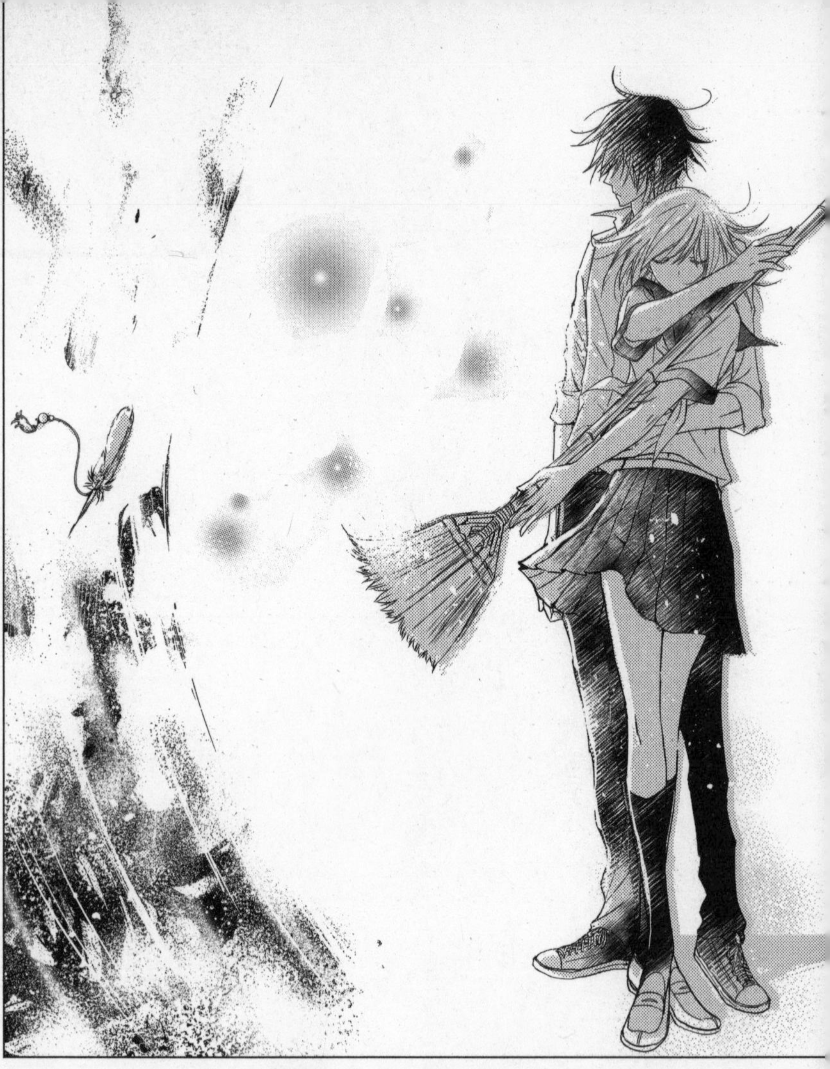

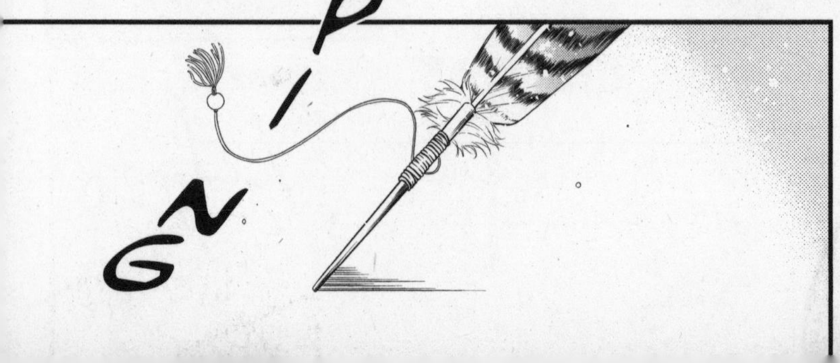
PING

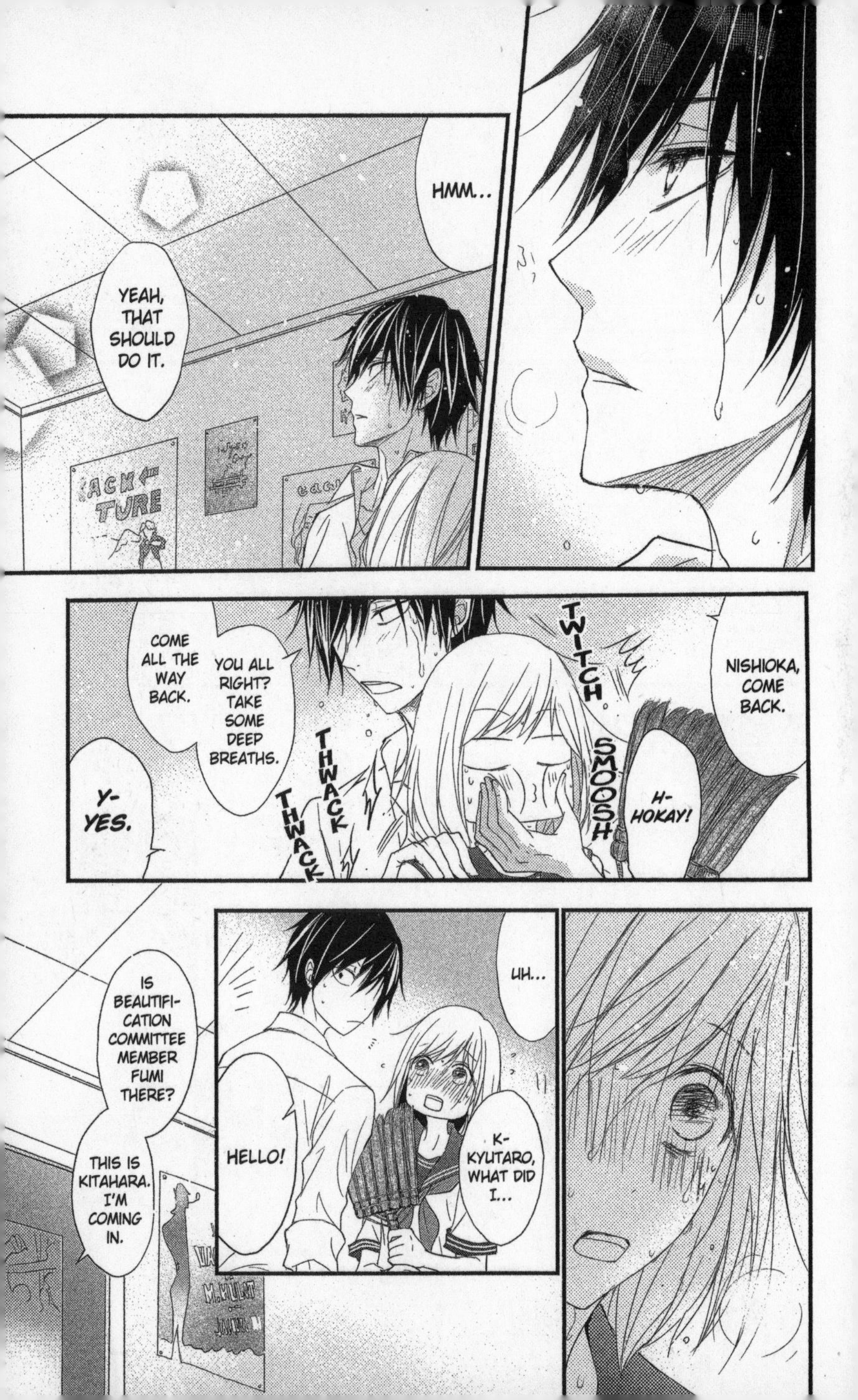
HMM...
YEAH, THAT SHOULD DO IT.
NISHIOKA, COME BACK.
TWITCH
H-HOKAY!
SMOOSH
YOU ALL RIGHT? TAKE SOME DEEP BREATHS.
COME ALL THE WAY BACK.
THWACK
THWACK
Y-YES.
UH...
K-KYUTARO, WHAT DID I...
HELLO!
IS BEAUTIFICATION COMMITTEE MEMBER FUMI THERE?
THIS IS KITAHARA. I'M COMING IN.

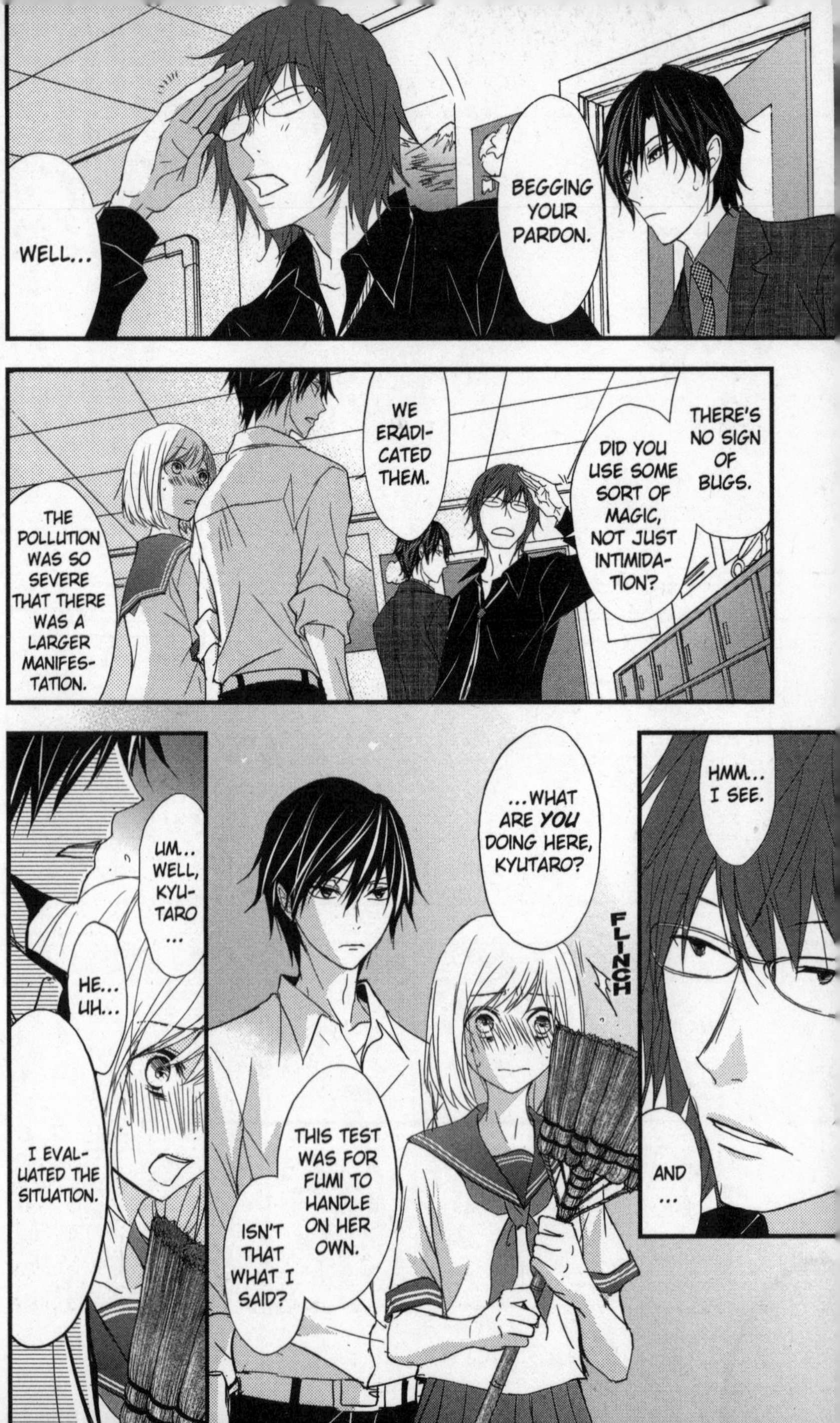
BEGGING YOUR PARDON.
WELL...
THERE'S NO SIGN OF BUGS.
DID YOU USE SOME SORT OF MAGIC, NOT JUST INTIMIDATION?
WE ERADICATED THEM.
THE POLLUTION WAS SO SEVERE THAT THERE WAS A LARGER MANIFESTATION.
HMM... I SEE.
AND ...
...WHAT ARE *YOU* DOING HERE, KYUTARO?
FLINCH
THIS TEST WAS FOR FUMI TO HANDLE ON HER OWN.
ISN'T THAT WHAT I SAID?
UM... WELL, KYUTARO ...
HE... UH...
I EVALUATED THE SITUATION.

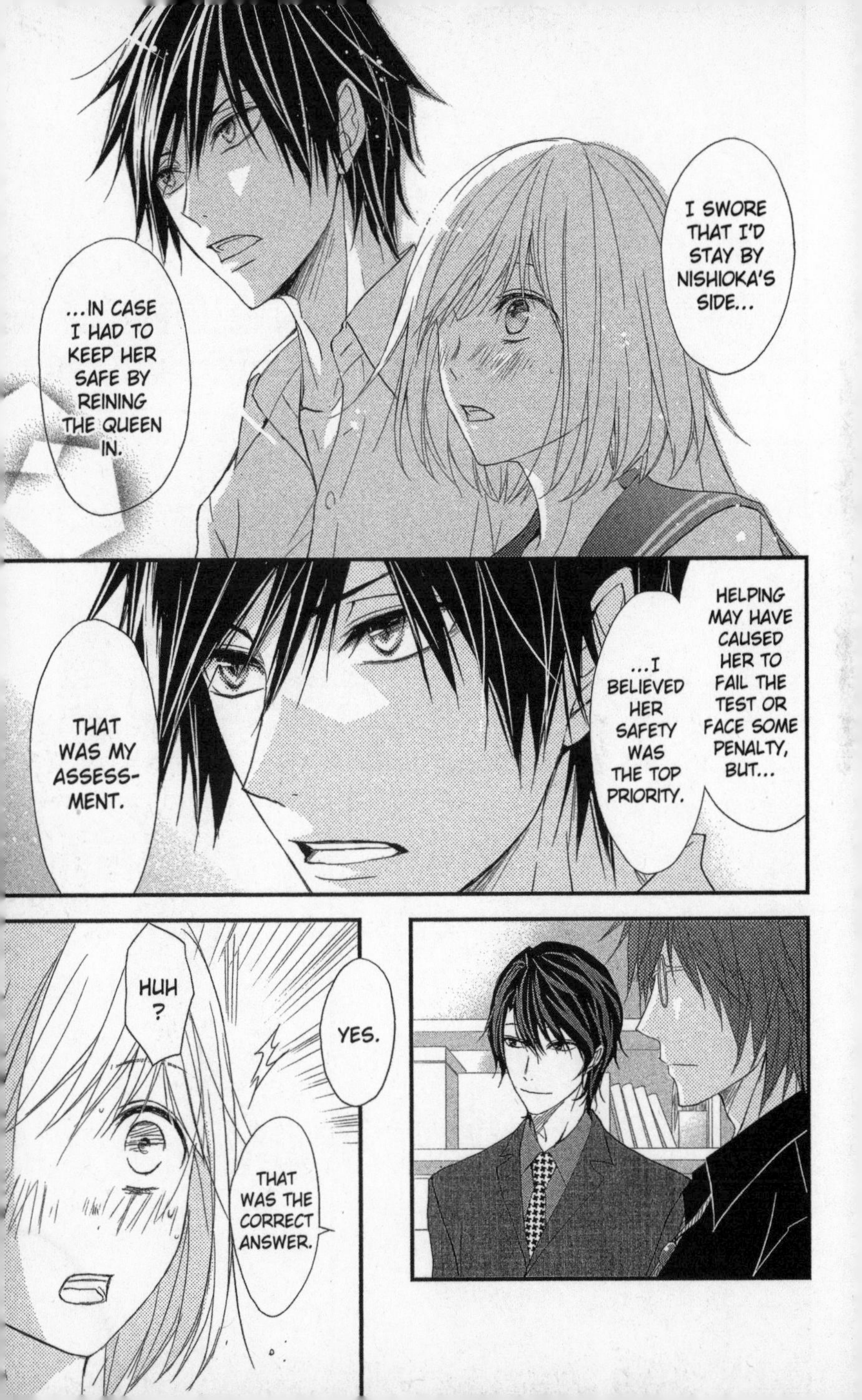
I SWORE THAT I'D STAY BY NISHIOKA'S SIDE...
...IN CASE I HAD TO KEEP HER SAFE BY REINING THE QUEEN IN.
HELPING MAY HAVE CAUSED HER TO FAIL THE TEST OR FACE SOME PENALTY, BUT...
...I BELIEVED HER SAFETY WAS THE TOP PRIORITY.
THAT WAS MY ASSESSMENT.
YES.
THAT WAS THE CORRECT ANSWER.
HUH?

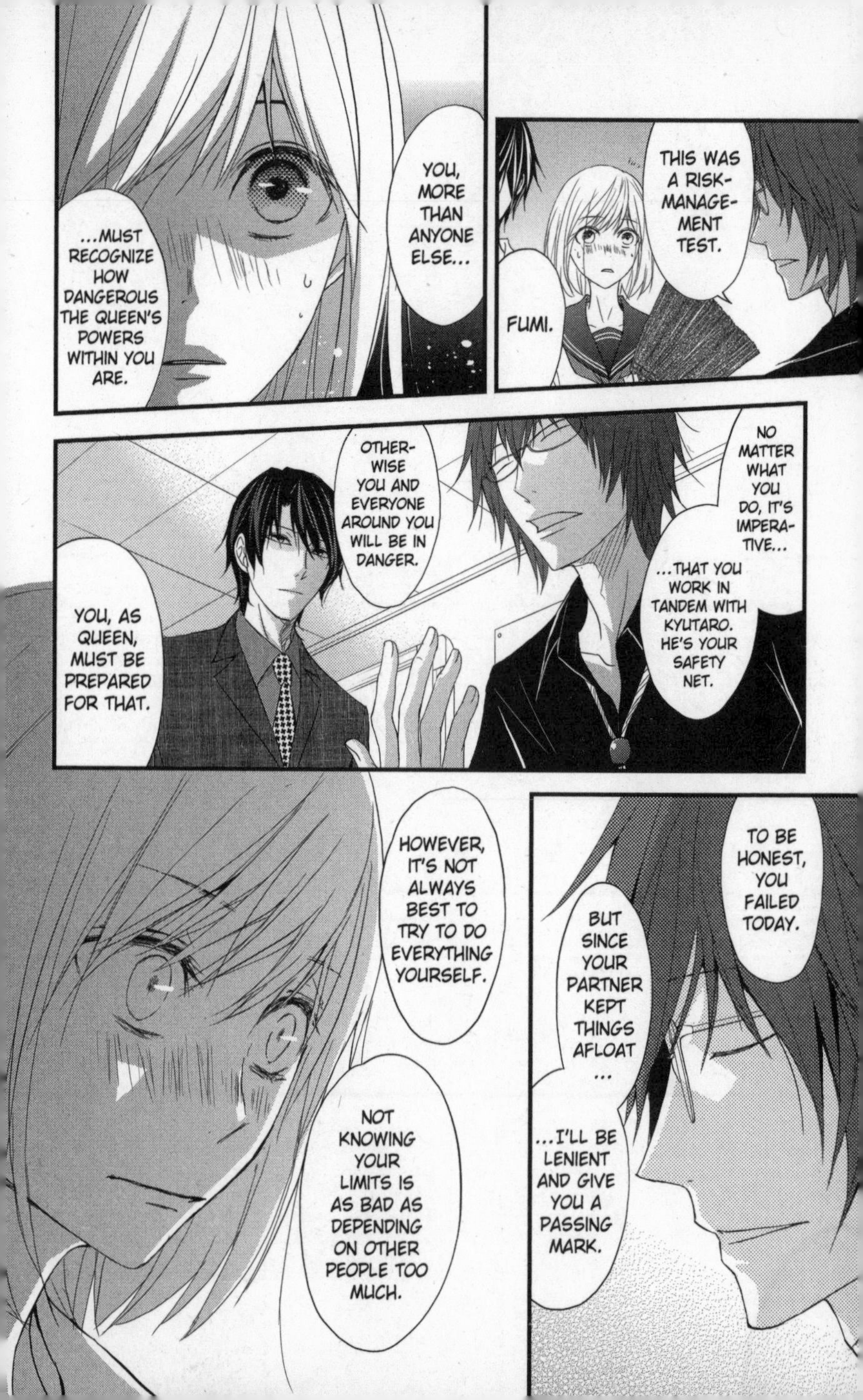
THIS WAS A RISK-MANAGEMENT TEST.
FUMI.
YOU, MORE THAN ANYONE ELSE...
...MUST RECOGNIZE HOW DANGEROUS THE QUEEN'S POWERS WITHIN YOU ARE.
NO MATTER WHAT YOU DO, IT'S IMPERATIVE...
...THAT YOU WORK IN TANDEM WITH KYUTARO. HE'S YOUR SAFETY NET.
OTHERWISE YOU AND EVERYONE AROUND YOU WILL BE IN DANGER.
YOU, AS QUEEN, MUST BE PREPARED FOR THAT.
TO BE HONEST, YOU FAILED TODAY.
BUT SINCE YOUR PARTNER KEPT THINGS AFLOAT...
...I'LL BE LENIENT AND GIVE YOU A PASSING MARK.
HOWEVER, IT'S NOT ALWAYS BEST TO TRY TO DO EVERYTHING YOURSELF.
NOT KNOWING YOUR LIMITS IS AS BAD AS DEPENDING ON OTHER PEOPLE TOO MUCH.

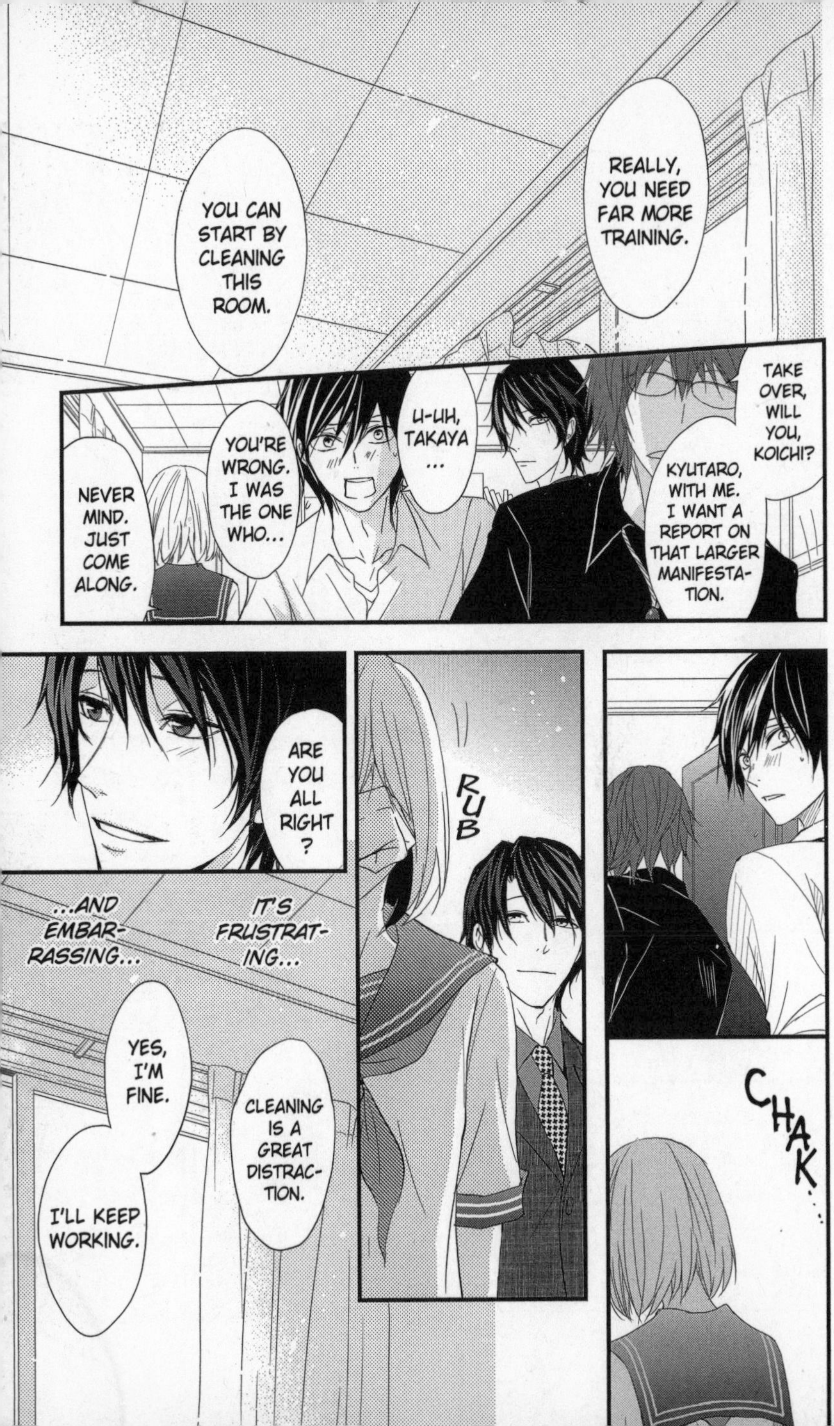
REALLY, YOU NEED FAR MORE TRAINING.
YOU CAN START BY CLEANING THIS ROOM.
TAKE OVER, WILL YOU, KOICHI?
KYUTARO, WITH ME. I WANT A REPORT ON THAT LARGER MANIFESTATION.
U-UH, TAKAYA...
YOU'RE WRONG. I WAS THE ONE WHO...
NEVER MIND. JUST COME ALONG.
CHAK...
RUB
ARE YOU ALL RIGHT?
IT'S FRUSTRATING...
...AND EMBARRASSING...
YES, I'M FINE.
CLEANING IS A GREAT DISTRACTION.
I'LL KEEP WORKING.

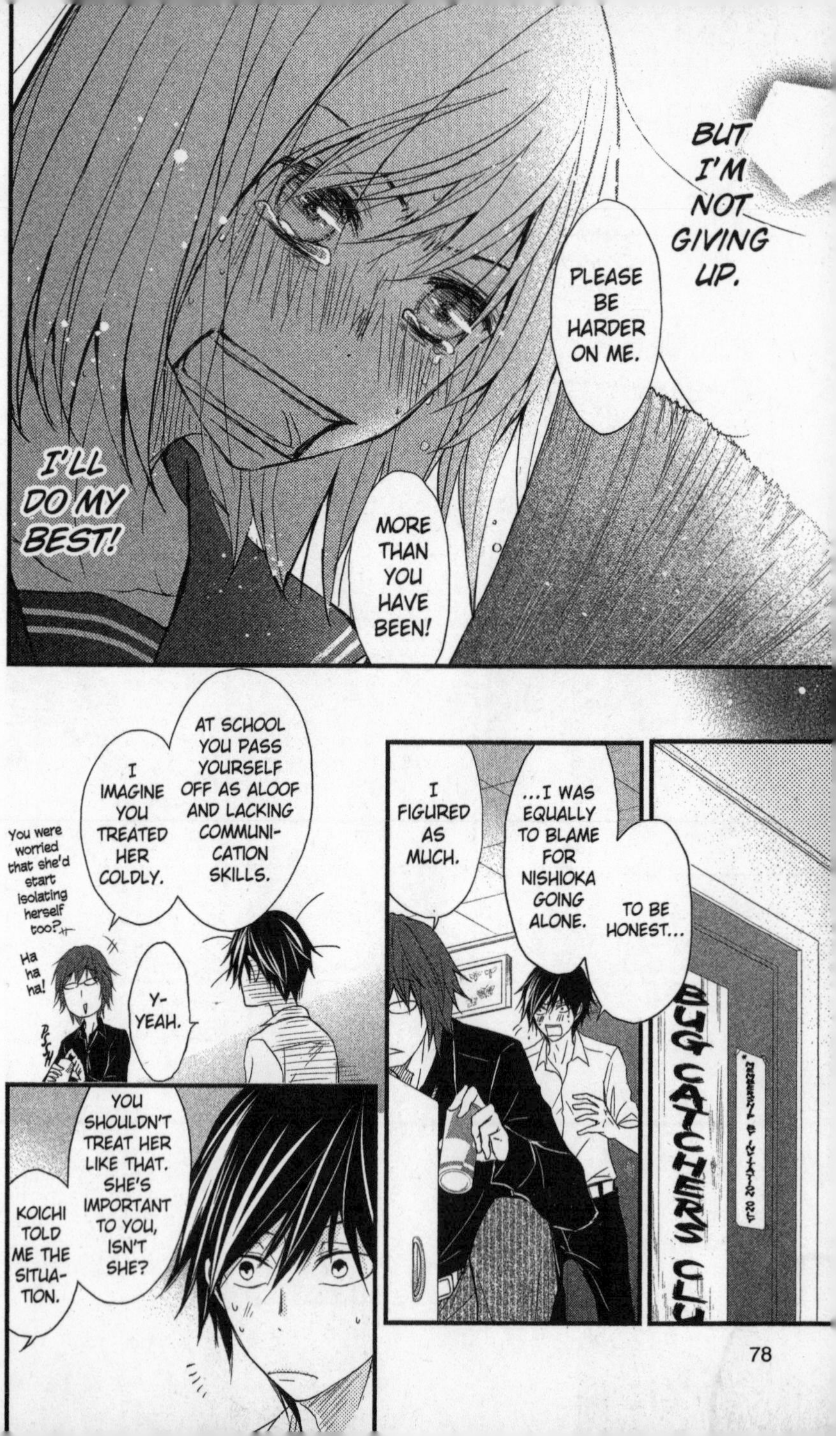
BUT I'M NOT GIVING UP.
PLEASE BE HARDER ON ME.
MORE THAN YOU HAVE BEEN!
I'LL DO MY BEST!
BUG CATCHERS' CLU
TO BE HONEST...
...I WAS EQUALLY TO BLAME FOR NISHIOKA GOING ALONE.
I FIGURED AS MUCH.
AT SCHOOL YOU PASS YOURSELF OFF AS ALOOF AND LACKING COMMUNICATION SKILLS.
I IMAGINE YOU TREATED HER COLDLY.
Y-YEAH.
You were worried that she'd start isolating herself too?
Ha ha ha!
YOU SHOULDN'T TREAT HER LIKE THAT. SHE'S IMPORTANT TO YOU, ISN'T SHE?
KOICHI TOLD ME THE SITUATION.

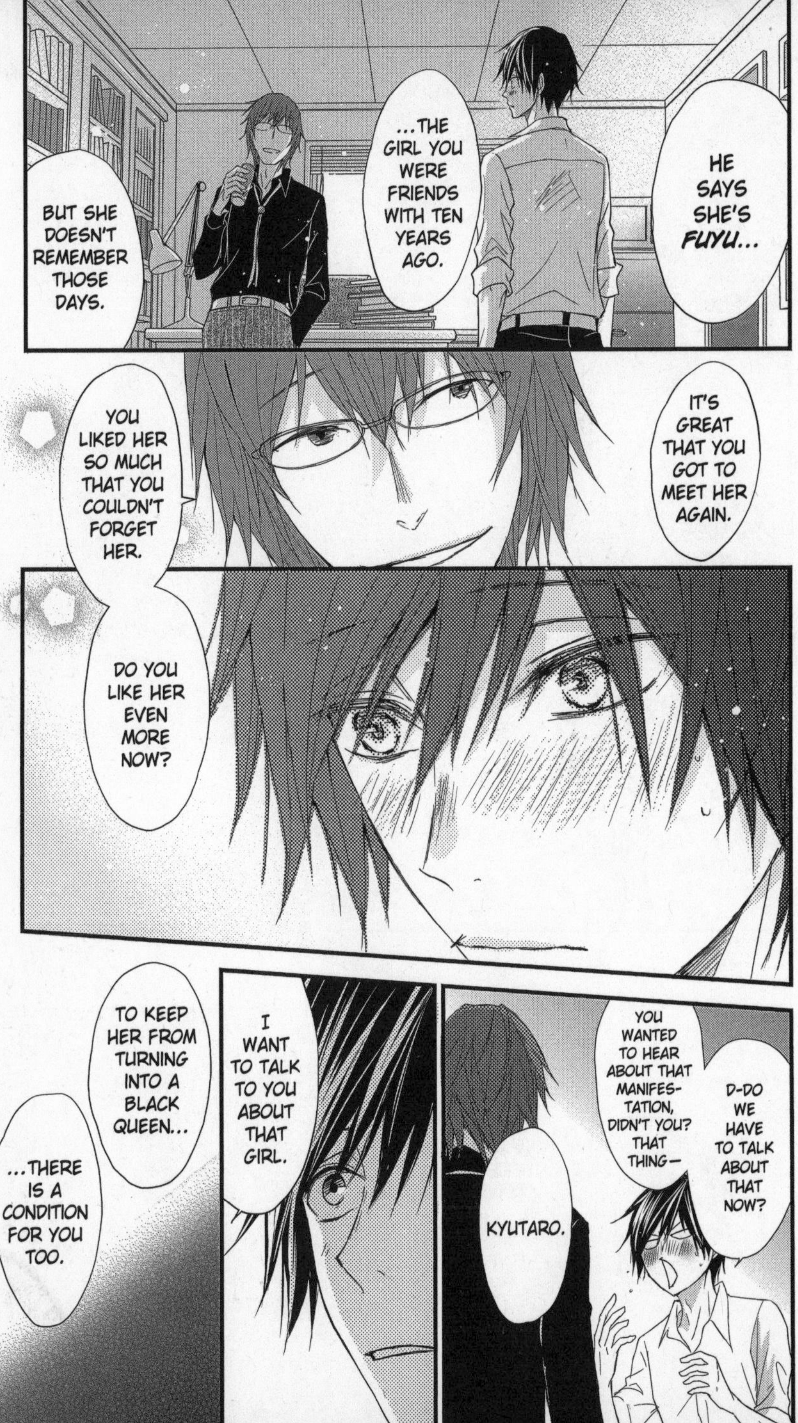
HE SAYS SHE'S FUYU...
...THE GIRL YOU WERE FRIENDS WITH TEN YEARS AGO.
BUT SHE DOESN'T REMEMBER THOSE DAYS.
IT'S GREAT THAT YOU GOT TO MEET HER AGAIN.
YOU LIKED HER SO MUCH THAT YOU COULDN'T FORGET HER.
DO YOU LIKE HER EVEN MORE NOW?
D-DO WE HAVE TO TALK ABOUT THAT NOW?
YOU WANTED TO HEAR ABOUT THAT MANIFES-TATION, DIDN'T YOU? THAT THING—
KYUTARO.
I WANT TO TALK TO YOU ABOUT THAT GIRL.
TO KEEP HER FROM TURNING INTO A BLACK QUEEN...
...THERE IS A CONDITION FOR YOU TOO.

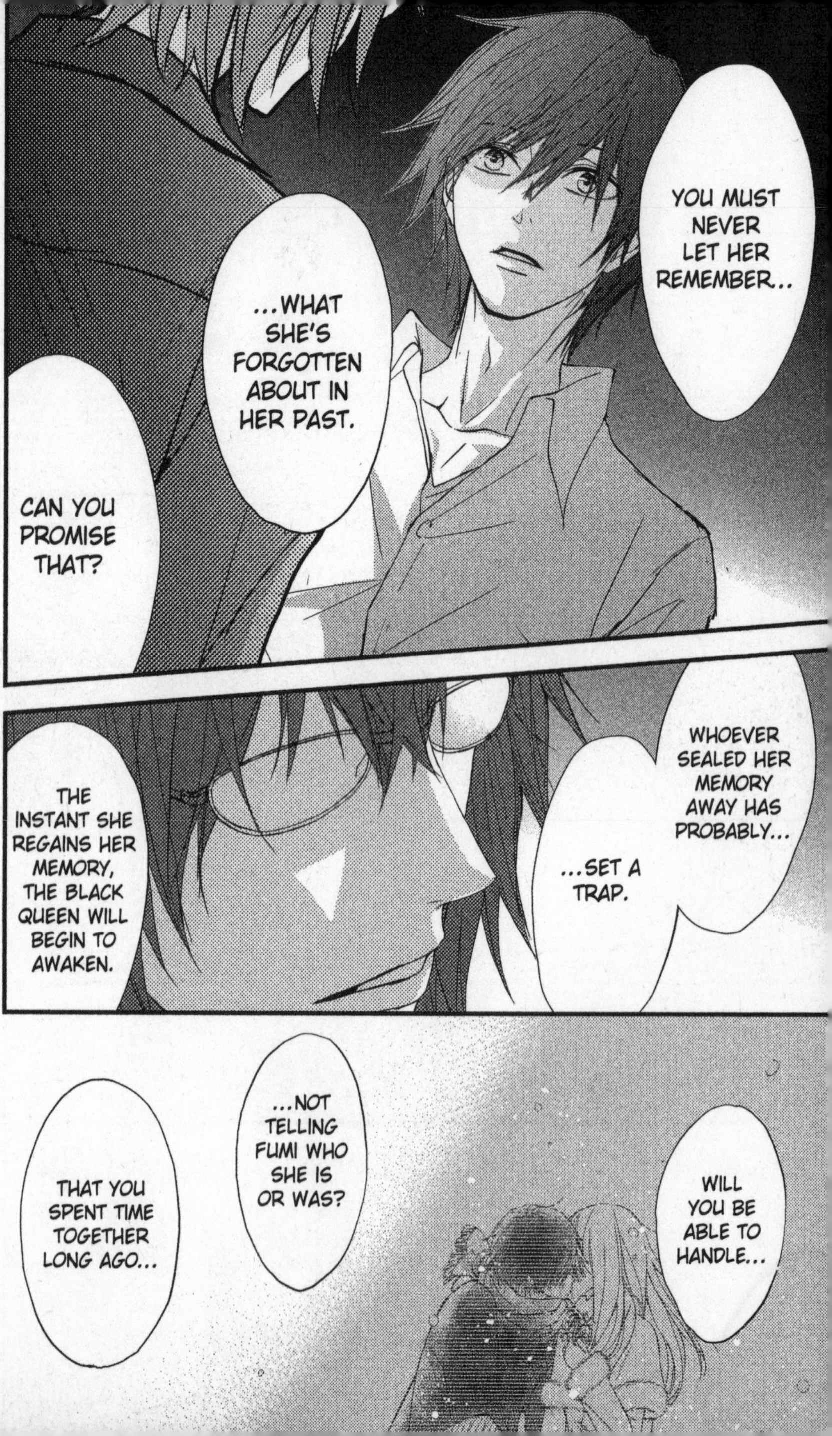
YOU MUST NEVER LET HER REMEMBER...
...WHAT SHE'S FORGOTTEN ABOUT IN HER PAST.
CAN YOU PROMISE THAT?
WHOEVER SEALED HER MEMORY AWAY HAS PROBABLY...
...SET A TRAP.
THE INSTANT SHE REGAINS HER MEMORY, THE BLACK QUEEN WILL BEGIN TO AWAKEN.
WILL YOU BE ABLE TO HANDLE...
...NOT TELLING FUMI WHO SHE IS OR WAS?
THAT YOU SPENT TIME TOGETHER LONG AGO...

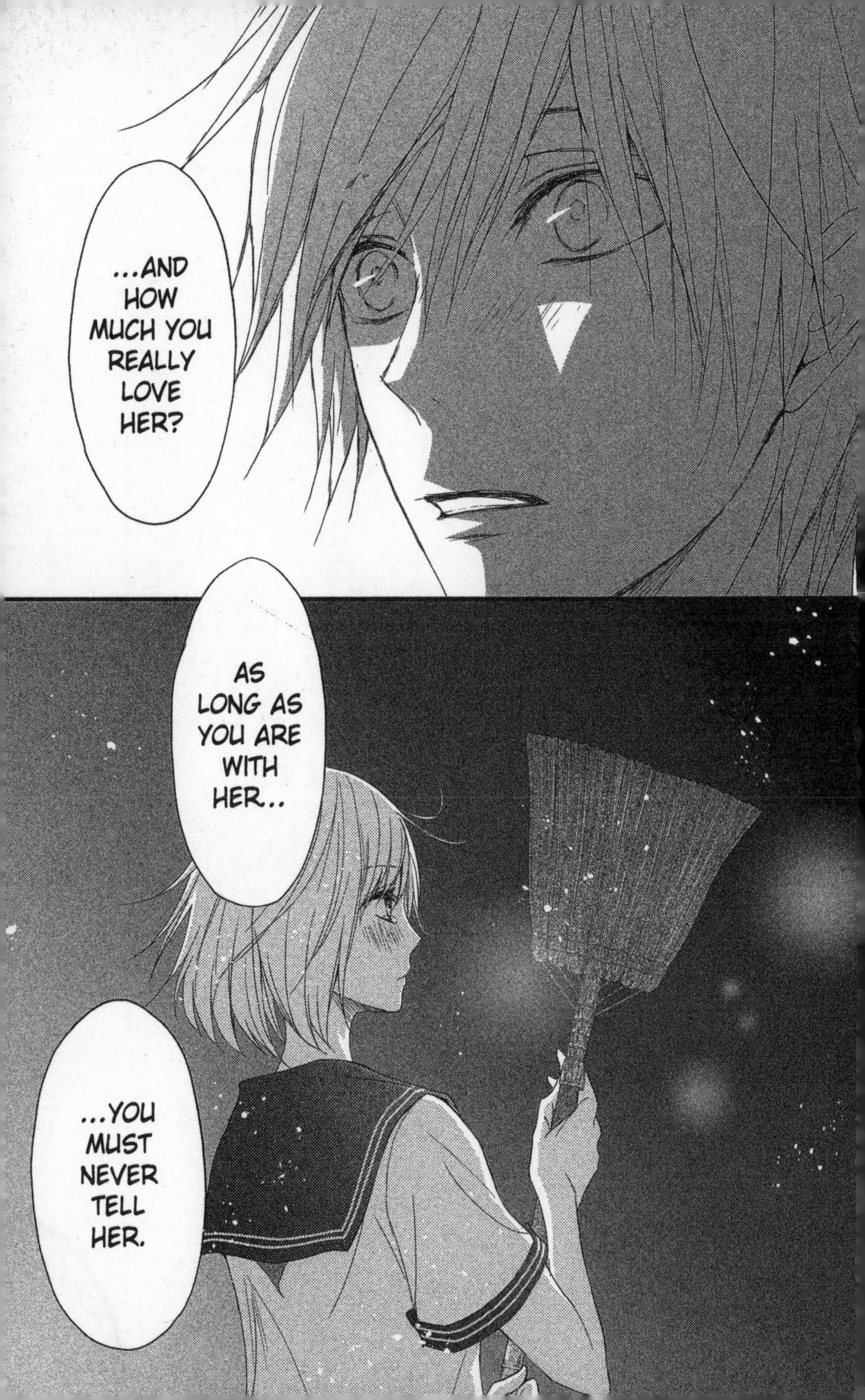
...AND HOW MUCH YOU REALLY LOVE HER?
AS LONG AS YOU ARE WITH HER...
...YOU MUST NEVER TELL HER.

Follow me on Twitter! @motomikyosuke

Basically you'll just hear me muttering about my boring life, but on the days ***Betsucomi*** comes out, you might find illustrations like this one.

↓ *(This is from when QQ vol. 1 came out.)*

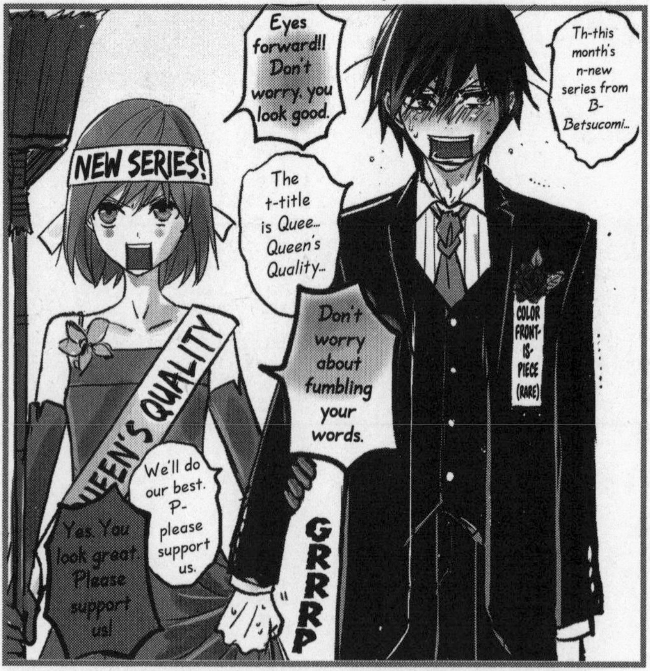
Th-this month's n-new series from B-Betsucomi...
COLOR FRONT-IS-PIECE (RARE)
Eyes forward!! Don't worry, you look good.
The t-title is Quee... Queen's Quality...
Don't worry about fumbling your words.
GRRRP
NEW SERIES!
UEEN'S QUALITY
We'll do our best. P-please support us.
Yes. You look great. Please support us!

Sometimes you'll see illustrations cut from older works or occasionally artwork created just for posting. Please take a look when you can!

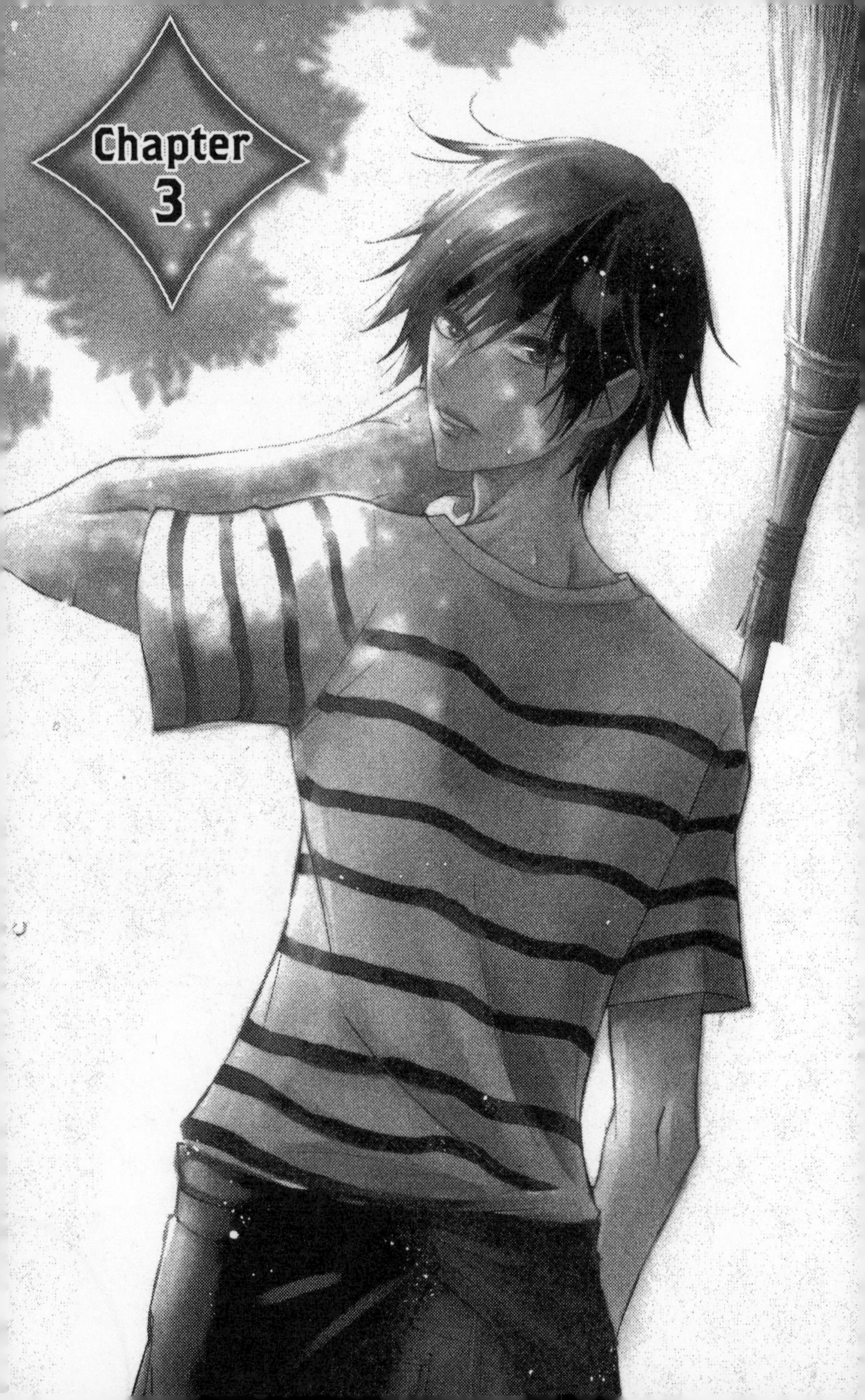
Chapter
3

TAKE
THAT!

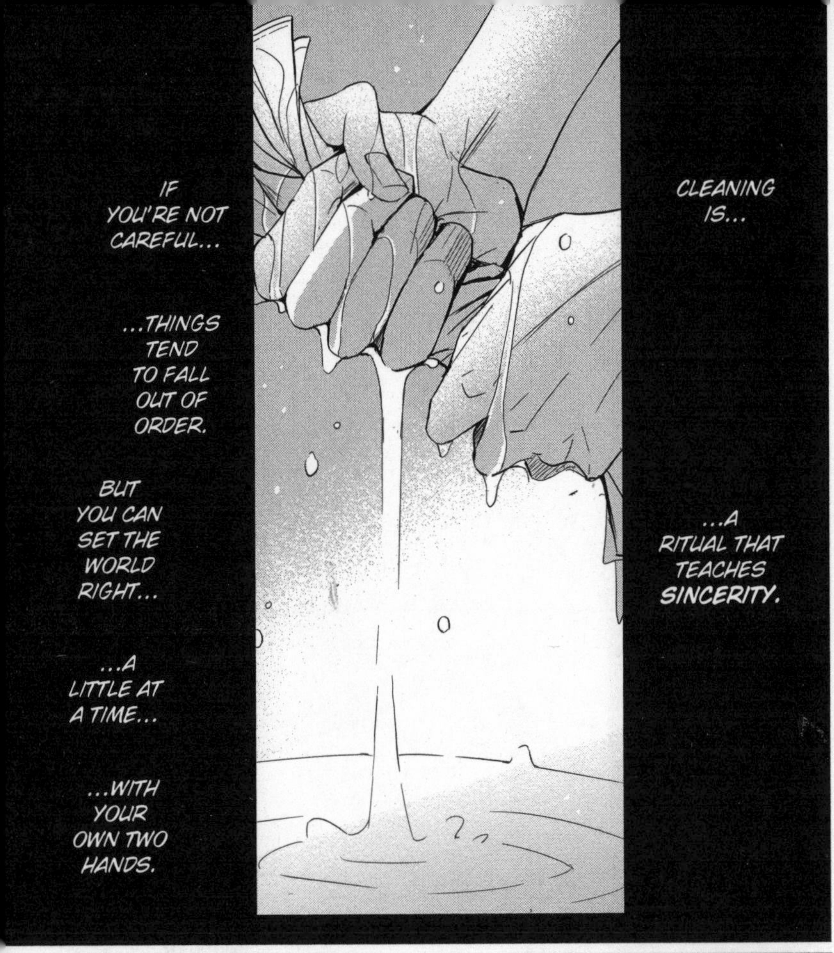
CLEANING IS...
...A RITUAL THAT TEACHES **SINCERITY.**
IF YOU'RE NOT CAREFUL...
...THINGS TEND TO FALL OUT OF ORDER.
BUT YOU CAN SET THE WORLD RIGHT...
...A LITTLE AT A TIME...
...WITH YOUR OWN TWO HANDS.

Kyutaro's weapon in chapter 2 (what he threw at the bug) is a tool called a *haboki*, which is used in tea ceremony.
That one was tied to a metal chopstick, also from tea ceremony.
It seems like a pain to carry around—even juvenile. There aren't many cleaning tools that take so much energy to use. Why not just whack everything with a vacuum cleaner...?

I thought of having him throw a feather duster like this one, but that's so commonly used by manga artists that I thought it might be too comical.

Of course, it's also funny that he throws a haboki!

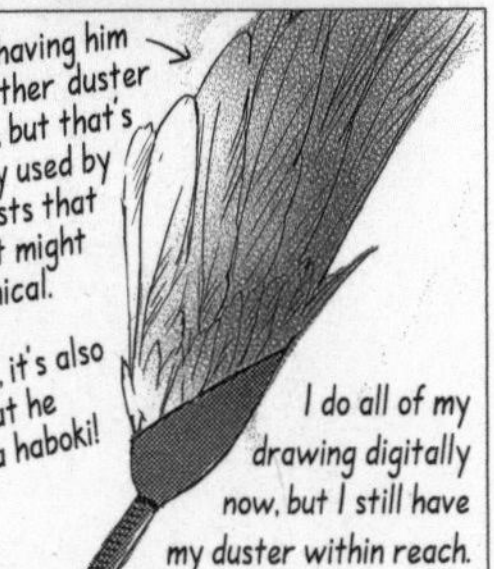

I do all of my drawing digitally now, but I still have my duster within reach. It's great for cleaning my keyboard!!!

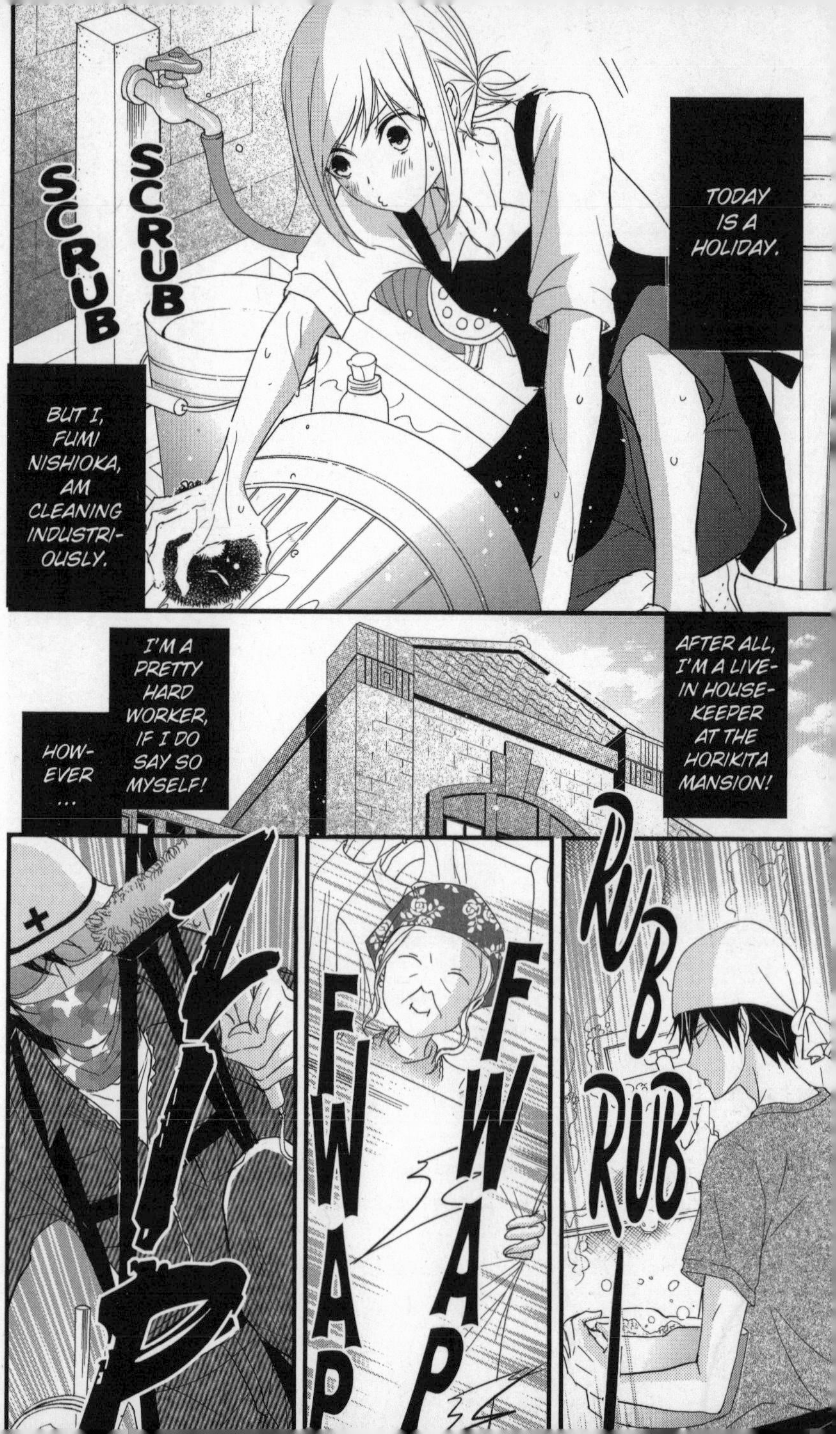
TODAY IS A HOLIDAY.
SCRUB
SCRUB
BUT I, FUMI NISHIOKA, AM CLEANING INDUSTRIOUSLY.
AFTER ALL, I'M A LIVE-IN HOUSEKEEPER AT THE HORIKITA MANSION!
I'M A PRETTY HARD WORKER, IF I DO SAY SO MYSELF!
HOWEVER...
RUB
RUB
FWAP
FWAP

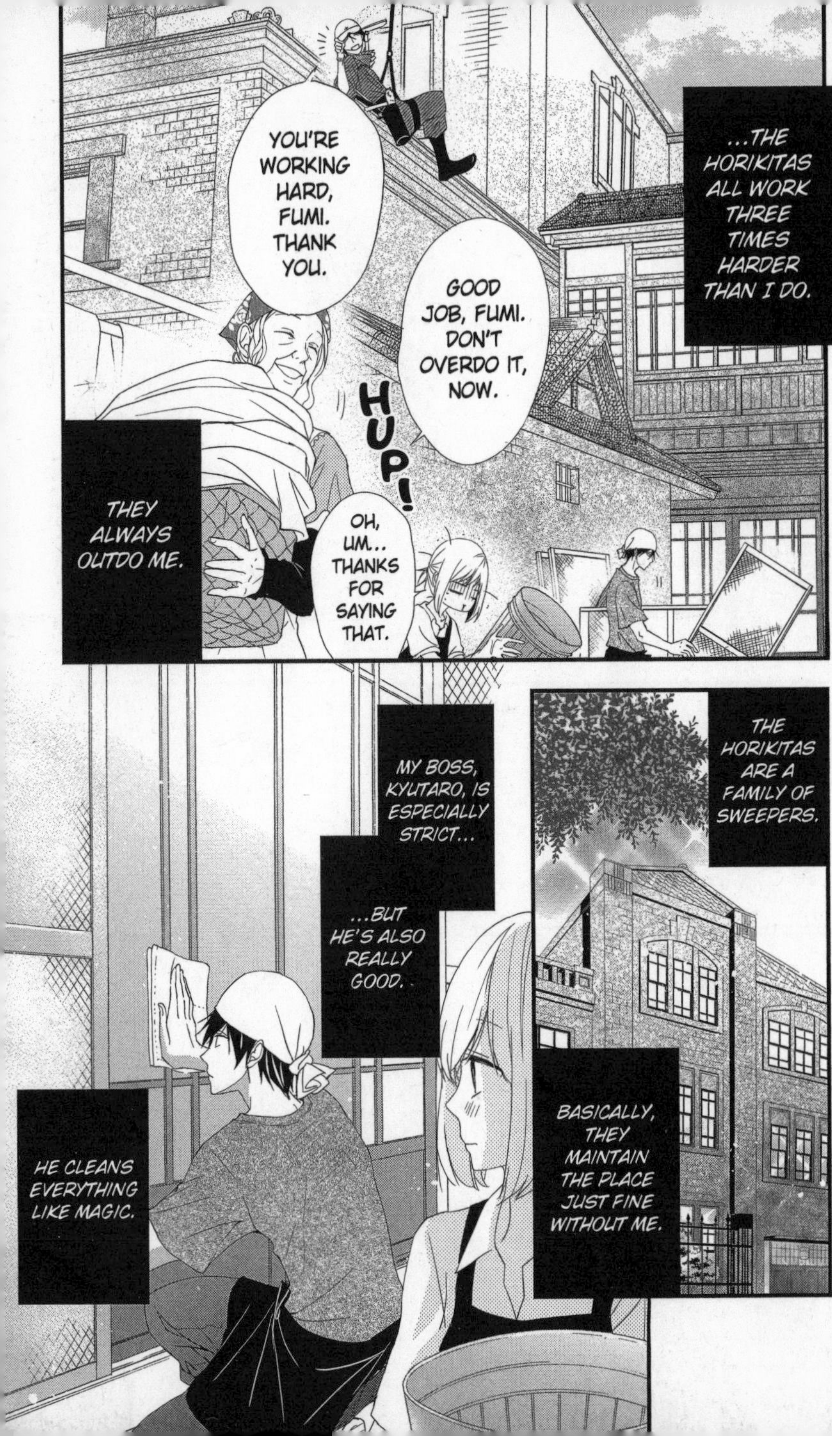
...THE HORIKITAS ALL WORK THREE TIMES HARDER THAN I DO.
YOU'RE WORKING HARD, FUMI. THANK YOU.
GOOD JOB, FUMI. DON'T OVERDO IT, NOW.
HUP!
OH, UM... THANKS FOR SAYING THAT.
THEY ALWAYS OUTDO ME.
THE HORIKITAS ARE A FAMILY OF SWEEPERS.
BASICALLY, THEY MAINTAIN THE PLACE JUST FINE WITHOUT ME.
MY BOSS, KYUTARO, IS ESPECIALLY STRICT...
...BUT HE'S ALSO REALLY GOOD.
HE CLEANS EVERYTHING LIKE MAGIC.

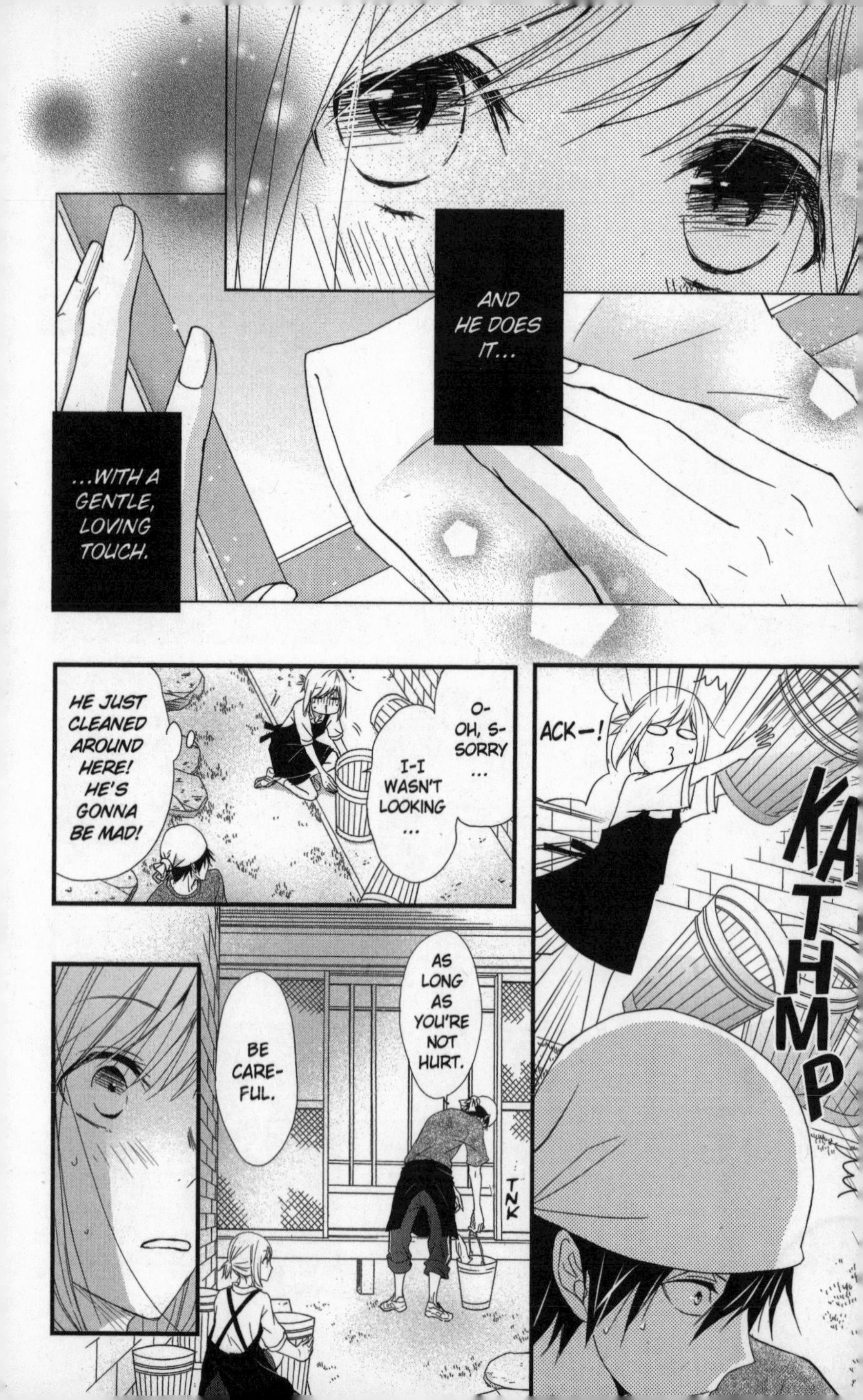
AND HE DOES IT...
...WITH A GENTLE, LOVING TOUCH.
ACK—!
KATHMP
O-OH, S-SORRY...
I-I WASN'T LOOKING...
HE JUST CLEANED AROUND HERE! HE'S GONNA BE MAD!
AS LONG AS YOU'RE NOT HURT.
BE CAREFUL.
TNK

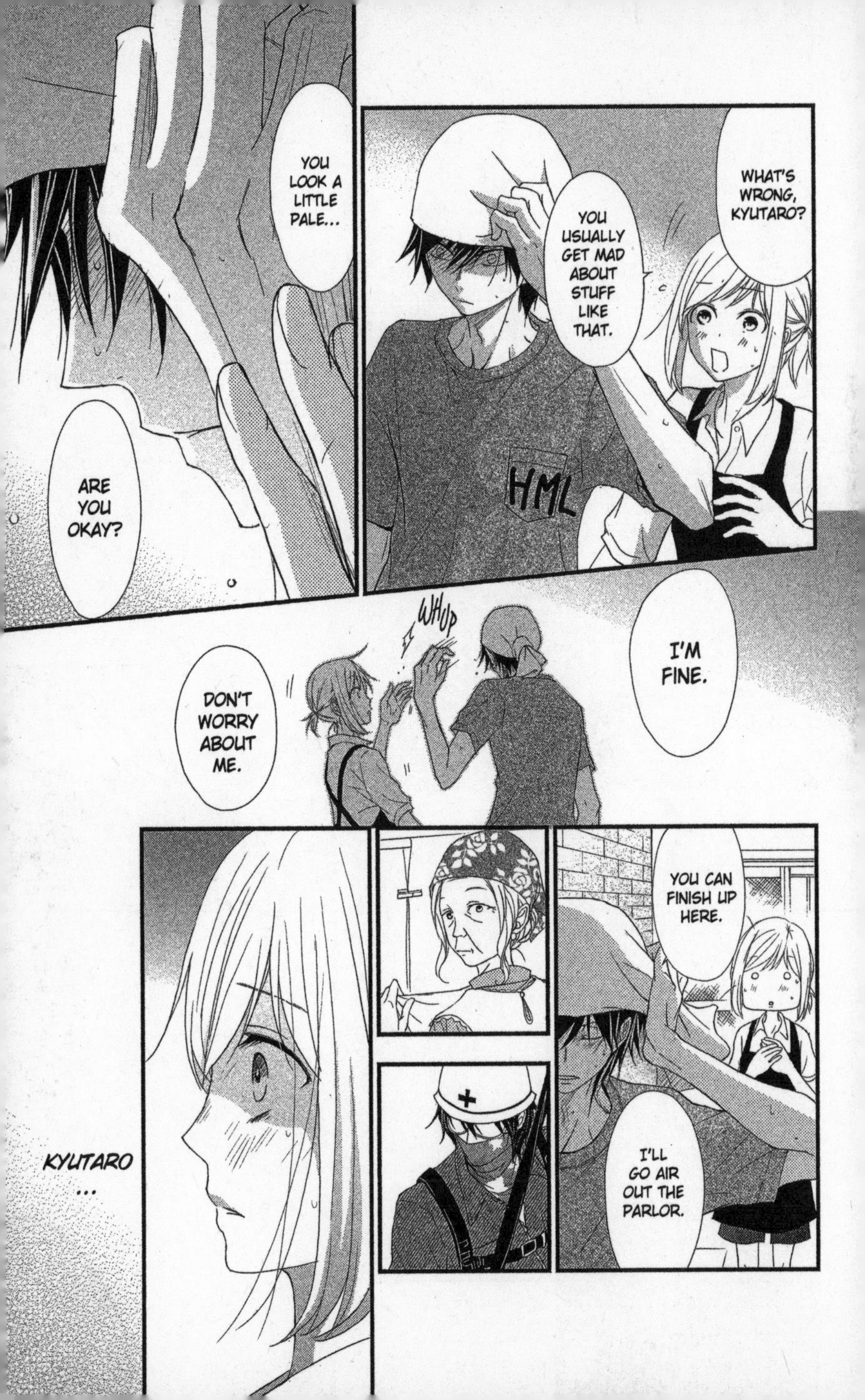
WHAT'S WRONG, KYUTARO?
YOU USUALLY GET MAD ABOUT STUFF LIKE THAT.
HML
YOU LOOK A LITTLE PALE...
ARE YOU OKAY?
I'M FINE.
WHUP
DON'T WORRY ABOUT ME.
YOU CAN FINISH UP HERE.
I'LL GO AIR OUT THE PARLOR.
KYUTARO ...

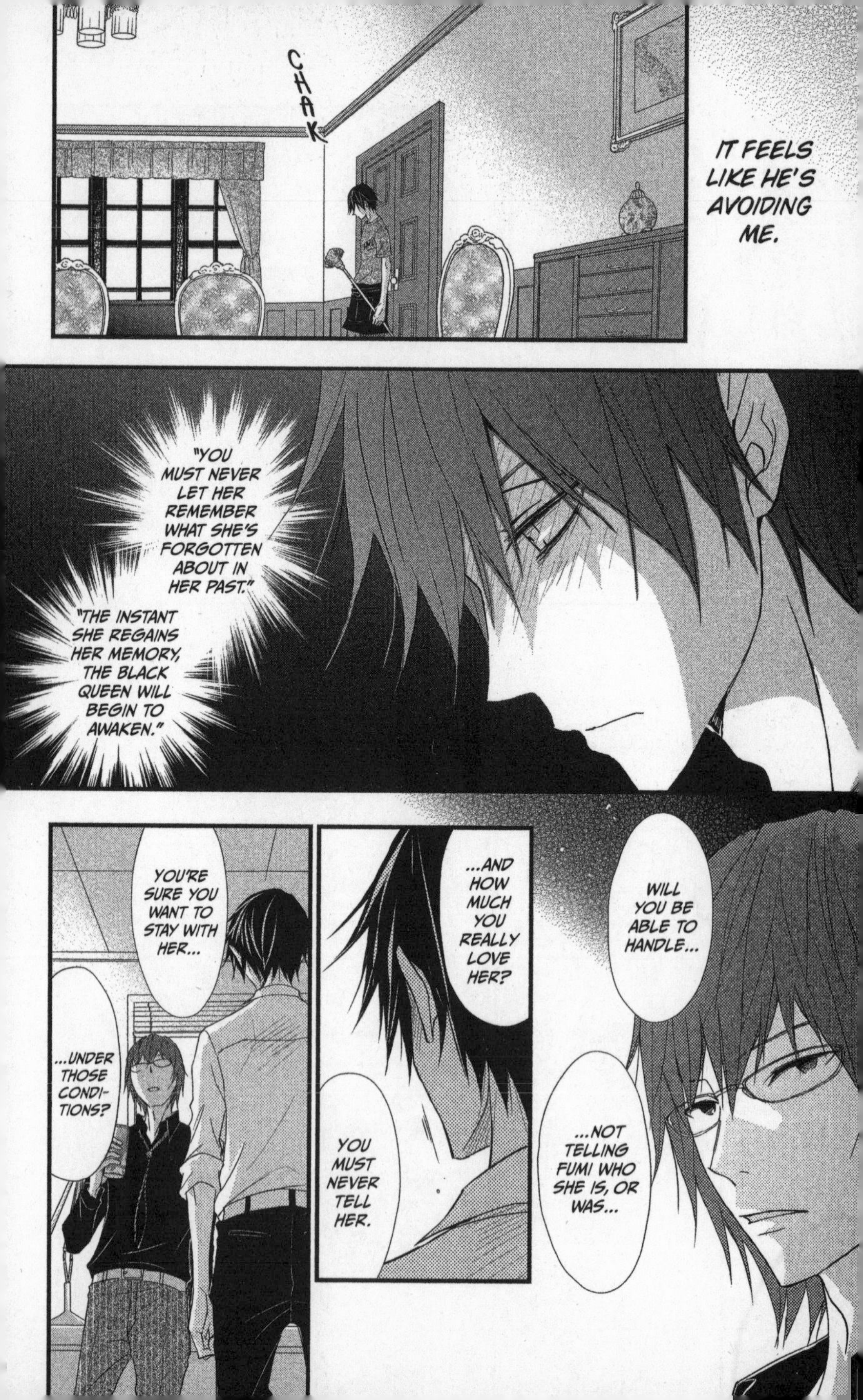
IT FEELS LIKE HE'S AVOIDING ME.
CHAK
"YOU MUST NEVER LET HER REMEMBER WHAT SHE'S FORGOTTEN ABOUT IN HER PAST."
"THE INSTANT SHE REGAINS HER MEMORY, THE BLACK QUEEN WILL BEGIN TO AWAKEN."
WILL YOU BE ABLE TO HANDLE...
...NOT TELLING FUMI WHO SHE IS, OR WAS...
...AND HOW MUCH YOU REALLY LOVE HER?
YOU MUST NEVER TELL HER.
YOU'RE SURE YOU WANT TO STAY WITH HER...
...UNDER THOSE CONDITIONS?

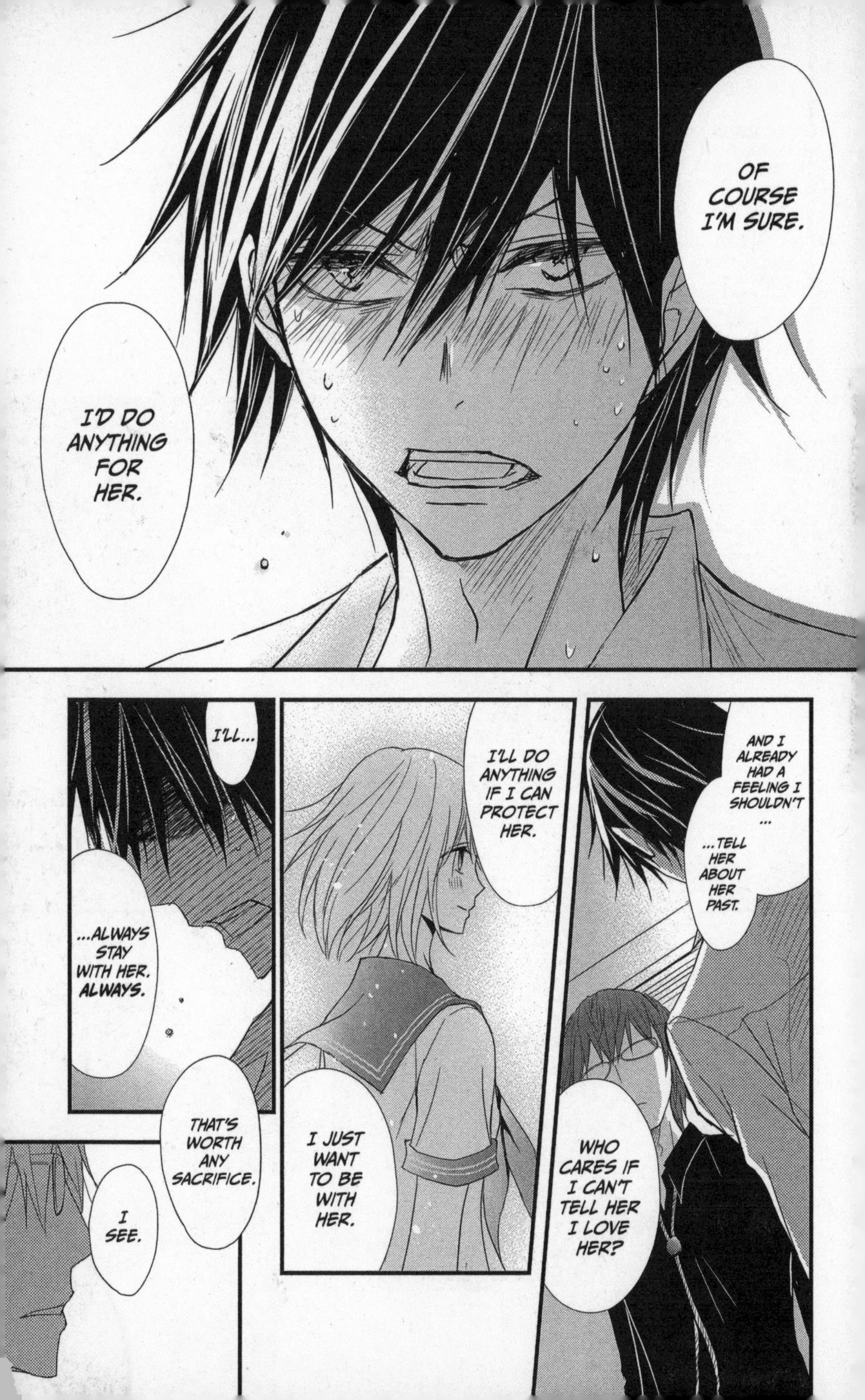

OF COURSE I'M SURE.
I'D DO ANYTHING FOR HER.
AND I ALREADY HAD A FEELING I SHOULDN'T ...
...TELL HER ABOUT HER PAST.
WHO CARES IF I CAN'T TELL HER I LOVE HER?
I'LL DO ANYTHING IF I CAN PROTECT HER.
I JUST WANT TO BE WITH HER.
I'LL...
...ALWAYS STAY WITH HER. ALWAYS.
THAT'S WORTH ANY SACRIFICE.
I SEE.

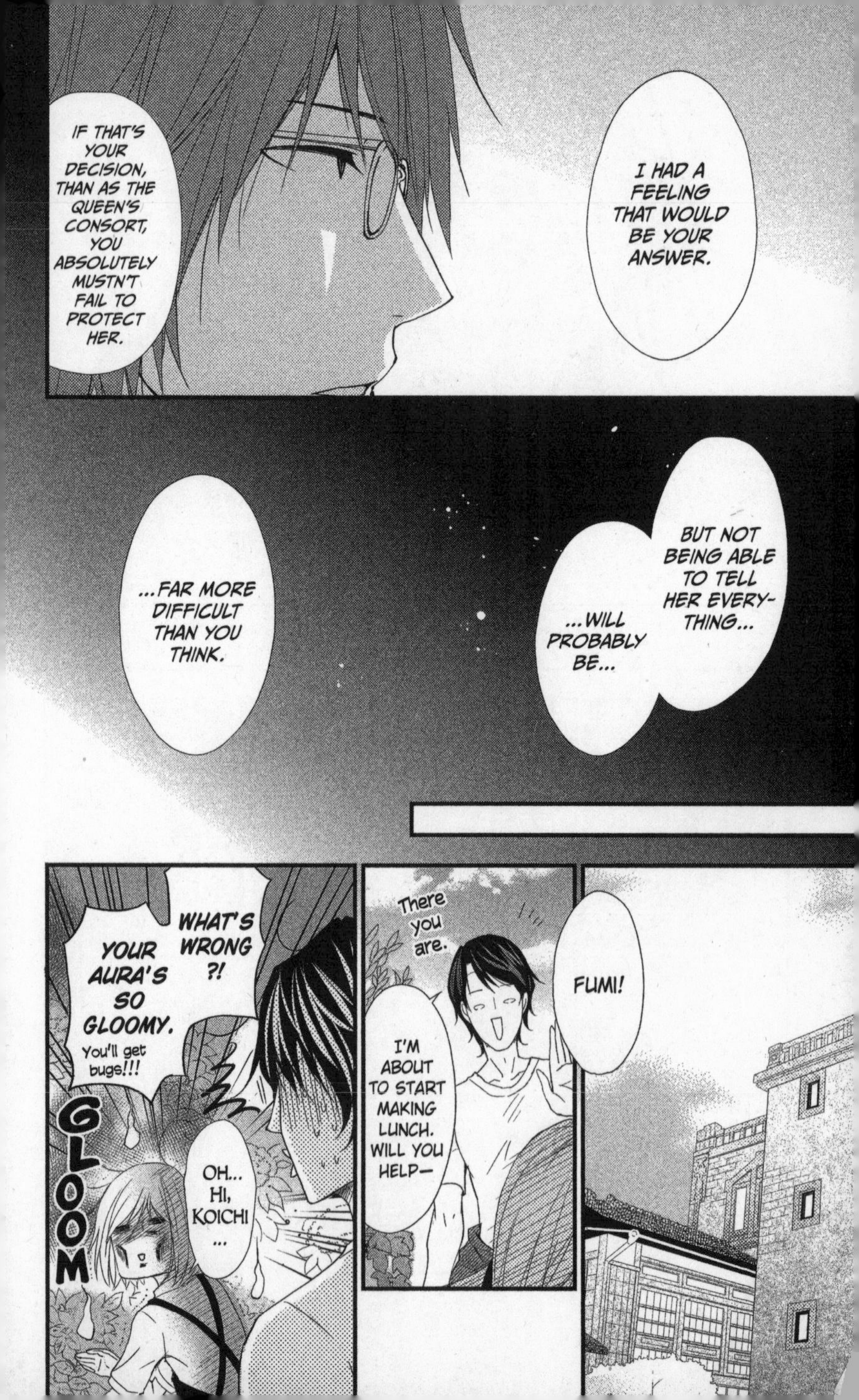
I HAD A FEELING THAT WOULD BE YOUR ANSWER.
IF THAT'S YOUR DECISION, THAN AS THE QUEEN'S CONSORT, YOU ABSOLUTELY MUSTN'T FAIL TO PROTECT HER.
BUT NOT BEING ABLE TO TELL HER EVERY-THING...
...WILL PROBABLY BE...
...FAR MORE DIFFICULT THAN YOU THINK.
FUMI!
There you are.
I'M ABOUT TO START MAKING LUNCH. WILL YOU HELP—
WHAT'S WRONG ?!
YOUR AURA'S SO GLOOMY.
You'll get bugs!!!
GLOOM
OH... HI, KOICHI ...

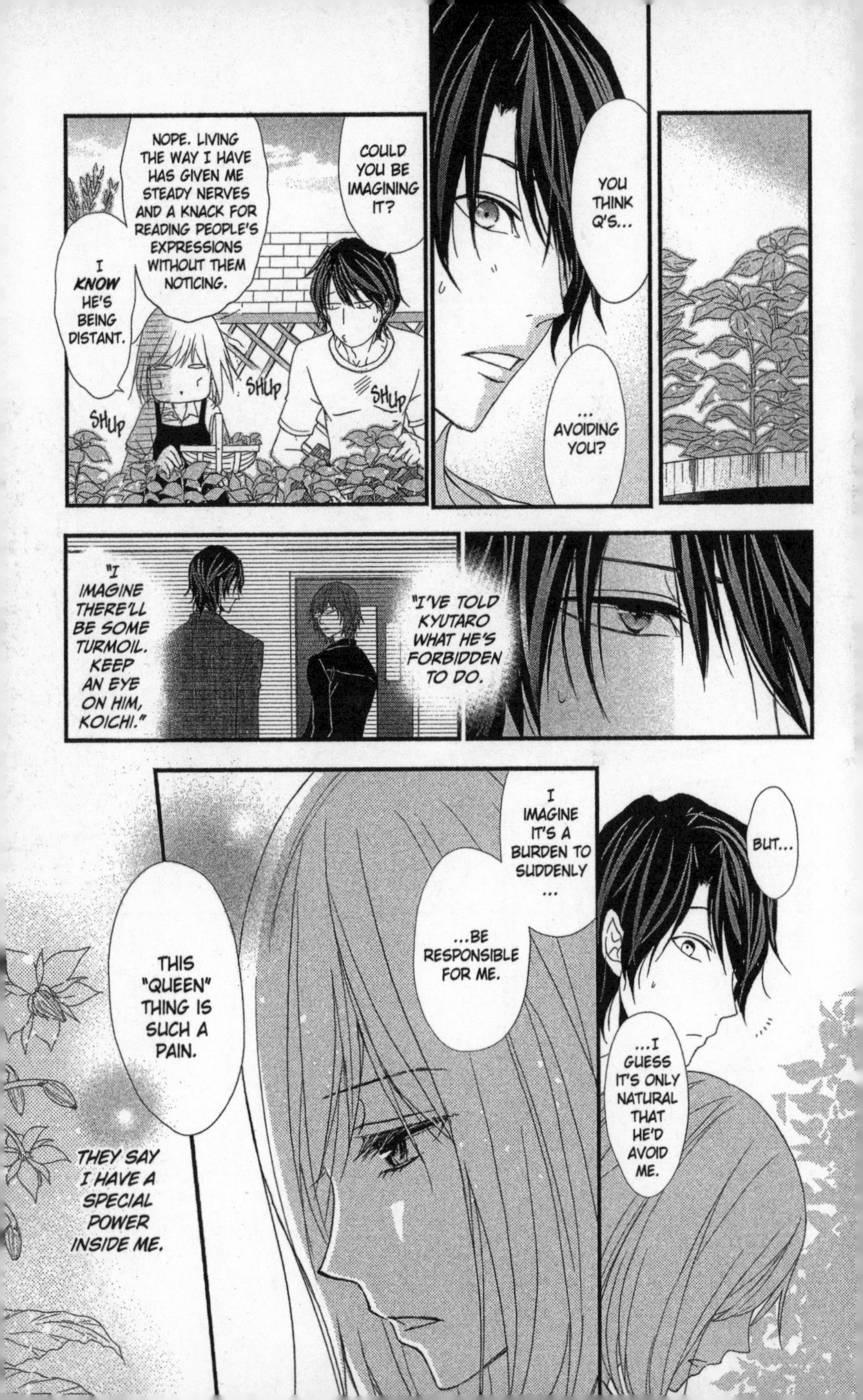
YOU THINK Q'S...
...AVOIDING YOU?
COULD YOU BE IMAGINING IT?
NOPE. LIVING THE WAY I HAVE HAS GIVEN ME STEADY NERVES AND A KNACK FOR READING PEOPLE'S EXPRESSIONS WITHOUT THEM NOTICING.
I *KNOW* HE'S BEING DISTANT.
SHUP
SHUP
SHUP
"I'VE TOLD KYUTARO WHAT HE'S FORBIDDEN TO DO.
"I IMAGINE THERE'LL BE SOME TURMOIL. KEEP AN EYE ON HIM, KOICHI."
BUT...
I IMAGINE IT'S A BURDEN TO SUDDENLY...
...BE RESPONSIBLE FOR ME.
...I GUESS IT'S ONLY NATURAL THAT HE'D AVOID ME.
THIS "QUEEN" THING IS SUCH A PAIN.
THEY SAY I HAVE A SPECIAL POWER INSIDE ME.

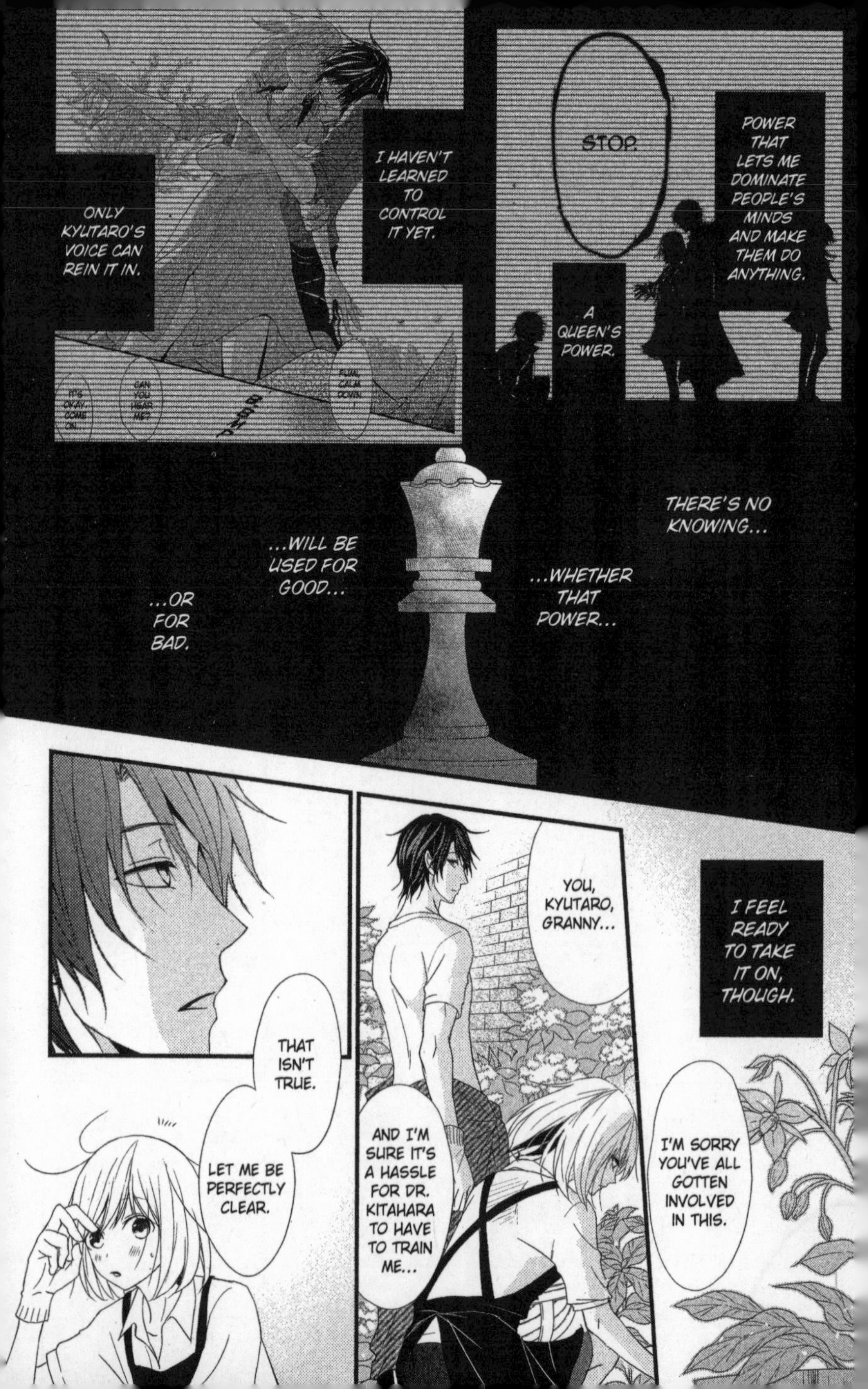

STOP.
POWER THAT LETS ME DOMINATE PEOPLE'S MINDS AND MAKE THEM DO ANYTHING.
A QUEEN'S POWER.
I HAVEN'T LEARNED TO CONTROL IT YET.
ONLY KYUTARO'S VOICE CAN REIN IT IN.
FUJI, CALM DOWN!
CAN YOU HEAR ME?
IT'S OKAY. COME ON.
THERE'S NO KNOWING...
...WHETHER THAT POWER...
...WILL BE USED FOR GOOD...
...OR FOR BAD.
I FEEL READY TO TAKE IT ON, THOUGH.
YOU, KYUTARO, GRANNY...
I'M SORRY YOU'VE ALL GOTTEN INVOLVED IN THIS.
AND I'M SURE IT'S A HASSLE FOR DR. KITAHARA TO HAVE TO TRAIN ME...
THAT ISN'T TRUE.
LET ME BE PERFECTLY CLEAR.

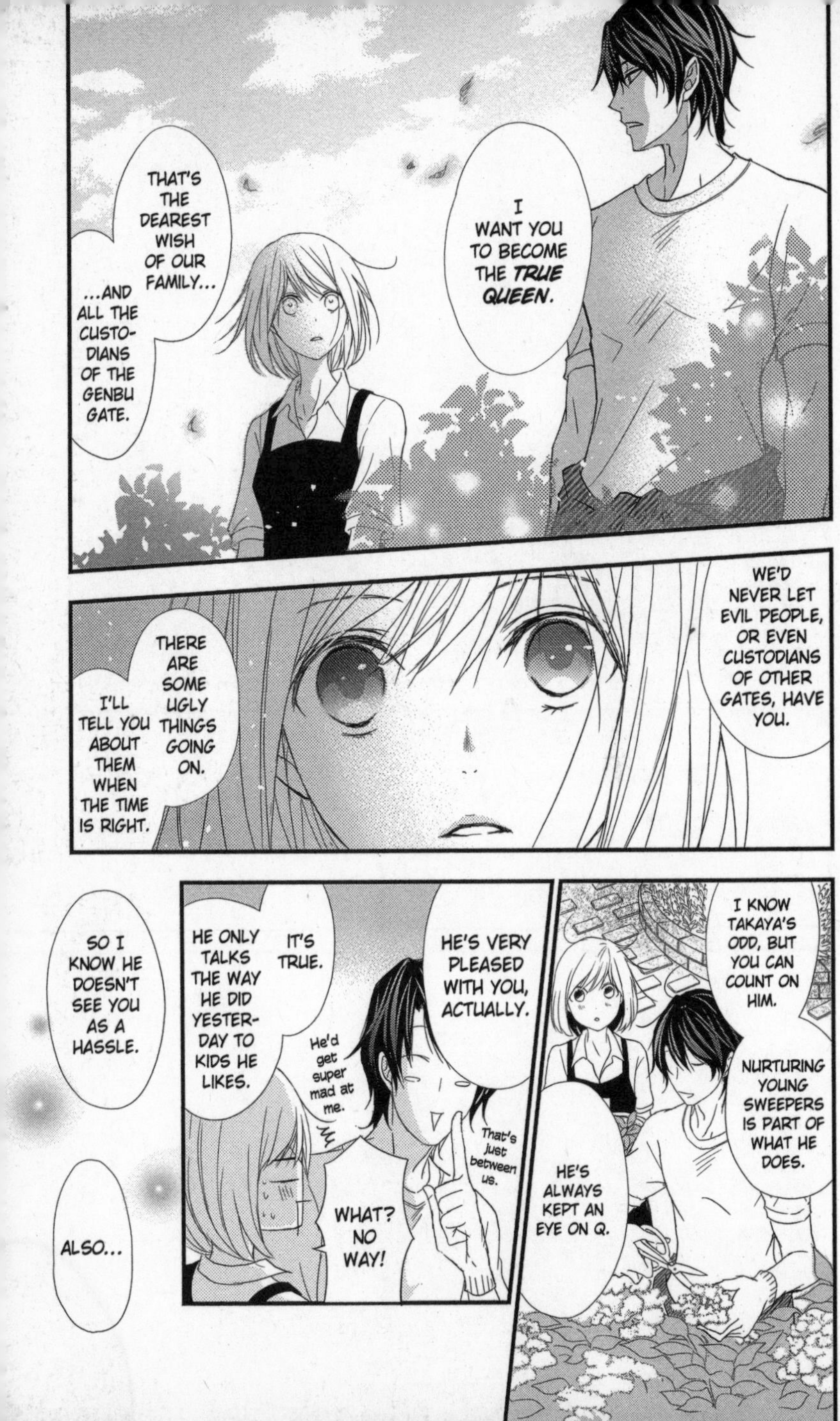
I WANT YOU TO BECOME THE TRUE QUEEN.
THAT'S THE DEAREST WISH OF OUR FAMILY...
...AND ALL THE CUSTODIANS OF THE GENBU GATE.
WE'D NEVER LET EVIL PEOPLE, OR EVEN CUSTODIANS OF OTHER GATES, HAVE YOU.
THERE ARE SOME UGLY THINGS GOING ON.
I'LL TELL YOU ABOUT THEM WHEN THE TIME IS RIGHT.
I KNOW TAKAYA'S ODD, BUT YOU CAN COUNT ON HIM.
NURTURING YOUNG SWEEPERS IS PART OF WHAT HE DOES.
HE'S ALWAYS KEPT AN EYE ON Q.
HE'S VERY PLEASED WITH YOU, ACTUALLY.
IT'S TRUE.
HE ONLY TALKS THE WAY HE DID YESTERDAY TO KIDS HE LIKES.
He'd get super mad at me.
That's just between us.
WHAT? NO WAY!
SO I KNOW HE DOESN'T SEE YOU AS A HASSLE.
ALSO...

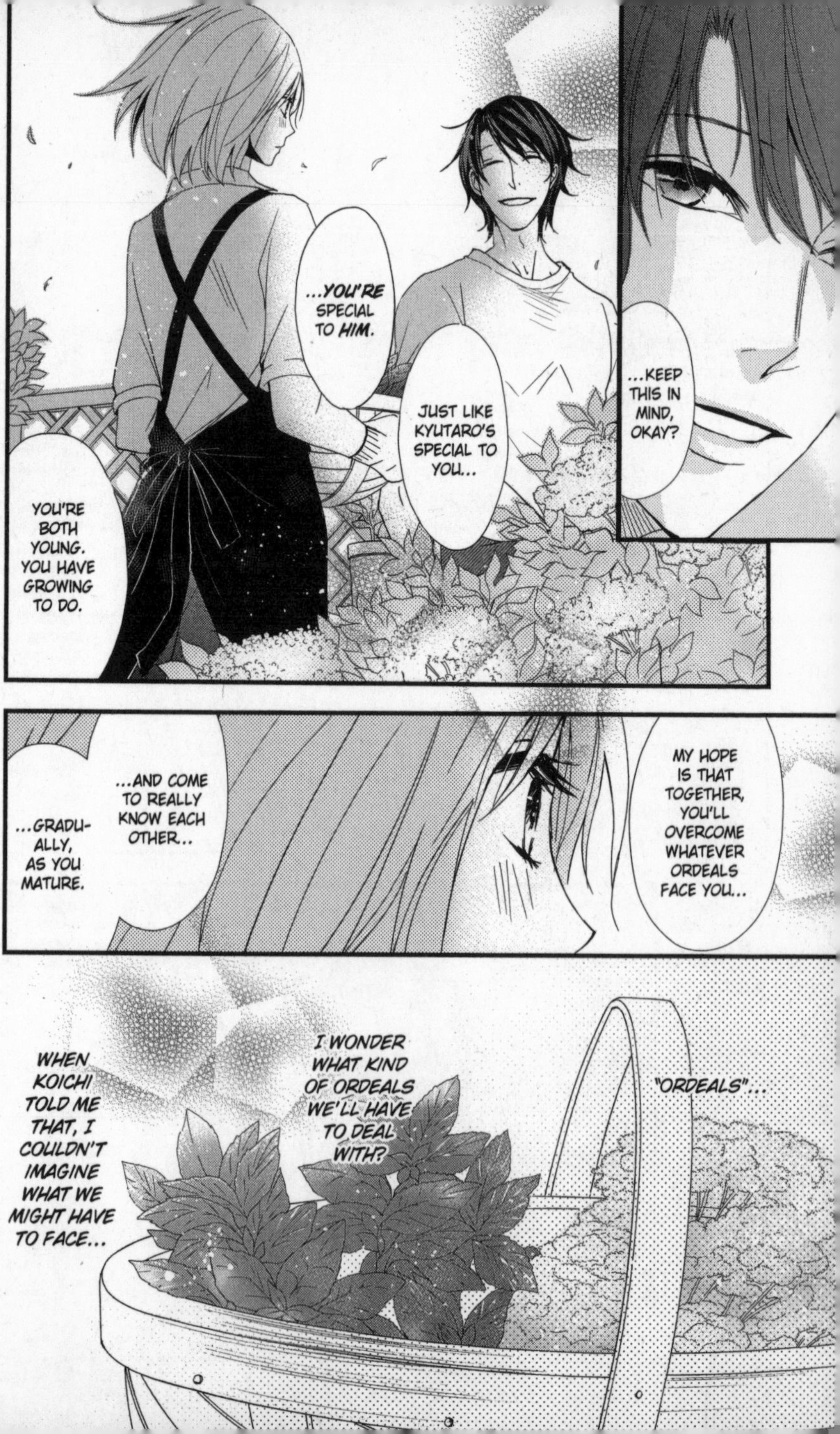
...KEEP THIS IN MIND, OKAY?
JUST LIKE KYUTARO'S SPECIAL TO YOU...
...YOU'RE SPECIAL TO HIM.
YOU'RE BOTH YOUNG. YOU HAVE GROWING TO DO.
MY HOPE IS THAT TOGETHER, YOU'LL OVERCOME WHATEVER ORDEALS FACE YOU...
...AND COME TO REALLY KNOW EACH OTHER...
...GRADU-ALLY, AS YOU MATURE.
"ORDEALS"...
I WONDER WHAT KIND OF ORDEALS WE'LL HAVE TO DEAL WITH?
WHEN KOICHI TOLD ME THAT, I COULDN'T IMAGINE WHAT WE MIGHT HAVE TO FACE...

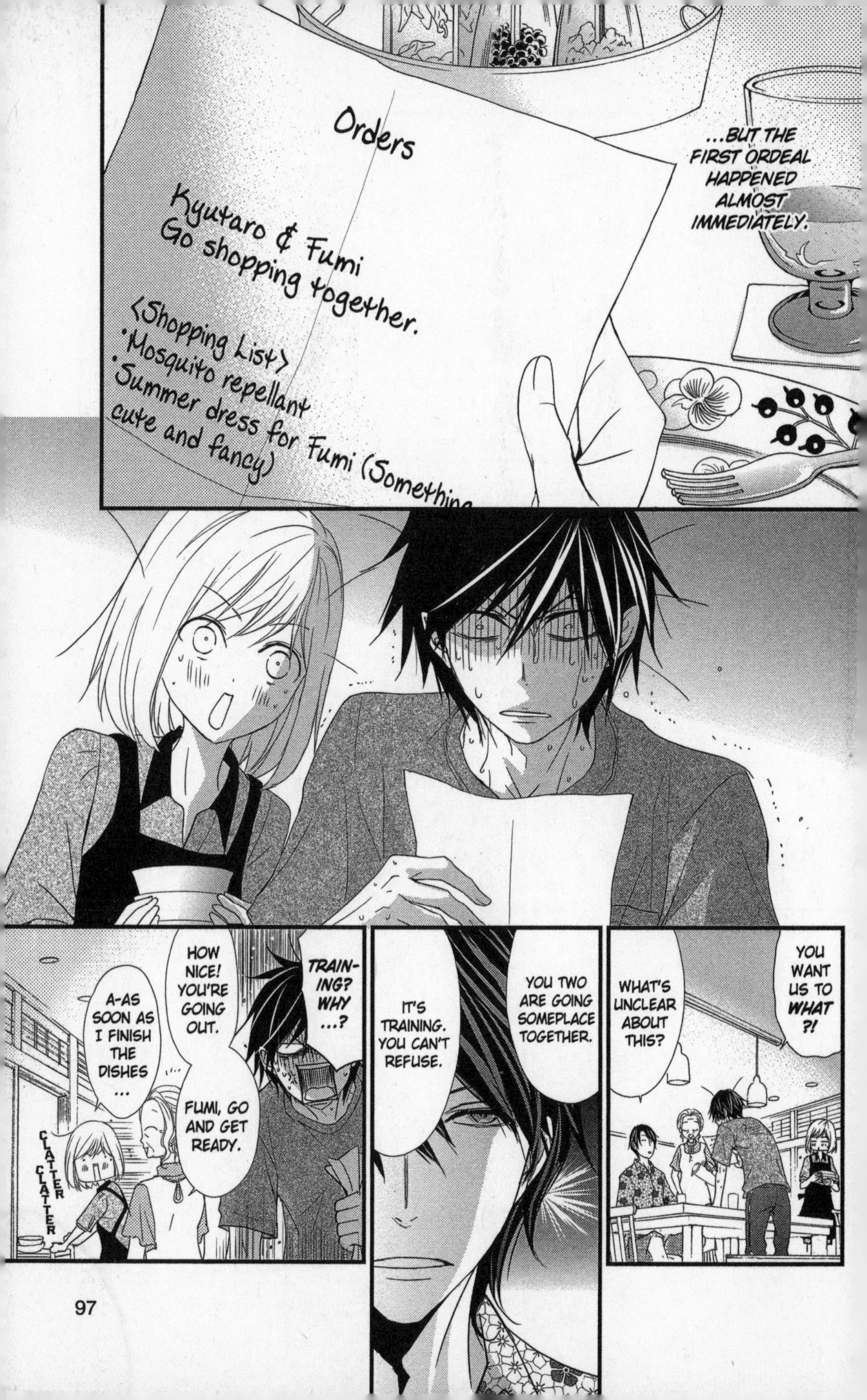
...BUT THE FIRST ORDEAL HAPPENED ALMOST IMMEDIATELY.
Orders
Kyutaro & Fumi Go shopping together.
<Shopping List>
•Mosquito repellant
•Summer dress for Fumi (Something cute and fancy)
YOU WANT US TO WHAT?!
WHAT'S UNCLEAR ABOUT THIS?
YOU TWO ARE GOING SOMEPLACE TOGETHER.
IT'S TRAINING. YOU CAN'T REFUSE.
TRAIN-ING? WHY...?
HOW NICE! YOU'RE GOING OUT.
FUMI, GO AND GET READY.
A-AS SOON AS I FINISH THE DISHES...
CLATTER CLATTER

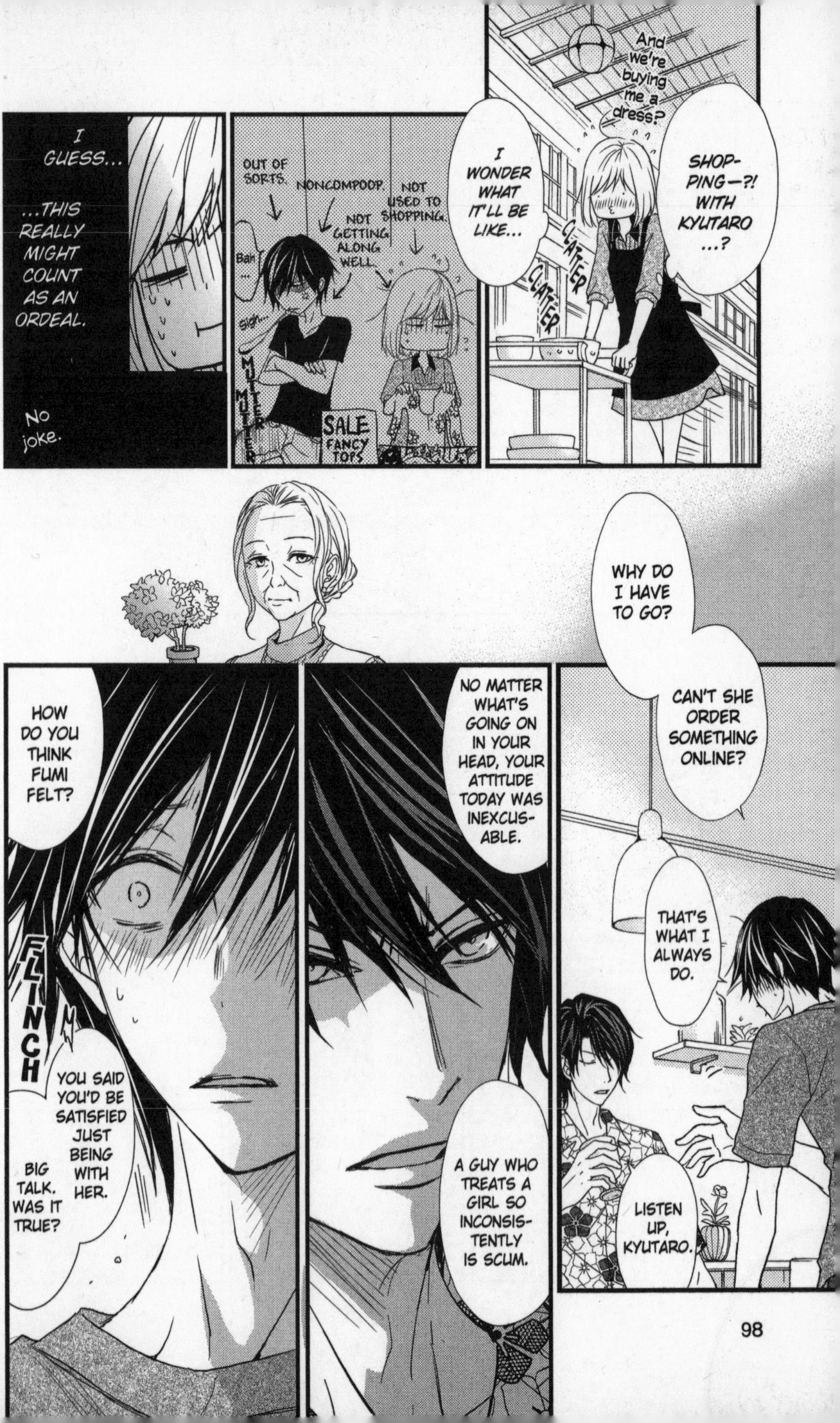

And we're buying me a dress?
SHOP-PING—?! WITH KYUTARO ...?
I WONDER WHAT IT'LL BE LIKE...
CLATTER
CLATTER
NOT USED TO SHOPPING.
NOT GETTING ALONG WELL.
NONCOMPOOP.
OUT OF SORTS.
Bah...
Sigh...
MUTTER
MUTTER
SALE
FANCY TOPS
I GUESS...
...THIS REALLY MIGHT COUNT AS AN ORDEAL.
No joke.
WHY DO I HAVE TO GO?
CAN'T SHE ORDER SOMETHING ONLINE?
THAT'S WHAT I ALWAYS DO.
LISTEN UP, KYUTARO.
NO MATTER WHAT'S GOING ON IN YOUR HEAD, YOUR ATTITUDE TODAY WAS INEXCUS-ABLE.
A GUY WHO TREATS A GIRL SO INCONSIS-TENTLY IS SCUM.
HOW DO YOU THINK FUMI FELT?
FLINCH
YOU SAID YOU'D BE SATISFIED JUST BEING WITH HER.
BIG TALK. WAS IT TRUE?

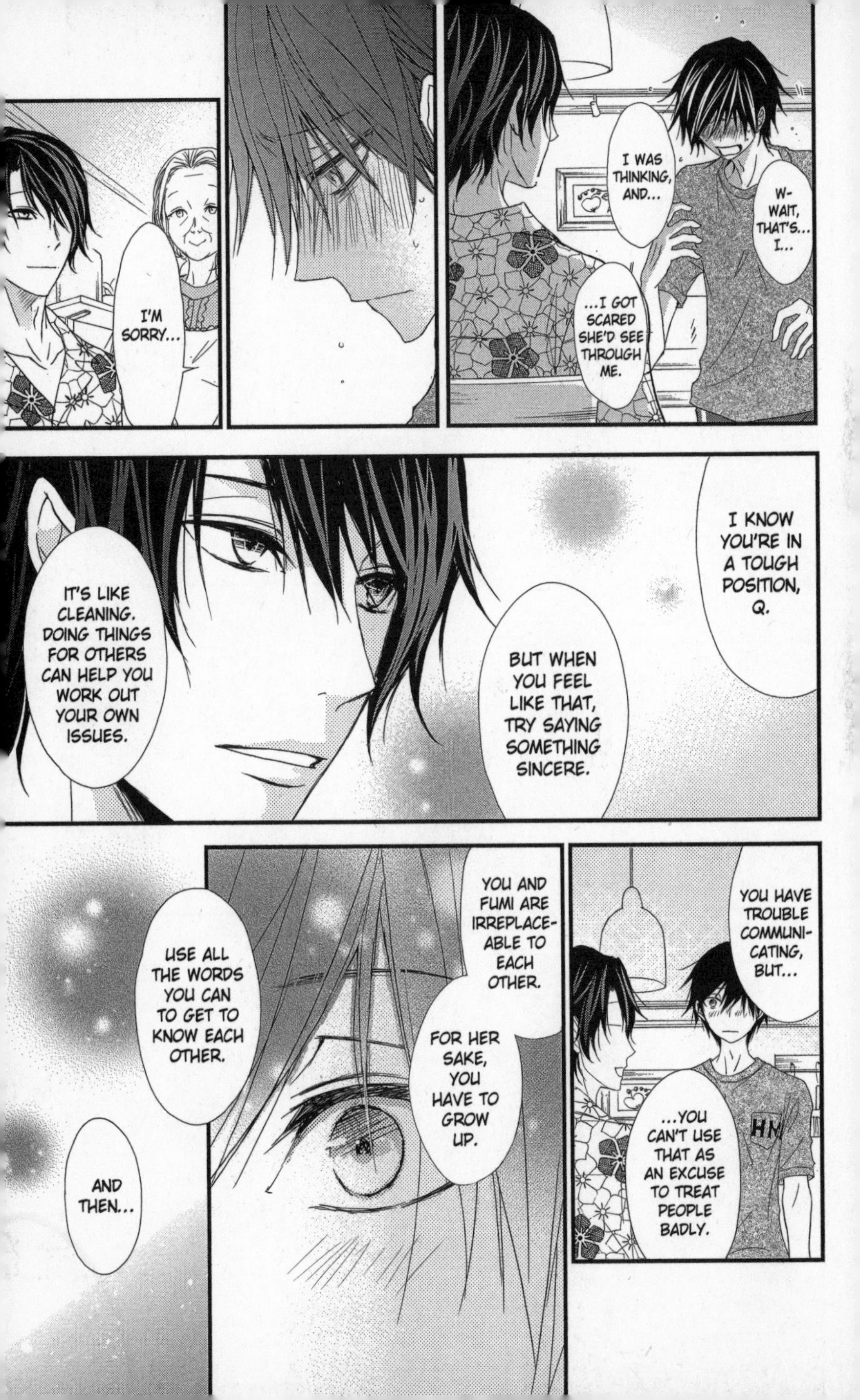
W-WAIT, THAT'S... I...
I WAS THINKING, AND...
...I GOT SCARED SHE'D SEE THROUGH ME.
I'M SORRY...
I KNOW YOU'RE IN A TOUGH POSITION, Q.
BUT WHEN YOU FEEL LIKE THAT, TRY SAYING SOMETHING SINCERE.
IT'S LIKE CLEANING. DOING THINGS FOR OTHERS CAN HELP YOU WORK OUT YOUR OWN ISSUES.
YOU HAVE TROUBLE COMMUNICATING, BUT...
...YOU CAN'T USE THAT AS AN EXCUSE TO TREAT PEOPLE BADLY.
YOU AND FUMI ARE IRREPLACEABLE TO EACH OTHER.
FOR HER SAKE, YOU HAVE TO GROW UP.
USE ALL THE WORDS YOU CAN TO GET TO KNOW EACH OTHER.
AND THEN...
HM

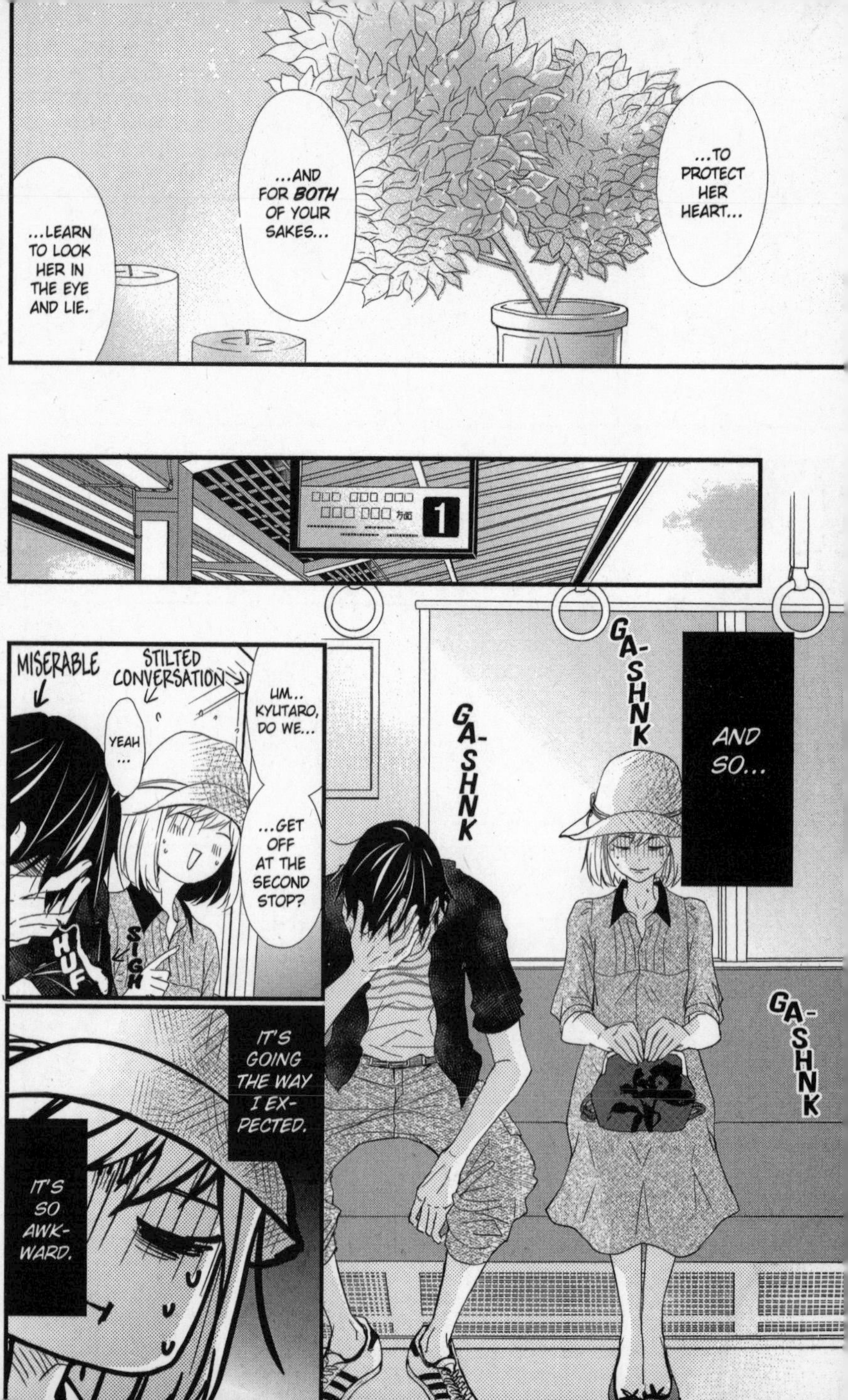
...TO PROTECT HER HEART...
...AND FOR BOTH OF YOUR SAKES...
...LEARN TO LOOK HER IN THE EYE AND LIE.
1
AND SO...
GA-SHNK
GA-SHNK
GA-SHNK
UM... KYUTARO, DO WE...
...GET OFF AT THE SECOND STOP?
YEAH...
STILTED CONVERSATION
MISERABLE
SIGH
HUF
IT'S GOING THE WAY I EXPECTED.
IT'S SO AWKWARD.

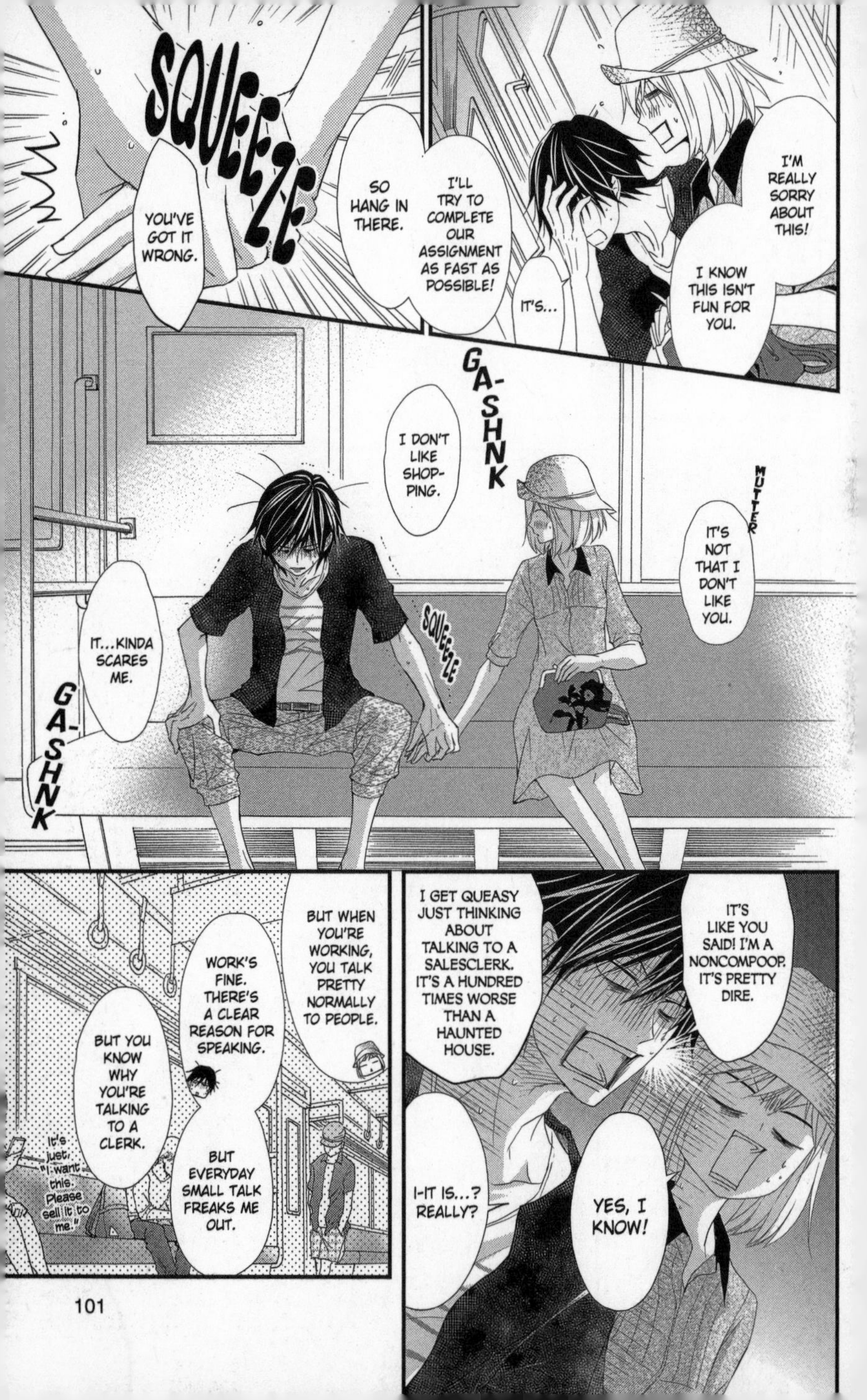
I'M REALLY SORRY ABOUT THIS!
I KNOW THIS ISN'T FUN FOR YOU.
IT'S...
I'LL TRY TO COMPLETE OUR ASSIGNMENT AS FAST AS POSSIBLE!
SO HANG IN THERE.
SQUEEZE
YOU'VE GOT IT WRONG.
GA-SHNK
I DON'T LIKE SHOP-PING.
MUTTER
IT'S NOT THAT I DON'T LIKE YOU.
SQUEEZE
IT...KINDA SCARES ME.
GA-SHNK
IT'S LIKE YOU SAID! I'M A NONCOMPOOP. IT'S PRETTY DIRE.
I GET QUEASY JUST THINKING ABOUT TALKING TO A SALESCLERK. IT'S A HUNDRED TIMES WORSE THAN A HAUNTED HOUSE.
YES, I KNOW!
I-IT IS...? REALLY?
BUT WHEN YOU'RE WORKING, YOU TALK PRETTY NORMALLY TO PEOPLE.
WORK'S FINE. THERE'S A CLEAR REASON FOR SPEAKING.
BUT YOU KNOW WHY YOU'RE TALKING TO A CLERK.
BUT EVERYDAY SMALL TALK FREAKS ME OUT.
It's just, "I want this. Please sell it to me."

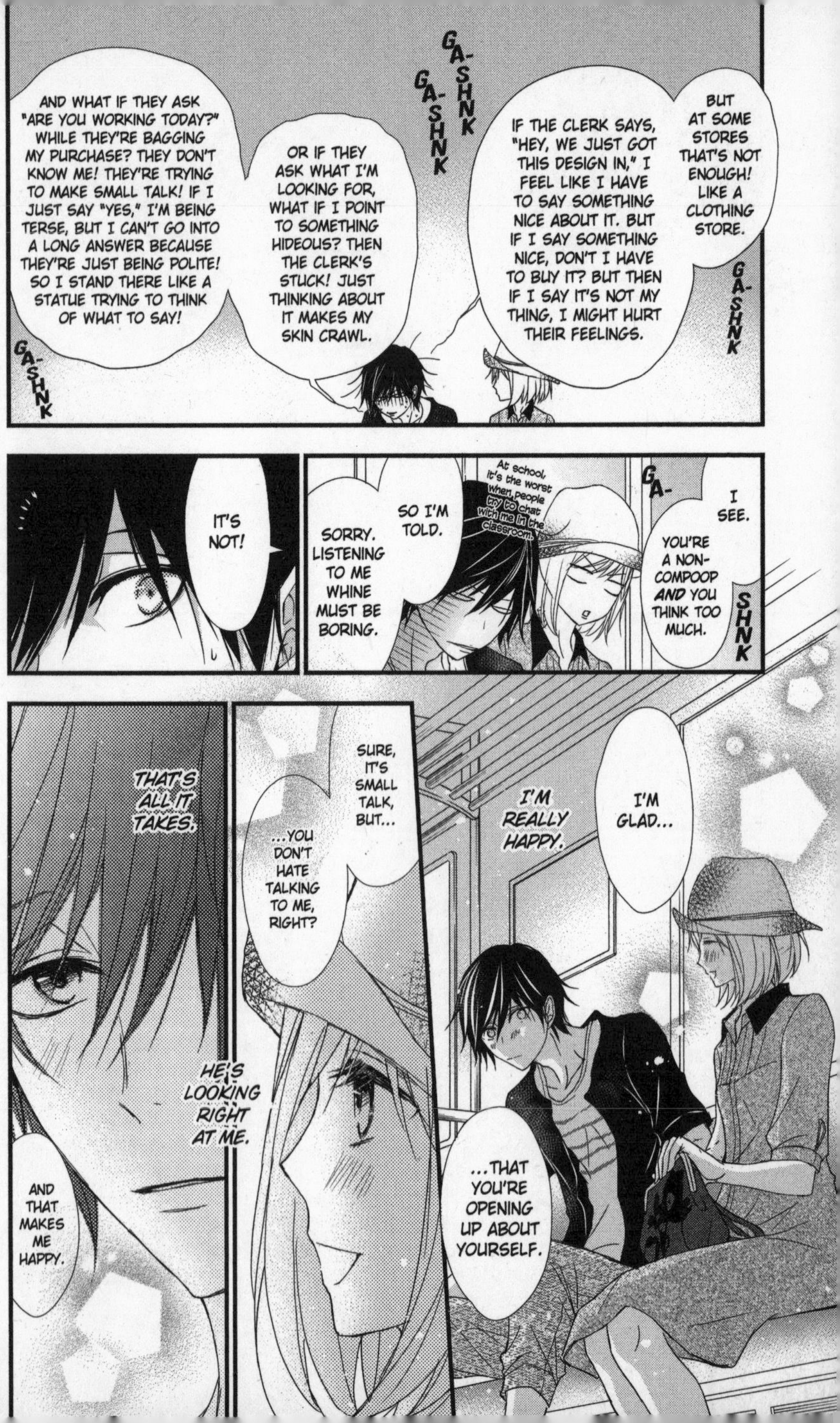
BUT AT SOME STORES THAT'S NOT ENOUGH! LIKE A CLOTHING STORE.
GA-SHNK
IF THE CLERK SAYS, "HEY, WE JUST GOT THIS DESIGN IN," I FEEL LIKE I HAVE TO SAY SOMETHING NICE ABOUT IT. BUT IF I SAY SOMETHING NICE, DON'T I HAVE TO BUY IT? BUT THEN IF I SAY IT'S NOT MY THING, I MIGHT HURT THEIR FEELINGS.
GA-SHNK
GA-SHNK
OR IF THEY ASK WHAT I'M LOOKING FOR, WHAT IF I POINT TO SOMETHING HIDEOUS? THEN THE CLERK'S STUCK! JUST THINKING ABOUT IT MAKES MY SKIN CRAWL.
AND WHAT IF THEY ASK "ARE YOU WORKING TODAY?" WHILE THEY'RE BAGGING MY PURCHASE? THEY DON'T KNOW ME! THEY'RE TRYING TO MAKE SMALL TALK! IF I JUST SAY "YES," I'M BEING TERSE, BUT I CAN'T GO INTO A LONG ANSWER BECAUSE THEY'RE JUST BEING POLITE! SO I STAND THERE LIKE A STATUE TRYING TO THINK OF WHAT TO SAY!
GA-SHNK
GA-
SHNK
I SEE.
YOU'RE A NON-COMPOOP AND YOU THINK TOO MUCH.
At school, it's the worst when people try to chat with me in the classroom.
SO I'M TOLD.
SORRY. LISTENING TO ME WHINE MUST BE BORING.
IT'S NOT!
I'M GLAD...
I'M REALLY HAPPY.
...THAT YOU'RE OPENING UP ABOUT YOURSELF.
SURE, IT'S SMALL TALK, BUT...
...YOU DON'T HATE TALKING TO ME, RIGHT?
THAT'S ALL IT TAKES.
HE'S LOOKING RIGHT AT ME.
AND THAT MAKES ME HAPPY.

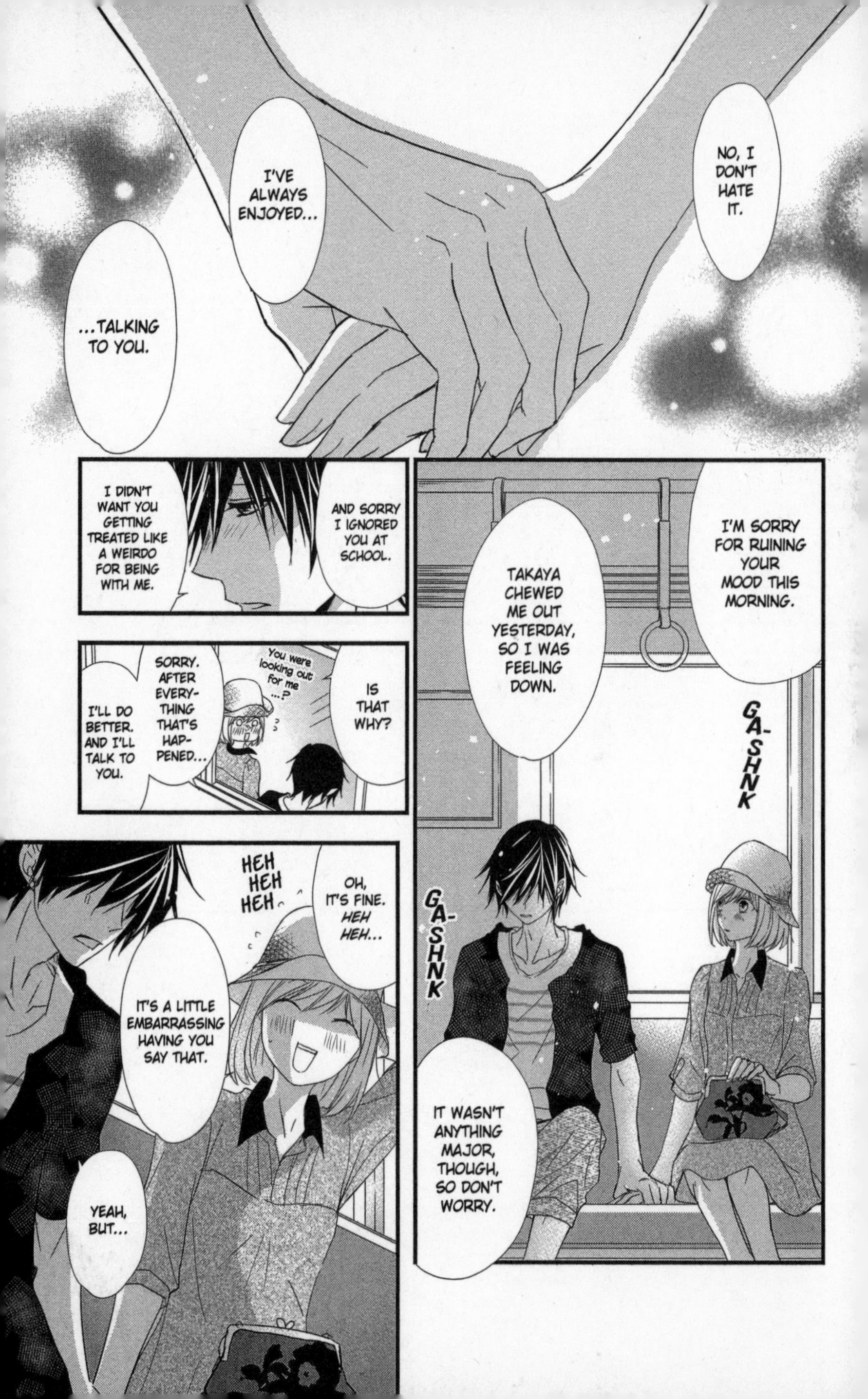
NO, I DON'T HATE IT.
I'VE ALWAYS ENJOYED...
...TALKING TO YOU.
I'M SORRY FOR RUINING YOUR MOOD THIS MORNING.
TAKAYA CHEWED ME OUT YESTERDAY, SO I WAS FEELING DOWN.
GA-SHNK
GA-SHNK
IT WASN'T ANYTHING MAJOR, THOUGH, SO DON'T WORRY.
AND SORRY I IGNORED YOU AT SCHOOL.
I DIDN'T WANT YOU GETTING TREATED LIKE A WEIRDO FOR BEING WITH ME.
IS THAT WHY?
You were looking out for me ...?
SORRY. AFTER EVERY-THING THAT'S HAP-PENED...
I'LL DO BETTER. AND I'LL TALK TO YOU.
OH, IT'S FINE. *HEH HEH...*
HEH HEH HEH
IT'S A LITTLE EMBARRASSING HAVING YOU SAY THAT.
YEAH, BUT...

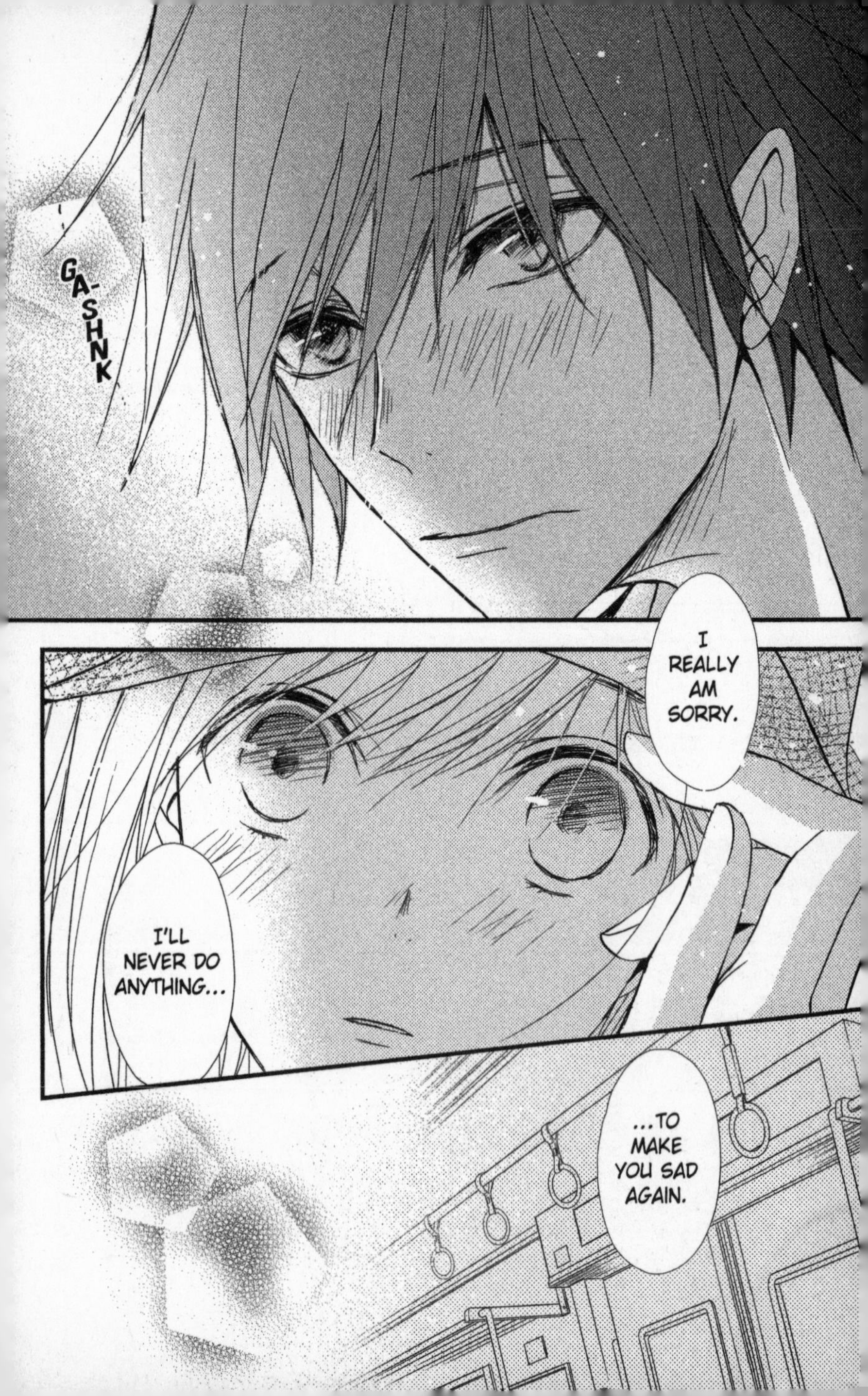
GA-SHNK
I REALLY AM SORRY.
I'LL NEVER DO ANYTHING...
...TO MAKE YOU SAD AGAIN.

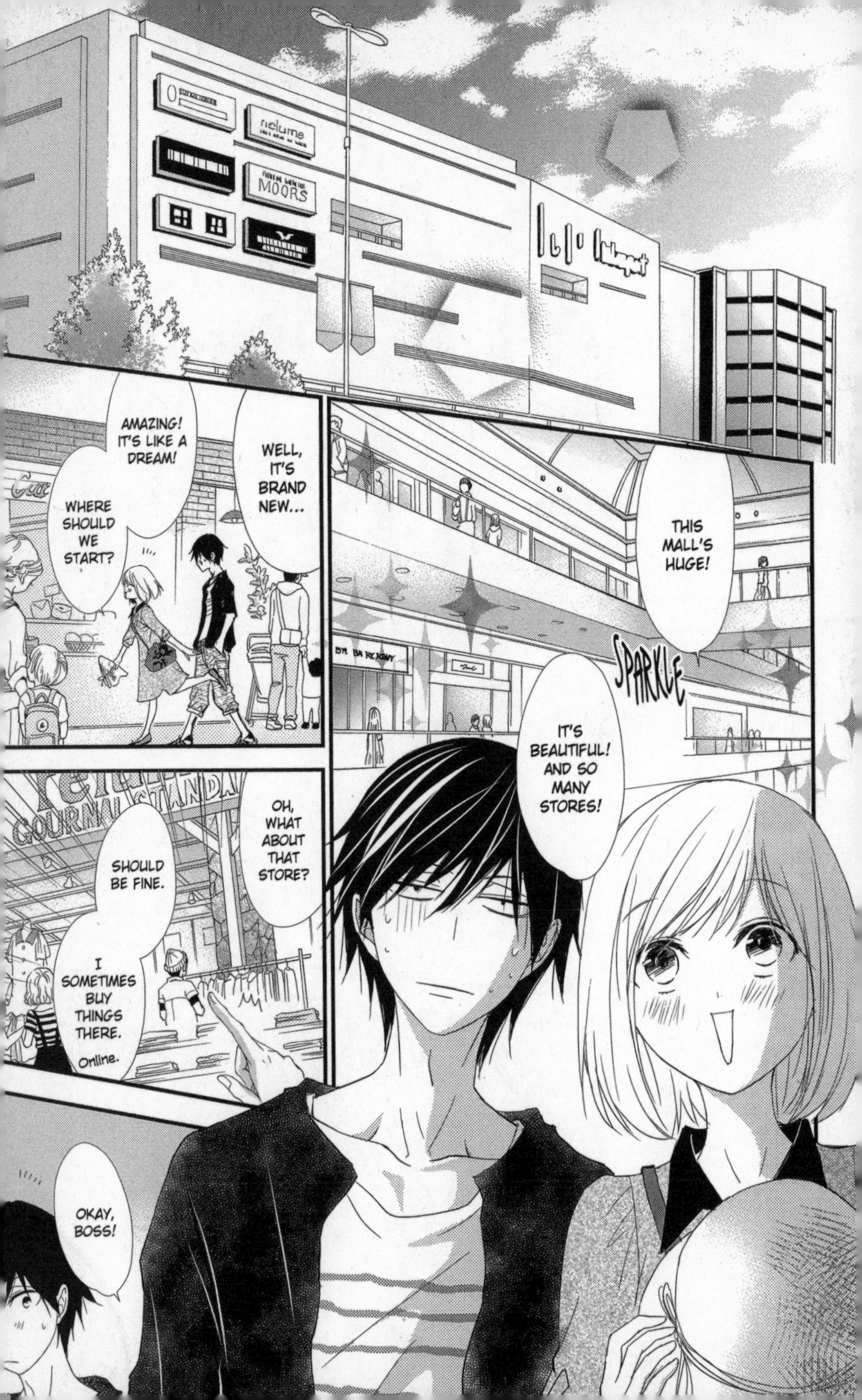
relume
MOORS
THIS MALL'S HUGE!
SPARKLE
IT'S BEAUTIFUL! AND SO MANY STORES!
WELL, IT'S BRAND NEW...
AMAZING! IT'S LIKE A DREAM!
WHERE SHOULD WE START?
OH, WHAT ABOUT THAT STORE?
SHOULD BE FINE.
I SOMETIMES BUY THINGS THERE.
Online.
OKAY, BOSS!

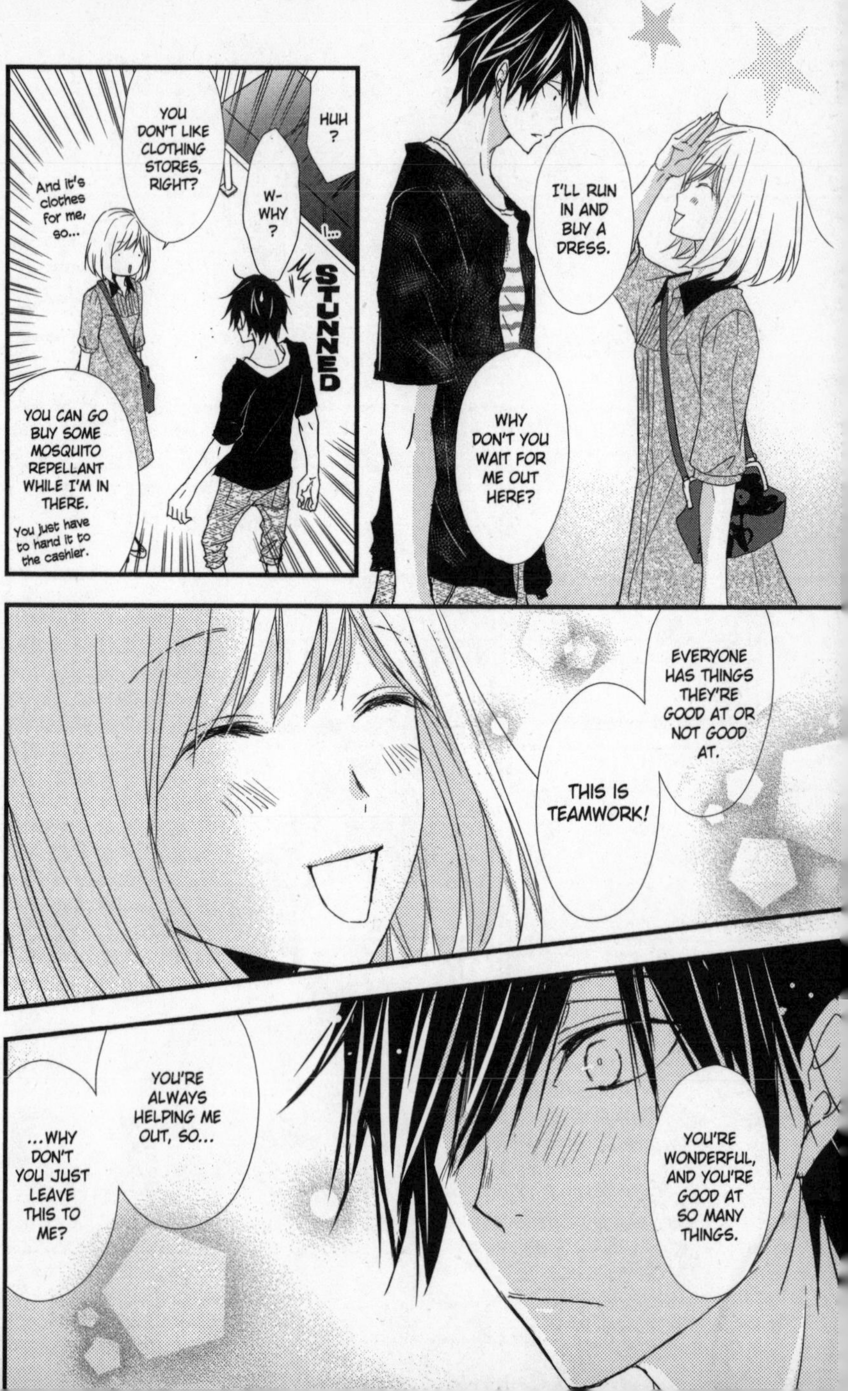
I'LL RUN IN AND BUY A DRESS.
WHY DON'T YOU WAIT FOR ME OUT HERE?
HUH?
W-WHY?
I...
STUNNED
YOU DON'T LIKE CLOTHING STORES, RIGHT?
And it's clothes for me, so...
YOU CAN GO BUY SOME MOSQUITO REPELLANT WHILE I'M IN THERE.
You just have to hand it to the cashier.
EVERYONE HAS THINGS THEY'RE GOOD AT OR NOT GOOD AT.
THIS IS TEAMWORK!
YOU'RE WONDERFUL, AND YOU'RE GOOD AT SO MANY THINGS.
YOU'RE ALWAYS HELPING ME OUT, SO...
...WHY DON'T YOU JUST LEAVE THIS TO ME?

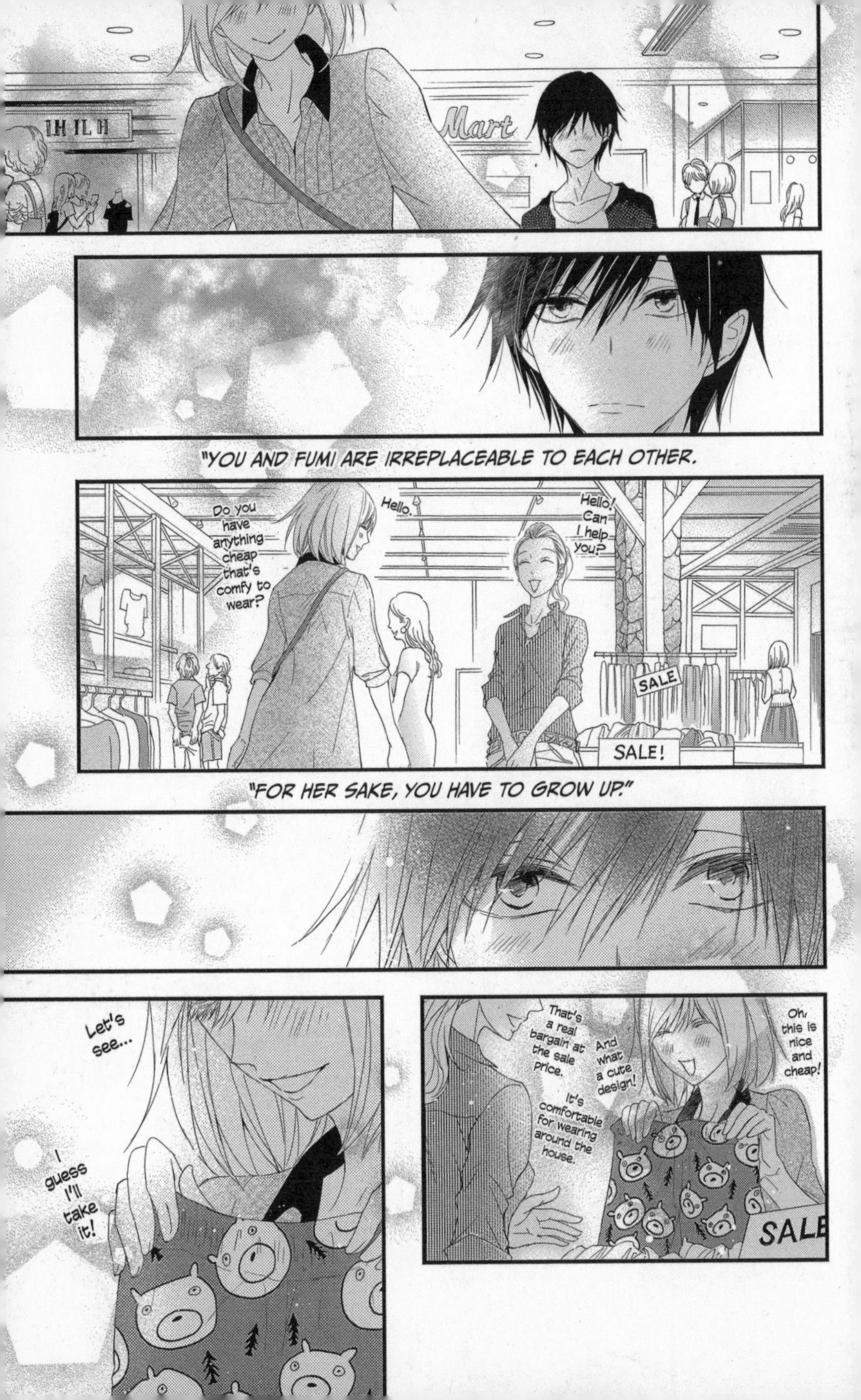
Mart
"YOU AND FUMI ARE IRREPLACEABLE TO EACH OTHER.
Hello! Can I help you?
Hello.
Do you have anything cheap that's comfy to wear?
SALE
SALE!
"FOR HER SAKE, YOU HAVE TO GROW UP."
Oh, this is nice and cheap!
And what a cute design!
That's a real bargain at the sale price.
It's comfortable for wearing around the house.
SALE
Let's see...
I guess I'll take it!

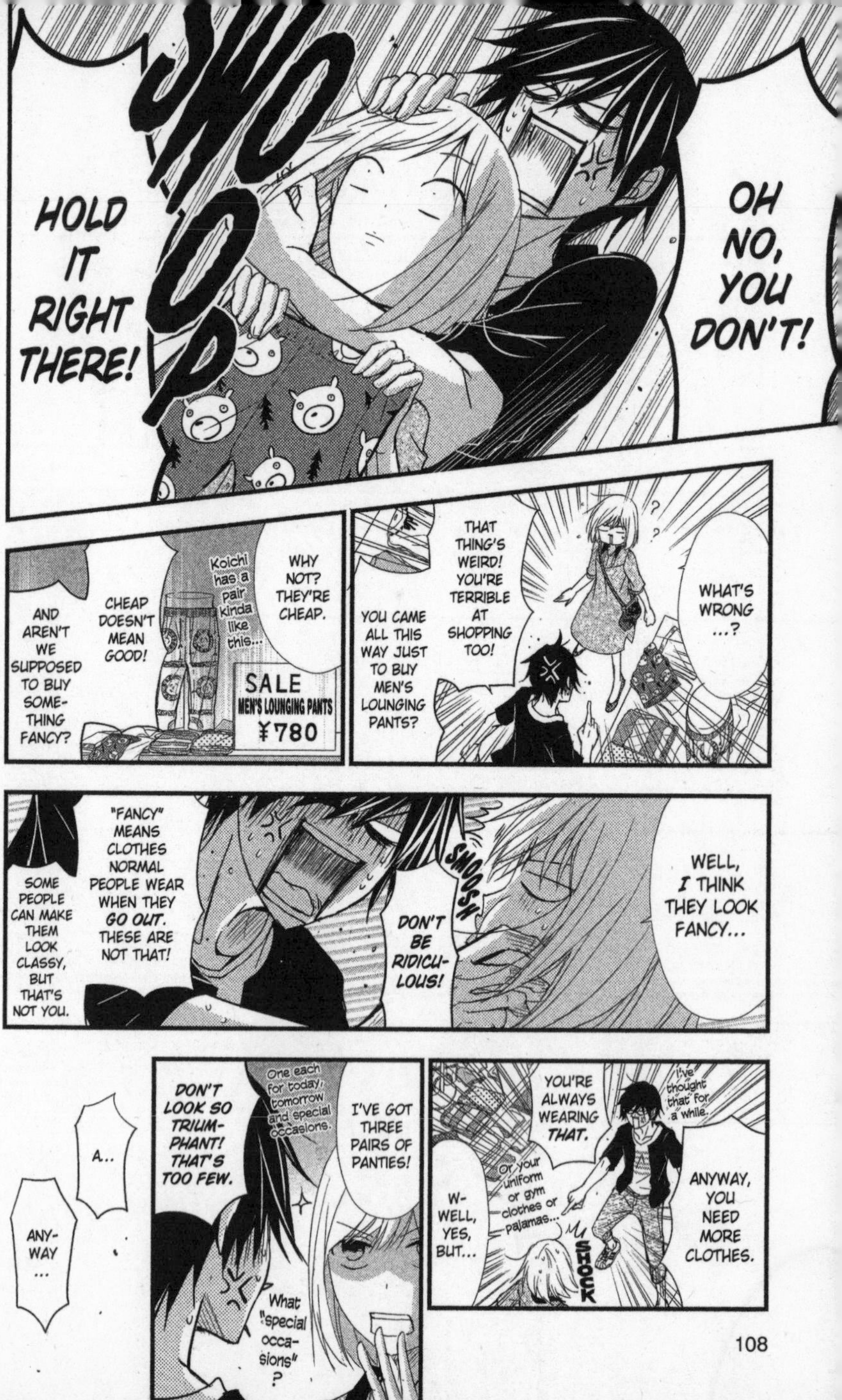
OH NO, YOU DON'T!
SWOOP
HOLD IT RIGHT THERE!
WHAT'S WRONG ...?
THAT THING'S WEIRD! YOU'RE TERRIBLE AT SHOPPING TOO!
YOU CAME ALL THIS WAY JUST TO BUY MEN'S LOUNGING PANTS?
WHY NOT? THEY'RE CHEAP.
Koichi has a pair kinda like this...
SALE
MEN'S LOUNGING PANTS
¥780
CHEAP DOESN'T MEAN GOOD!
AND AREN'T WE SUPPOSED TO BUY SOMETHING FANCY?
WELL, I THINK THEY LOOK FANCY...
SHOOSH
DON'T BE RIDICULOUS!
"FANCY" MEANS CLOTHES NORMAL PEOPLE WEAR WHEN THEY GO OUT. THESE ARE NOT THAT!
SOME PEOPLE CAN MAKE THEM LOOK CLASSY, BUT THAT'S NOT YOU.
I've thought that for a while.
YOU'RE ALWAYS WEARING THAT.
Or your uniform or gym clothes or pajamas...
ANYWAY, YOU NEED MORE CLOTHES.
SHOCK
W-WELL, YES, BUT...
I'VE GOT THREE PAIRS OF PANTIES!
One each for today, tomorrow and special occasions.
DON'T LOOK SO TRIUMPHANT! THAT'S TOO FEW.
What "special occasions"?
A...
ANYWAY...

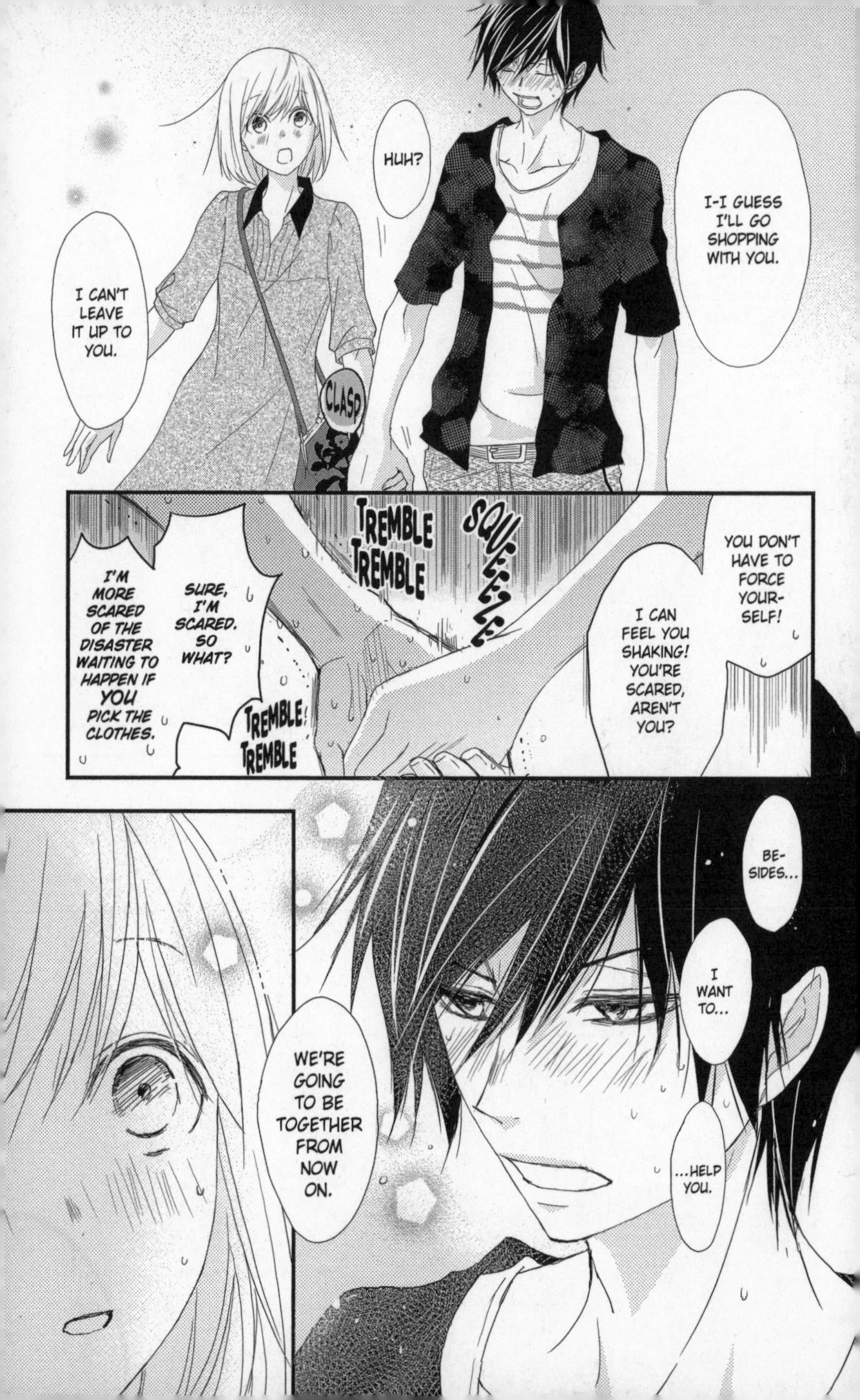
I-I GUESS I'LL GO SHOPPING WITH YOU.
HUH?
CLASP
I CAN'T LEAVE IT UP TO YOU.
YOU DON'T HAVE TO FORCE YOUR-SELF!
I CAN FEEL YOU SHAKING! YOU'RE SCARED, AREN'T YOU?
SQUEEZE
TREMBLE TREMBLE
SURE, I'M SCARED. SO WHAT?
I'M MORE SCARED OF THE DISASTER WAITING TO HAPPEN IF YOU PICK THE CLOTHES.
TREMBLE TREMBLE
BE-SIDES...
I WANT TO...
...HELP YOU.
WE'RE GOING TO BE TOGETHER FROM NOW ON.

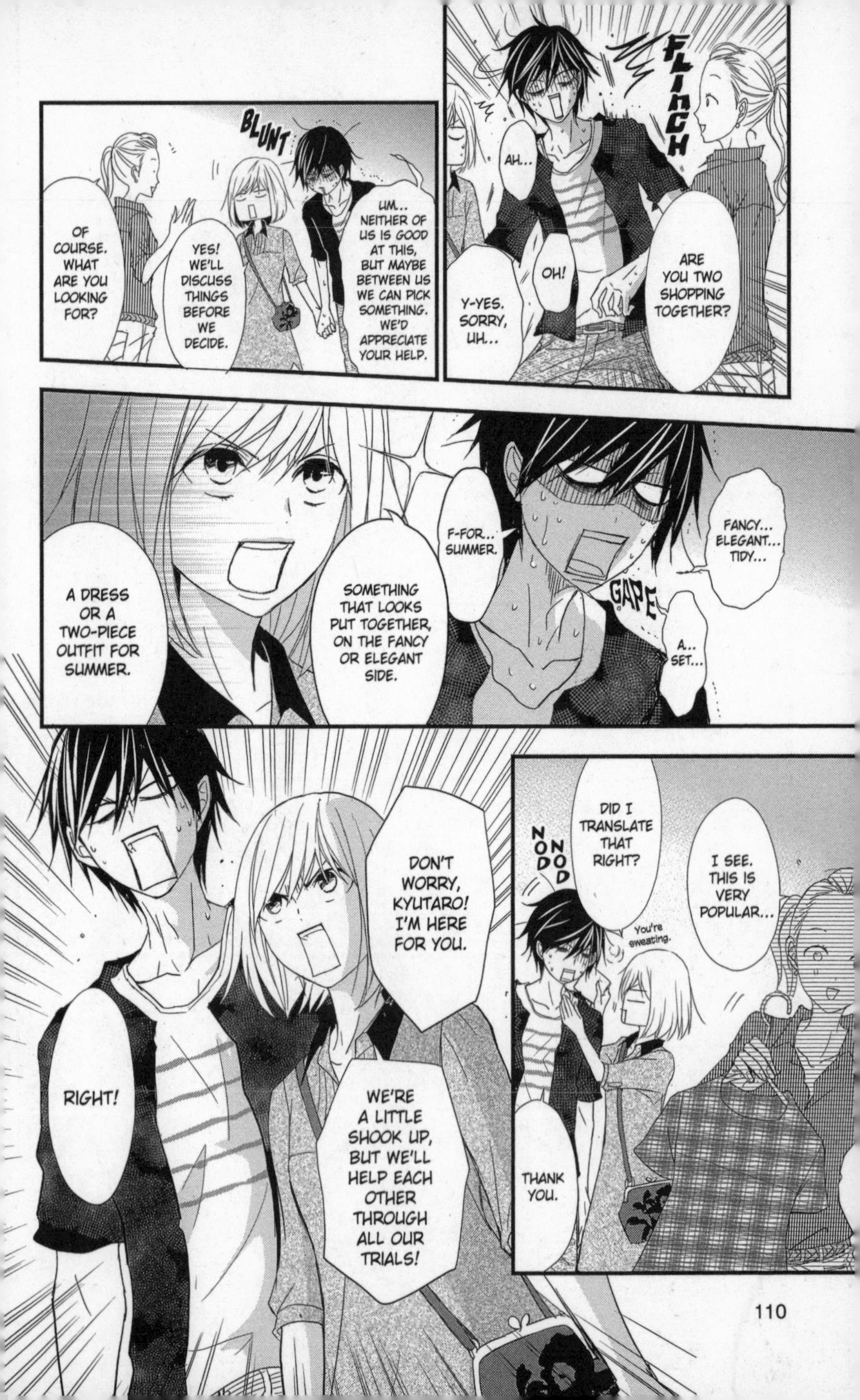
FLINCH
ARE YOU TWO SHOPPING TOGETHER?
AH...
OH!
Y-YES. SORRY, UH...
BLUNT
UM... NEITHER OF US IS GOOD AT THIS, BUT MAYBE BETWEEN US WE CAN PICK SOMETHING. WE'D APPRECIATE YOUR HELP.
YES! WE'LL DISCUSS THINGS BEFORE WE DECIDE.
OF COURSE. WHAT ARE YOU LOOKING FOR?
FANCY... ELEGANT... TIDY...
A... SET...
F-FOR.. SUMMER.
GAPE
SOMETHING THAT LOOKS PUT TOGETHER, ON THE FANCY OR ELEGANT SIDE.
A DRESS OR A TWO-PIECE OUTFIT FOR SUMMER.
I SEE. THIS IS VERY POPULAR...
DID I TRANSLATE THAT RIGHT?
NOD NOD
You're sweating.
THANK YOU.
DON'T WORRY, KYUTARO! I'M HERE FOR YOU.
WE'RE A LITTLE SHOOK UP, BUT WE'LL HELP EACH OTHER THROUGH ALL OUR TRIALS!
RIGHT!

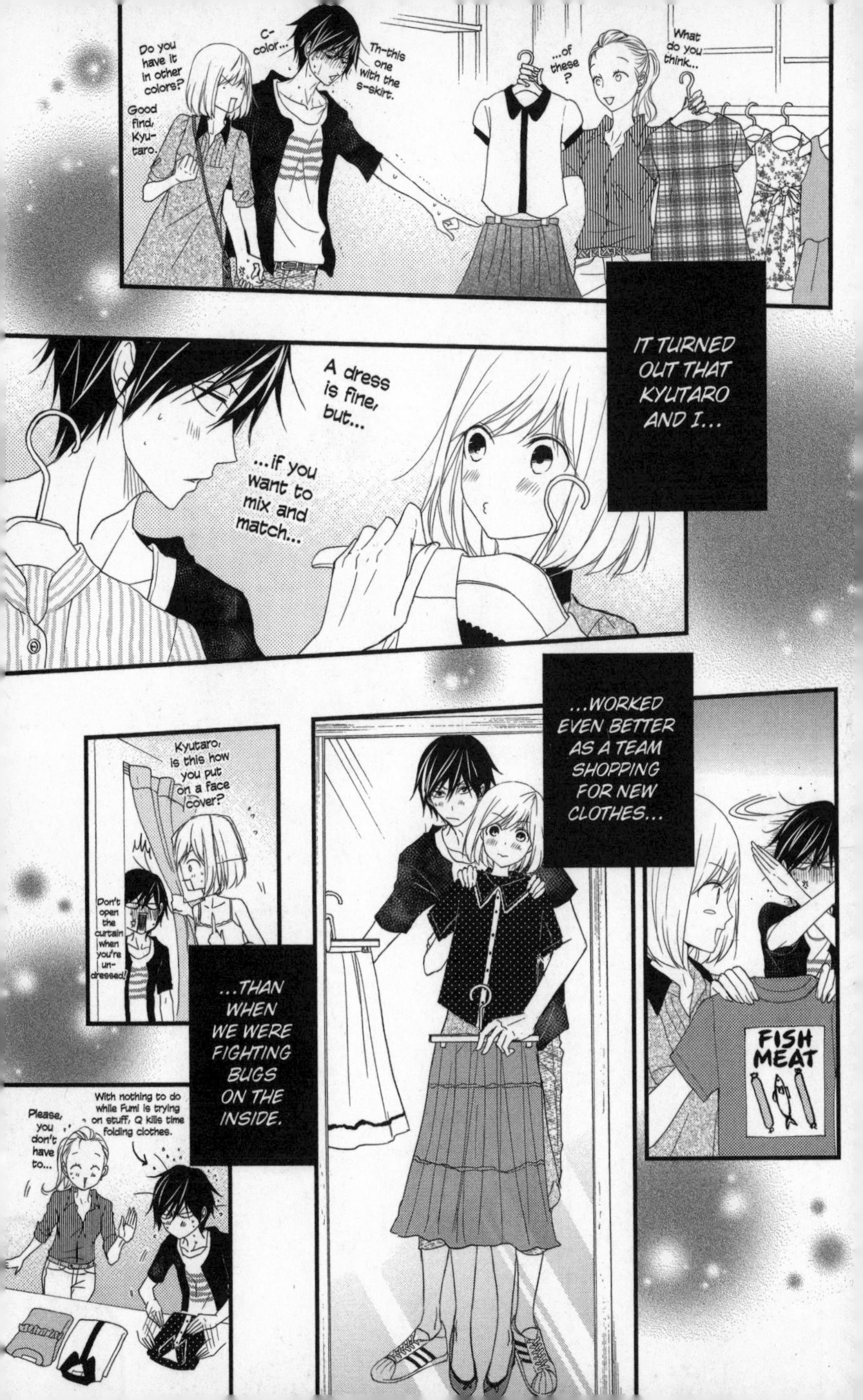
What do you think...
...of these?
Th-this one with the s-skirt.
C-color...
Do you have it in other colors?
Good find, Kyutaro.
IT TURNED OUT THAT KYUTARO AND I...
A dress is fine, but...
...if you want to mix and match...
...WORKED EVEN BETTER AS A TEAM SHOPPING FOR NEW CLOTHES...
FISH MEAT
Kyutaro, is this how you put on a face cover?
Don't open the curtain when you're undressed!
...THAN WHEN WE WERE FIGHTING BUGS ON THE INSIDE.
With nothing to do while Fumi is trying on stuff, Q kills time folding clothes.
Please, you don't have to...

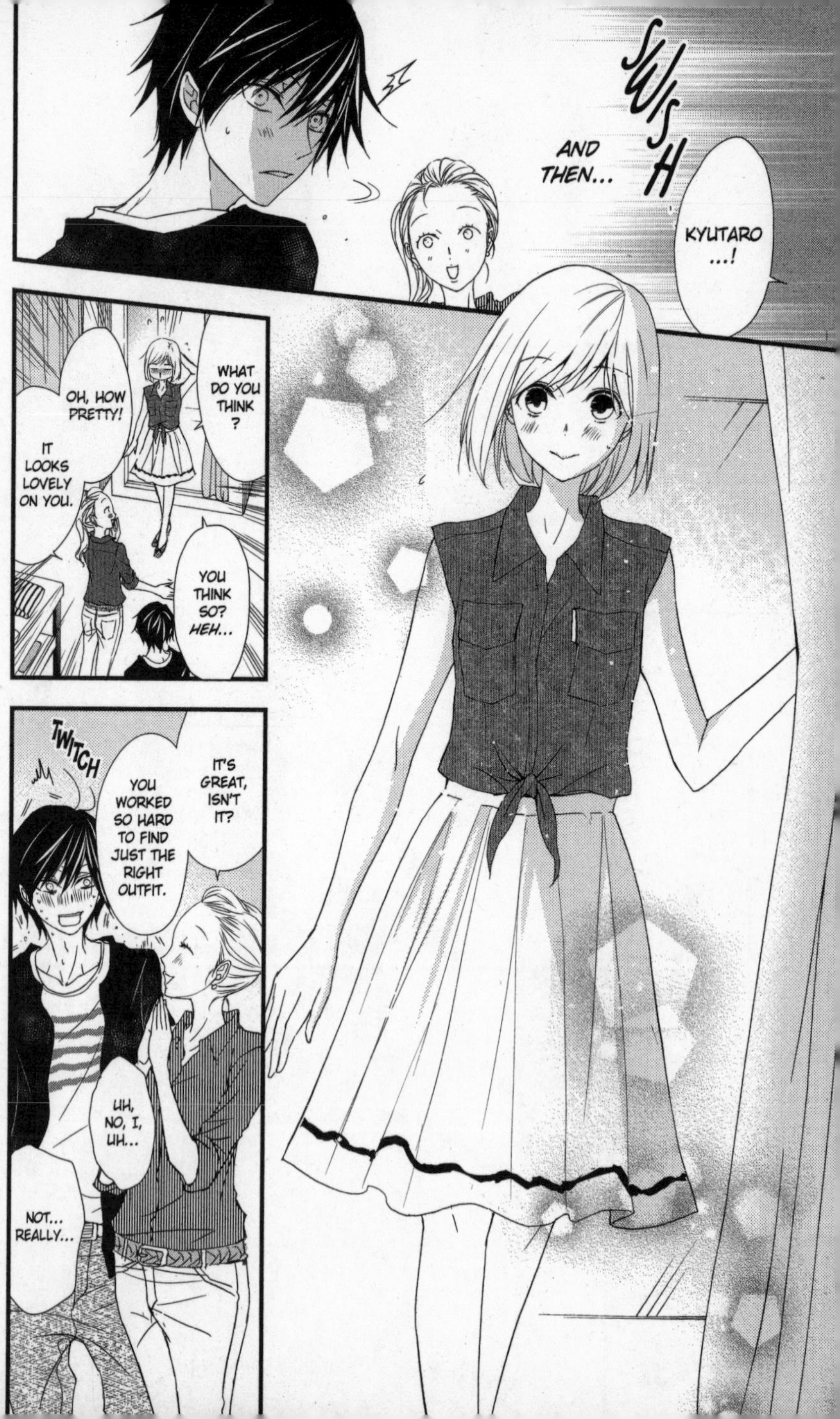
SWISH
AND THEN...
KYUTARO ...!
WHAT DO YOU THINK?
OH, HOW PRETTY!
IT LOOKS LOVELY ON YOU.
YOU THINK SO? HEH...
IT'S GREAT, ISN'T IT?
YOU WORKED SO HARD TO FIND JUST THE RIGHT OUTFIT.
TWITCH
UH, NO, I, UH...
NOT... REALLY...

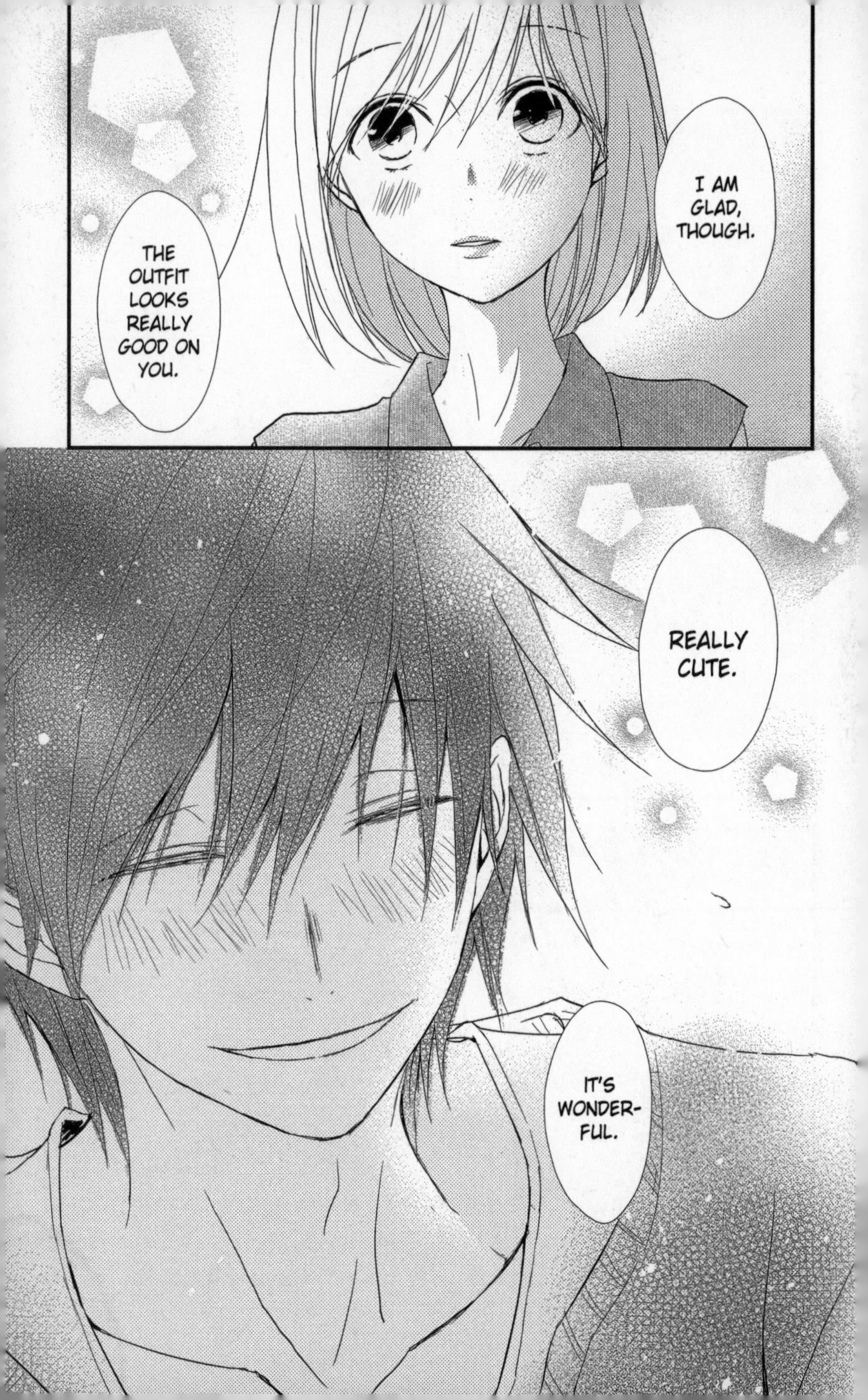
I AM GLAD, THOUGH.
THE OUTFIT LOOKS REALLY GOOD ON YOU.
REALLY CUTE.
IT'S WONDER-FUL.

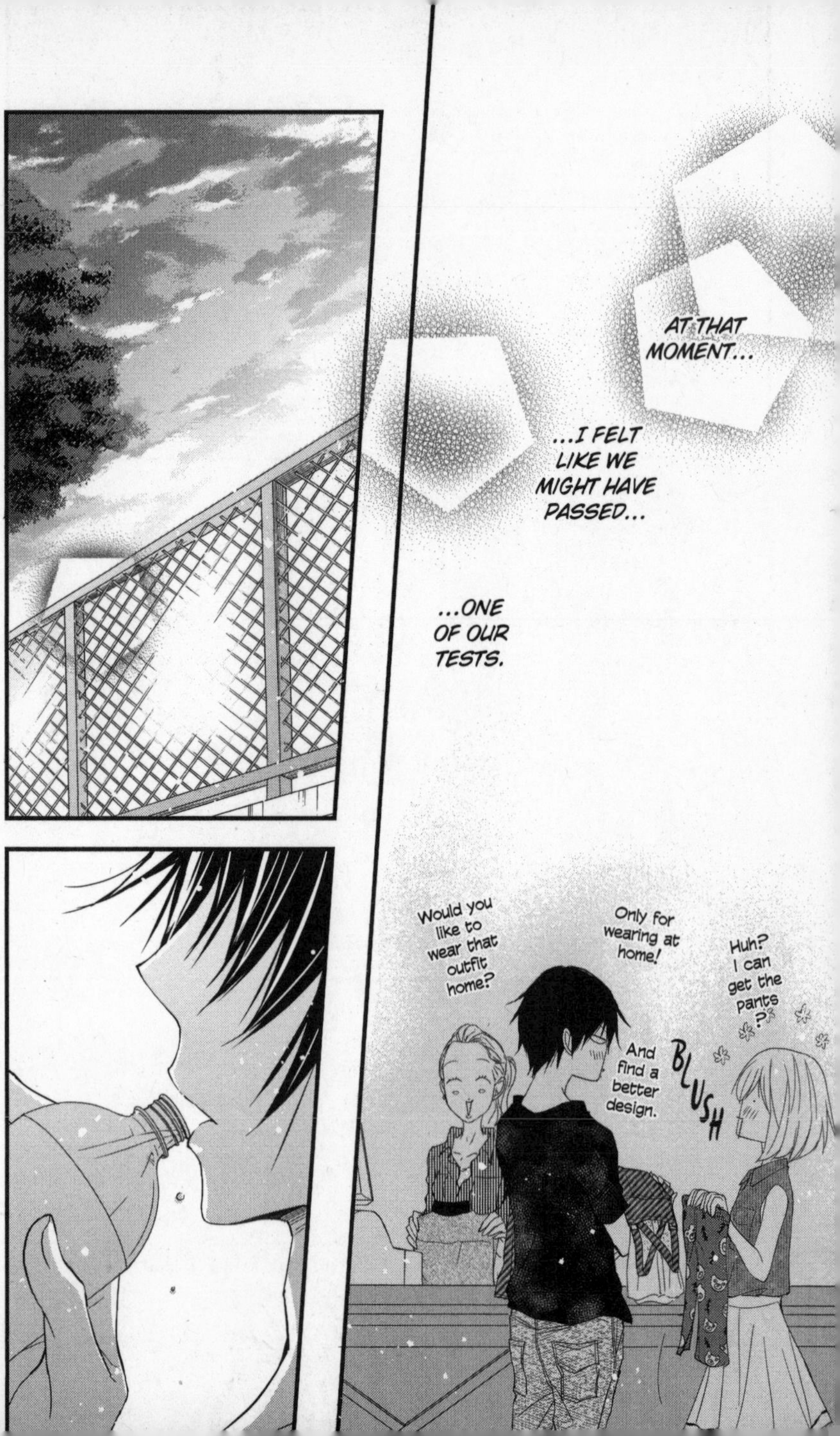
AT THAT MOMENT...
...I FELT LIKE WE MIGHT HAVE PASSED...
...ONE OF OUR TESTS.
Would you like to wear that outfit home?
Huh? I can get the pants?
Only for wearing at home!
And find a better design.
BLUSH

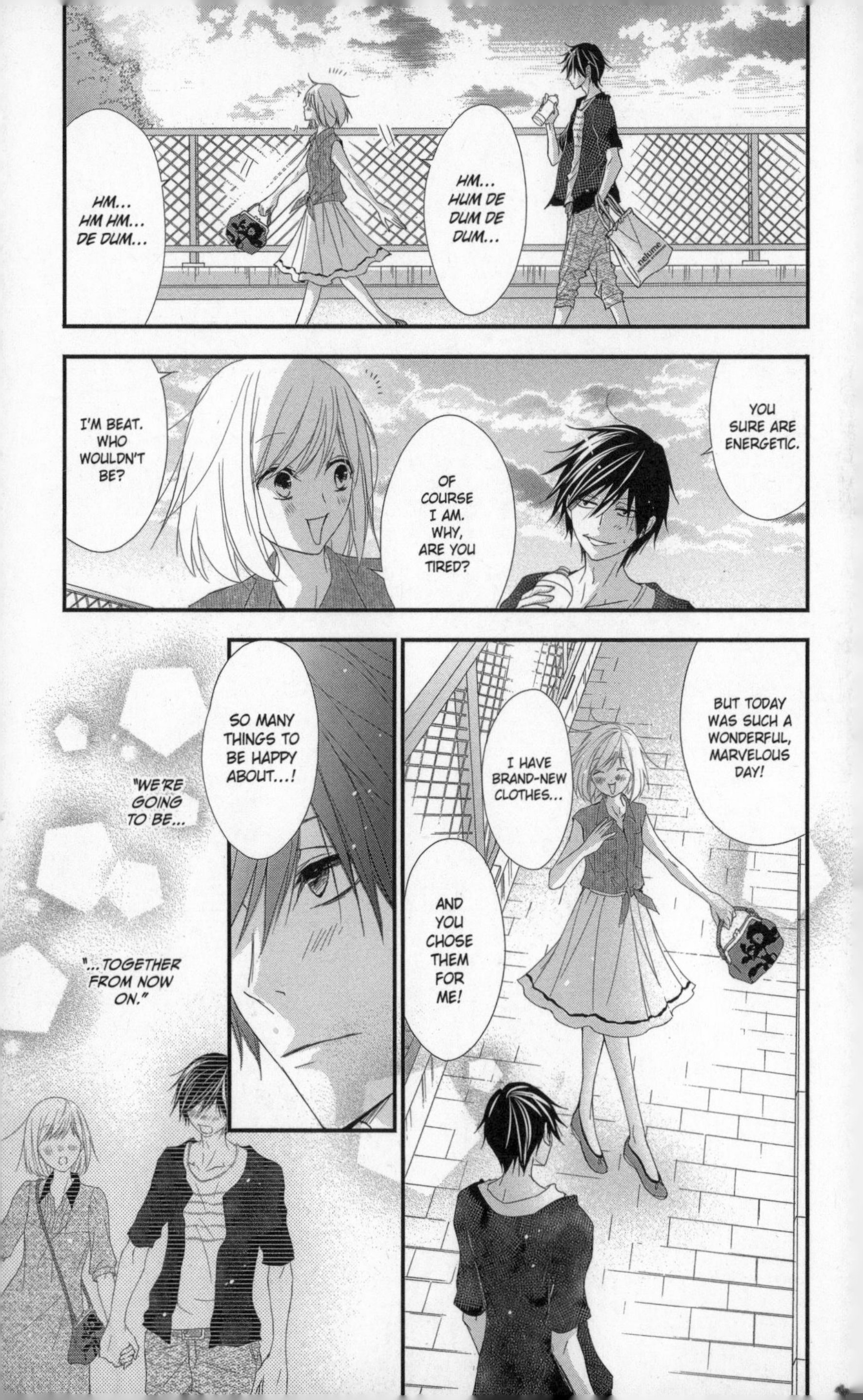
HM... HUM DE DUM DE DUM...
HM... HM HM... DE DUM...
YOU SURE ARE ENERGETIC.
OF COURSE I AM. WHY, ARE YOU TIRED?
I'M BEAT. WHO WOULDN'T BE?
BUT TODAY WAS SUCH A WONDERFUL, MARVELOUS DAY!
I HAVE BRAND-NEW CLOTHES...
AND YOU CHOSE THEM FOR ME!
SO MANY THINGS TO BE HAPPY ABOUT...!
"WE'RE GOING TO BE...
"...TOGETHER FROM NOW ON."

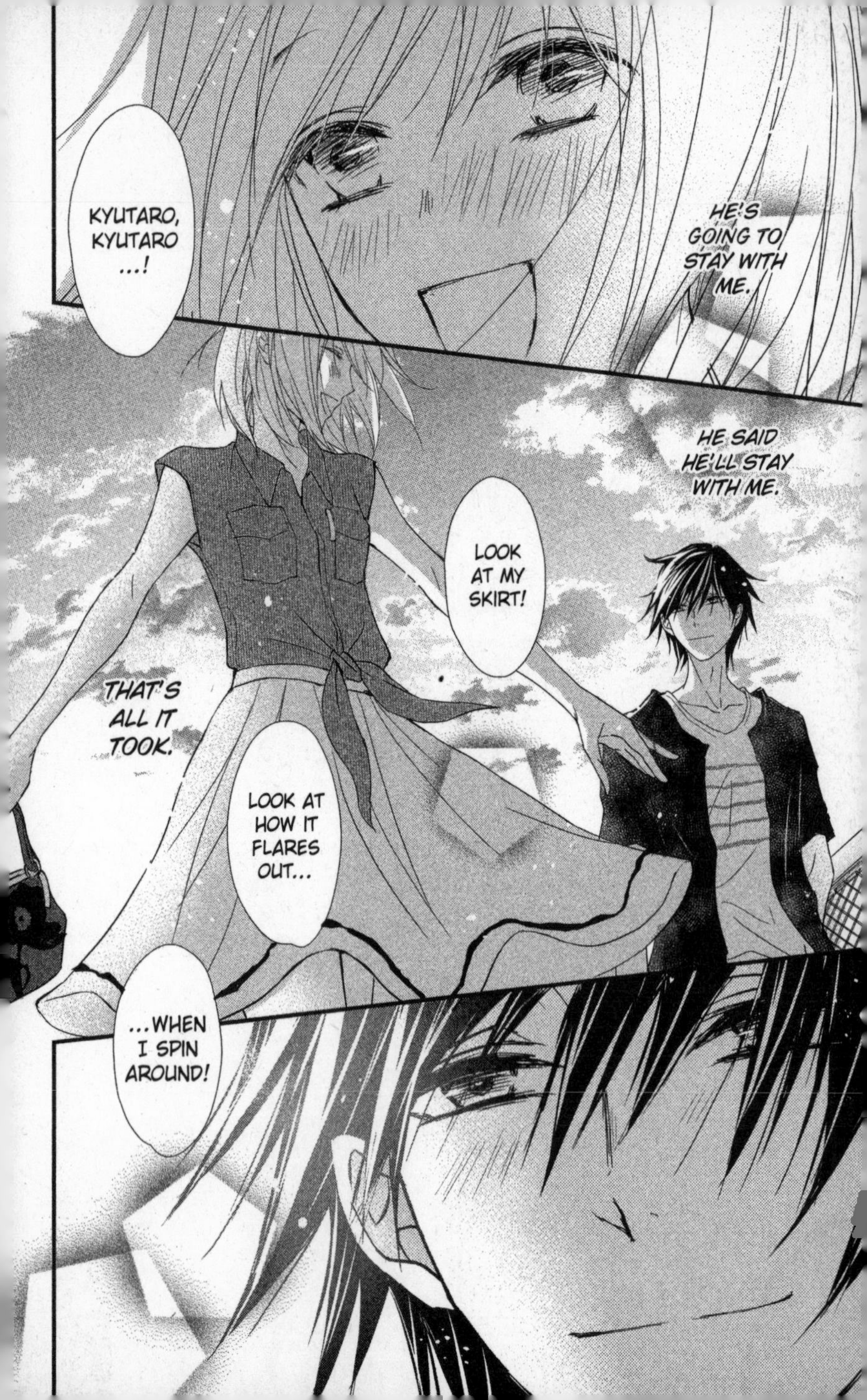
HE'S GOING TO STAY WITH ME.
KYUTARO, KYUTARO ...!
HE SAID HE'LL STAY WITH ME.
LOOK AT MY SKIRT!
THAT'S ALL IT TOOK.
LOOK AT HOW IT FLARES OUT...
...WHEN I SPIN AROUND!

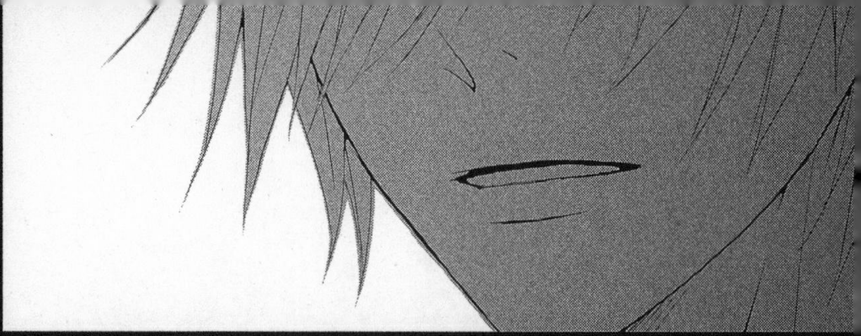

"WHO CARES IF I CAN'T TELL HER I LOVE HER?"

"IT WILL PROBABLY BE FAR MORE DIFFICULT THAN YOU THINK."

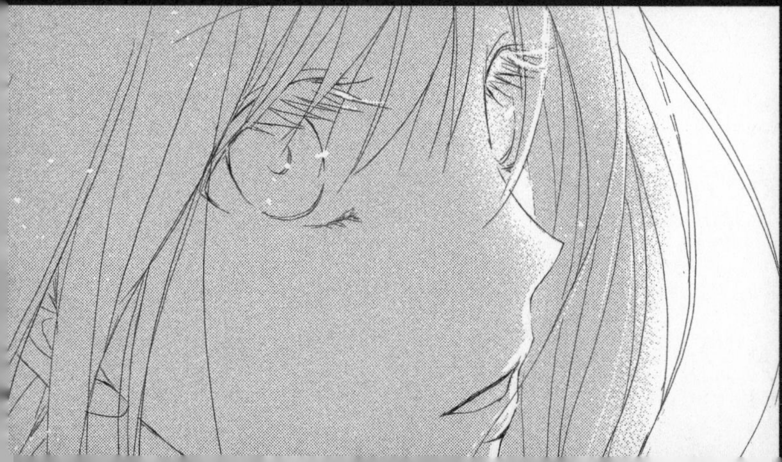

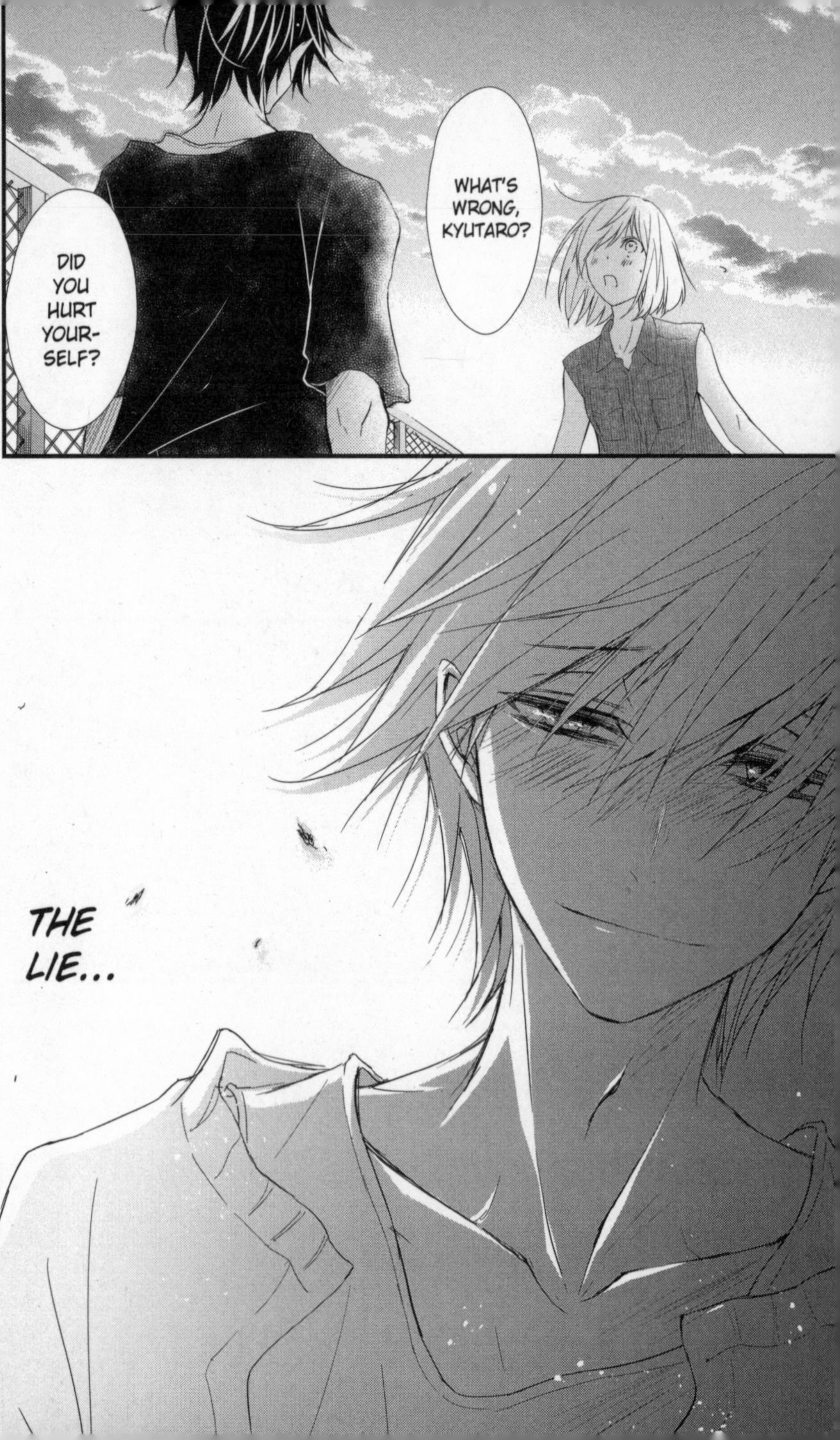
WHAT'S WRONG, KYUTARO?
DID YOU HURT YOURSELF?
THE LIE...

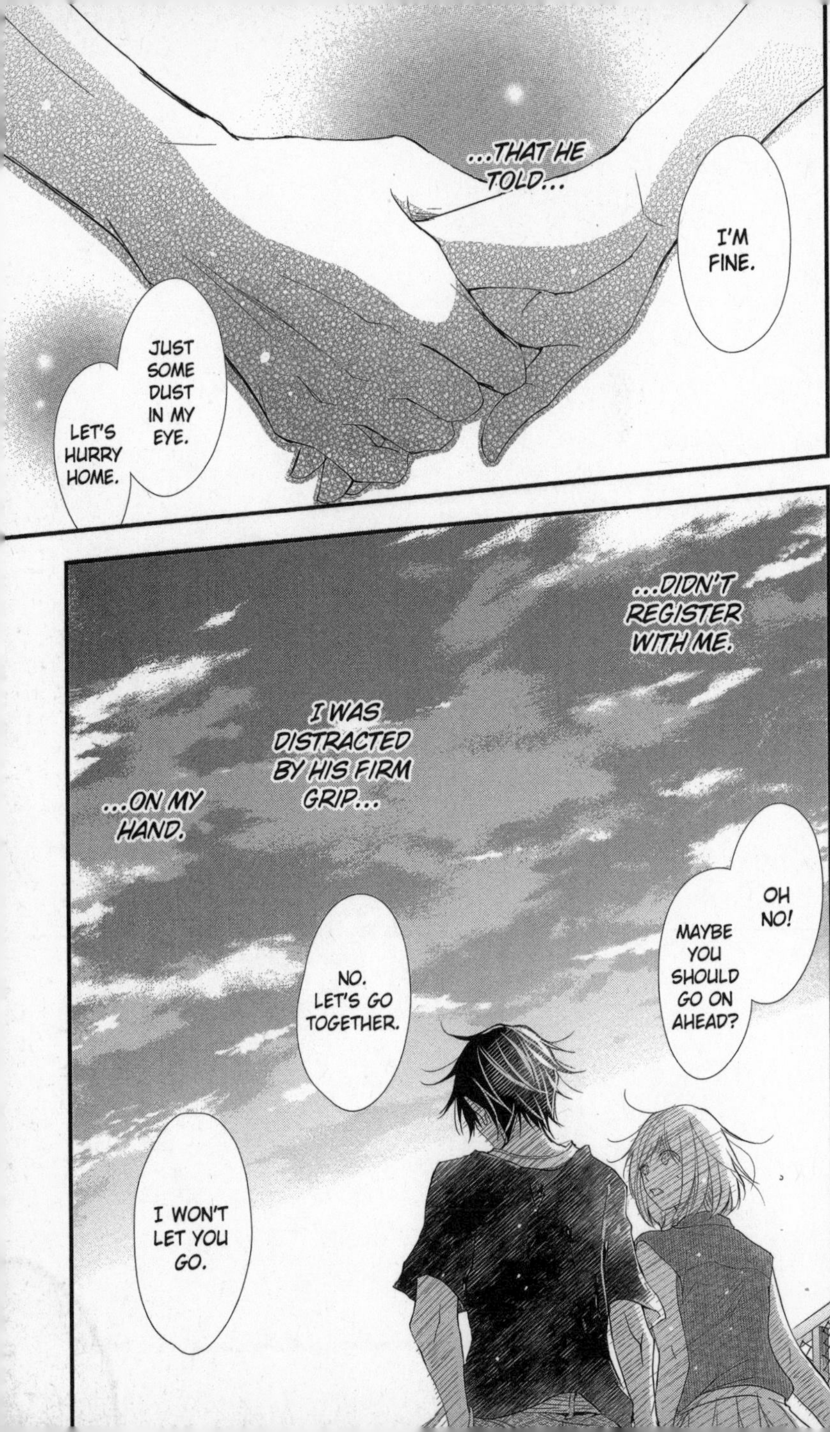

...THAT HE TOLD...
I'M FINE.
JUST SOME DUST IN MY EYE.
LET'S HURRY HOME.
...DIDN'T REGISTER WITH ME.
I WAS DISTRACTED BY HIS FIRM GRIP...
...ON MY HAND.
OH NO!
MAYBE YOU SHOULD GO ON AHEAD?
NO. LET'S GO TOGETHER.
I WON'T LET YOU GO.

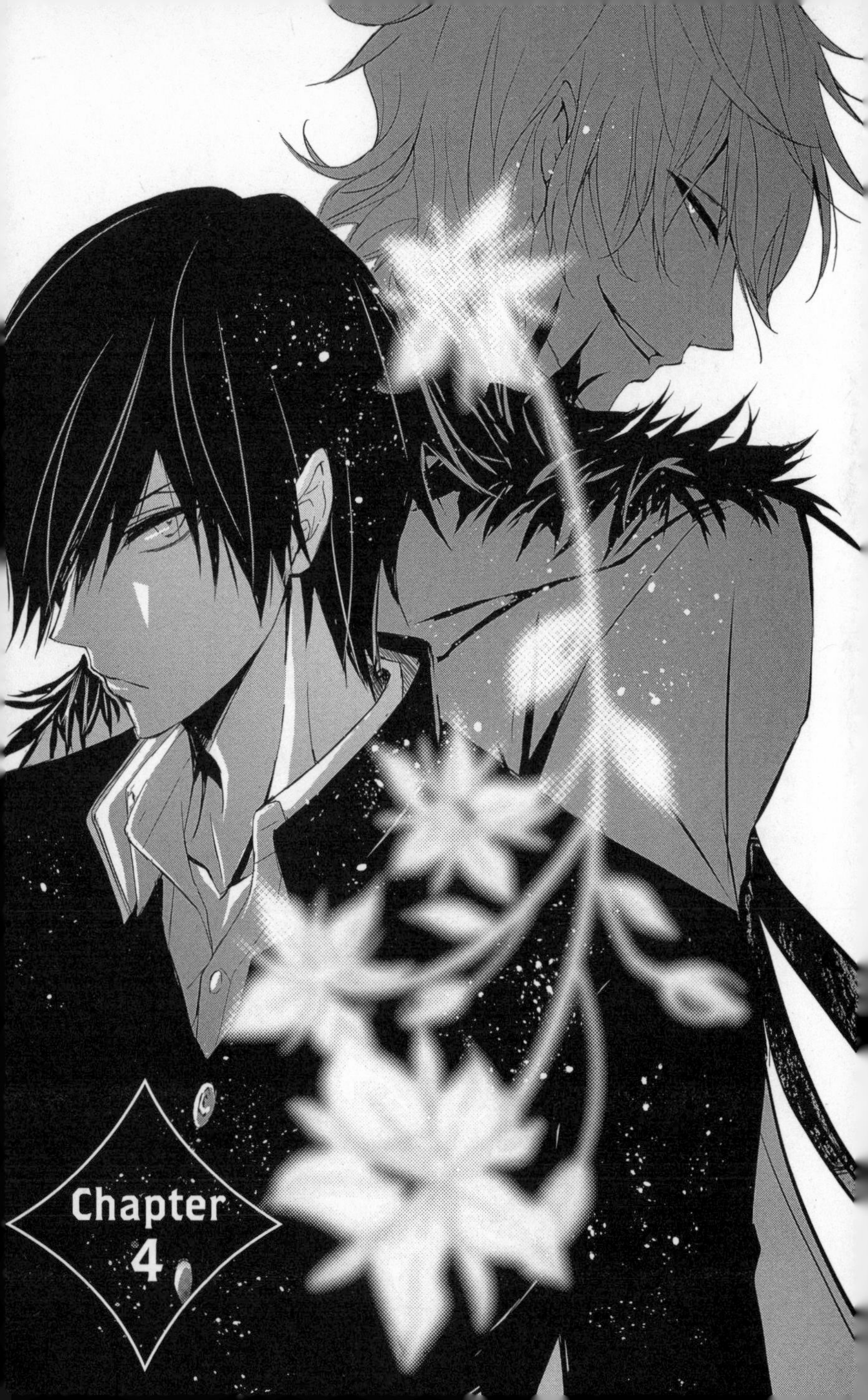
Chapter
4

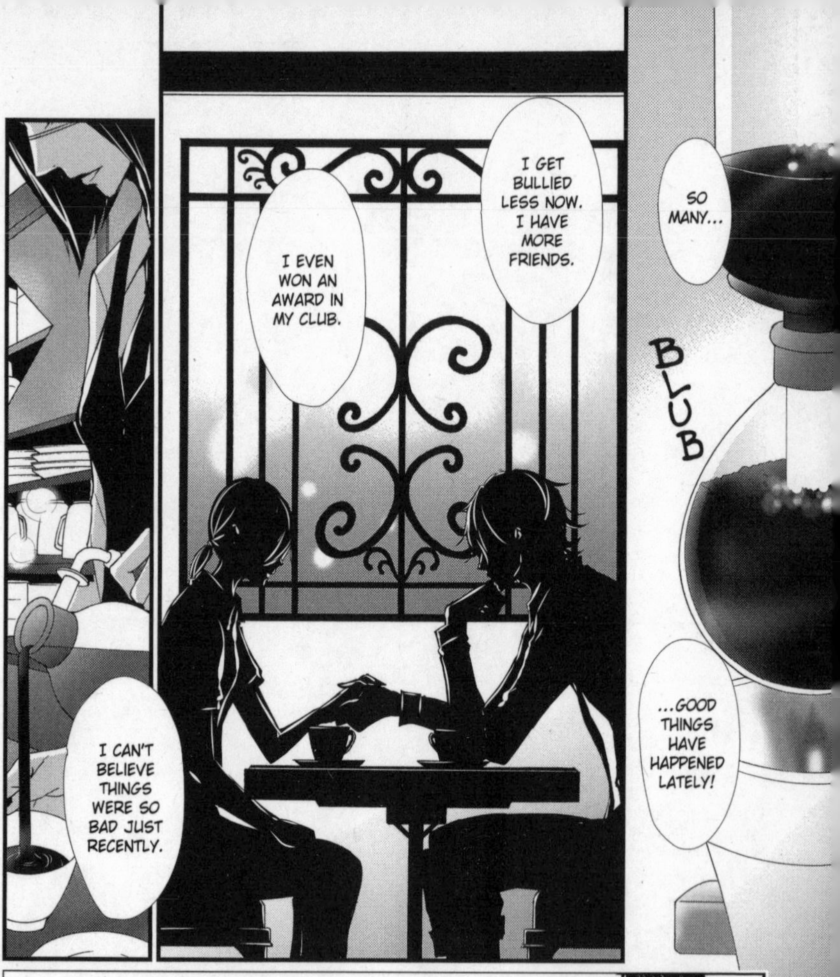
SO MANY...
BLUB
...GOOD THINGS HAVE HAPPENED LATELY!
I GET BULLIED LESS NOW. I HAVE MORE FRIENDS.
I EVEN WON AN AWARD IN MY CLUB.
I CAN'T BELIEVE THINGS WERE SO BAD JUST RECENTLY.

Lounging pants are great!
For someone like a manga artist,
who spends so much time indoors,
there's nothing more comfortable.
And isn't that bear design adorable?
My super-competent assistant
created it! I love it, so I decided
to showcase it in this story.

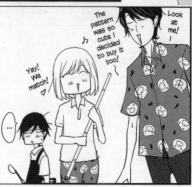

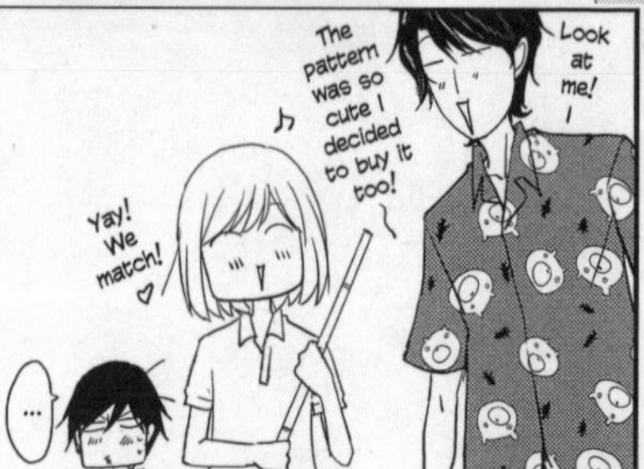
Look at me!
The pattern was so cute I decided to buy it too!
Yay! We match! ♡
...

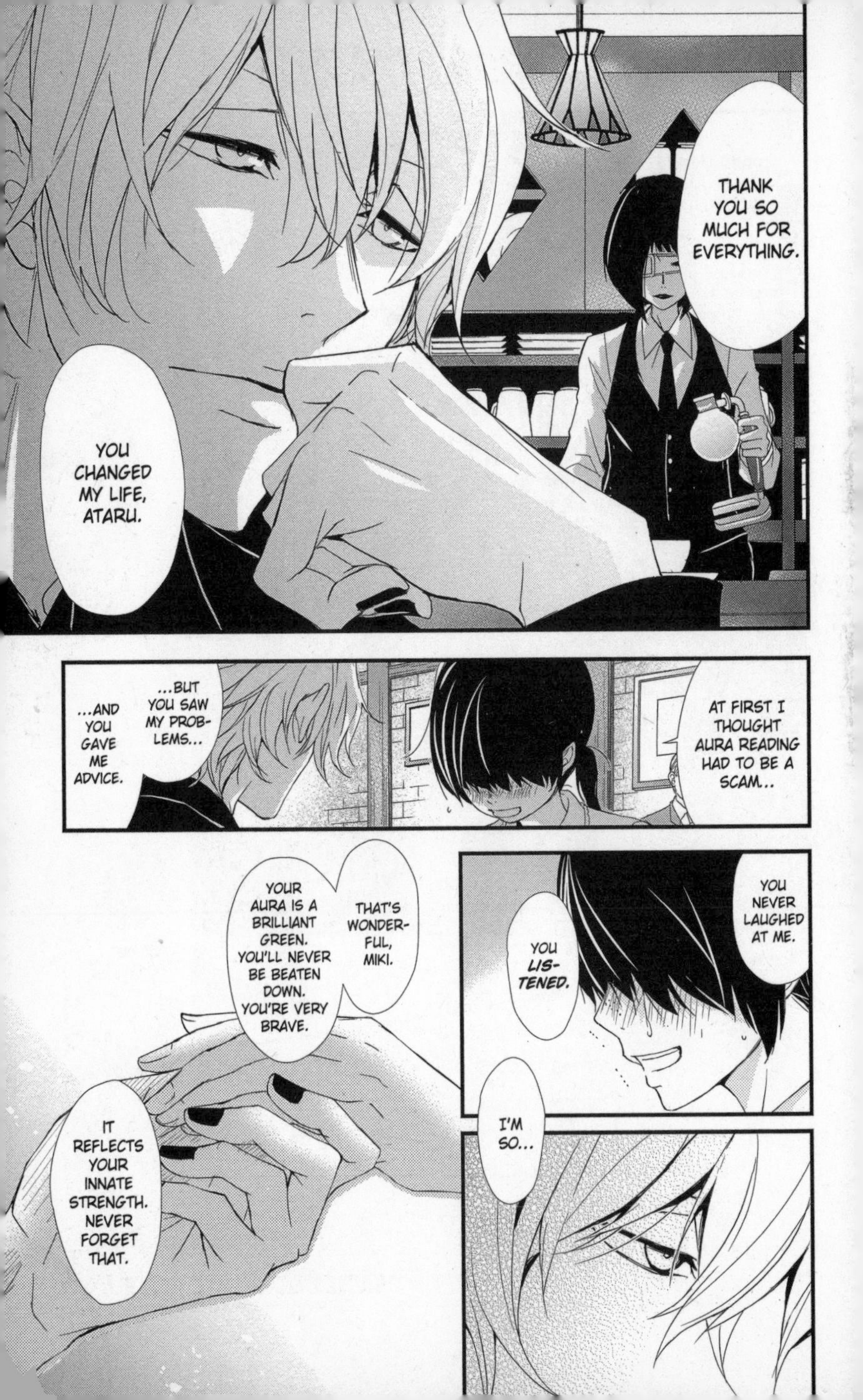
THANK YOU SO MUCH FOR EVERYTHING.
YOU CHANGED MY LIFE, ATARU.
AT FIRST I THOUGHT AURA READING HAD TO BE A SCAM...
...BUT YOU SAW MY PROBLEMS...
...AND YOU GAVE ME ADVICE.
YOU NEVER LAUGHED AT ME.
YOU *LISTENED.*
I'M SO...
THAT'S WONDERFUL, MIKI.
YOUR AURA IS A BRILLIANT GREEN. YOU'LL NEVER BE BEATEN DOWN. YOU'RE VERY BRAVE.
IT REFLECTS YOUR INNATE STRENGTH. NEVER FORGET THAT.

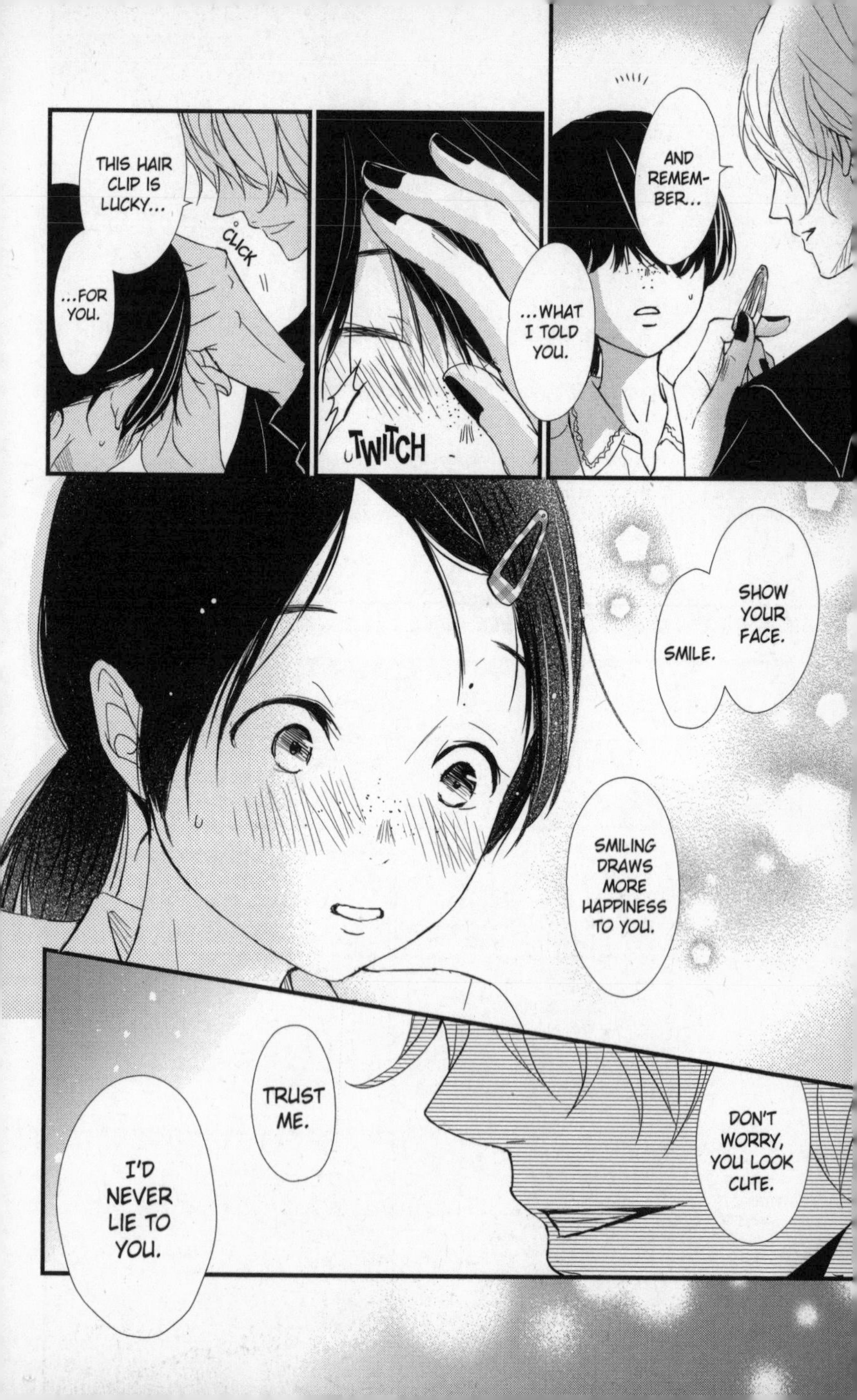
AND REMEM-BER...
...WHAT I TOLD YOU.
TWITCH
THIS HAIR CLIP IS LUCKY...
CLICK
...FOR YOU.
SHOW YOUR FACE.
SMILE.
SMILING DRAWS MORE HAPPINESS TO YOU.
DON'T WORRY, YOU LOOK CUTE.
TRUST ME.
I'D NEVER LIE TO YOU.

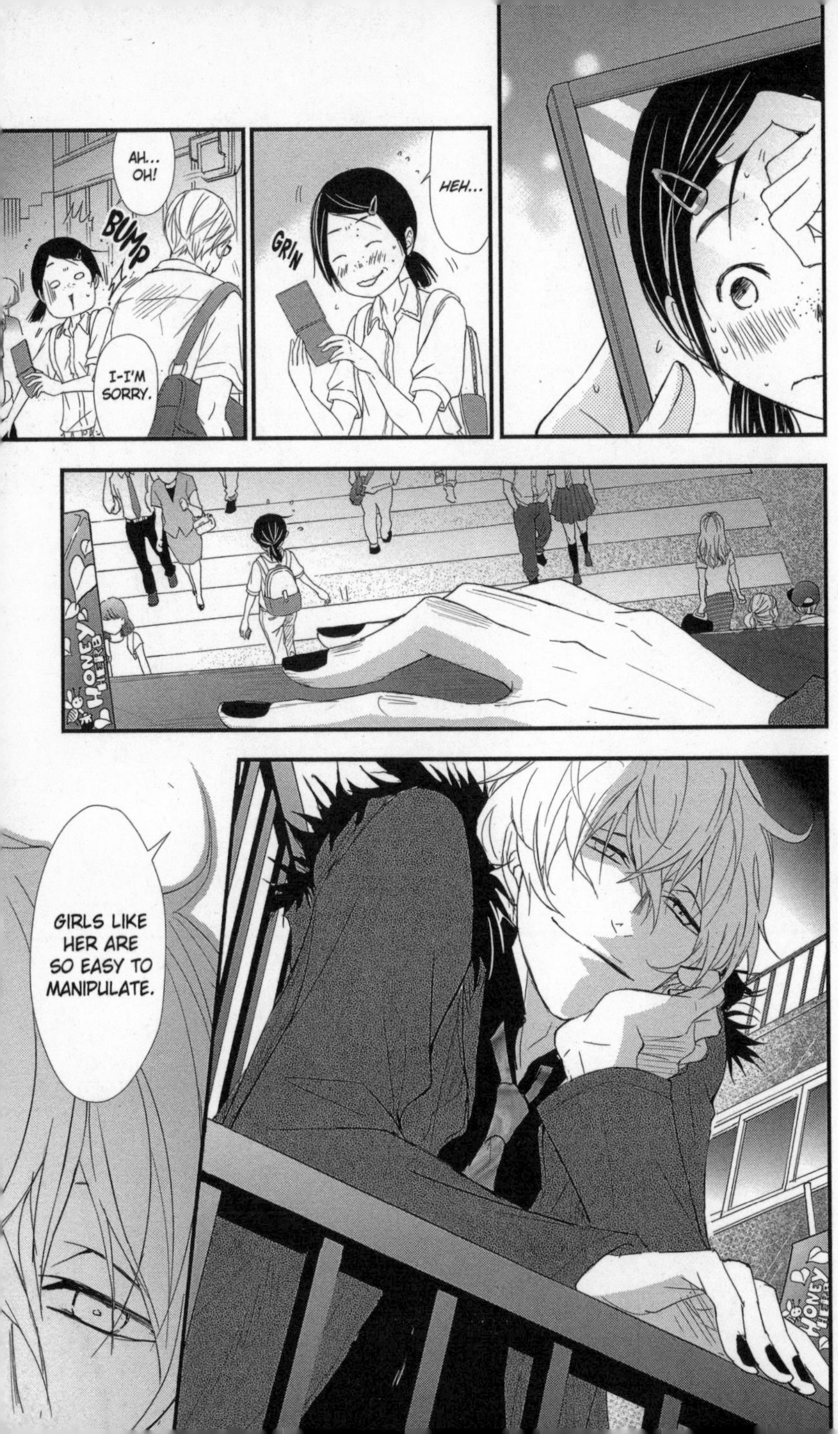
HEH...
GRIN
AH... OH!
BUMP
I-I'M SORRY.
HONEY HERB
GIRLS LIKE HER ARE SO EASY TO MANIPULATE.
HONEY HERB

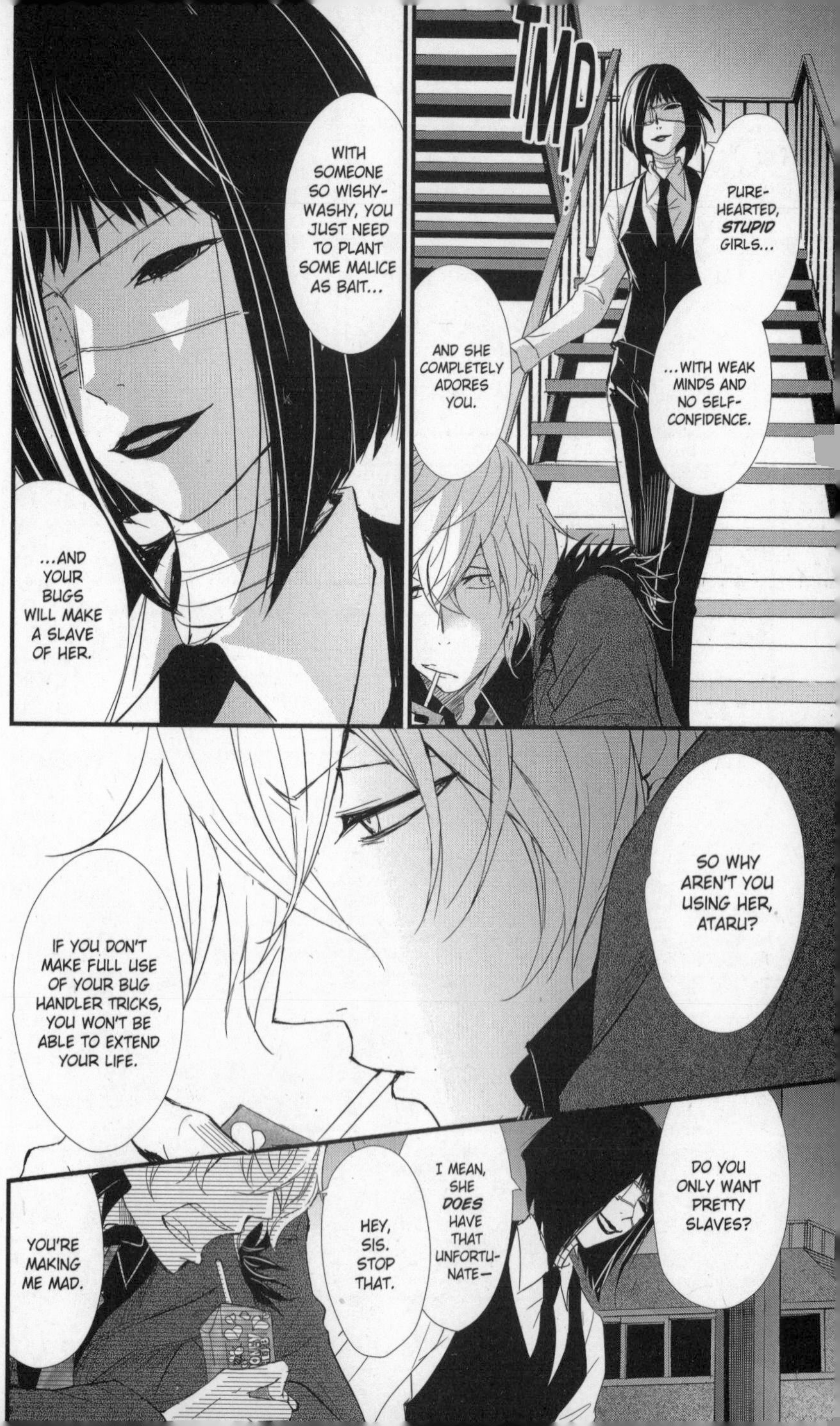
TMP
PURE-HEARTED, **STUPID** GIRLS...
...WITH WEAK MINDS AND NO SELF-CONFIDENCE.
AND SHE COMPLETELY ADORES YOU.
WITH SOMEONE SO WISHY-WASHY, YOU JUST NEED TO PLANT SOME MALICE AS BAIT...
...AND YOUR BUGS WILL MAKE A SLAVE OF HER.
SO WHY AREN'T YOU USING HER, ATARU?
IF YOU DON'T MAKE FULL USE OF YOUR BUG HANDLER TRICKS, YOU WON'T BE ABLE TO EXTEND YOUR LIFE.
DO YOU ONLY WANT PRETTY SLAVES?
I MEAN, SHE **DOES** HAVE THAT UNFORTU-NATE—
HEY, SIS. STOP THAT.
YOU'RE MAKING ME MAD.

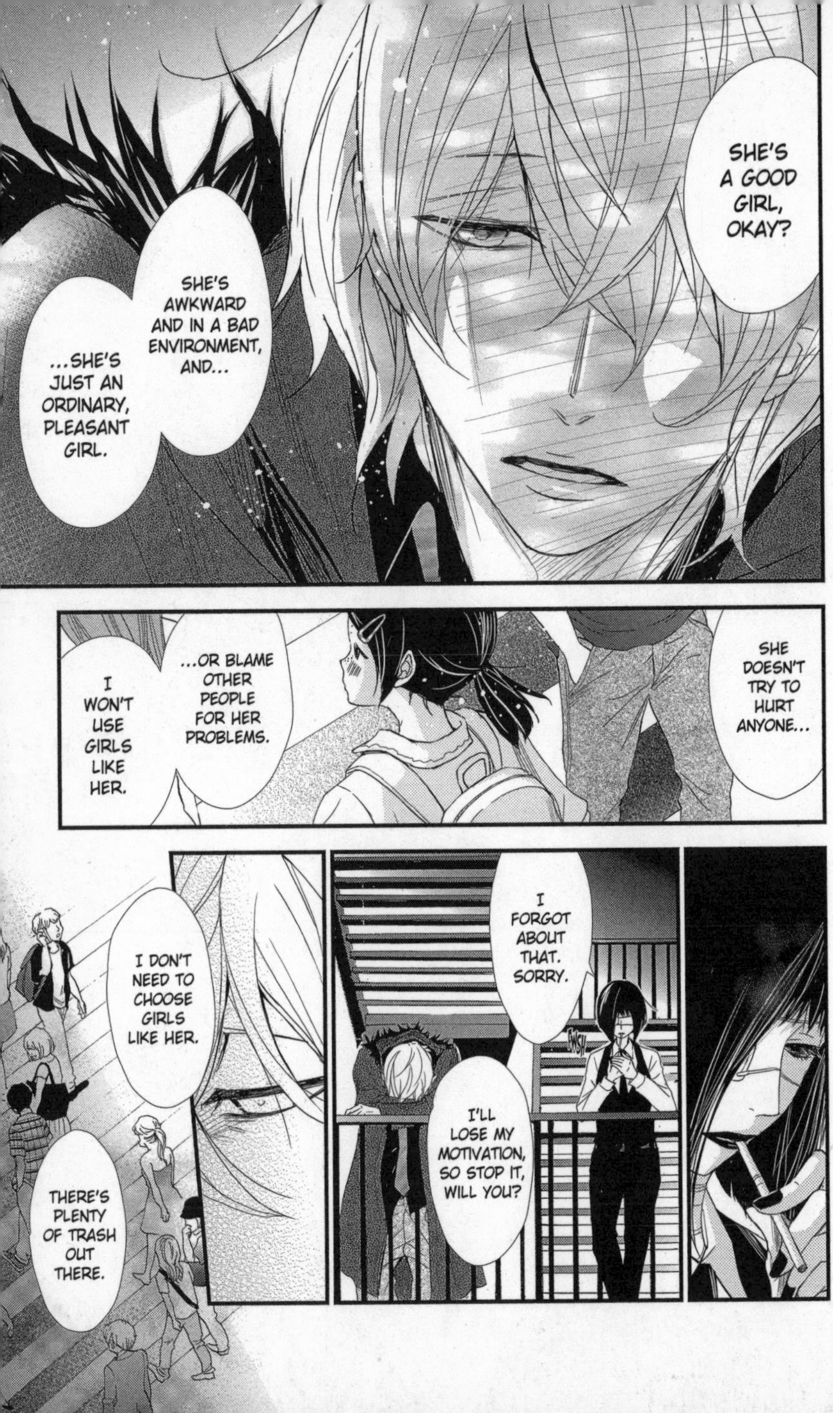
SHE'S A GOOD GIRL, OKAY?
SHE'S AWKWARD AND IN A BAD ENVIRONMENT, AND...
...SHE'S JUST AN ORDINARY, PLEASANT GIRL.
SHE DOESN'T TRY TO HURT ANYONE...
...OR BLAME OTHER PEOPLE FOR HER PROBLEMS.
I WON'T USE GIRLS LIKE HER.
I FORGOT ABOUT THAT. SORRY.
FWSH
I'LL LOSE MY MOTIVATION, SO STOP IT, WILL YOU?
I DON'T NEED TO CHOOSE GIRLS LIKE HER.
THERE'S PLENTY OF TRASH OUT THERE.

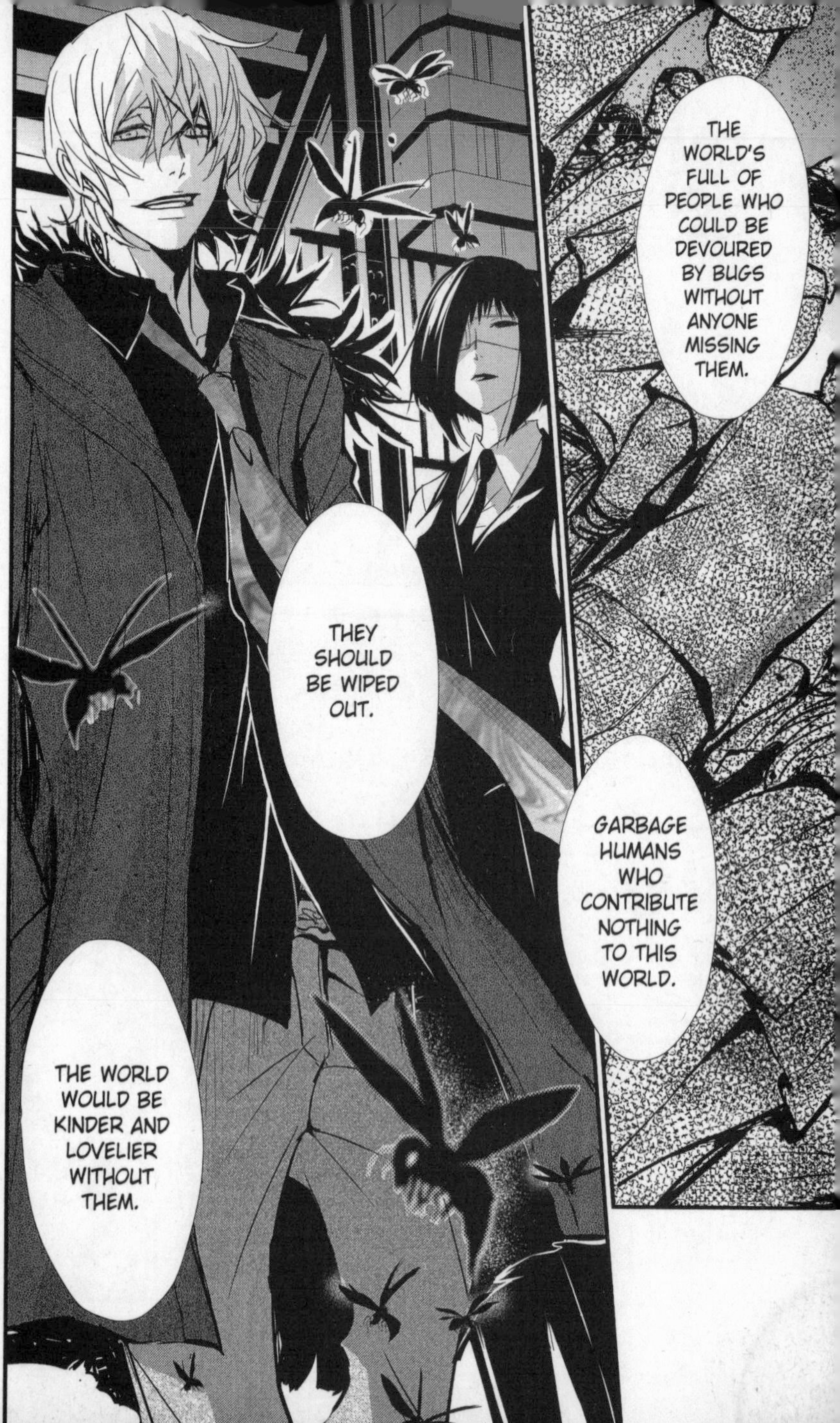
THE WORLD'S FULL OF PEOPLE WHO COULD BE DEVOURED BY BUGS WITHOUT ANYONE MISSING THEM.
GARBAGE HUMANS WHO CONTRIBUTE NOTHING TO THIS WORLD.
THEY SHOULD BE WIPED OUT.
THE WORLD WOULD BE KINDER AND LOVELIER WITHOUT THEM.

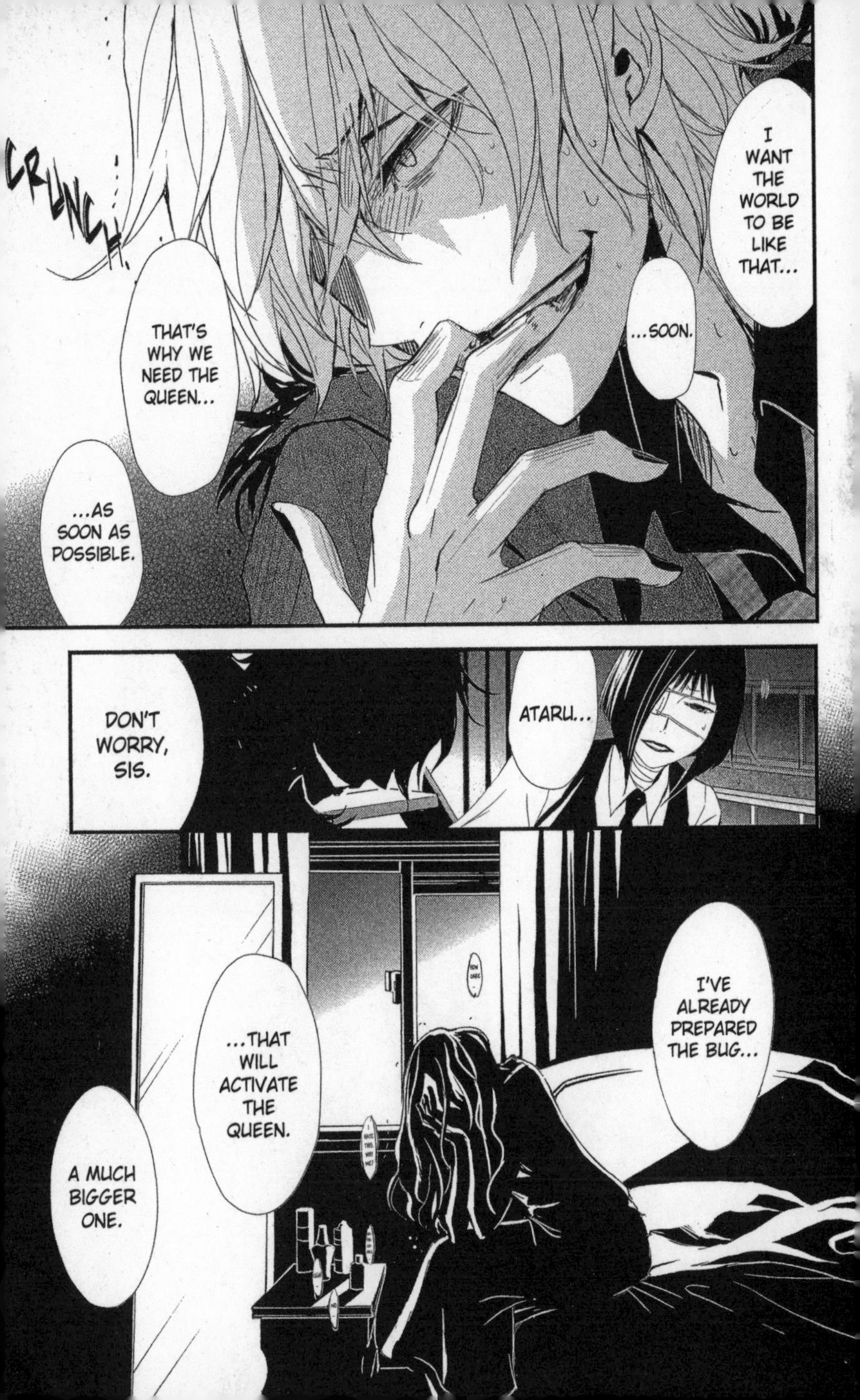
I WANT THE WORLD TO BE LIKE THAT...
...SOON.
CRUNCH
THAT'S WHY WE NEED THE QUEEN...
...AS SOON AS POSSIBLE.
ATARU...
DON'T WORRY, SIS.
I'VE ALREADY PREPARED THE BUG...
HOW DARE...
...THAT WILL ACTIVATE THE QUEEN.
I HATE THIS. WHY ME?
A MUCH BIGGER ONE.

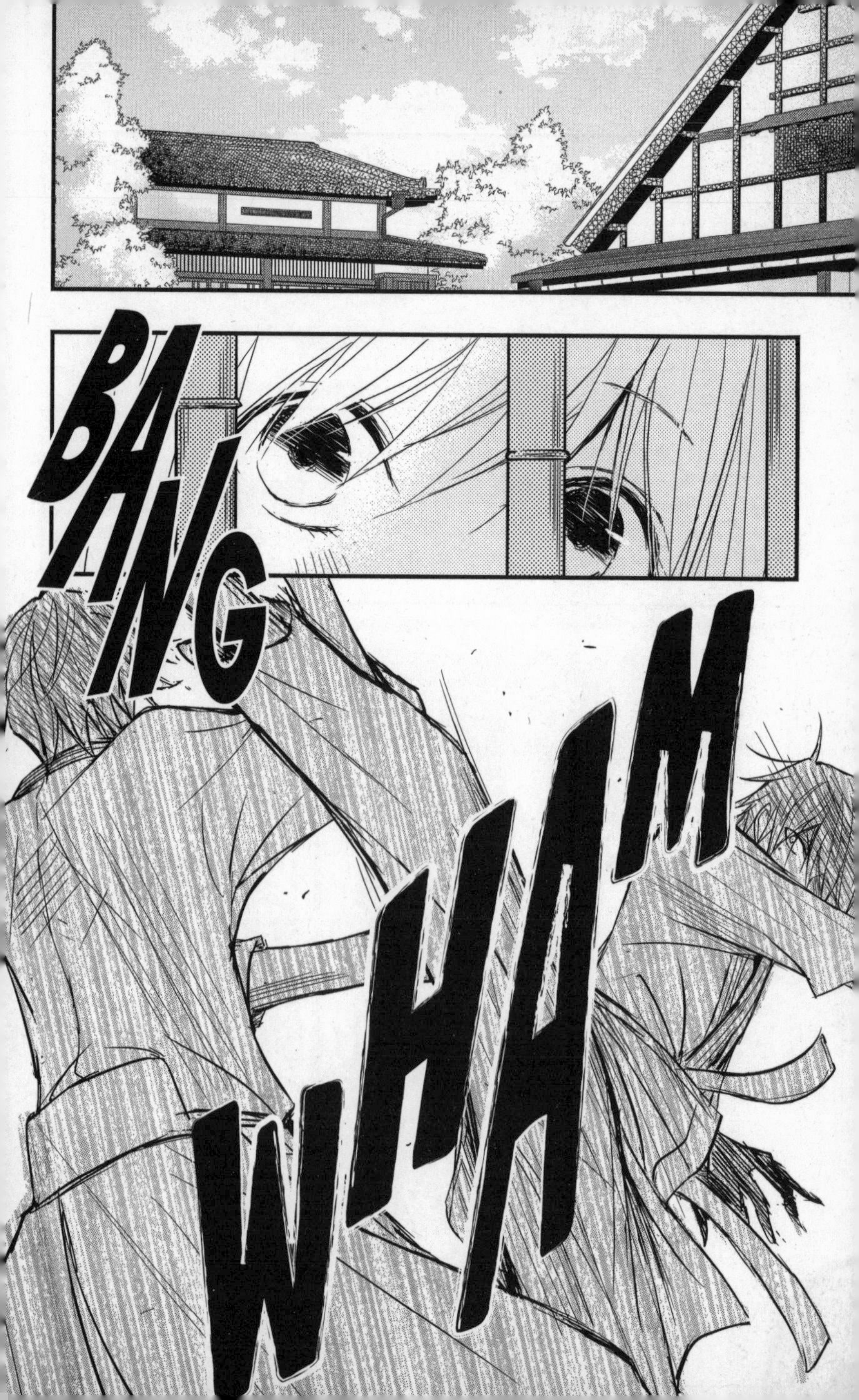
BANG
WHAM

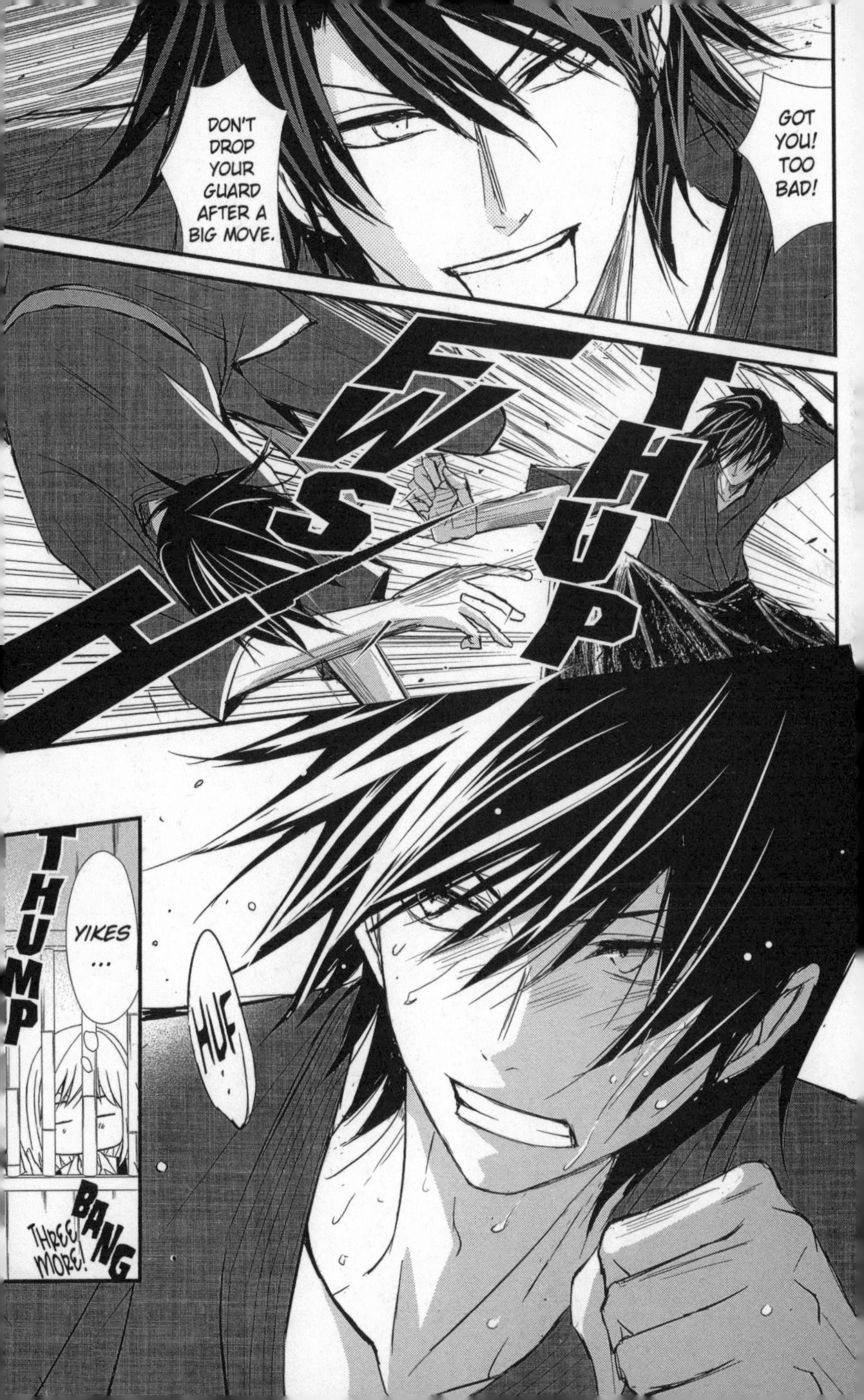
GOT YOU! TOO BAD!
DON'T DROP YOUR GUARD AFTER A BIG MOVE.
THUP
FWSH
HUF
YIKES...
THUMP
BANG
THREE MORE!

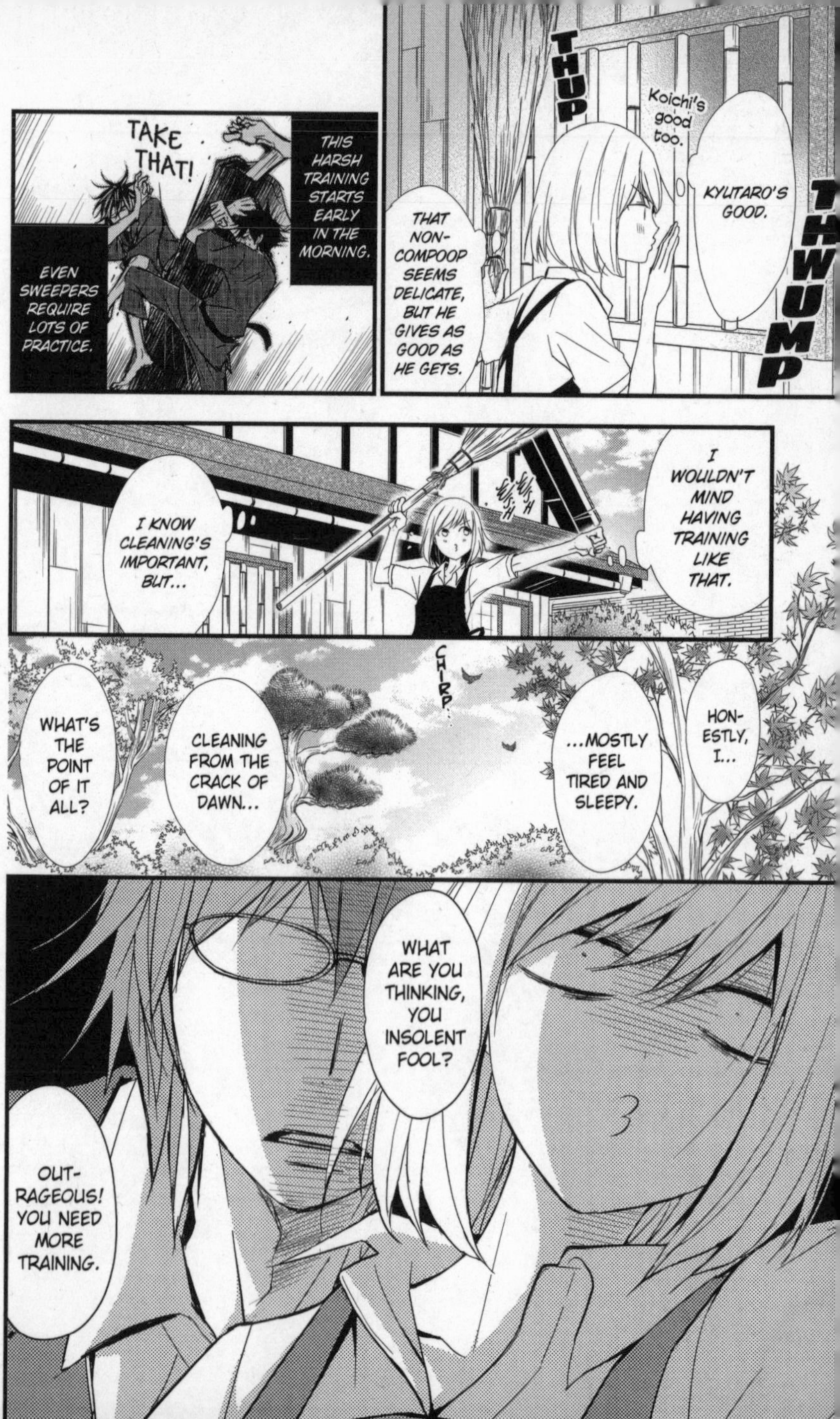
THWUMP
KYUTARO'S GOOD.
Koichi's good too.
THUP
THAT NON-COMPOOP SEEMS DELICATE, BUT HE GIVES AS GOOD AS HE GETS.
THIS HARSH TRAINING STARTS EARLY IN THE MORNING.
TAKE THAT!
EVEN SWEEPERS REQUIRE LOTS OF PRACTICE.
I WOULDN'T MIND HAVING TRAINING LIKE THAT.
SWISH
SWISH
I KNOW CLEANING'S IMPORTANT, BUT...
HON-ESTLY, I...
...MOSTLY FEEL TIRED AND SLEEPY.
CHIRP...
CLEANING FROM THE CRACK OF DAWN...
WHAT'S THE POINT OF IT ALL?
WHAT ARE YOU THINKING, YOU INSOLENT FOOL?
OUT-RAGEOUS! YOU NEED MORE TRAINING.

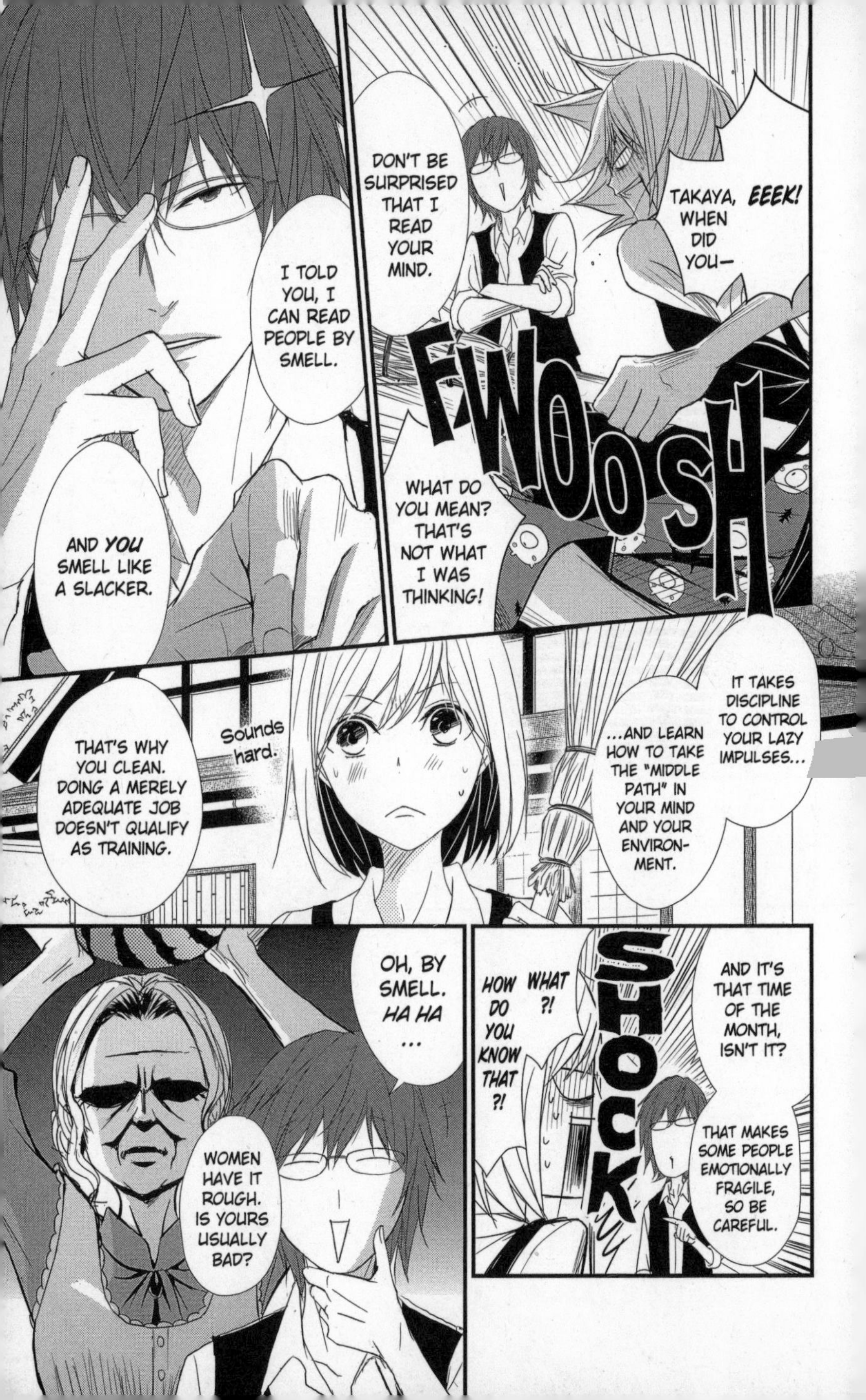
TAKAYA, WHEN DID YOU—
EEEK!
FWOOSH
DON'T BE SURPRISED THAT I READ YOUR MIND.
WHAT DO YOU MEAN? THAT'S NOT WHAT I WAS THINKING!
I TOLD YOU, I CAN READ PEOPLE BY SMELL.
AND *YOU* SMELL LIKE A SLACKER.
IT TAKES DISCIPLINE TO CONTROL YOUR LAZY IMPULSES...
...AND LEARN HOW TO TAKE THE "MIDDLE PATH" IN YOUR MIND AND YOUR ENVIRONMENT.
Sounds hard.
THAT'S WHY YOU CLEAN. DOING A MERELY ADEQUATE JOB DOESN'T QUALIFY AS TRAINING.
AND IT'S THAT TIME OF THE MONTH, ISN'T IT?
SHOCK
WHAT?!
HOW DO YOU KNOW THAT?!
THAT MAKES SOME PEOPLE EMOTIONALLY FRAGILE, SO BE CAREFUL.
OH, BY SMELL. HA HA ...
WOMEN HAVE IT ROUGH. IS YOURS USUALLY BAD?

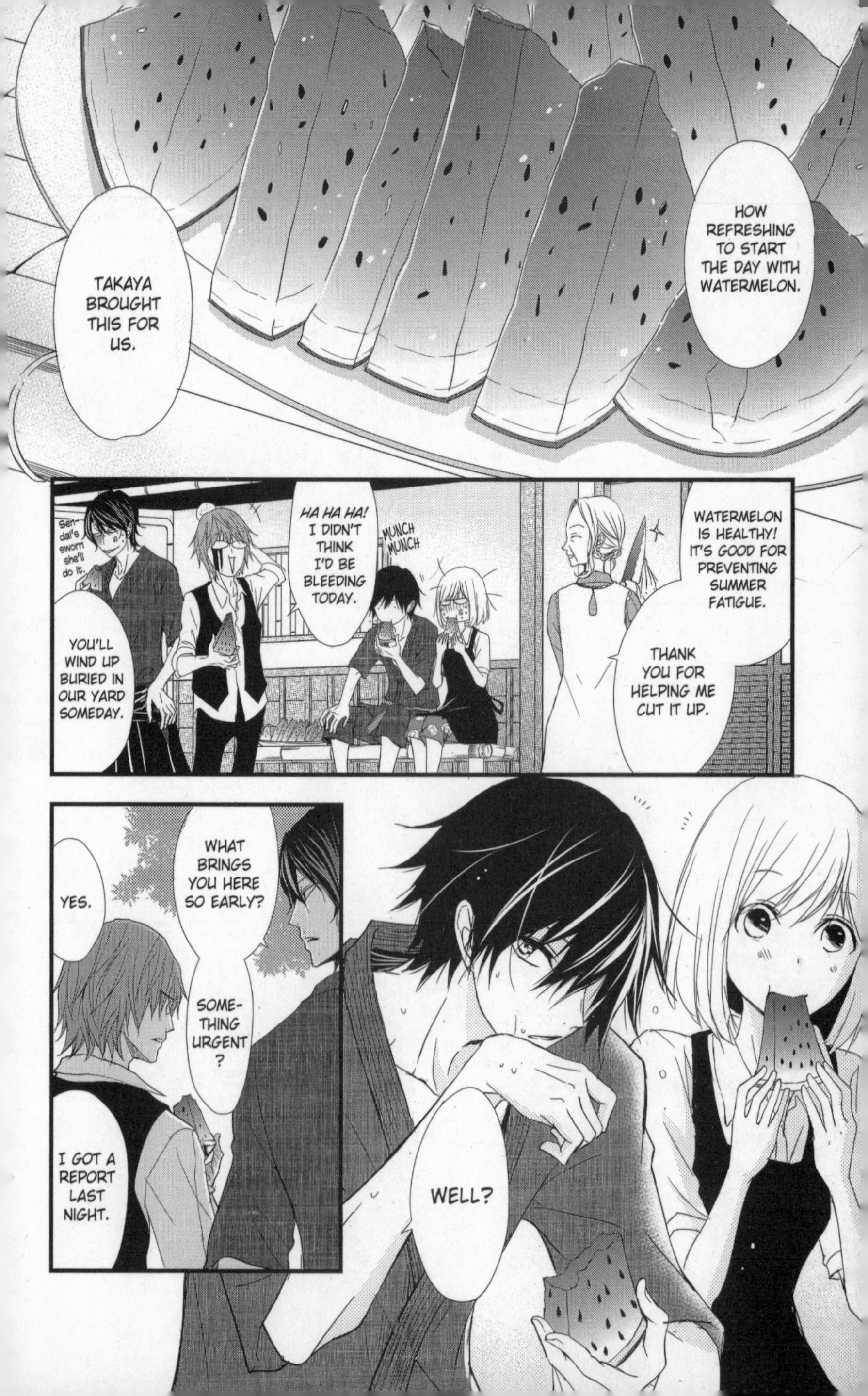
HOW REFRESHING TO START THE DAY WITH WATERMELON.
TAKAYA BROUGHT THIS FOR US.
WATERMELON IS HEALTHY! IT'S GOOD FOR PREVENTING SUMMER FATIGUE.
THANK YOU FOR HELPING ME CUT IT UP.
MUNCH MUNCH
HA HA HA! I DIDN'T THINK I'D BE BLEEDING TODAY.
Sen-dai's sworn she'll do it.
YOU'LL WIND UP BURIED IN OUR YARD SOMEDAY.
WELL?
WHAT BRINGS YOU HERE SO EARLY?
YES.
SOME-THING URGENT?
I GOT A REPORT LAST NIGHT.

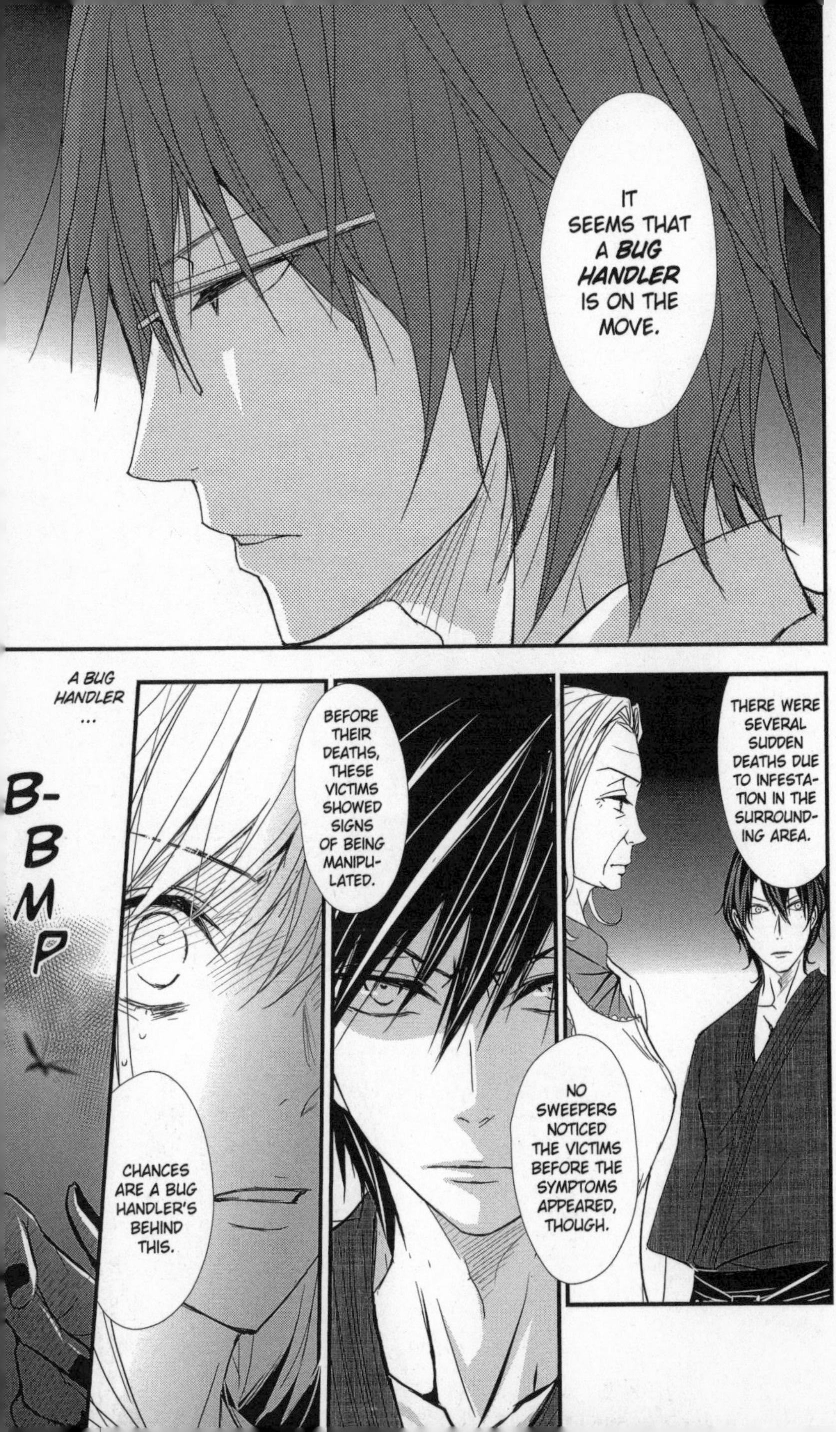
IT SEEMS THAT A **BUG HANDLER** IS ON THE MOVE.
THERE WERE SEVERAL SUDDEN DEATHS DUE TO INFESTATION IN THE SURROUNDING AREA.
BEFORE THEIR DEATHS, THESE VICTIMS SHOWED SIGNS OF BEING MANIPULATED.
NO SWEEPERS NOTICED THE VICTIMS BEFORE THE SYMPTOMS APPEARED, THOUGH.
A BUG HANDLER...
B-BMP
CHANCES ARE A BUG HANDLER'S BEHIND THIS.

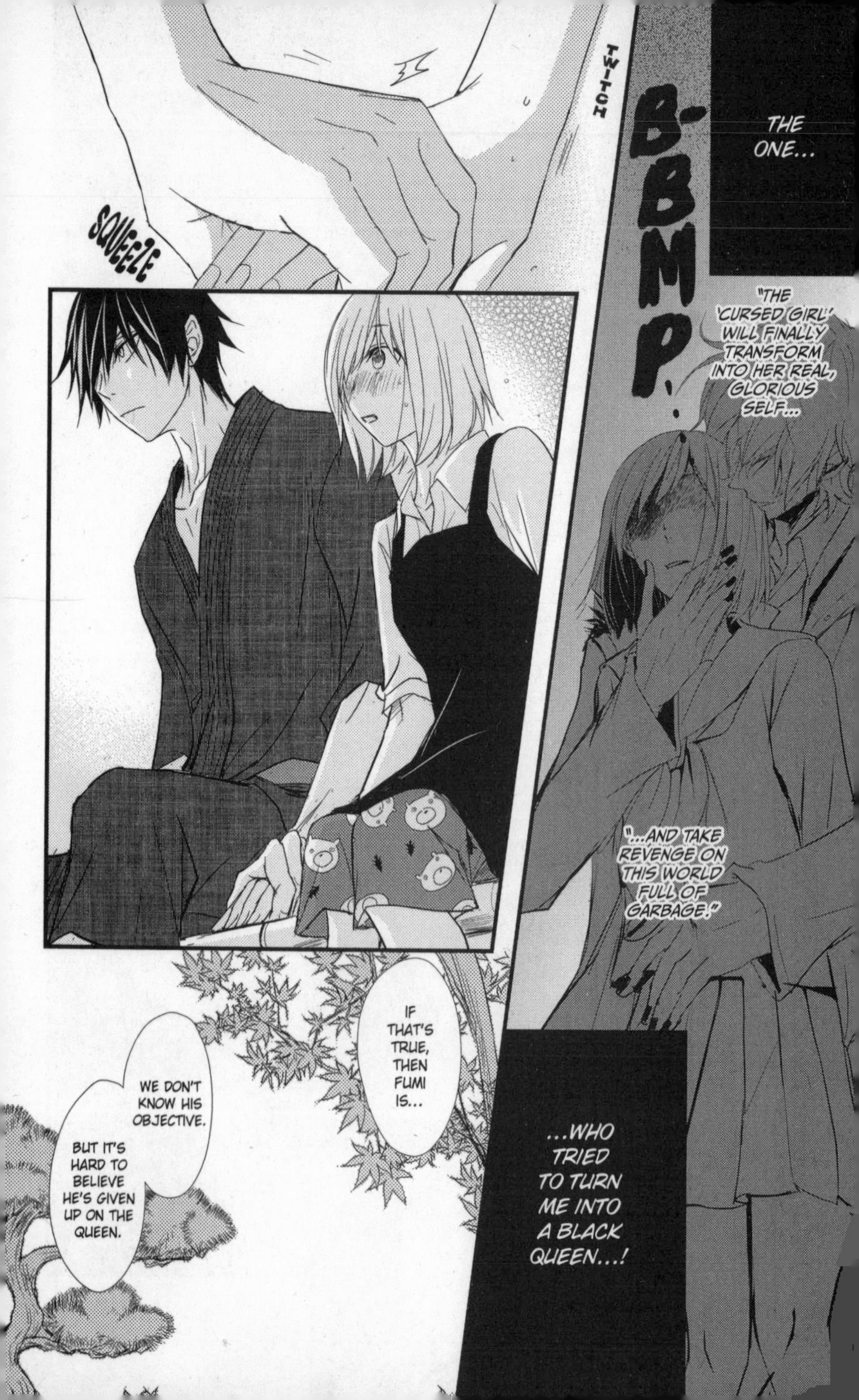
THE ONE...
B-BMP
"THE 'CURSED GIRL' WILL FINALLY TRANSFORM INTO HER REAL, GLORIOUS SELF...
"...AND TAKE REVENGE ON THIS WORLD FULL OF GARBAGE."
...WHO TRIED TO TURN ME INTO A BLACK QUEEN...!
TWITCH
SQUEEZE
IF THAT'S TRUE, THEN FUMI IS...
WE DON'T KNOW HIS OBJECTIVE.
BUT IT'S HARD TO BELIEVE HE'S GIVEN UP ON THE QUEEN.

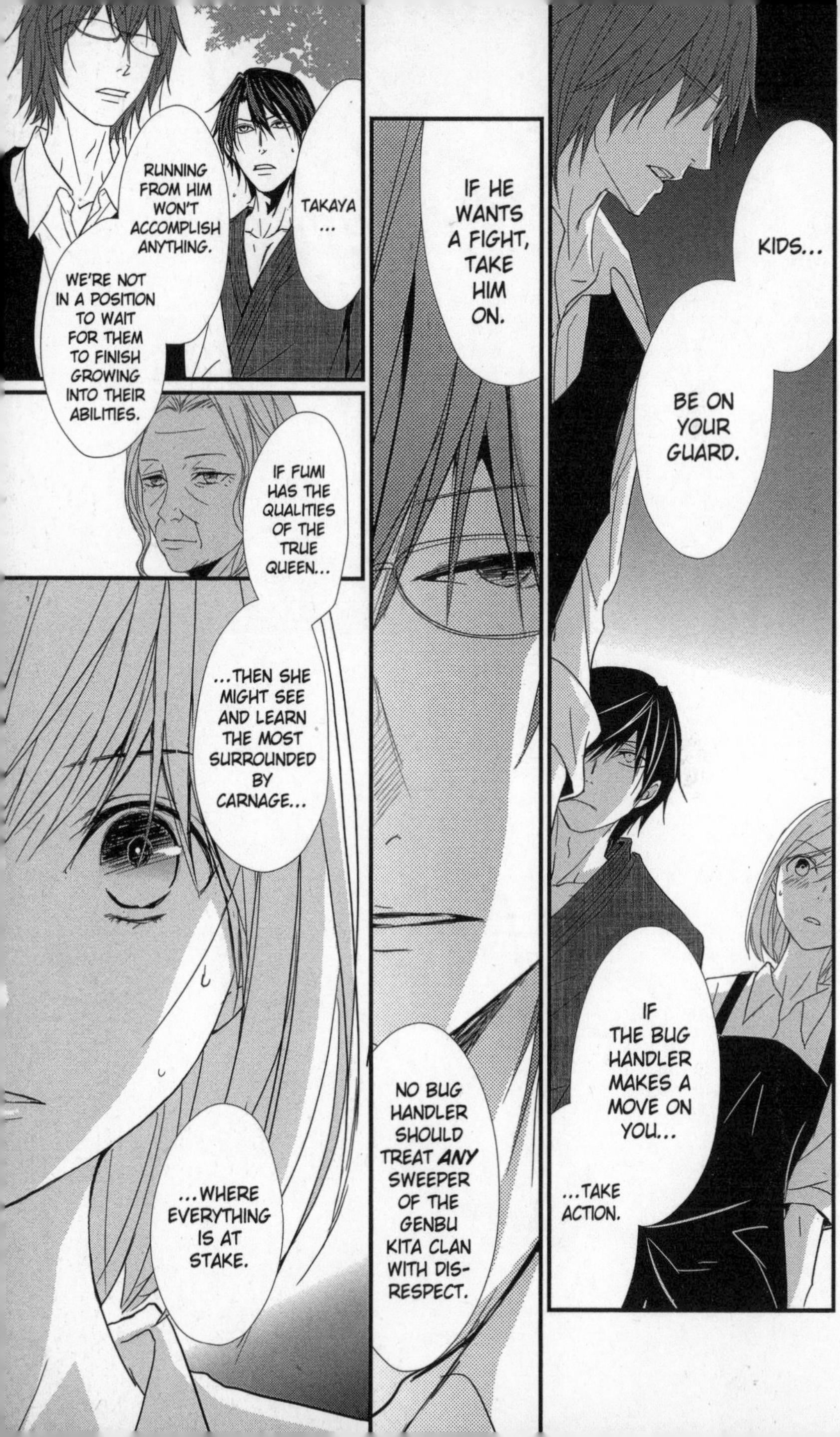
KIDS...
BE ON YOUR GUARD.
IF THE BUG HANDLER MAKES A MOVE ON YOU...
...TAKE ACTION.
IF HE WANTS A FIGHT, TAKE HIM ON.
NO BUG HANDLER SHOULD TREAT *ANY* SWEEPER OF THE GENBU KITA CLAN WITH DIS-RESPECT.
TAKAYA...
RUNNING FROM HIM WON'T ACCOMPLISH ANYTHING.
WE'RE NOT IN A POSITION TO WAIT FOR THEM TO FINISH GROWING INTO THEIR ABILITIES.
IF FUMI HAS THE QUALITIES OF THE TRUE QUEEN...
...THEN SHE MIGHT SEE AND LEARN THE MOST SURROUNDED BY CARNAGE...
...WHERE EVERYTHING IS AT STAKE.

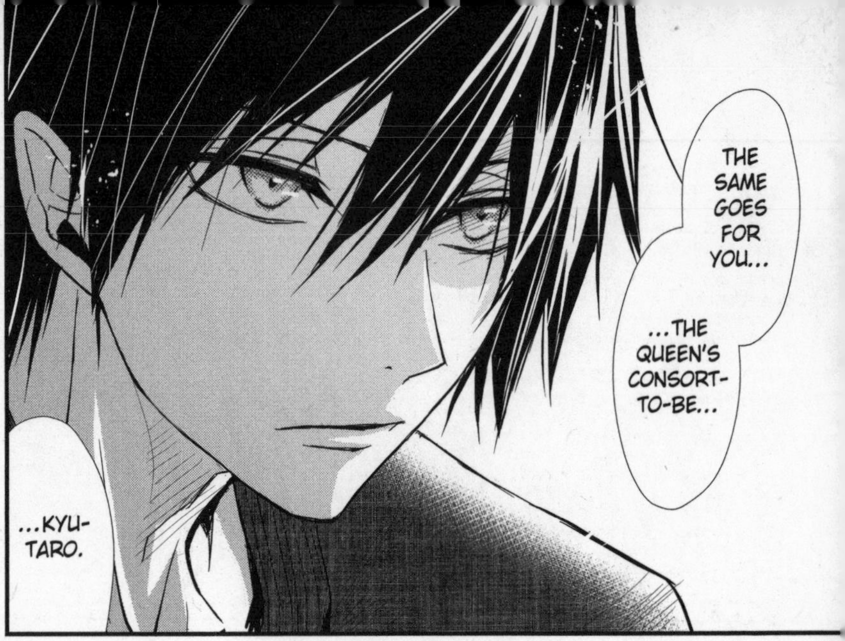
THE SAME GOES FOR YOU...
...THE QUEEN'S CONSORT-TO-BE...
...KYU-TARO.
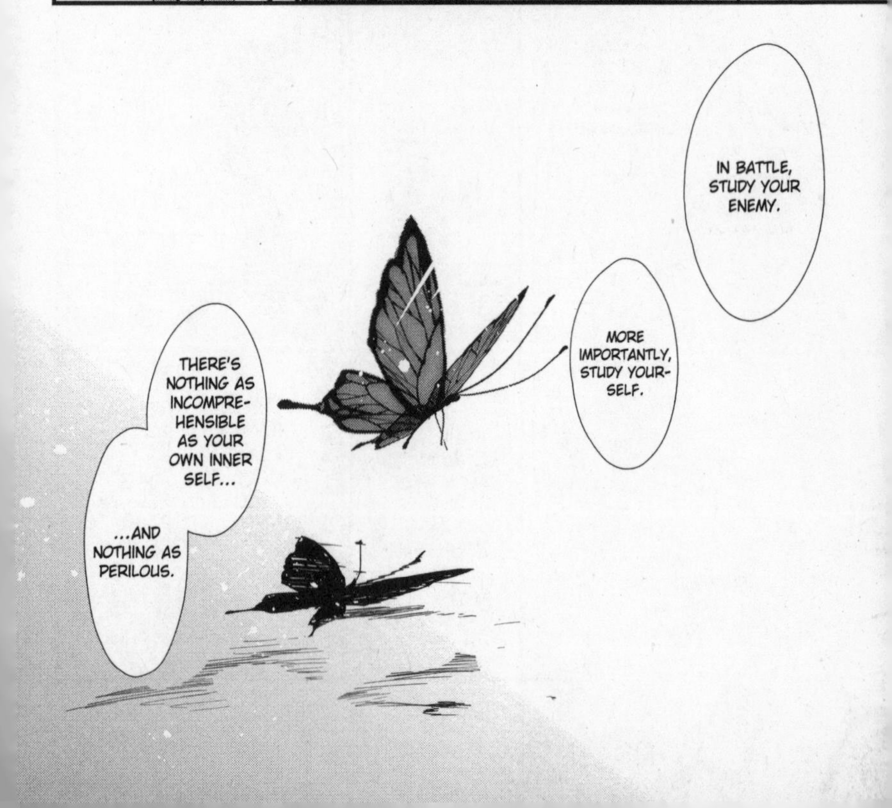
IN BATTLE, STUDY YOUR ENEMY.
MORE IMPORTANTLY, STUDY YOUR-SELF.
THERE'S NOTHING AS INCOMPRE-HENSIBLE AS YOUR OWN INNER SELF...
...AND NOTHING AS PERILOUS.

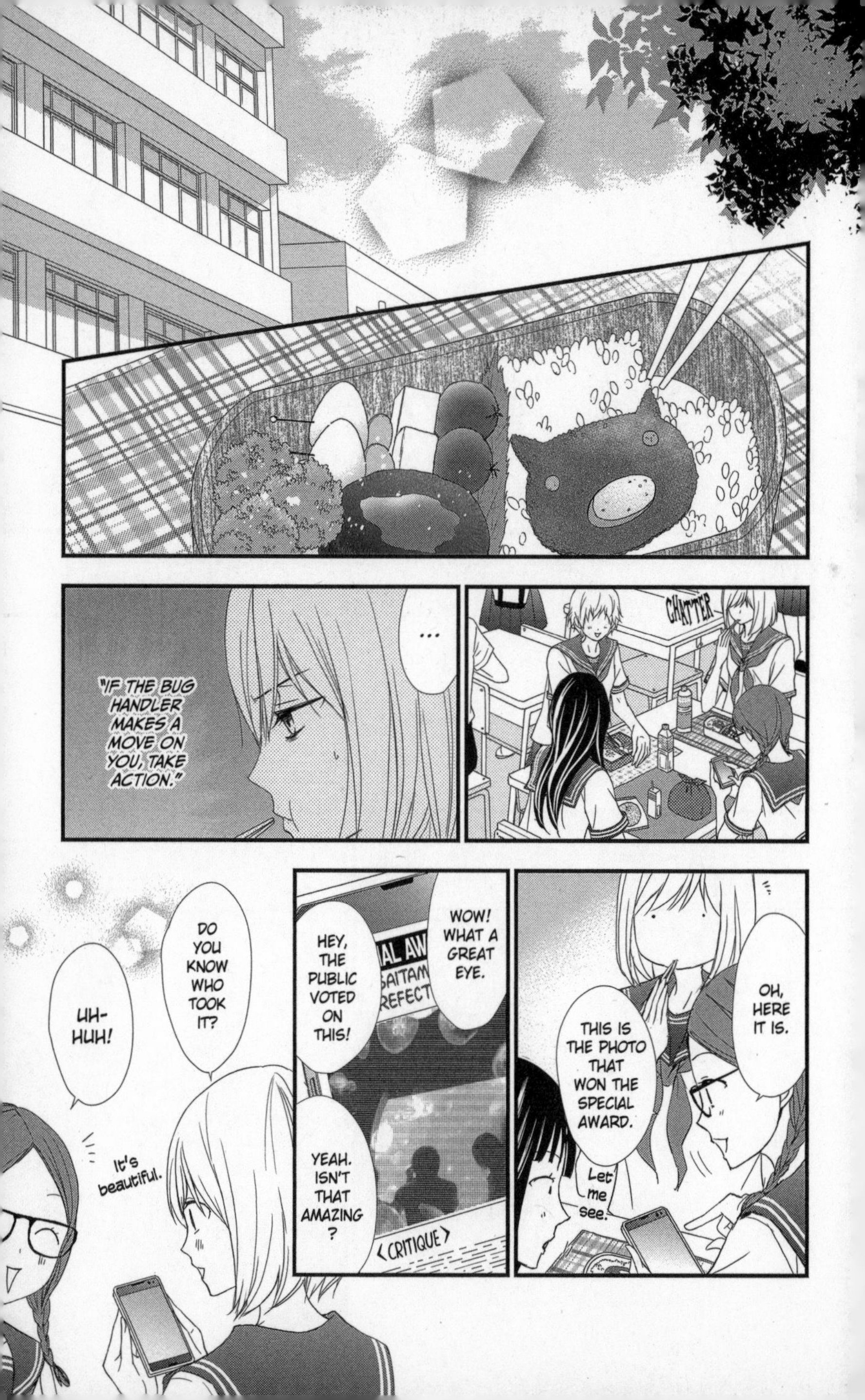
CHATTER
...
"IF THE BUG HANDLER MAKES A MOVE ON YOU, TAKE ACTION."
OH, HERE IT IS.
THIS IS THE PHOTO THAT WON THE SPECIAL AWARD.
Let me see.
WOW! WHAT A GREAT EYE.
HEY, THE PUBLIC VOTED ON THIS!
YEAH. ISN'T THAT AMAZING?
CRITIQUE
DO YOU KNOW WHO TOOK IT?
UH-HUH!
It's beautiful.

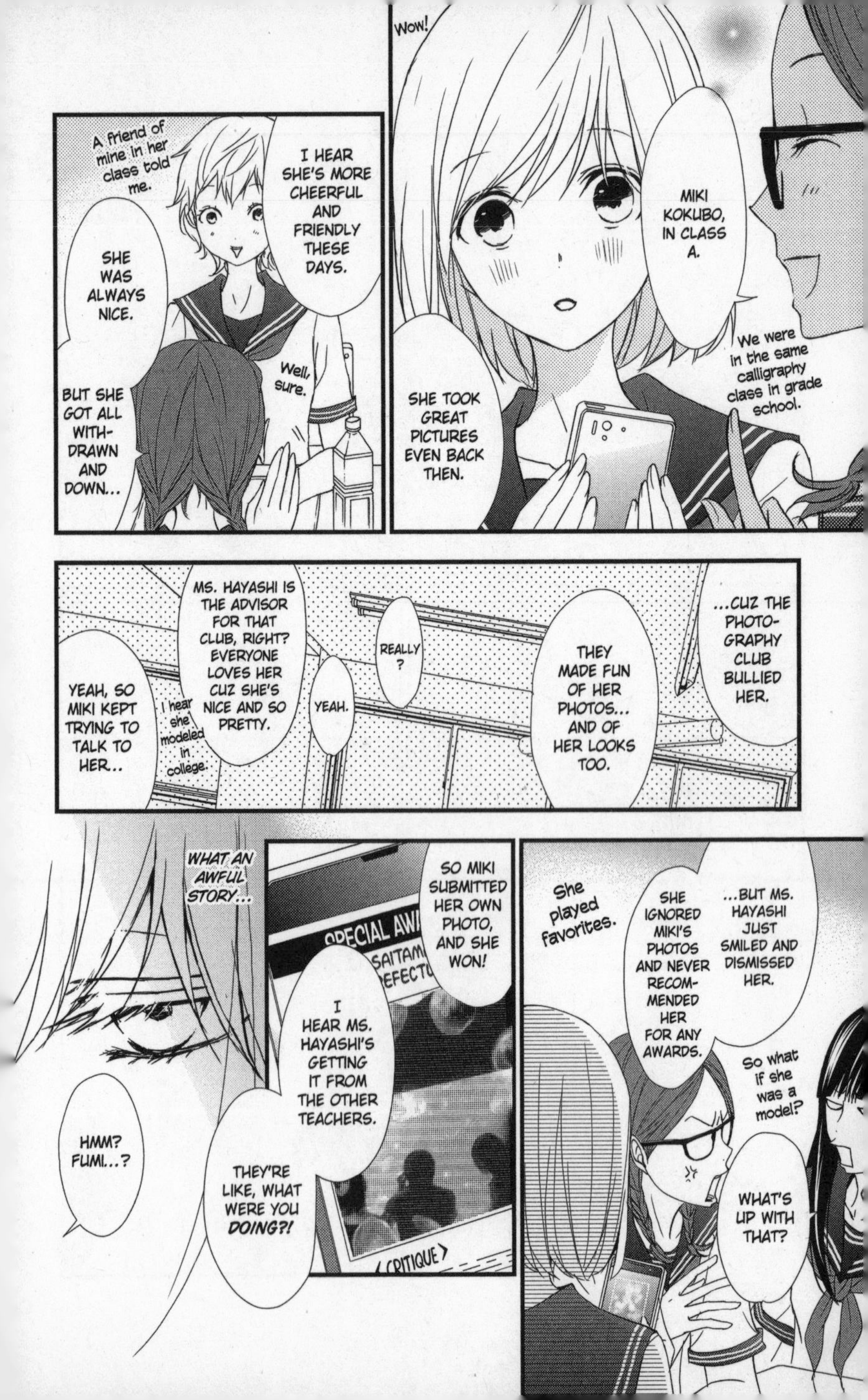
Wow!
MIKI KOKUBO, IN CLASS A.
We were in the same calligraphy class in grade school.
SHE TOOK GREAT PICTURES EVEN BACK THEN.
I HEAR SHE'S MORE CHEERFUL AND FRIENDLY THESE DAYS.
A friend of mine in her class told me.
SHE WAS ALWAYS NICE.
Well, sure.
BUT SHE GOT ALL WITH-DRAWN AND DOWN...
...CUZ THE PHOTO-GRAPHY CLUB BULLIED HER.
THEY MADE FUN OF HER PHOTOS... AND OF HER LOOKS TOO.
REALLY?
YEAH.
MS. HAYASHI IS THE ADVISOR FOR THAT CLUB, RIGHT? EVERYONE LOVES HER CUZ SHE'S NICE AND SO PRETTY.
I hear she modeled in college.
YEAH, SO MIKI KEPT TRYING TO TALK TO HER...
...BUT MS. HAYASHI JUST SMILED AND DISMISSED HER.
SHE IGNORED MIKI'S PHOTOS AND NEVER RECOM-MENDED HER FOR ANY AWARDS.
She played favorites.
So what if she was a model?
WHAT'S UP WITH THAT?
SO MIKI SUBMITTED HER OWN PHOTO, AND SHE WON!
I HEAR MS. HAYASHI'S GETTING IT FROM THE OTHER TEACHERS.
THEY'RE LIKE, WHAT WERE YOU *DOING?!*
‹CRITIQUE›
WHAT AN AWFUL STORY...
HMM? FUMI...?

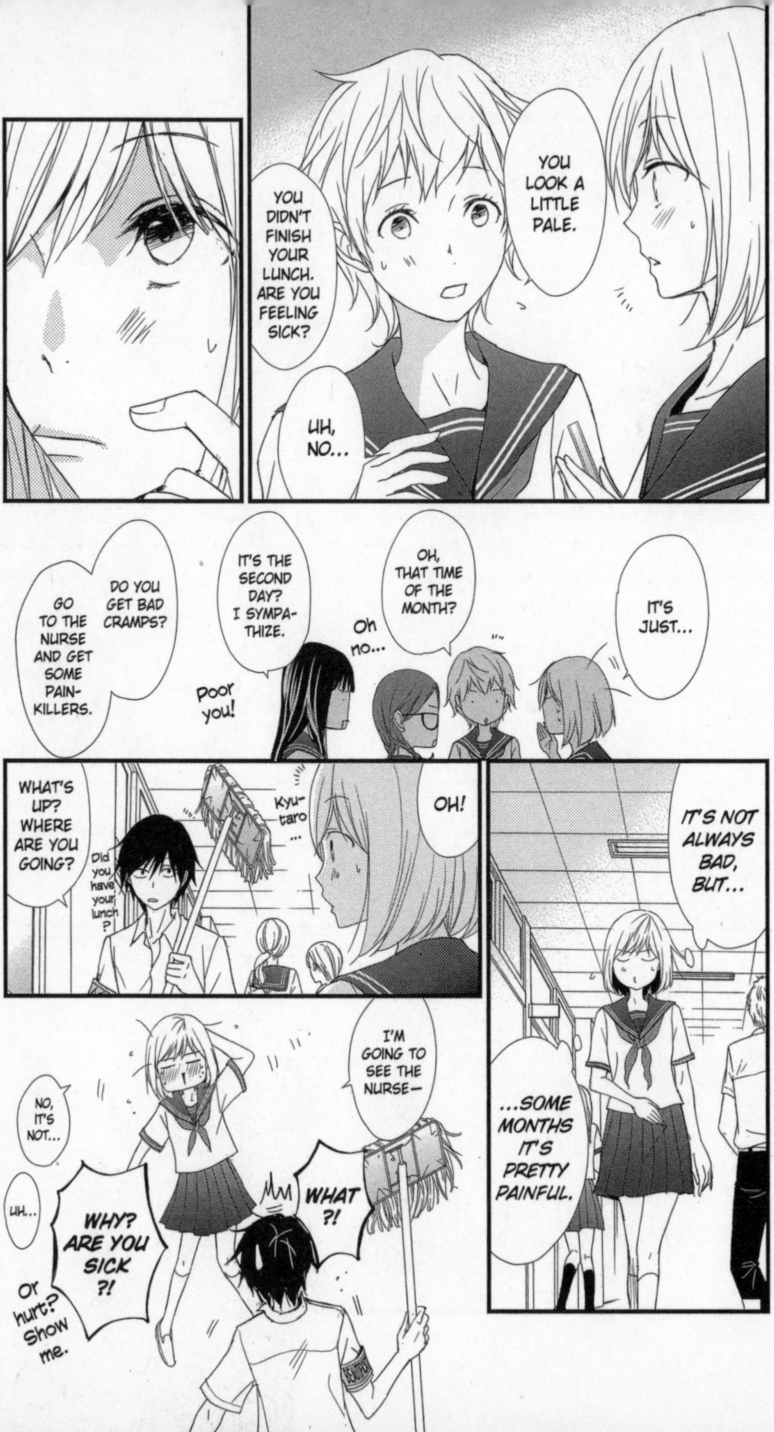
YOU LOOK A LITTLE PALE.
YOU DIDN'T FINISH YOUR LUNCH. ARE YOU FEELING SICK?
UH, NO...
IT'S JUST...
OH, THAT TIME OF THE MONTH?
Oh no...
IT'S THE SECOND DAY? I SYMPA-THIZE.
Poor you!
DO YOU GET BAD CRAMPS?
GO TO THE NURSE AND GET SOME PAIN-KILLERS.
IT'S NOT ALWAYS BAD, BUT...
...SOME MONTHS IT'S PRETTY PAINFUL.
OH!
Kyu-taro...
WHAT'S UP? WHERE ARE YOU GOING?
Did you have your lunch?
I'M GOING TO SEE THE NURSE—
WHAT?!
WHY? ARE YOU SICK?!
Or hurt? Show me.
NO, IT'S NOT...
UH...

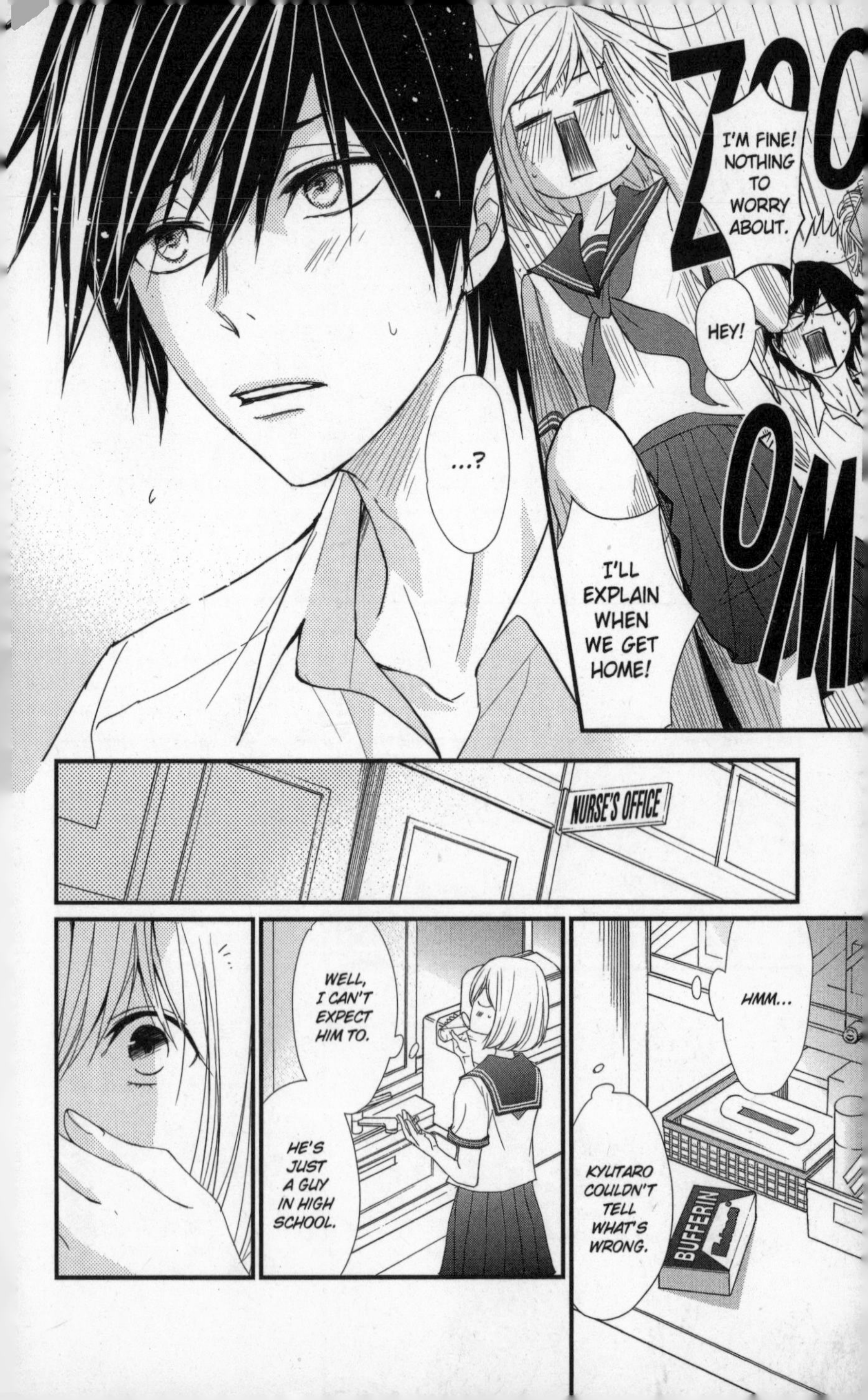

I'M FINE! NOTHING TO WORRY ABOUT.
HEY!
I'LL EXPLAIN WHEN WE GET HOME!
ZOO
OM
...?
NURSE'S OFFICE
HMM...
KYUTARO COULDN'T TELL WHAT'S WRONG.
BUFFERIN
WELL, I CAN'T EXPECT HIM TO.
HE'S JUST A GUY IN HIGH SCHOOL.

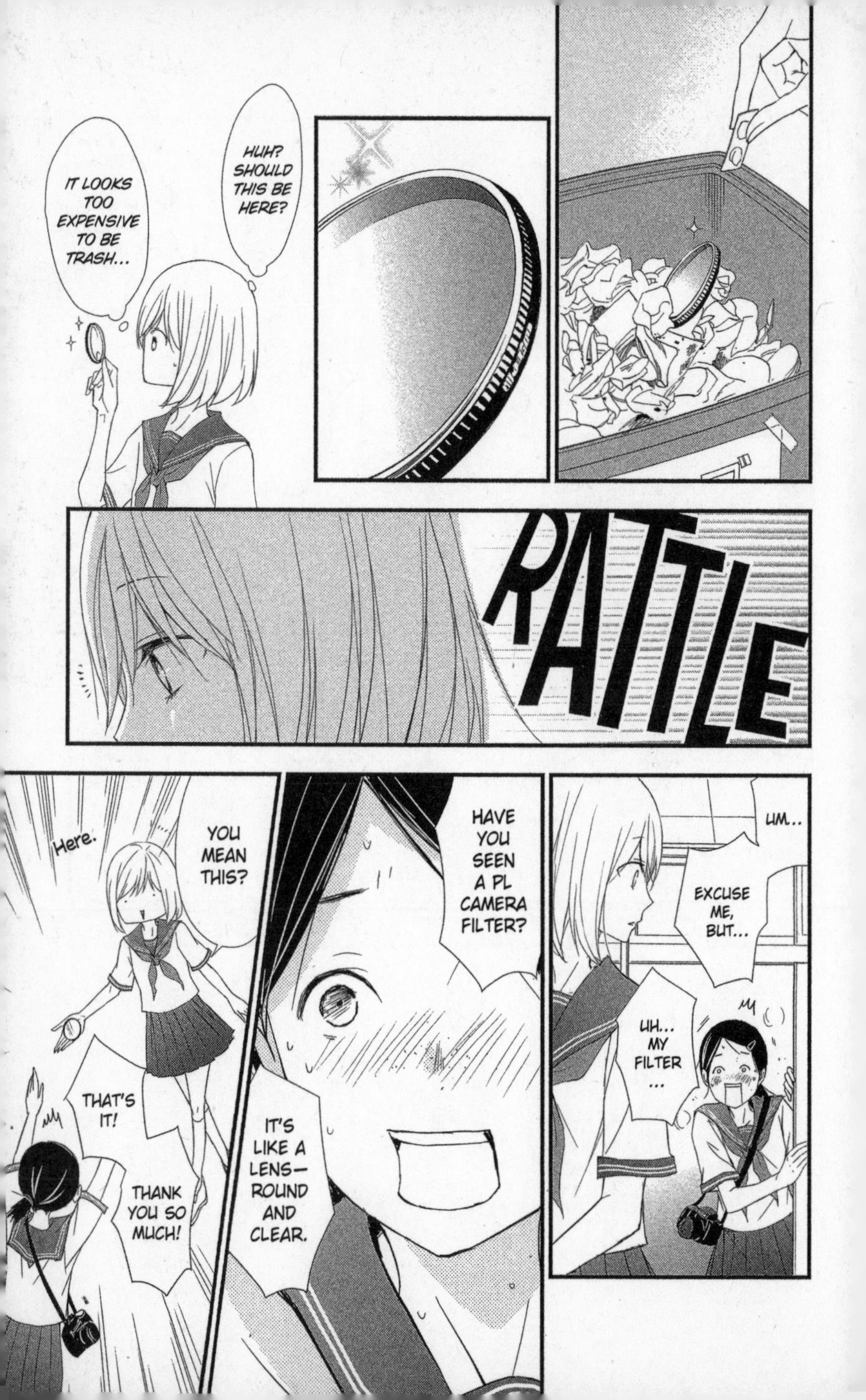
HUH? SHOULD THIS BE HERE?
IT LOOKS TOO EXPENSIVE TO BE TRASH...
RATTLE
UM..
EXCUSE ME, BUT...
UH... MY FILTER ...
HAVE YOU SEEN A PL CAMERA FILTER?
IT'S LIKE A LENS—ROUND AND CLEAR.
YOU MEAN THIS?
Here.
THAT'S IT!
THANK YOU SO MUCH!

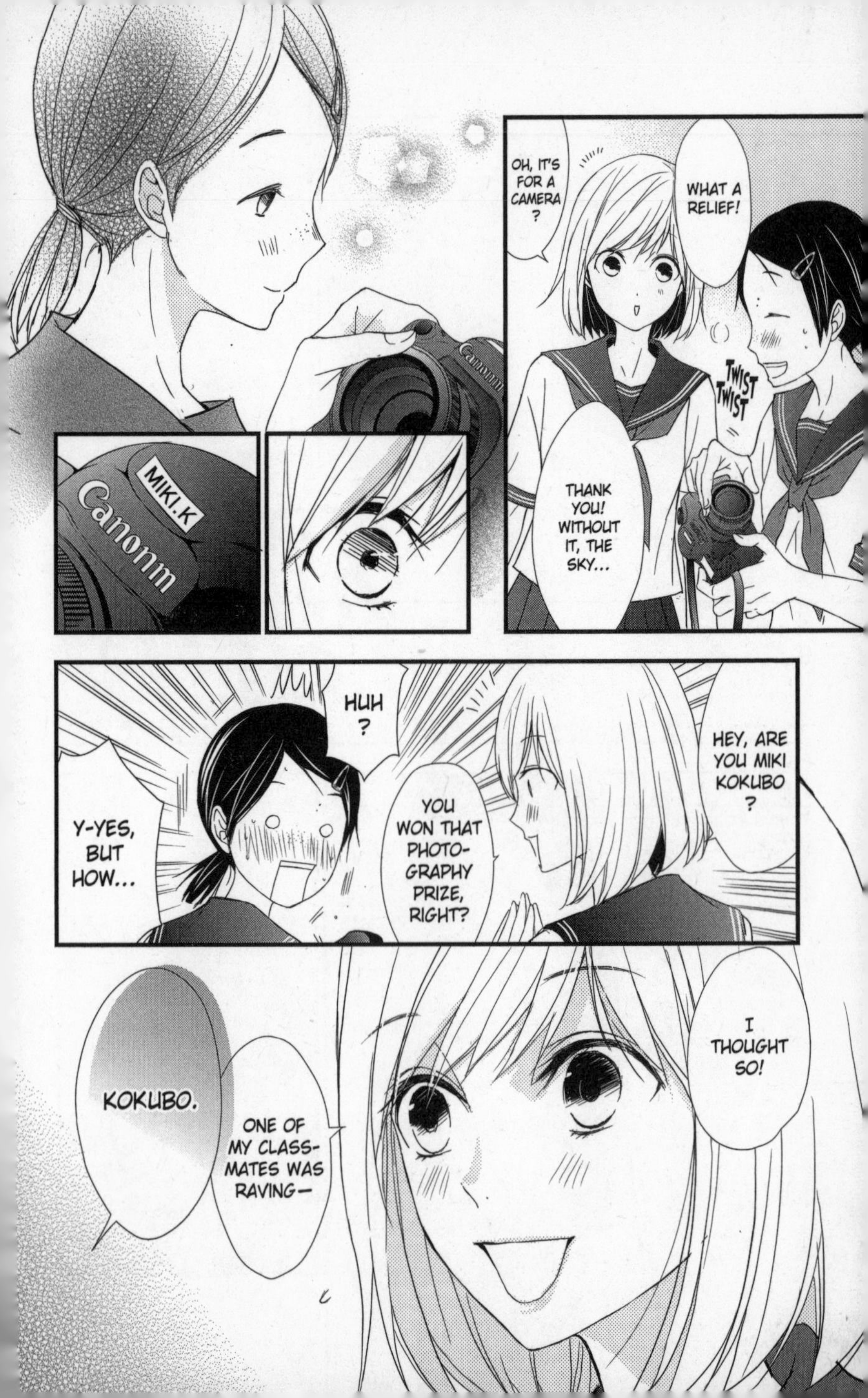
WHAT A RELIEF!
OH, IT'S FOR A CAMERA?
TWIST TWIST
THANK YOU! WITHOUT IT, THE SKY...
Canonm
MIKI.K
Canonm
HEY, ARE YOU MIKI KOKUBO?
HUH?
YOU WON THAT PHOTOGRAPHY PRIZE, RIGHT?
Y-YES, BUT HOW...
I THOUGHT SO!
ONE OF MY CLASSMATES WAS RAVING—
KOKUBO.

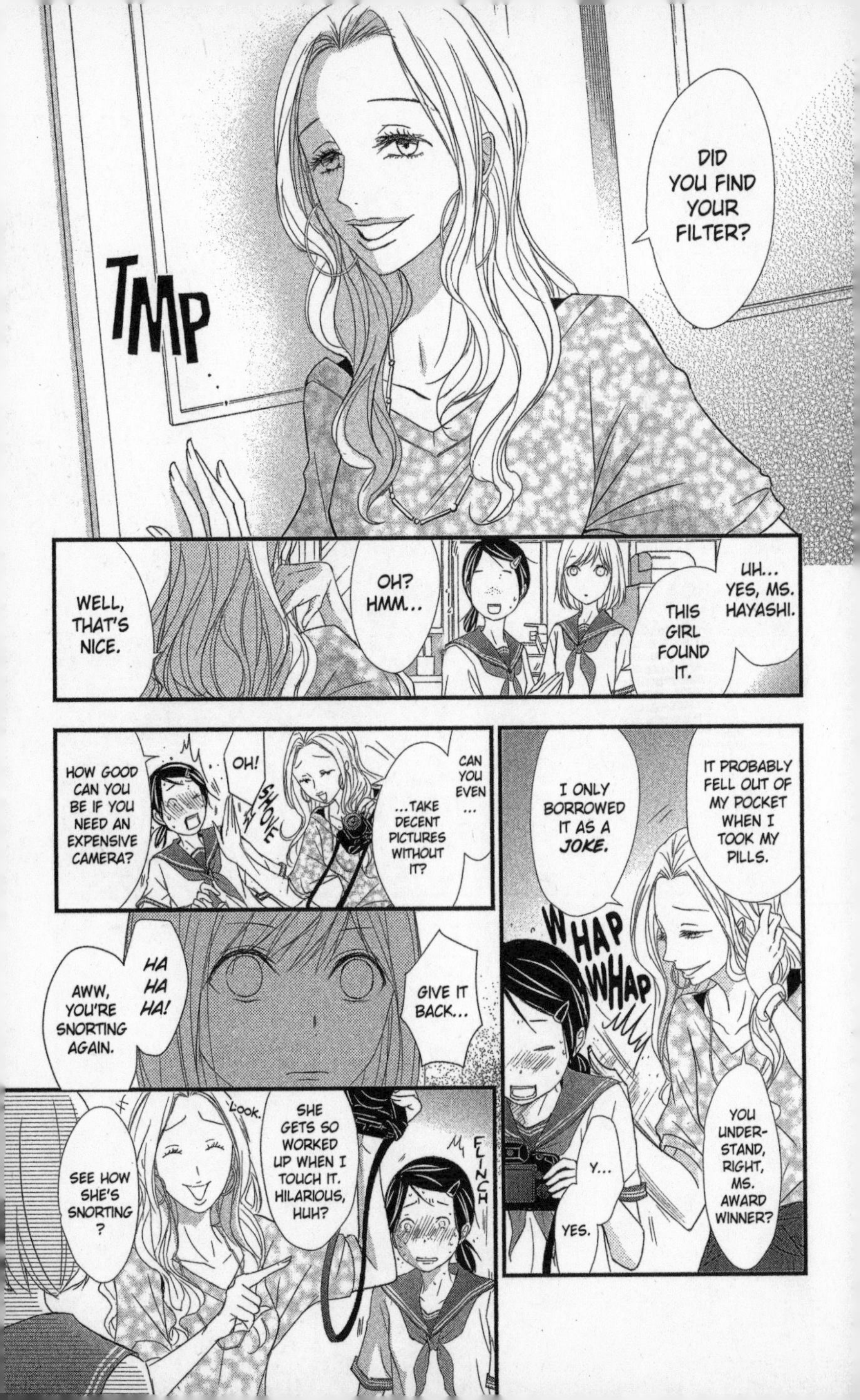
DID YOU FIND YOUR FILTER?
TMP
UH... YES, MS. HAYASHI.
THIS GIRL FOUND IT.
OH? HMM...
WELL, THAT'S NICE.
IT PROBABLY FELL OUT OF MY POCKET WHEN I TOOK MY PILLS.
I ONLY BORROWED IT AS A *JOKE.*
WHAP WHAP
YOU UNDER-STAND, RIGHT, MS. AWARD WINNER?
Y...
YES.
CAN YOU EVEN ...
...TAKE DECENT PICTURES WITHOUT IT?
SHOVE
OH!
HOW GOOD CAN YOU BE IF YOU NEED AN EXPENSIVE CAMERA?
GIVE IT BACK...
HA HA HA!
AWW, YOU'RE SNORTING AGAIN.
FLINCH
SHE GETS SO WORKED UP WHEN I TOUCH IT. HILARIOUS, HUH?
LOOK.
SEE HOW SHE'S SNORTING?

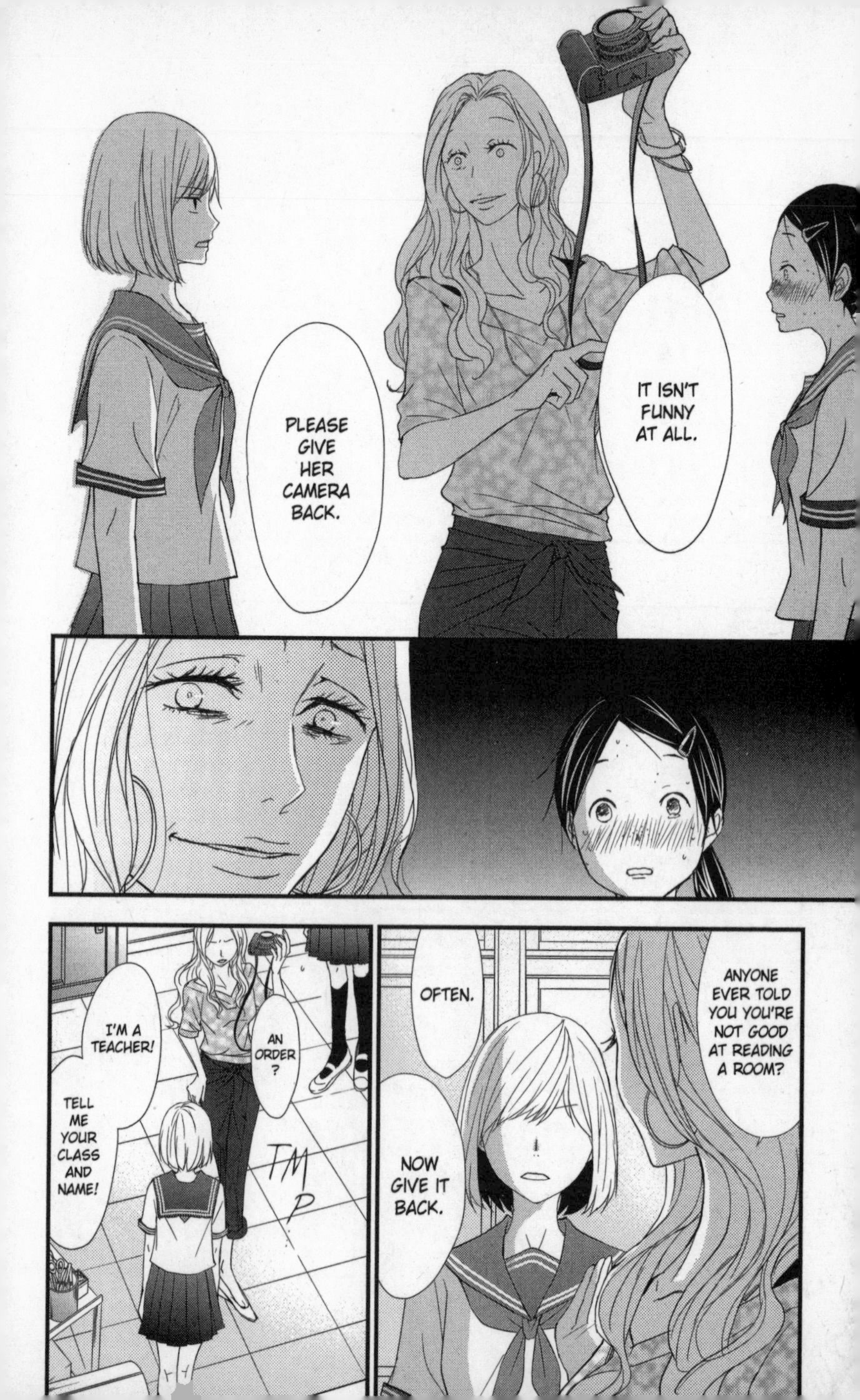
IT ISN'T FUNNY AT ALL.
PLEASE GIVE HER CAMERA BACK.
ANYONE EVER TOLD YOU YOU'RE NOT GOOD AT READING A ROOM?
OFTEN.
NOW GIVE IT BACK.
AN ORDER?
I'M A TEACHER!
TELL ME YOUR CLASS AND NAME!
TMP

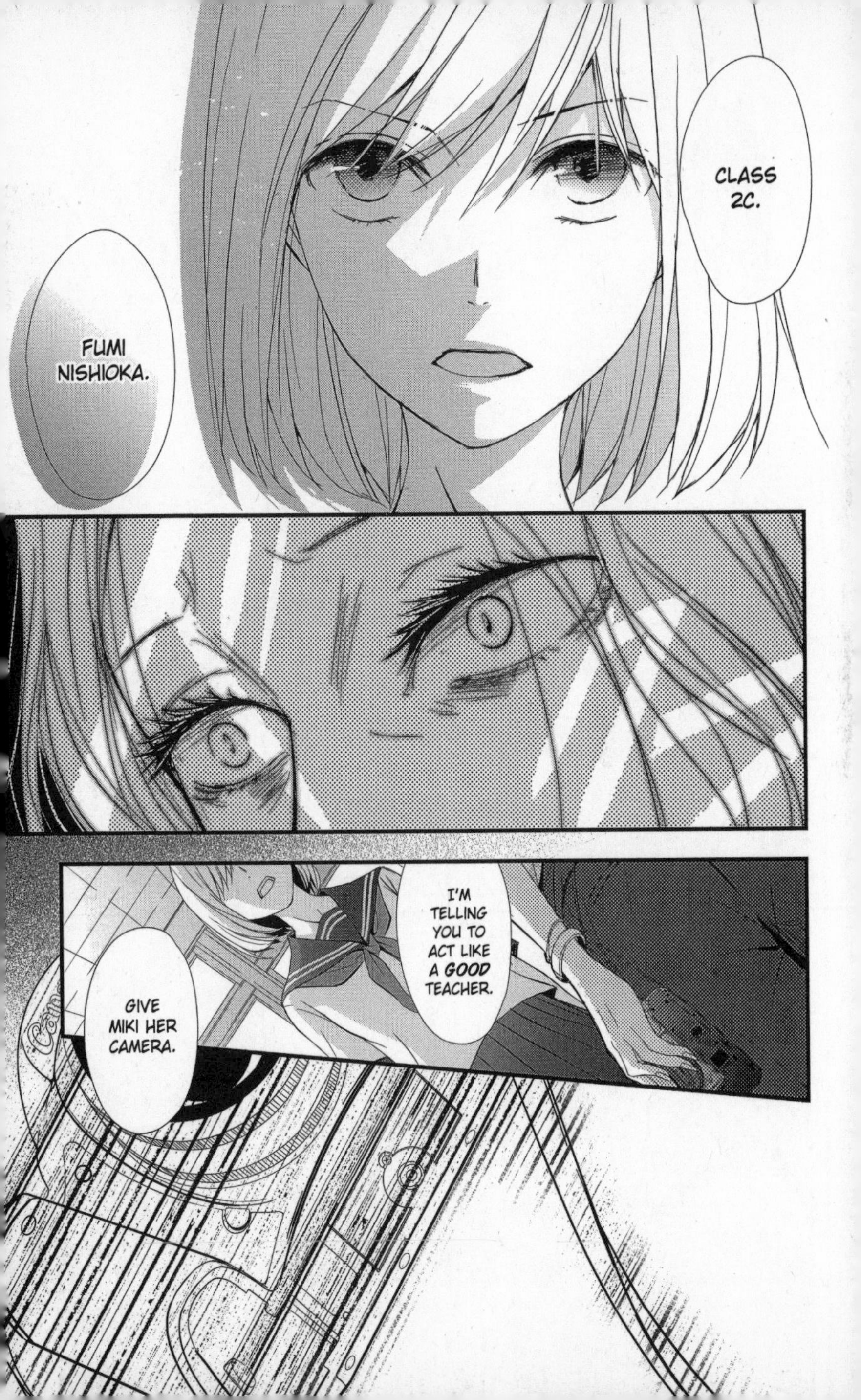
CLASS 2C.
FUMI NISHIOKA.
I'M TELLING YOU TO ACT LIKE A GOOD TEACHER.
GIVE MIKI HER CAMERA.

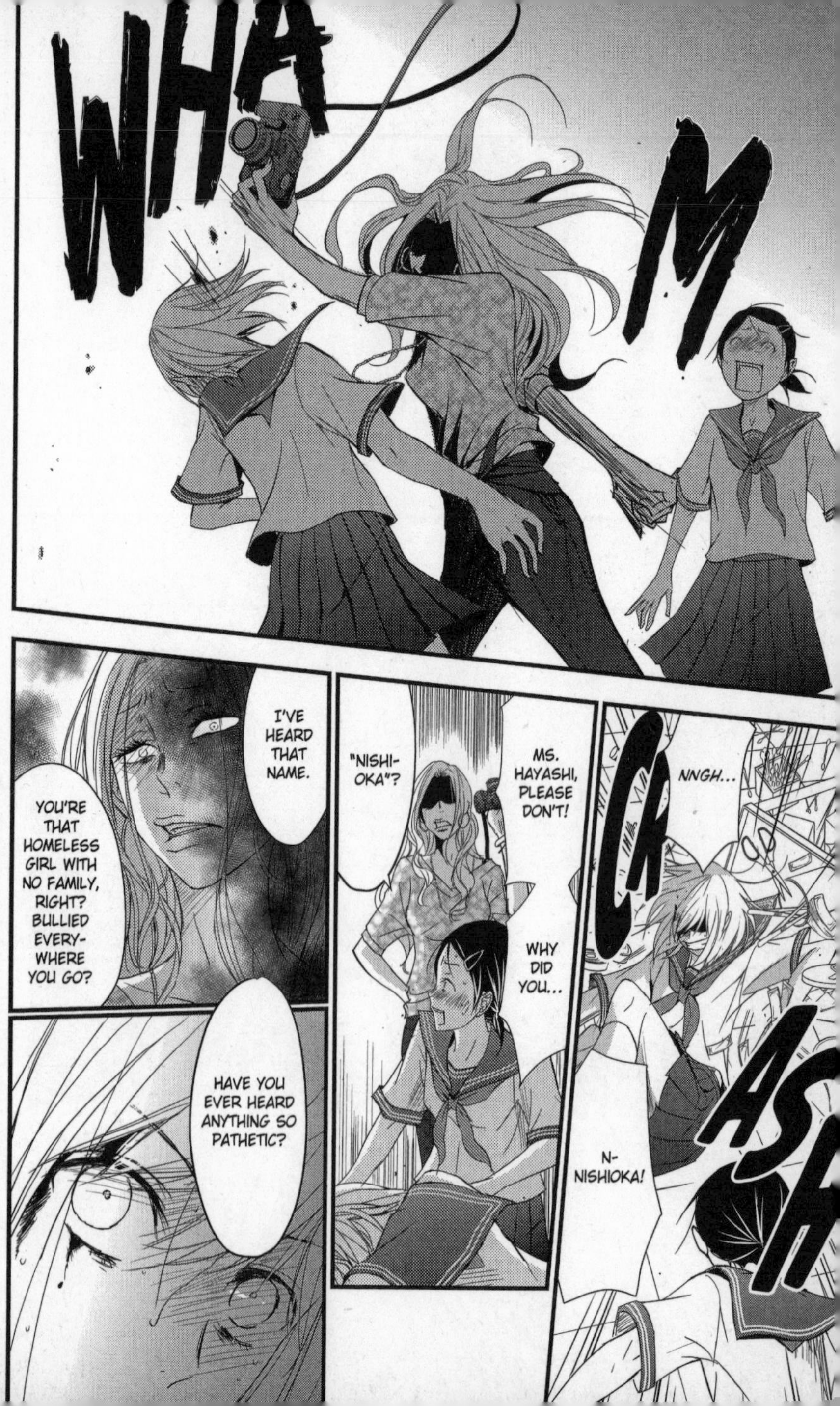
WHA
M
CR
NNGH...
ASH
N-NISHIOKA!
MS. HAYASHI, PLEASE DON'T!
WHY DID YOU...
"NISHI-OKA"?
I'VE HEARD THAT NAME.
YOU'RE THAT HOMELESS GIRL WITH NO FAMILY, RIGHT? BULLIED EVERY-WHERE YOU GO?
HAVE YOU EVER HEARD ANYTHING SO PATHETIC?

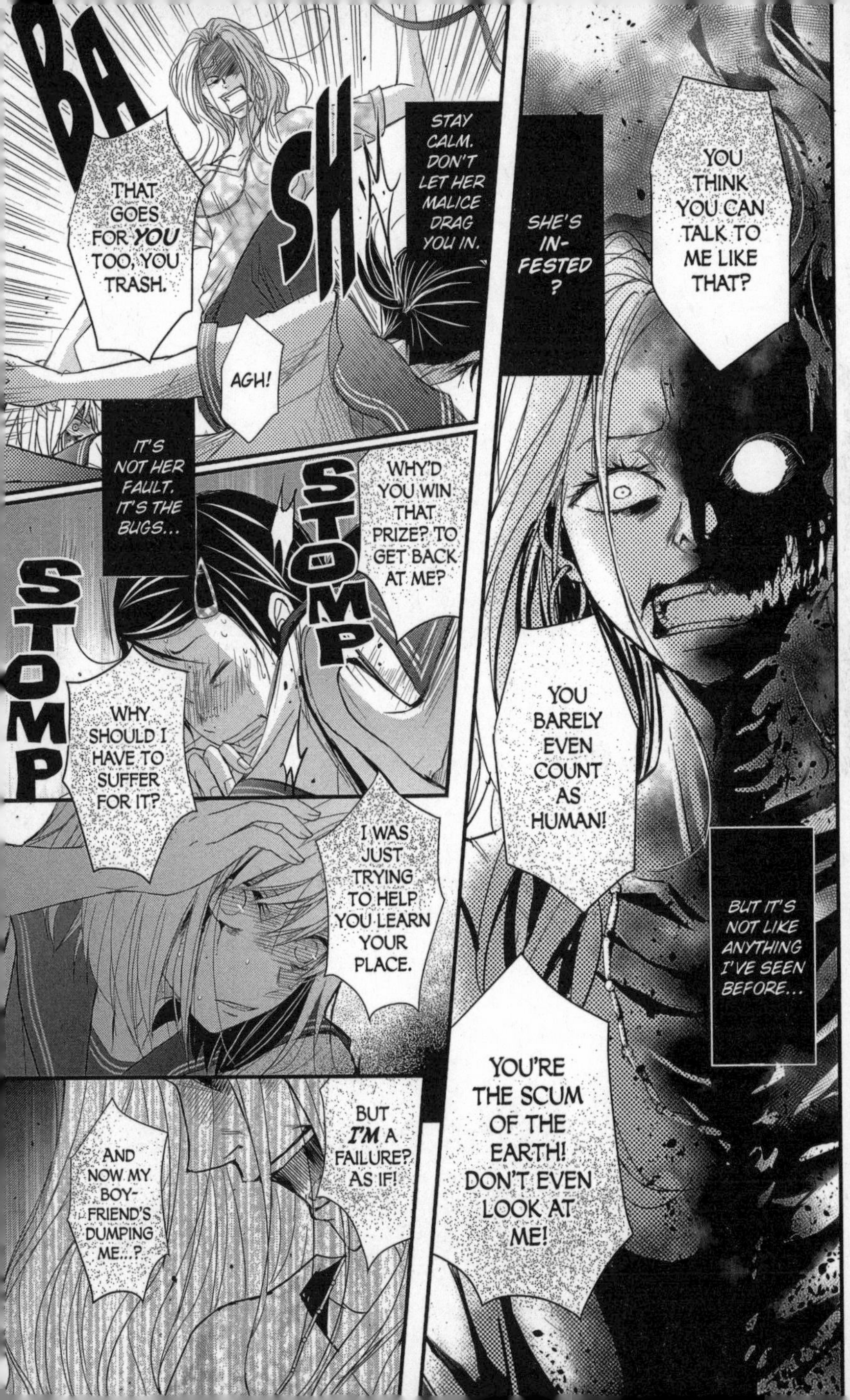
YOU THINK YOU CAN TALK TO ME LIKE THAT?
SHE'S IN-FESTED?
YOU BARELY EVEN COUNT AS HUMAN!
BUT IT'S NOT LIKE ANYTHING I'VE SEEN BEFORE...
YOU'RE THE SCUM OF THE EARTH! DON'T EVEN LOOK AT ME!
STAY CALM. DON'T LET HER MALICE DRAG YOU IN.
SH
BA
THAT GOES FOR *YOU* TOO, YOU TRASH.
AGH!
WHY'D YOU WIN THAT PRIZE? TO GET BACK AT ME?
STOMP
IT'S NOT HER FAULT. IT'S THE BUGS...
STOMP
WHY SHOULD I HAVE TO SUFFER FOR IT?
I WAS JUST TRYING TO HELP YOU LEARN YOUR PLACE.
BUT *I'M* A FAILURE? AS IF!
AND NOW MY BOY-FRIEND'S DUMPING ME...?

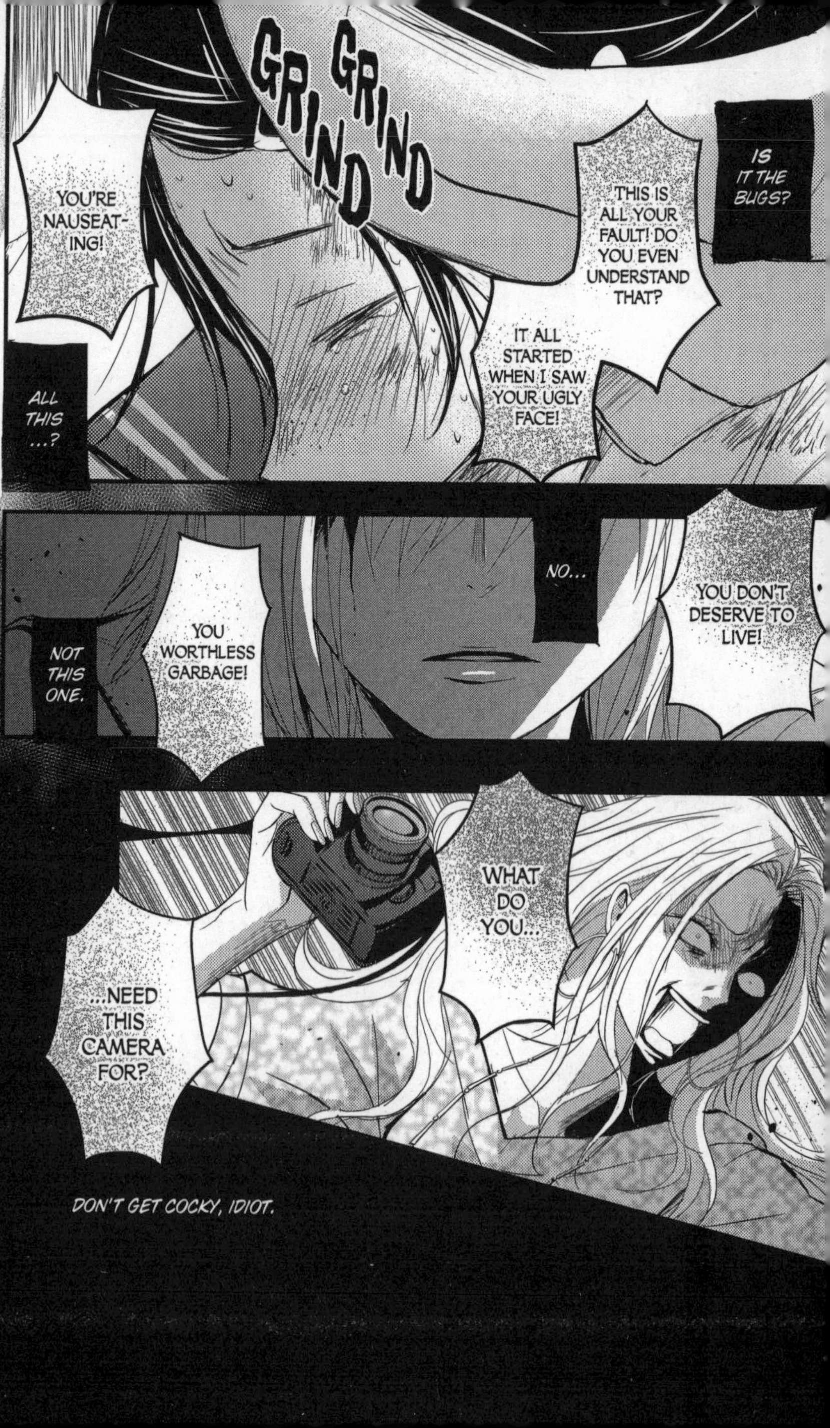

IS IT THE BUGS?
THIS IS ALL YOUR FAULT! DO YOU EVEN UNDERSTAND THAT?
GRIND GRIND
IT ALL STARTED WHEN I SAW YOUR UGLY FACE!
YOU'RE NAUSEAT-ING!
ALL THIS ...?
YOU DON'T DESERVE TO LIVE!
NO...
YOU WORTHLESS GARBAGE!
NOT THIS ONE.
WHAT DO YOU...
...NEED THIS CAMERA FOR?
DON'T GET COCKY, IDIOT.

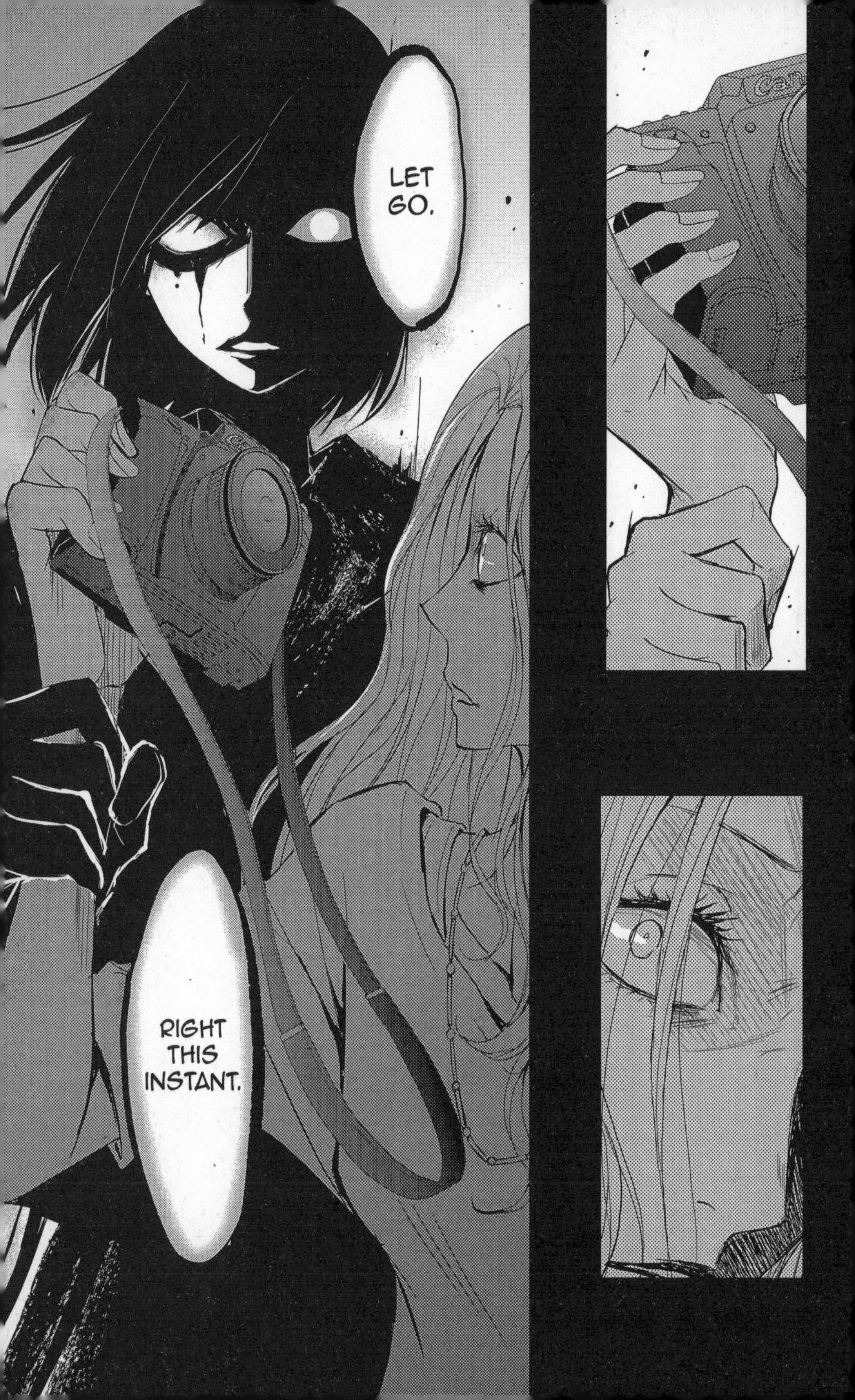
LET GO.
RIGHT THIS INSTANT.

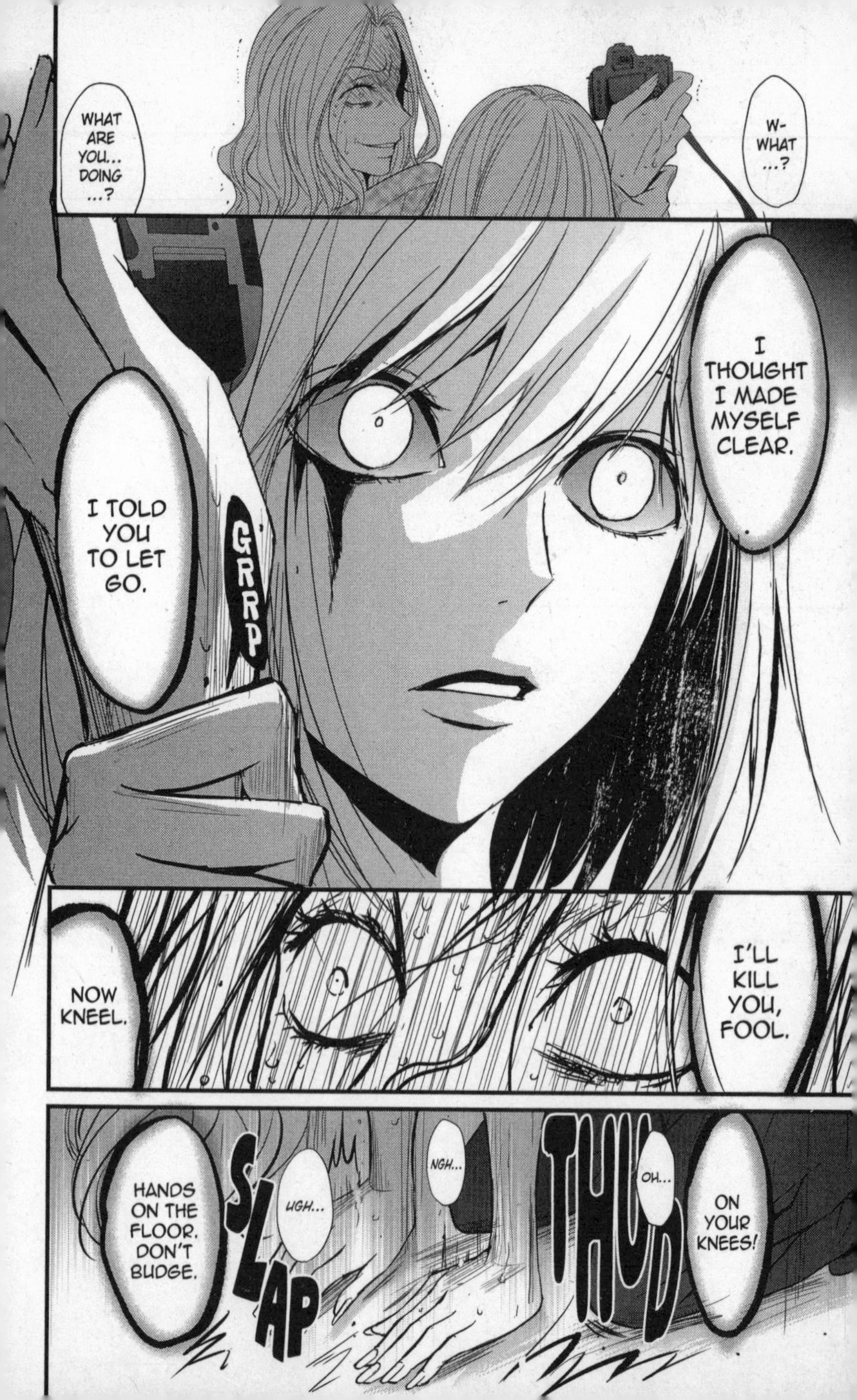
W-WHAT...?
WHAT ARE YOU... DOING...?
I THOUGHT I MADE MYSELF CLEAR.
GRRP
I TOLD YOU TO LET GO.
I'LL KILL YOU, FOOL.
NOW KNEEL.
ON YOUR KNEES!
OH...
THUD
NGH...
UGH...
SLAP
HANDS ON THE FLOOR. DON'T BUDGE.

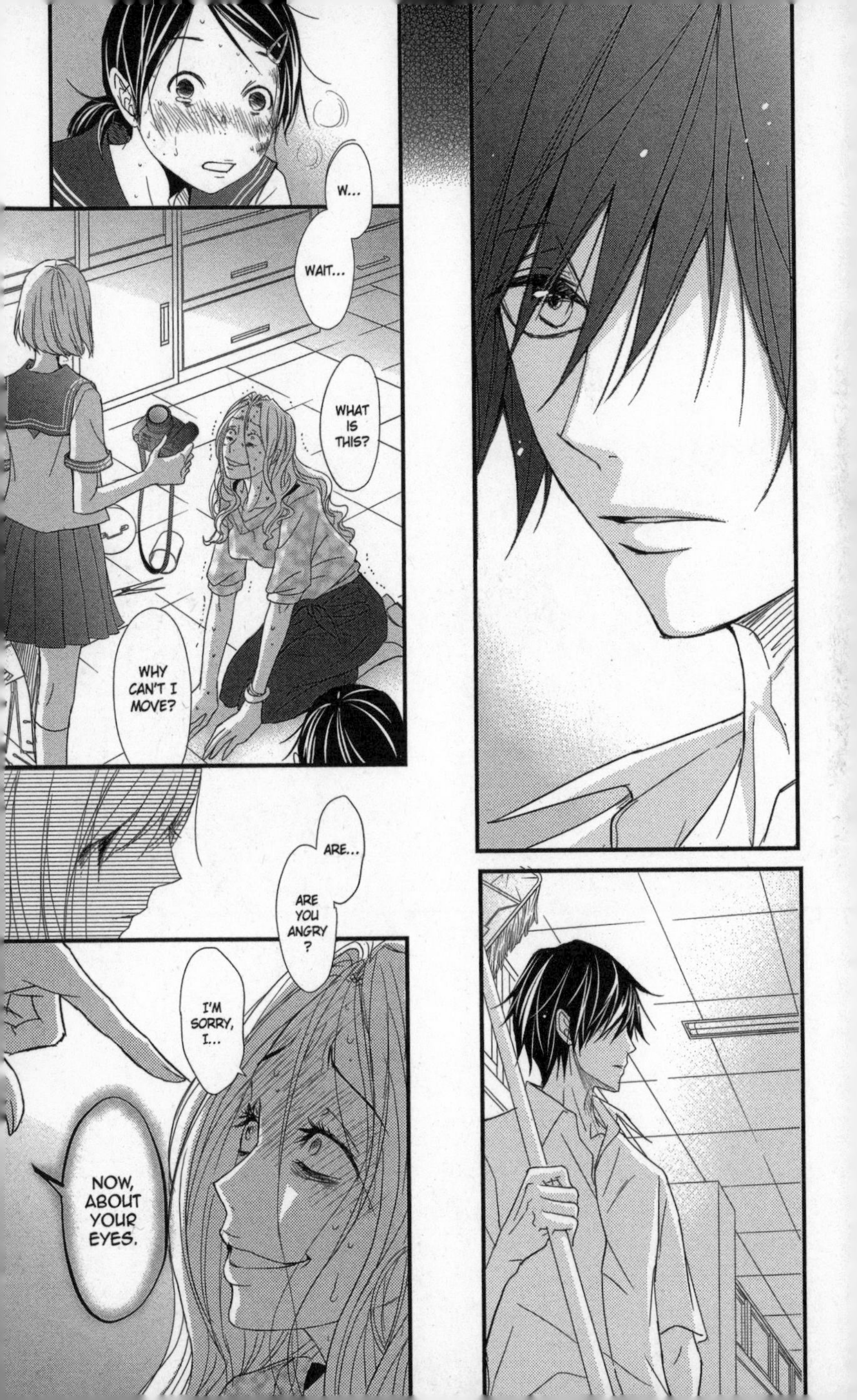
W...
WAIT...
WHAT IS THIS?
WHY CAN'T I MOVE?
ARE...
ARE YOU ANGRY?
I'M SORRY, I...
NOW, ABOUT YOUR EYES.

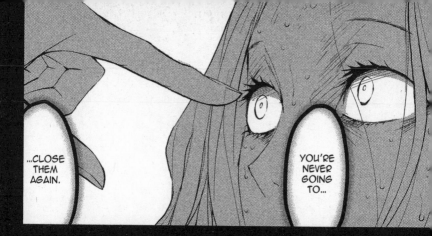

YOU'RE NEVER GOING TO...
...CLOSE THEM AGAIN.
WHAT AM I DOING?
WHY?
I DON'T FEEL WELL. I'M QUEASY.
BUT THAT DOESN'T MATTER. IT'S HER FAULT.
YOU SAID PEOPLE WHO ARE TRASH DON'T DESERVE TO LIVE, DIDN'T YOU?
WELL, *YOU'RE* TRASH.

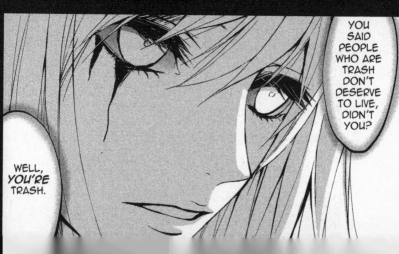

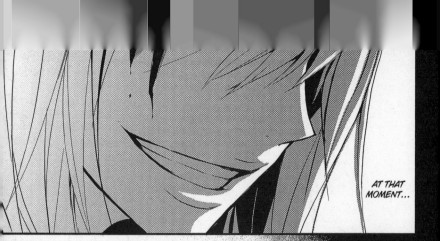

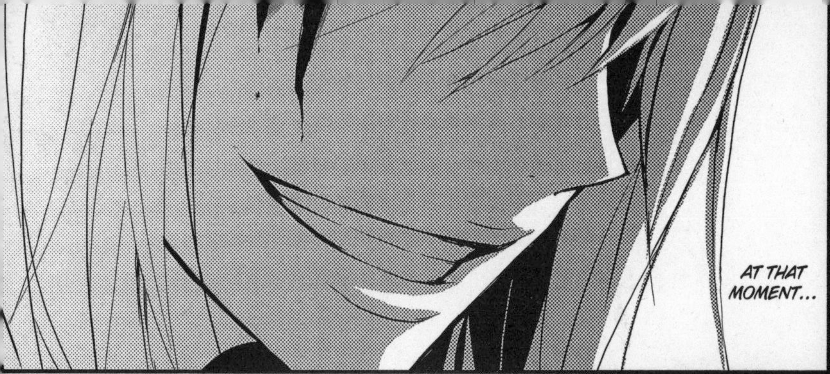
AT THAT MOMENT...
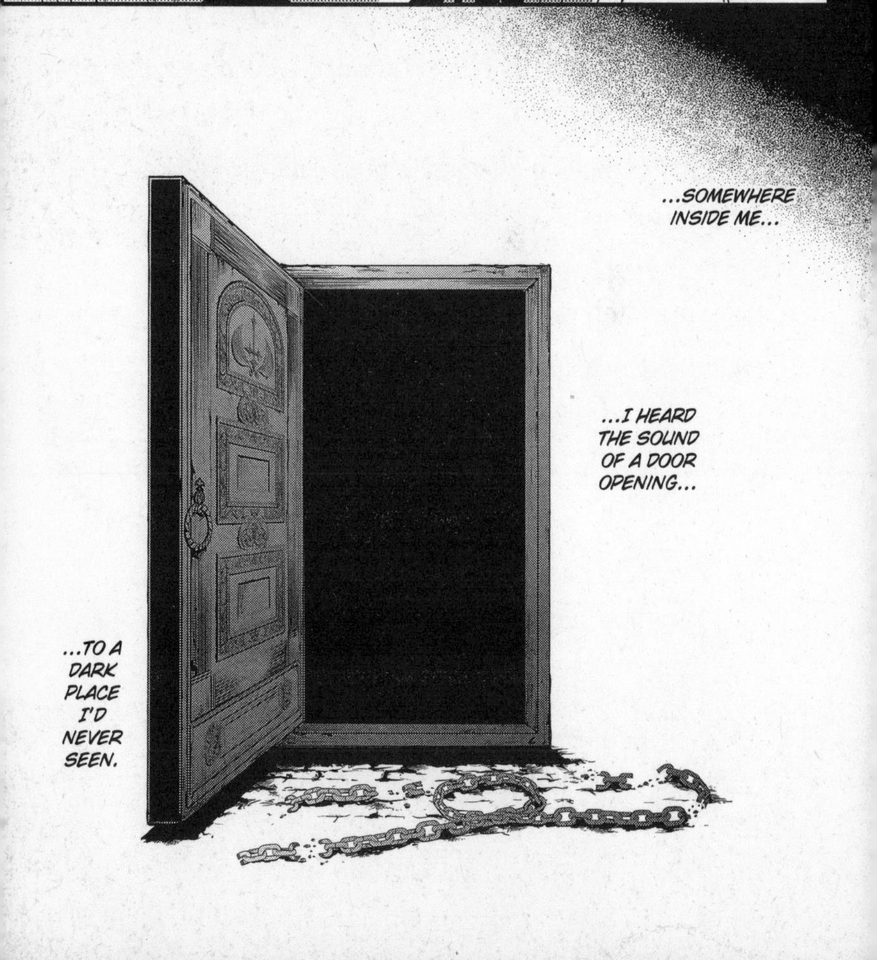
...SOMEWHERE INSIDE ME...
...I HEARD THE SOUND OF A DOOR OPENING...
...TO A DARK PLACE I'D NEVER SEEN.

Queen's Quality

Things are getting pretty dicey! And due to the layout of this volume, the afterword wound up here.

The story's moving along at a good and heavy pace now. Fumi, Kyutaro and I will keep doing our best from here on out. I hope you'll read to the end of this volume, and I look forward to seeing you in volume 2!

Kyousuke Motomi

Send your letters to: ♡

Kyousuke Motomi
c/o Queen's Quality Editor
Viz Media
P.O. Box 77010
San Francisco, CA 94107

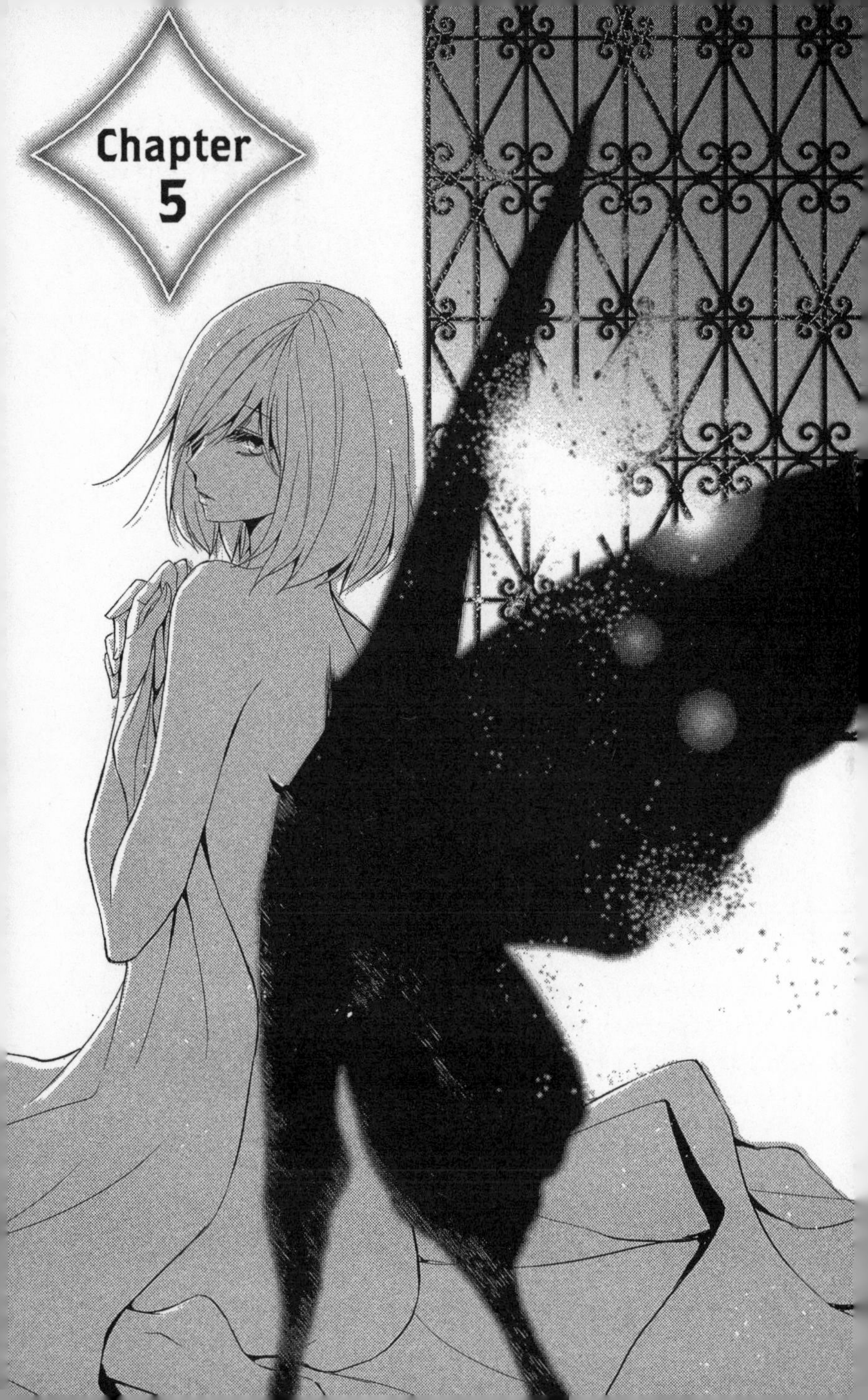
Chapter
5

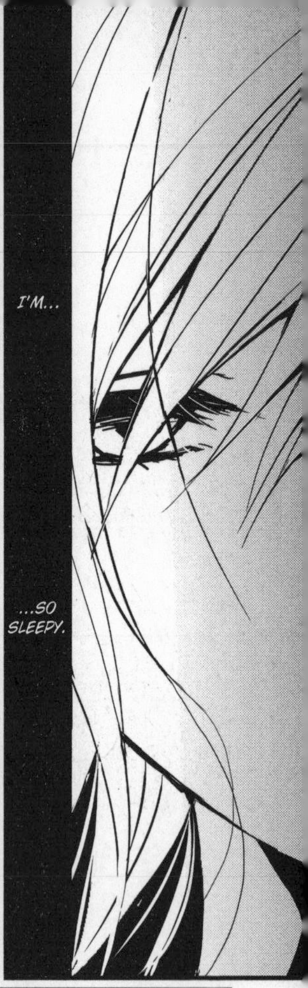
I'M...
...SO SLEEPY.
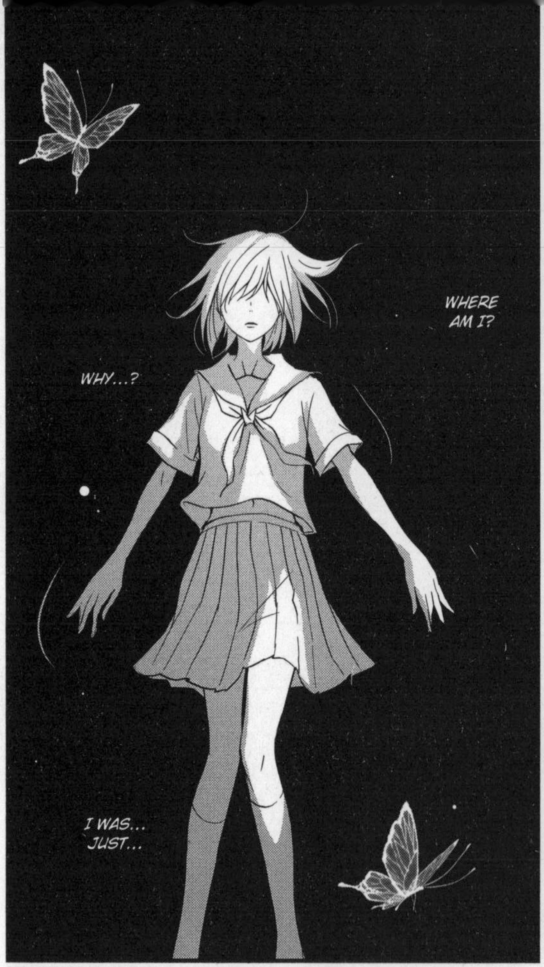
WHERE AM I?
WHY...?
I WAS... JUST...
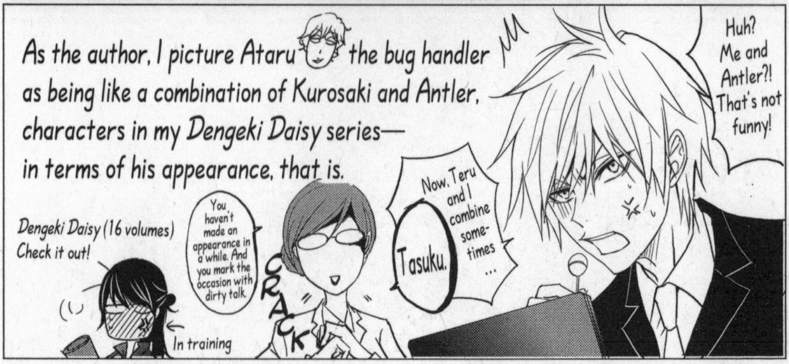
Huh? Me and Antler?! That's not funny!
As the author, I picture Ataru the bug handler as being like a combination of Kurosaki and Antler, characters in my Dengeki Daisy series—in terms of his appearance, that is.
Now, Teru and I combine some-times...
Tasuku.
You haven't made an appearance in a while. And you mark the occasion with dirty talk.
CRACK
Dengeki Daisy (16 volumes) Check it out!
In training

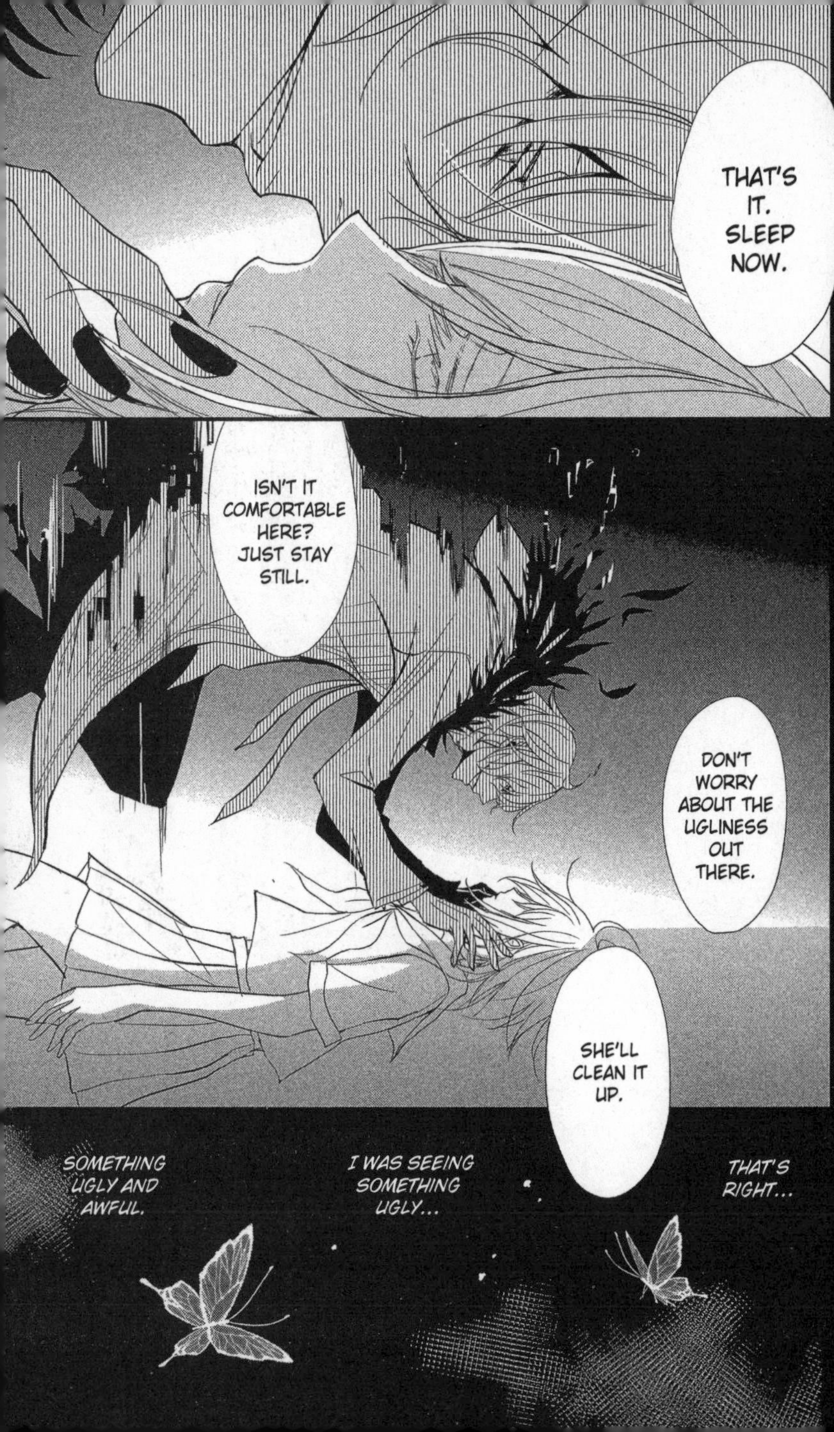
THAT'S IT. SLEEP NOW.
ISN'T IT COMFORTABLE HERE? JUST STAY STILL.
DON'T WORRY ABOUT THE UGLINESS OUT THERE.
SHE'LL CLEAN IT UP.
THAT'S RIGHT...
I WAS SEEING SOMETHING UGLY...
SOMETHING UGLY AND AWFUL.

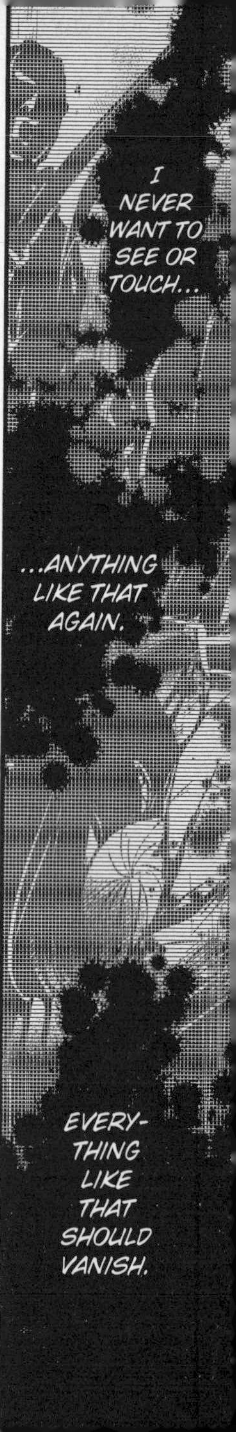
I NEVER WANT TO SEE OR TOUCH...
...ANYTHING LIKE THAT AGAIN.
EVERYTHING LIKE THAT SHOULD VANISH.
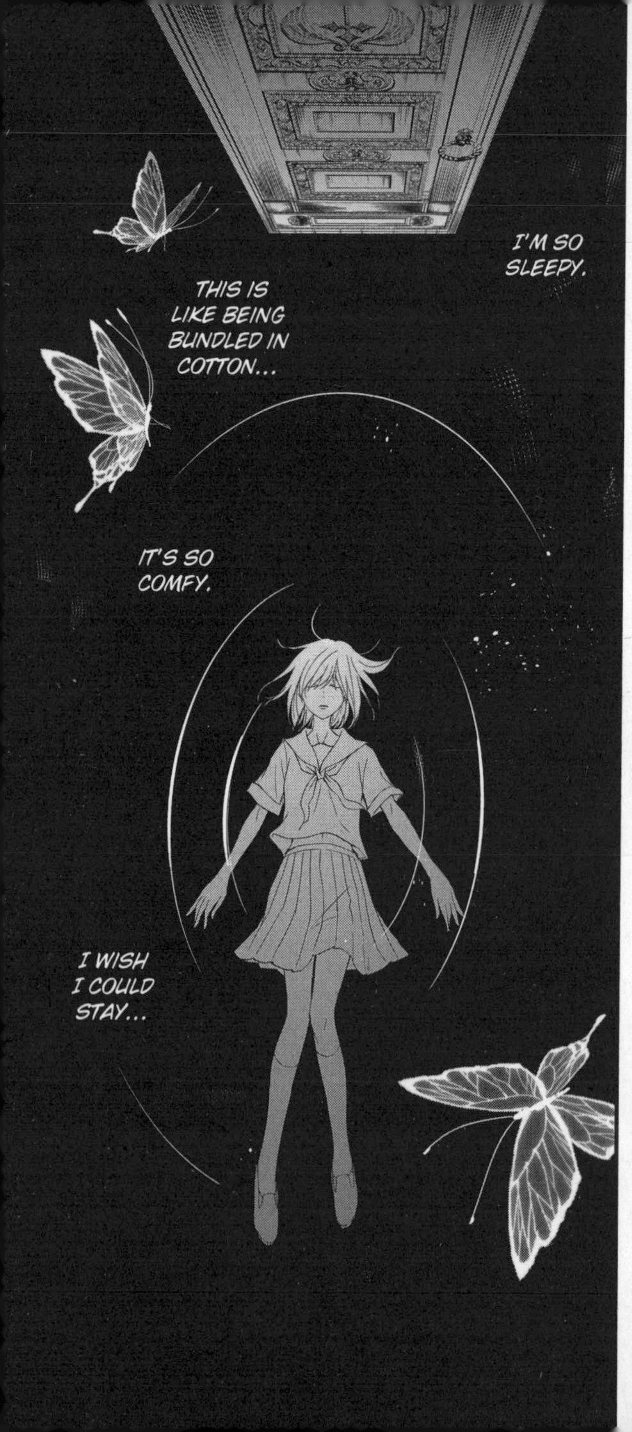
I'M SO SLEEPY.
THIS IS LIKE BEING BUNDLED IN COTTON...
IT'S SO COMFY.
I WISH I COULD STAY...

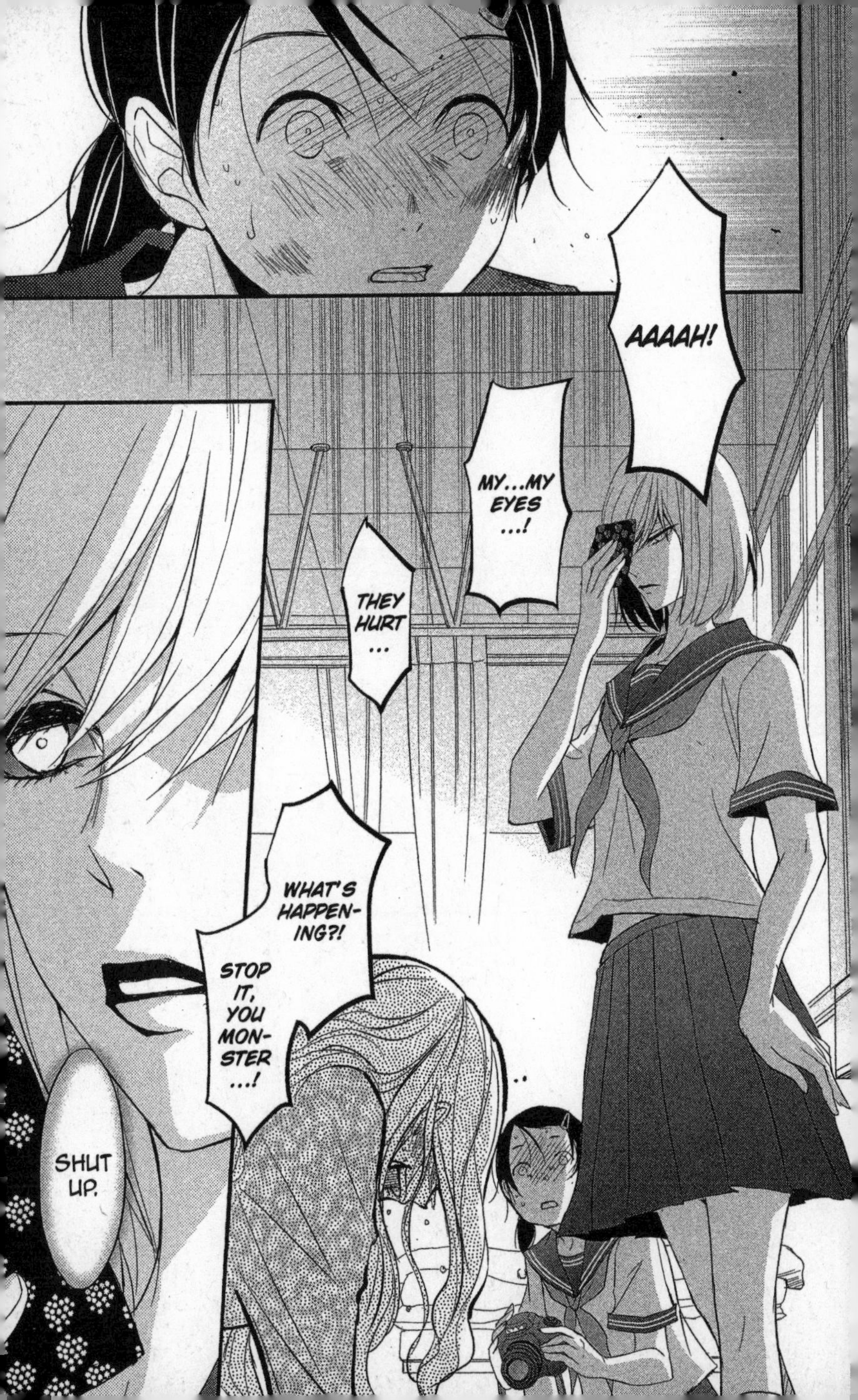
AAAAH!
MY...MY EYES...!
THEY HURT...
WHAT'S HAPPEN-ING?!
STOP IT, YOU MON-STER...!
..
SHUT UP.

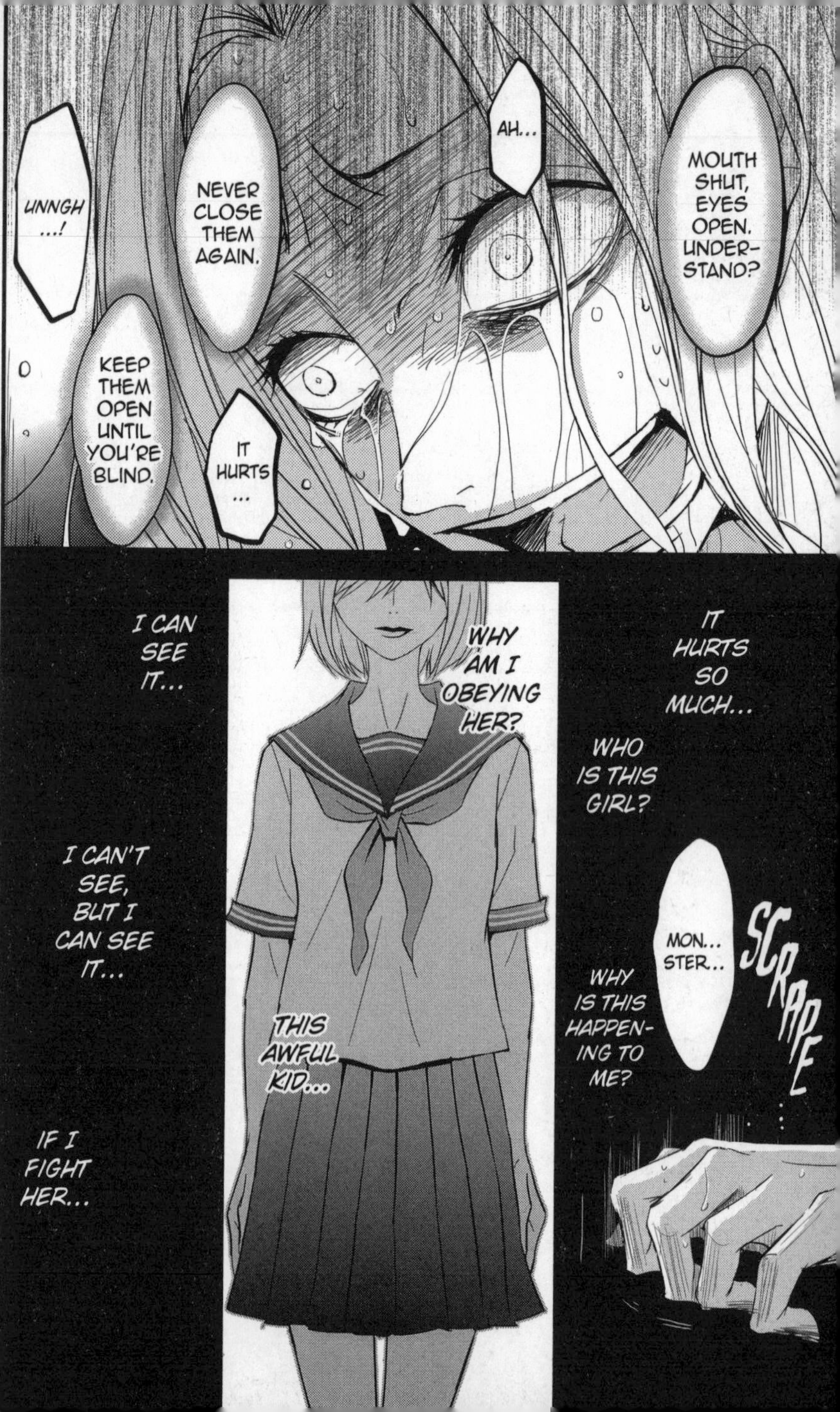
MOUTH SHUT, EYES OPEN. UNDERSTAND?
AH...
NEVER CLOSE THEM AGAIN.
UNNGH ...!
IT HURTS ...
KEEP THEM OPEN UNTIL YOU'RE BLIND.
IT HURTS SO MUCH...
WHO IS THIS GIRL?
MON... STER...
SCRAPE...
WHY IS THIS HAPPENING TO ME?
WHY AM I OBEYING HER?
THIS AWFUL KID...
I CAN SEE IT...
I CAN'T SEE, BUT I CAN SEE IT...
IF I FIGHT HER...

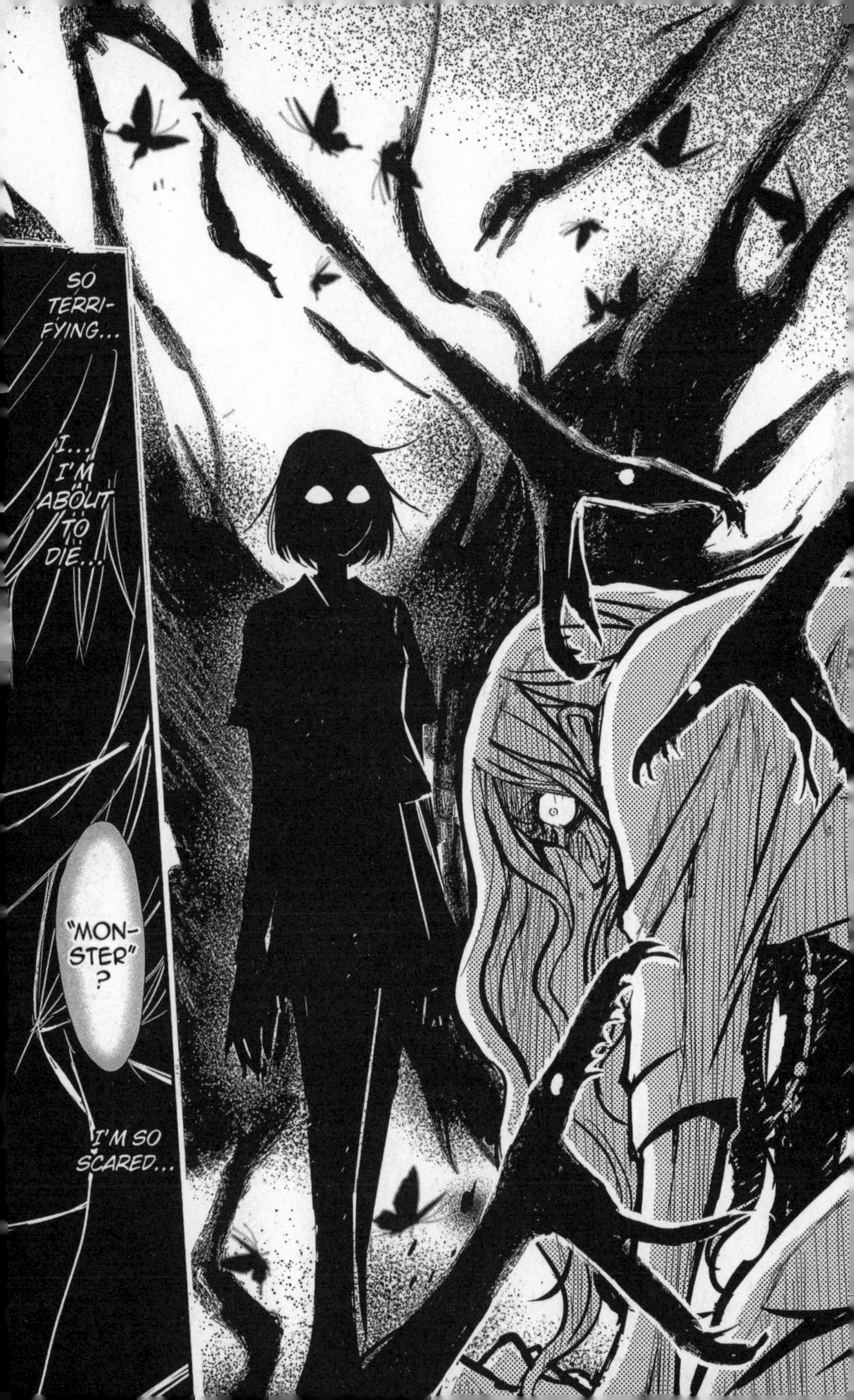
SO TERRI-FYING...
I... I'M ABOUT TO DIE...
"MON-STER"?
I'M SO SCARED...

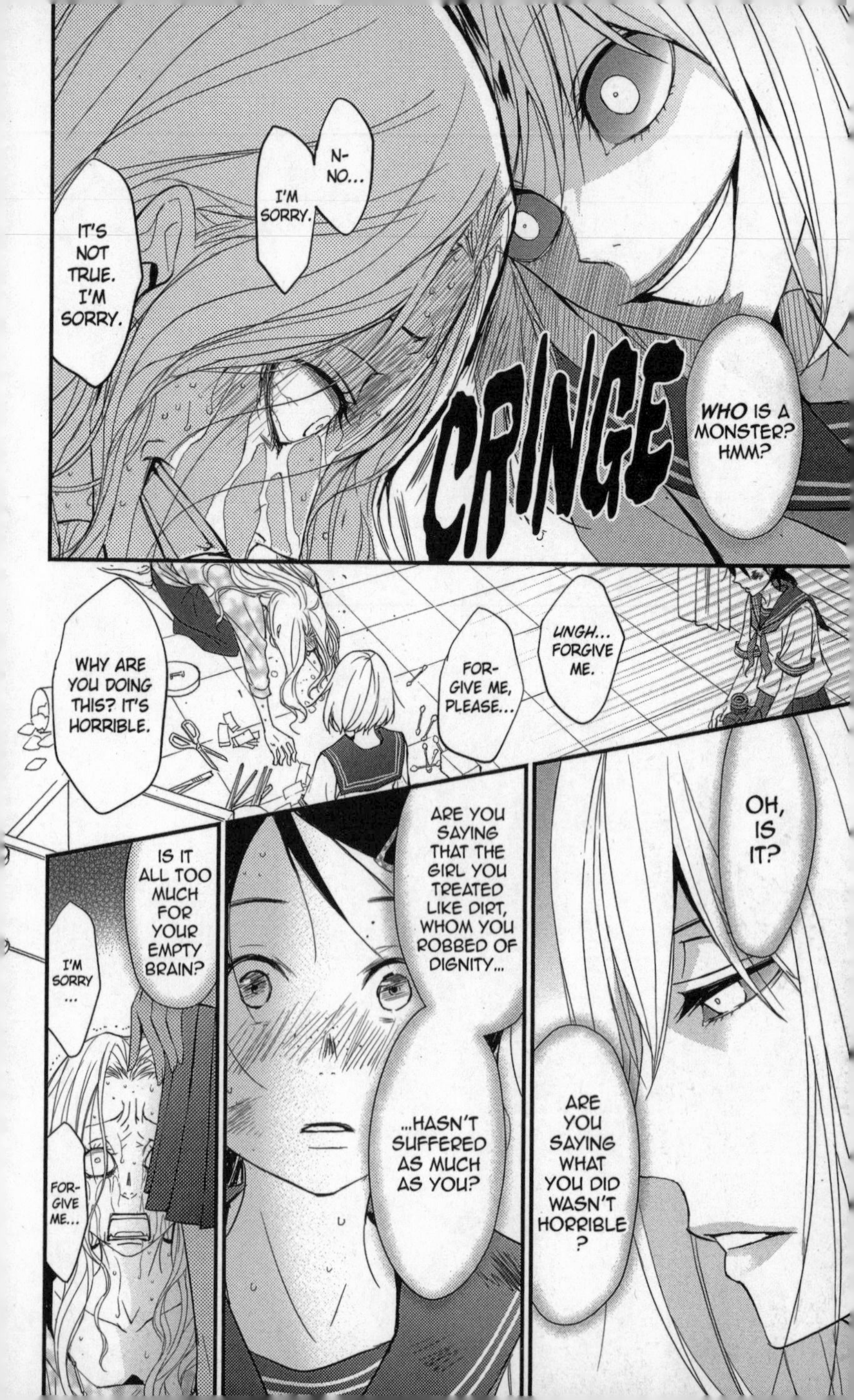
WHO IS A MONSTER? HMM?
CRINGE
N-NO... I'M SORRY.
IT'S NOT TRUE. I'M SORRY.
UNGH... FORGIVE ME.
FOR-GIVE ME, PLEASE...
WHY ARE YOU DOING THIS? IT'S HORRIBLE.
OH, IS IT?
ARE YOU SAYING WHAT YOU DID WASN'T HORRIBLE?
ARE YOU SAYING THAT THE GIRL YOU TREATED LIKE DIRT, WHOM YOU ROBBED OF DIGNITY...
...HASN'T SUFFERED AS MUCH AS YOU?
IS IT ALL TOO MUCH FOR YOUR EMPTY BRAIN?
I'M SORRY...
FOR-GIVE ME...

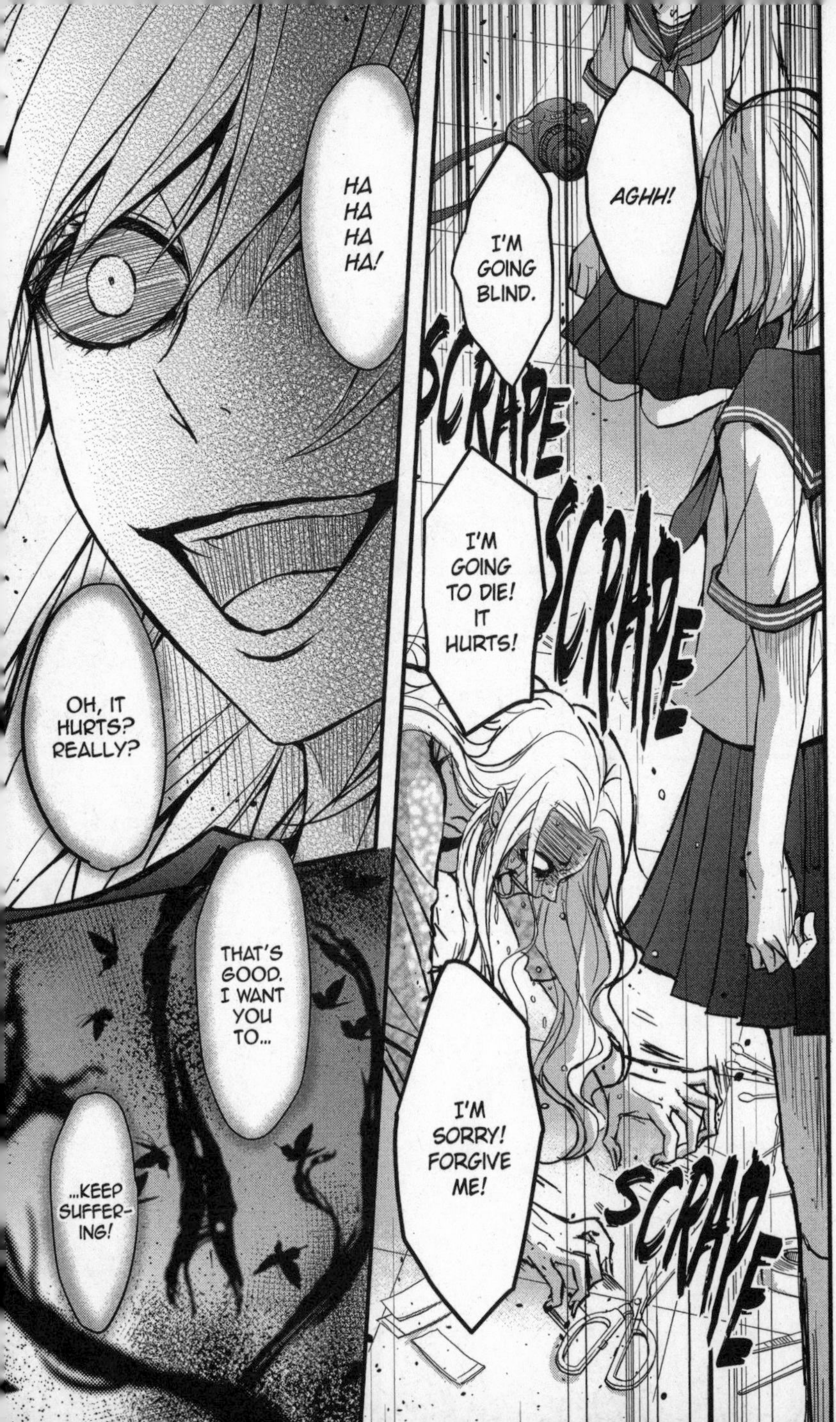
AGHH!
I'M GOING BLIND.
SCRAPE
SCRAPE
I'M GOING TO DIE! IT HURTS!
I'M SORRY! FORGIVE ME!
SCRAPE
HA HA HA HA!
OH, IT HURTS? REALLY?
THAT'S GOOD. I WANT YOU TO...
...KEEP SUFFER-ING!

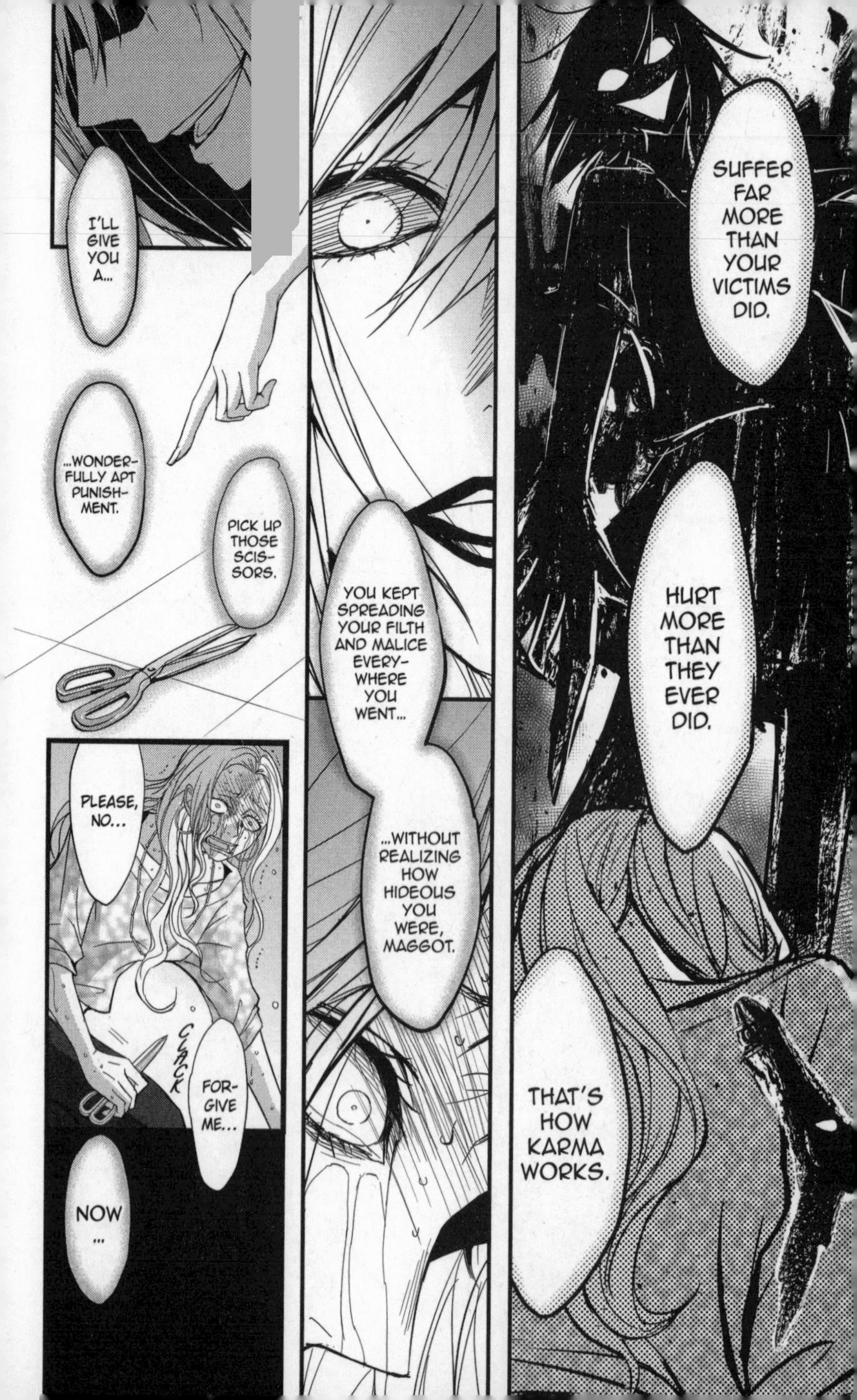
SUFFER FAR MORE THAN YOUR VICTIMS DID.
HURT MORE THAN THEY EVER DID.
THAT'S HOW KARMA WORKS.
YOU KEPT SPREADING YOUR FILTH AND MALICE EVERY-WHERE YOU WENT...
...WITHOUT REALIZING HOW HIDEOUS YOU WERE, MAGGOT.
I'LL GIVE YOU A...
...WONDER-FULLY APT PUNISH-MENT.
PICK UP THOSE SCIS-SORS.
PLEASE, NO...
CLACK
FOR-GIVE ME...
NOW...

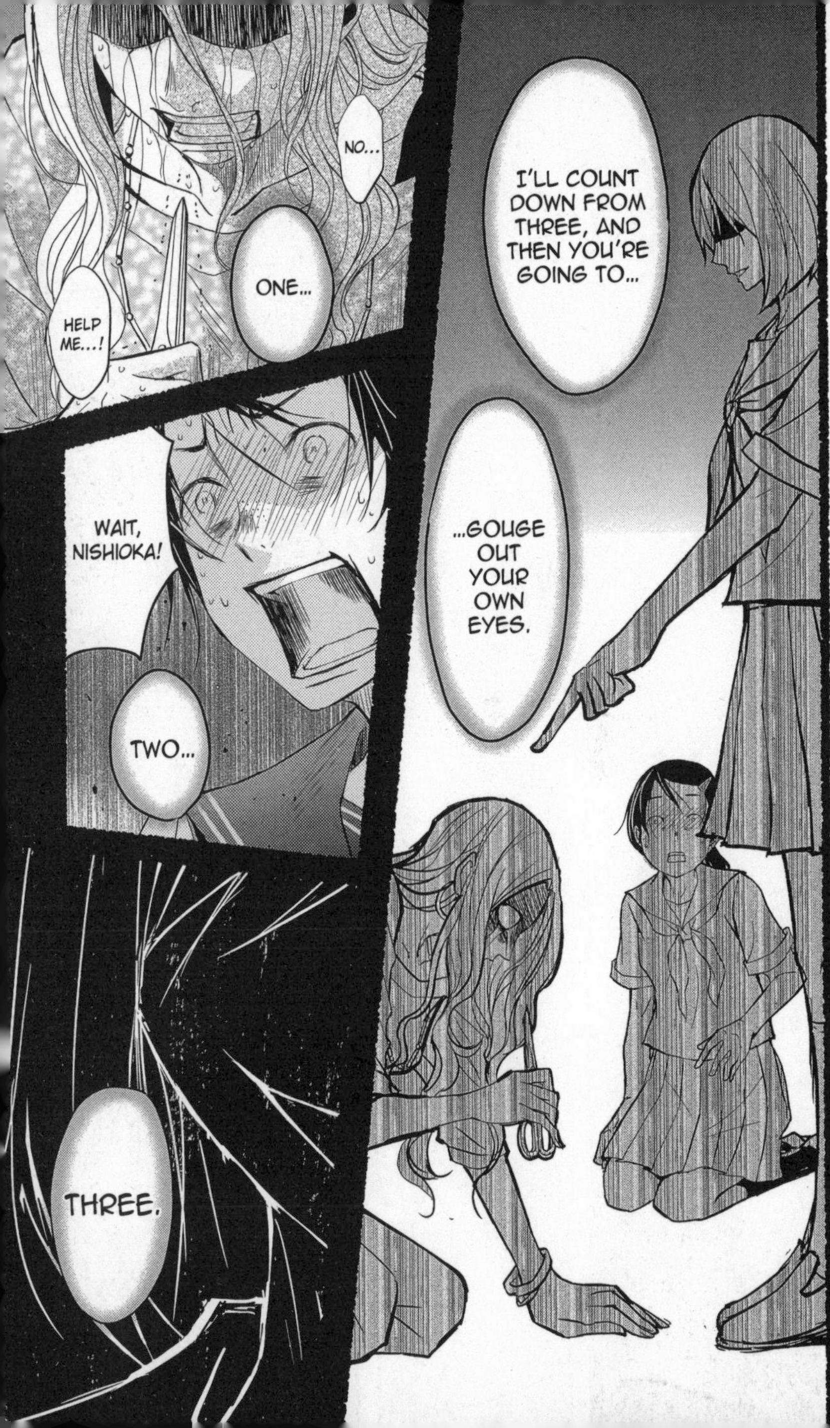
I'LL COUNT DOWN FROM THREE, AND THEN YOU'RE GOING TO...
...GOUGE OUT YOUR OWN EYES.
NO...
ONE...
HELP ME...!
WAIT, NISHIOKA!
TWO...
THREE.

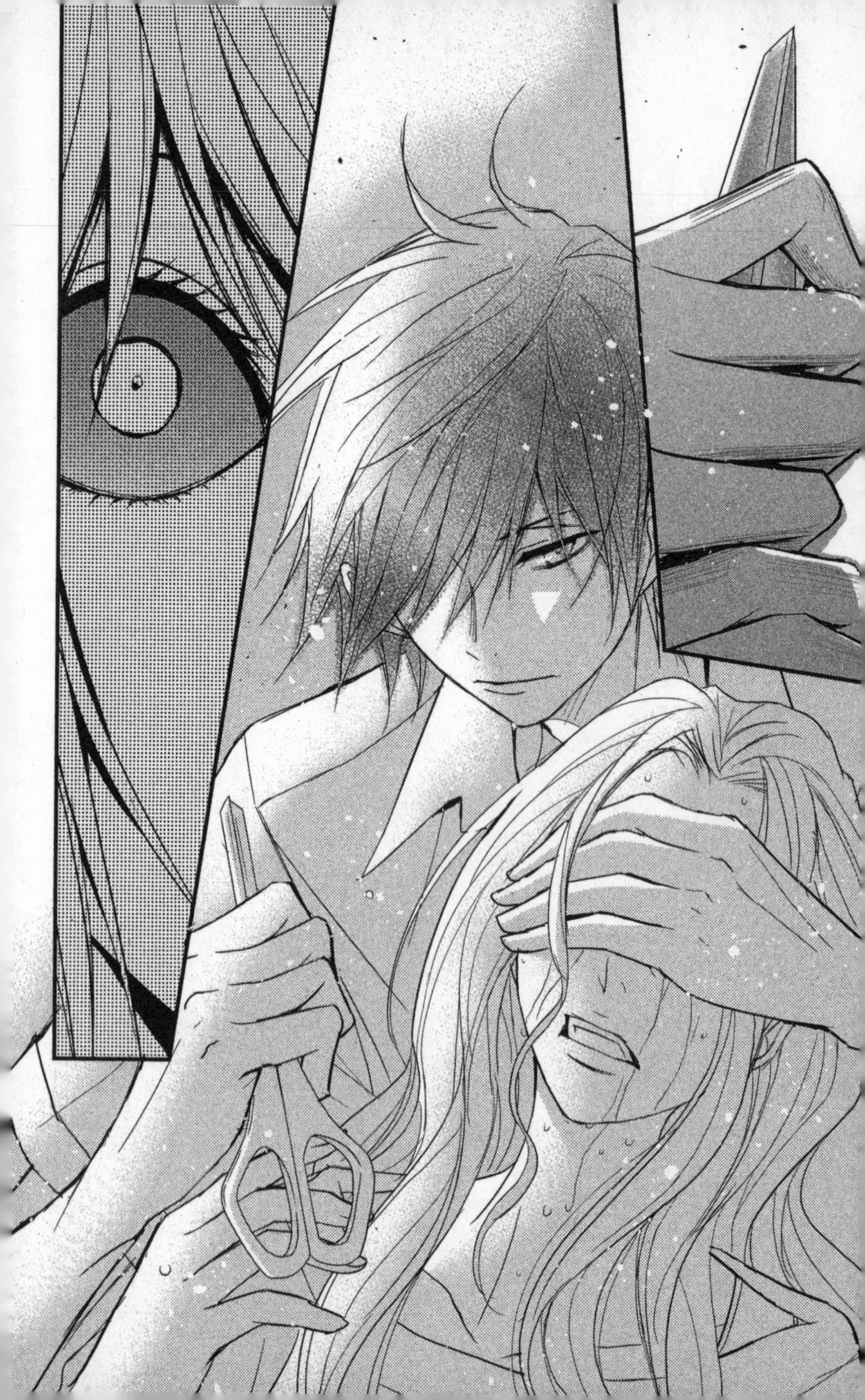

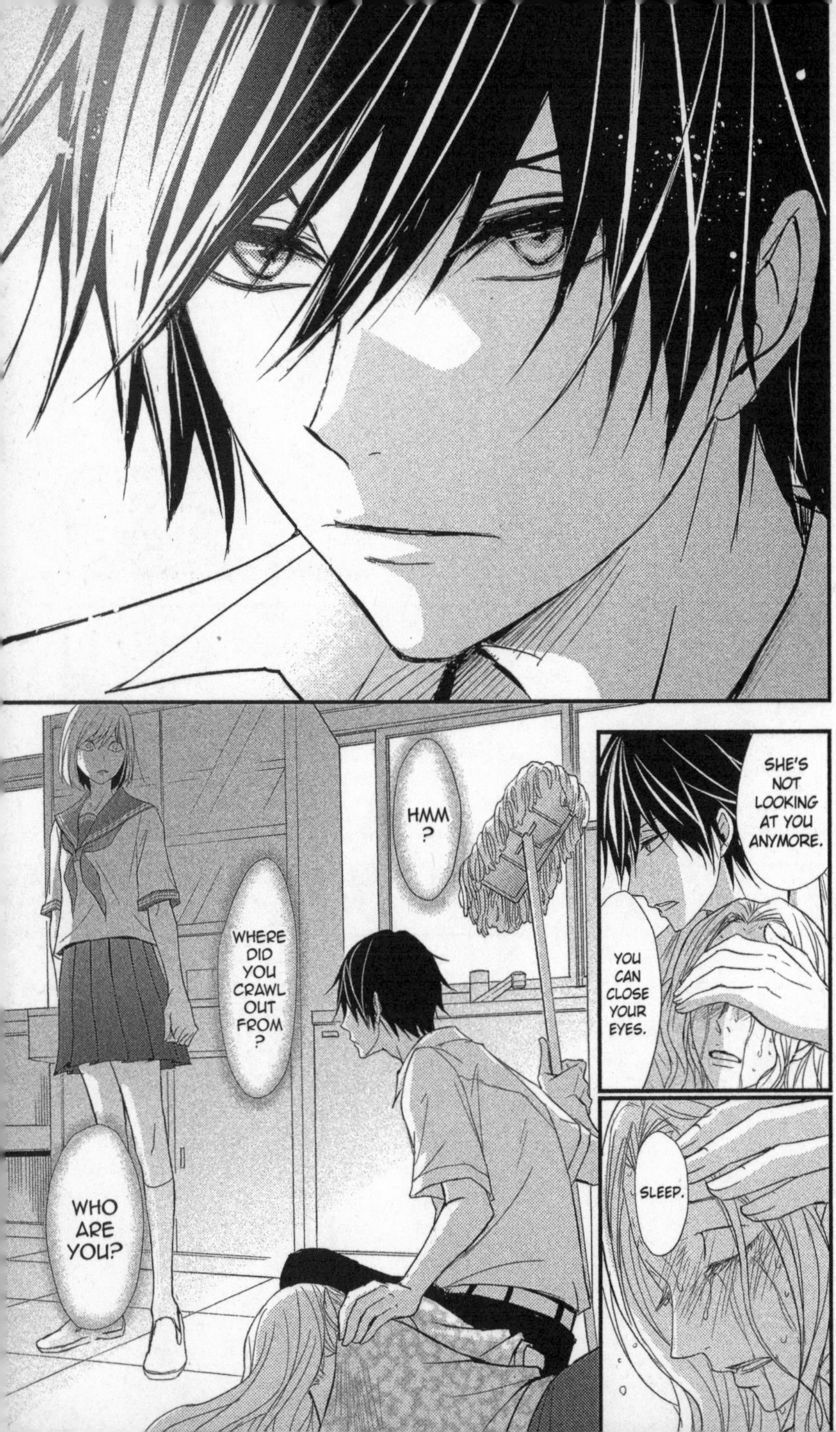

SHE'S NOT LOOKING AT YOU ANYMORE.
YOU CAN CLOSE YOUR EYES.
SLEEP.
HMM?
WHERE DID YOU CRAWL OUT FROM?
WHO ARE YOU?

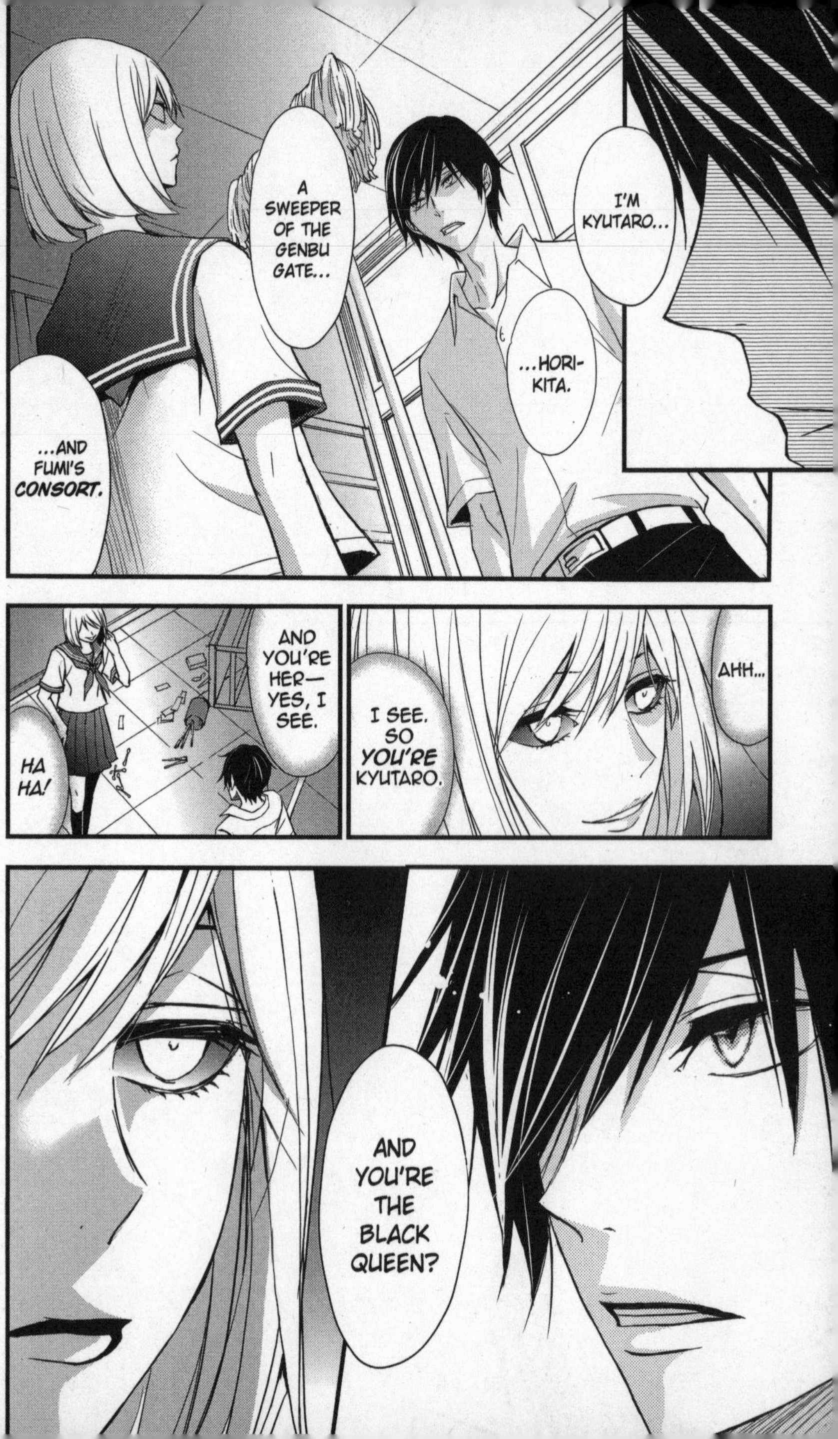
I'M KYUTARO...
...HORI-KITA.
A SWEEPER OF THE GENBU GATE...
...AND FUMI'S CONSORT.
AHH...
I SEE. SO YOU'RE KYUTARO.
AND YOU'RE HER— YES, I SEE.
HA HA!
AND YOU'RE THE BLACK QUEEN?

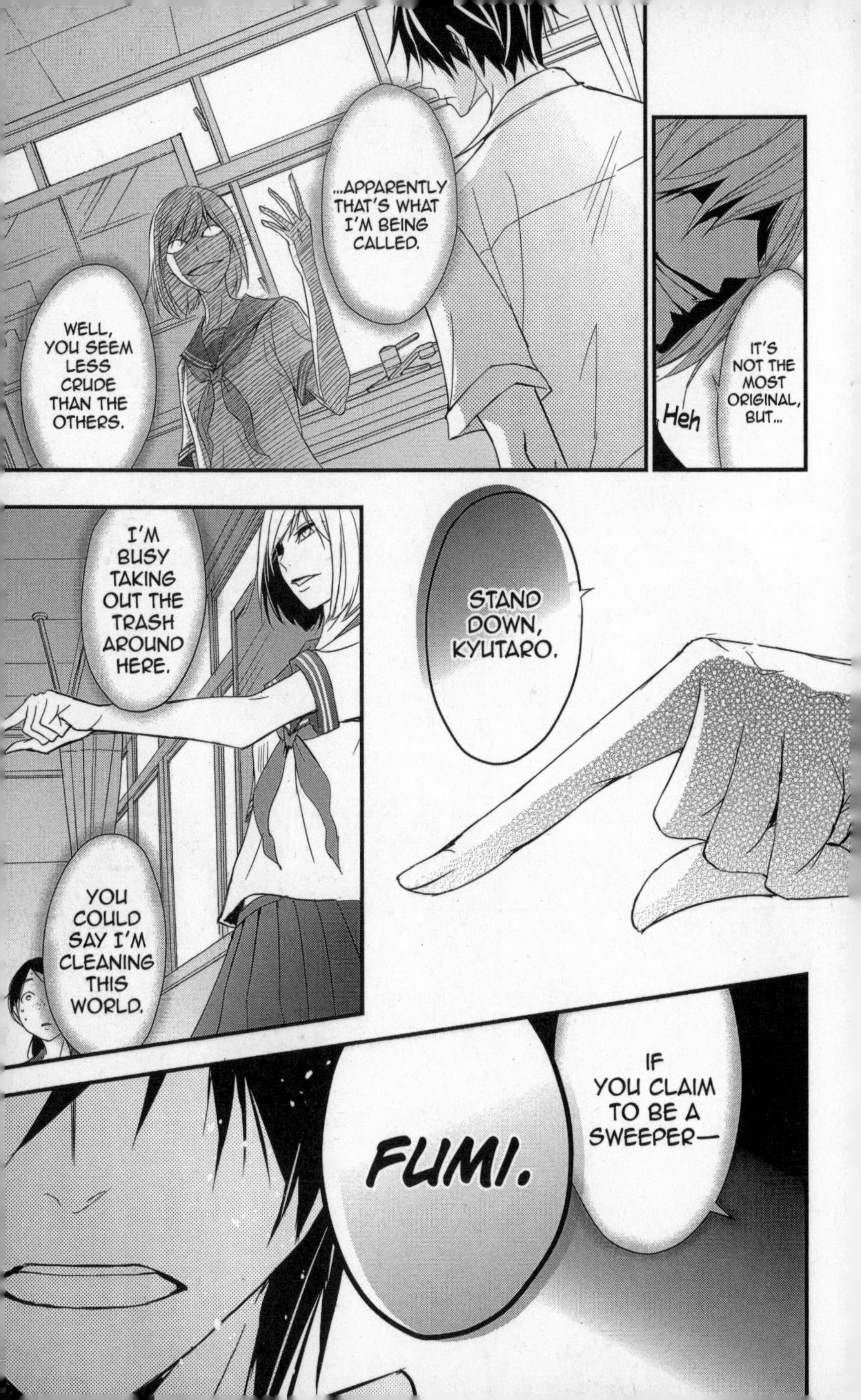
Heh
IT'S NOT THE MOST ORIGINAL, BUT...
...APPARENTLY THAT'S WHAT I'M BEING CALLED.
WELL, YOU SEEM LESS CRUDE THAN THE OTHERS.
STAND DOWN, KYUTARO.
I'M BUSY TAKING OUT THE TRASH AROUND HERE.
YOU COULD SAY I'M CLEANING THIS WORLD.
IF YOU CLAIM TO BE A SWEEPER—
FUMI.

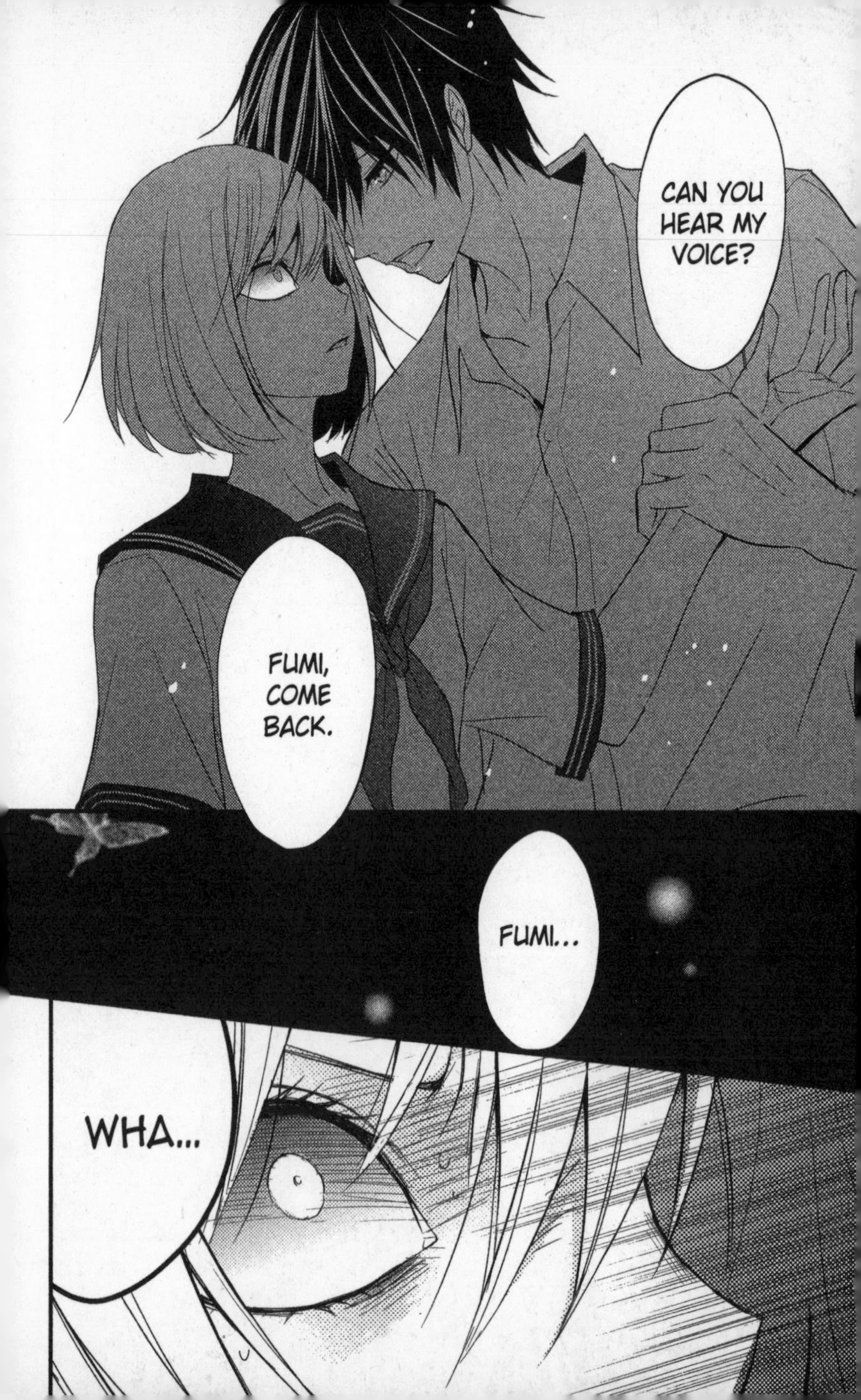
CAN YOU HEAR MY VOICE?
FUMI, COME BACK.
FUMI...
WHA...

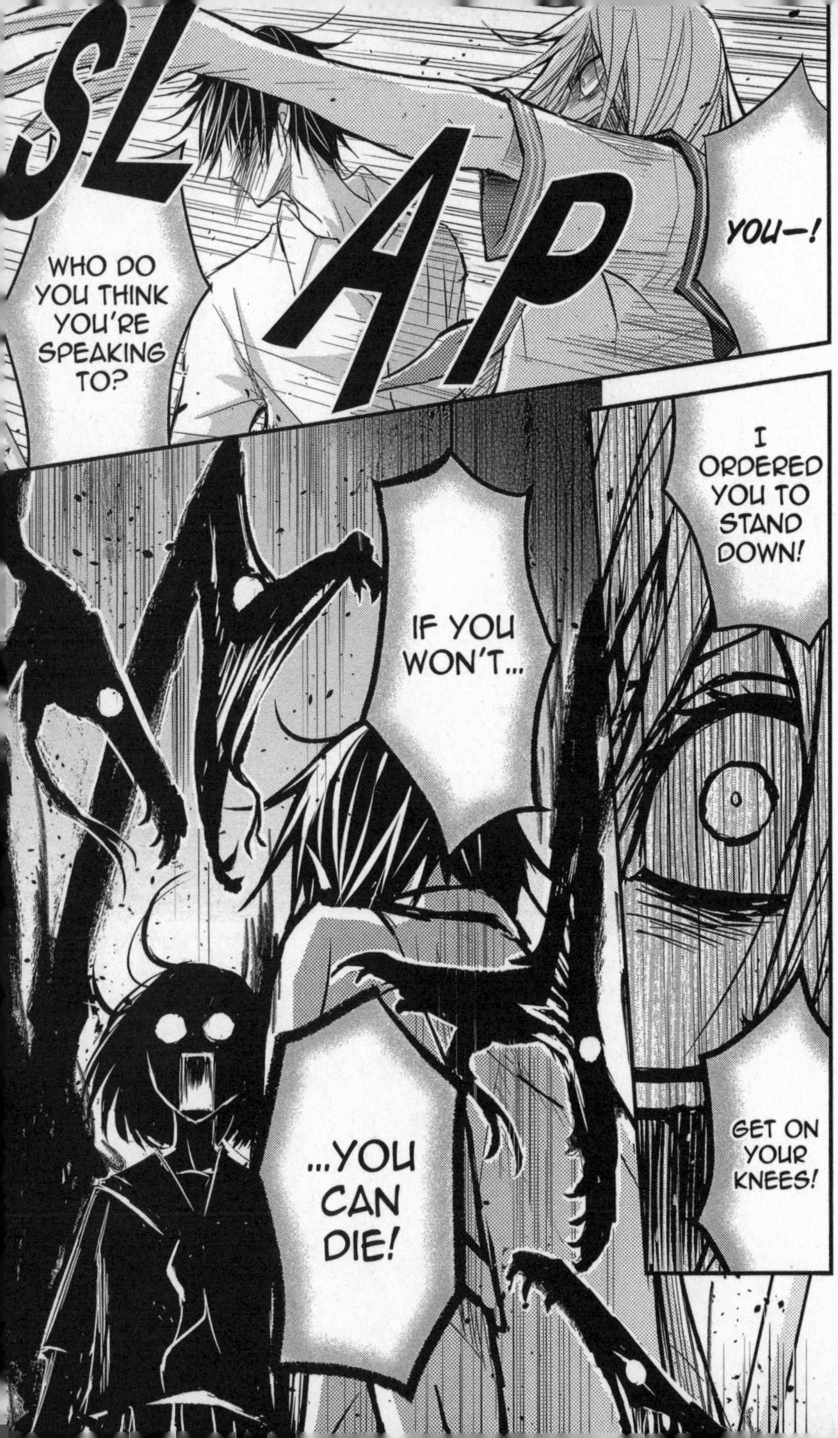
YOU—!
SLAP
WHO DO YOU THINK YOU'RE SPEAKING TO?
I ORDERED YOU TO STAND DOWN!
GET ON YOUR KNEES!
IF YOU WON'T...
...YOU CAN DIE!

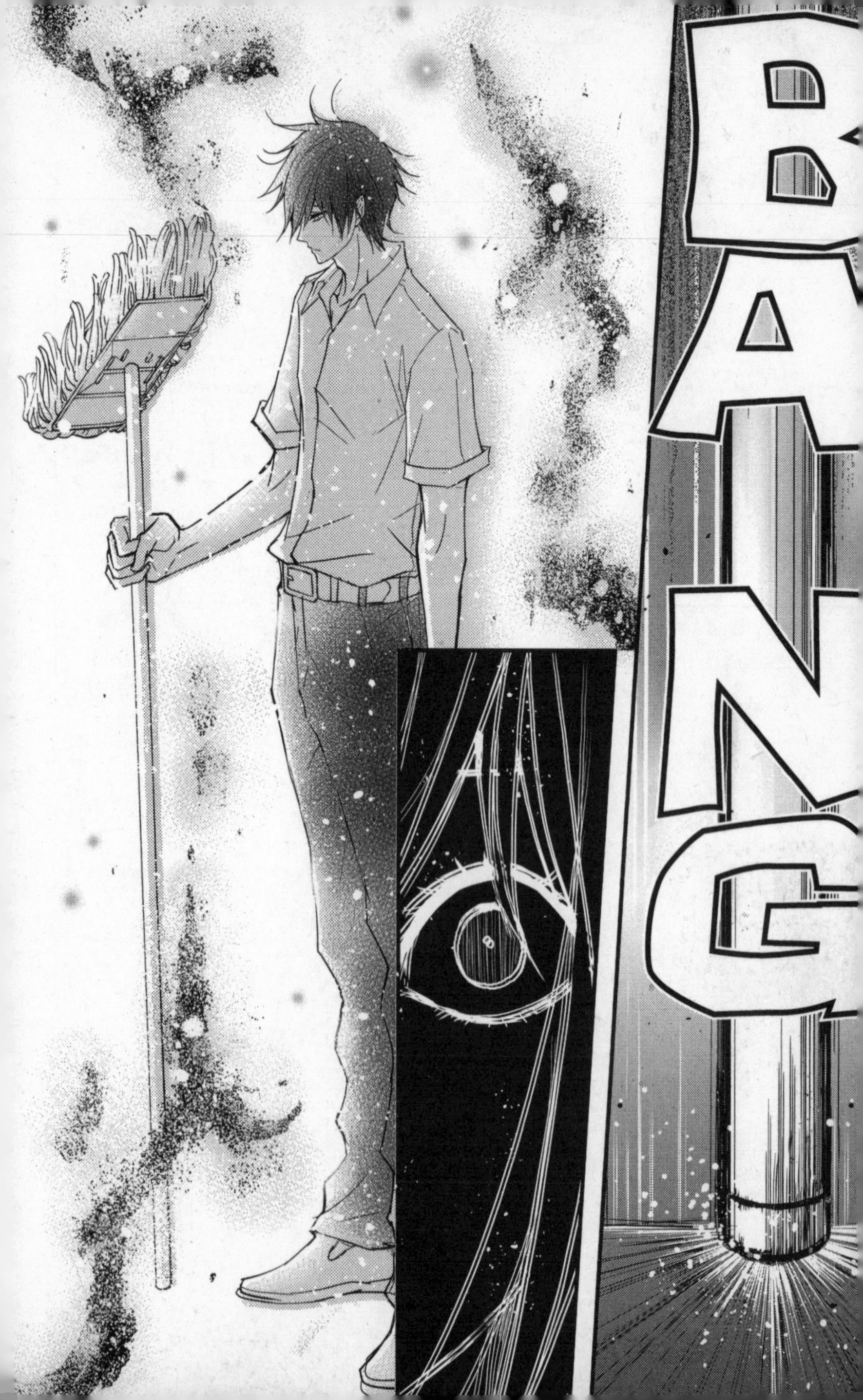
BANG

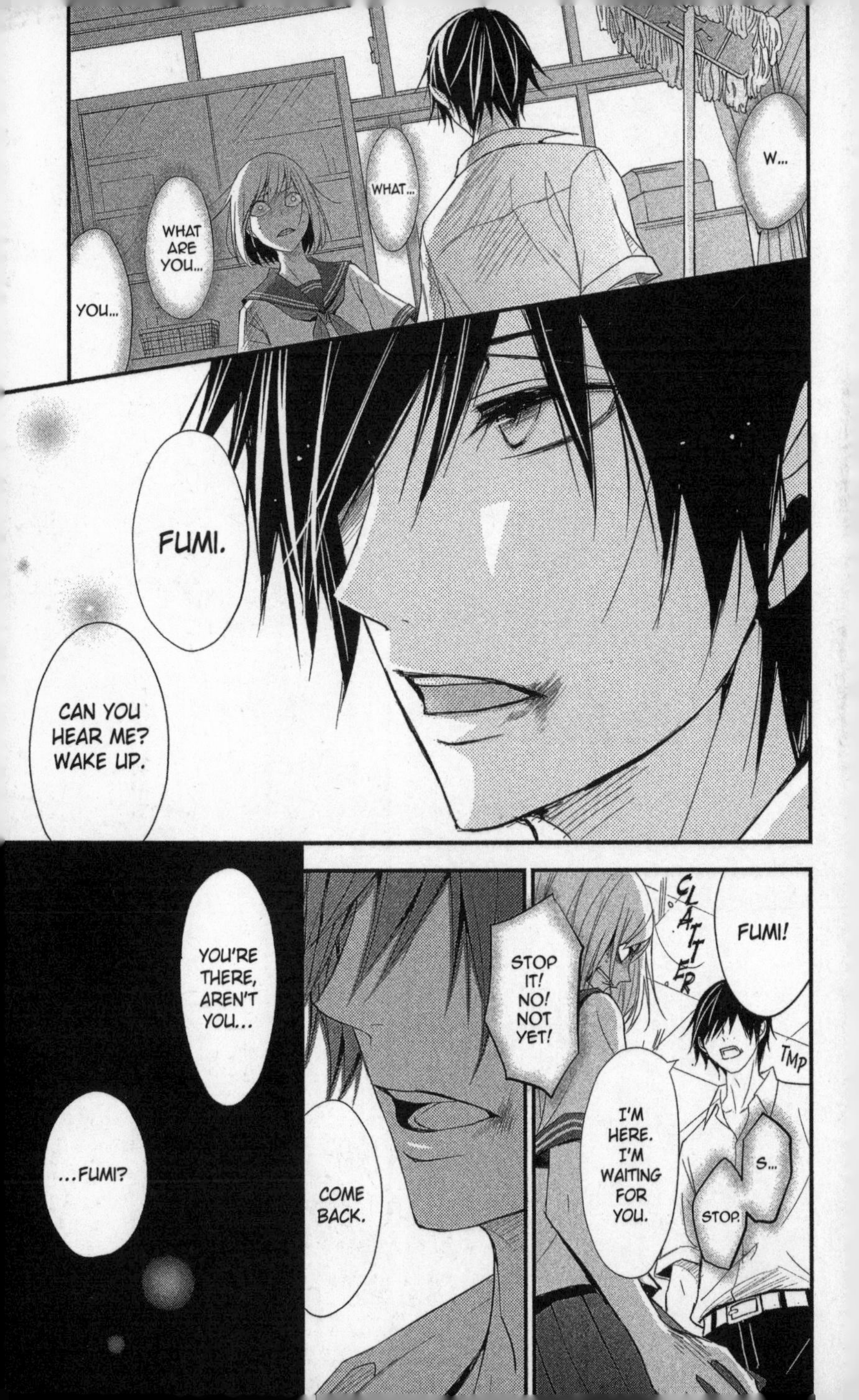
W...
WHAT...
WHAT ARE YOU...
YOU...
FUMI.
CAN YOU HEAR ME? WAKE UP.
FUMI!
CLATTER
STOP IT! NO! NOT YET!
TMP
I'M HERE. I'M WAITING FOR YOU.
S...
STOP.
COME BACK.
YOU'RE THERE, AREN'T YOU...
...FUMI?

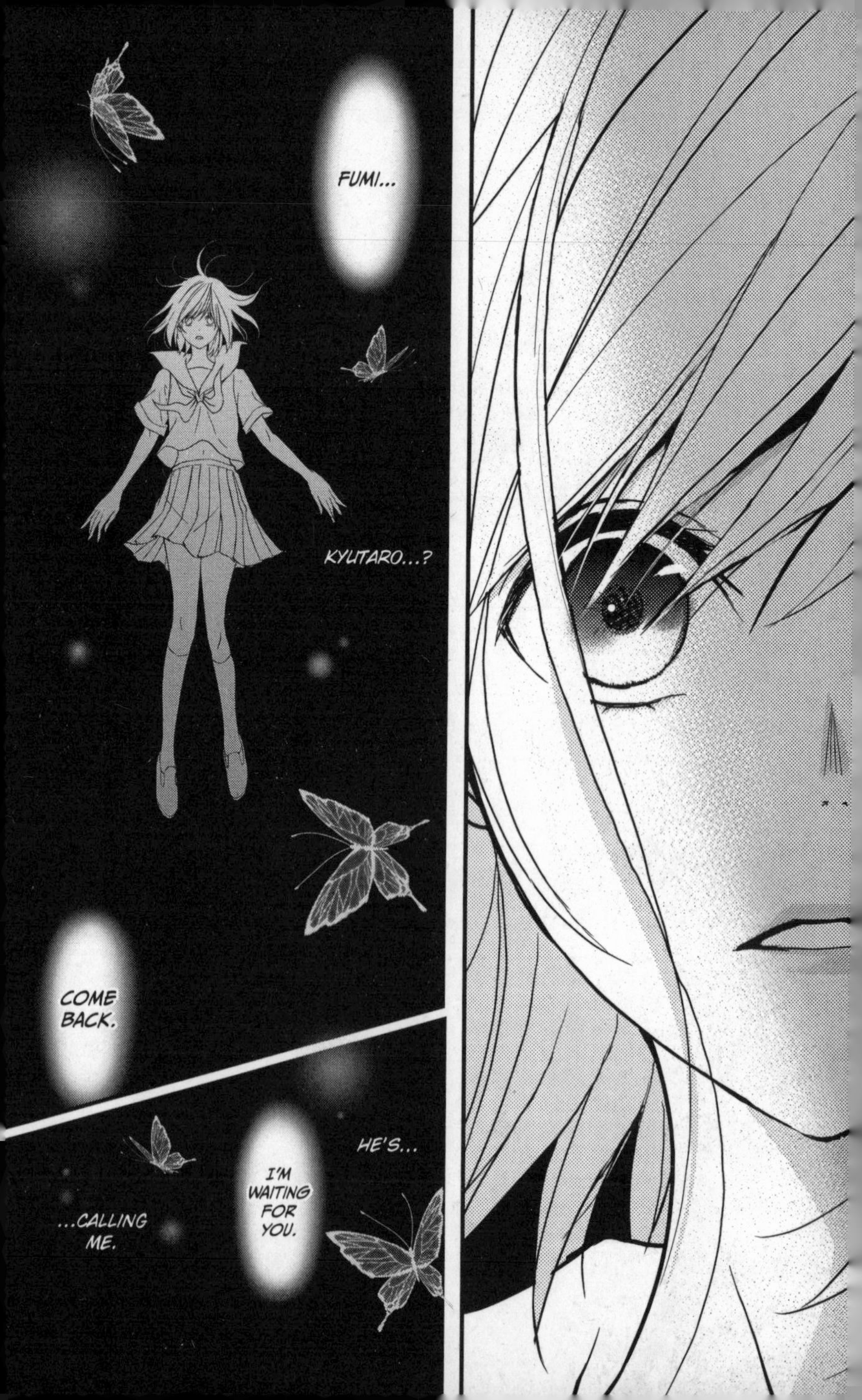
FUMI...
KYUTARO...?
COME BACK.
HE'S...
I'M WAITING FOR YOU.
...CALLING ME.

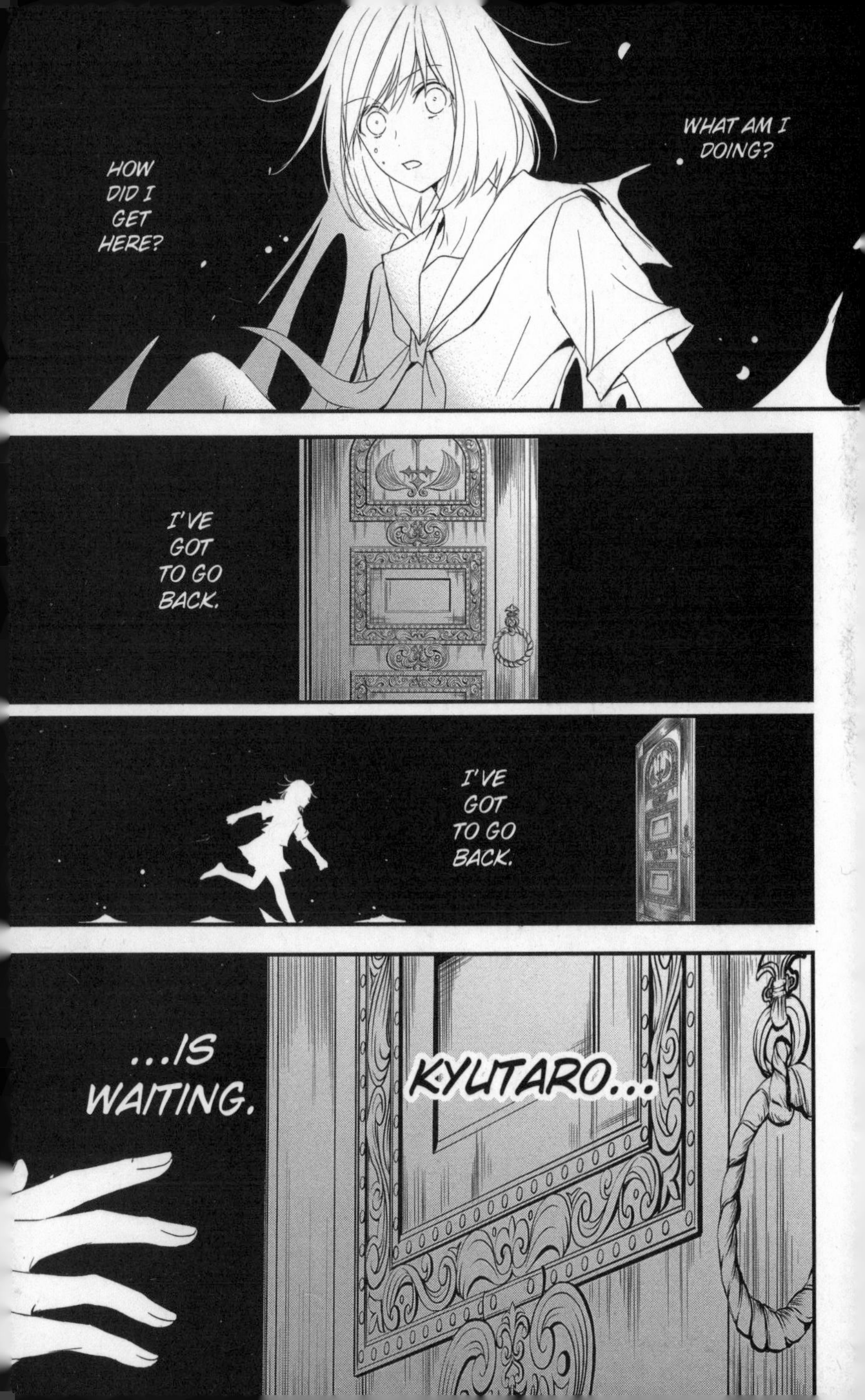
WHAT AM I DOING?
HOW DID I GET HERE?
I'VE GOT TO GO BACK.
I'VE GOT TO GO BACK.
KYUTARO...
...IS WAITING.

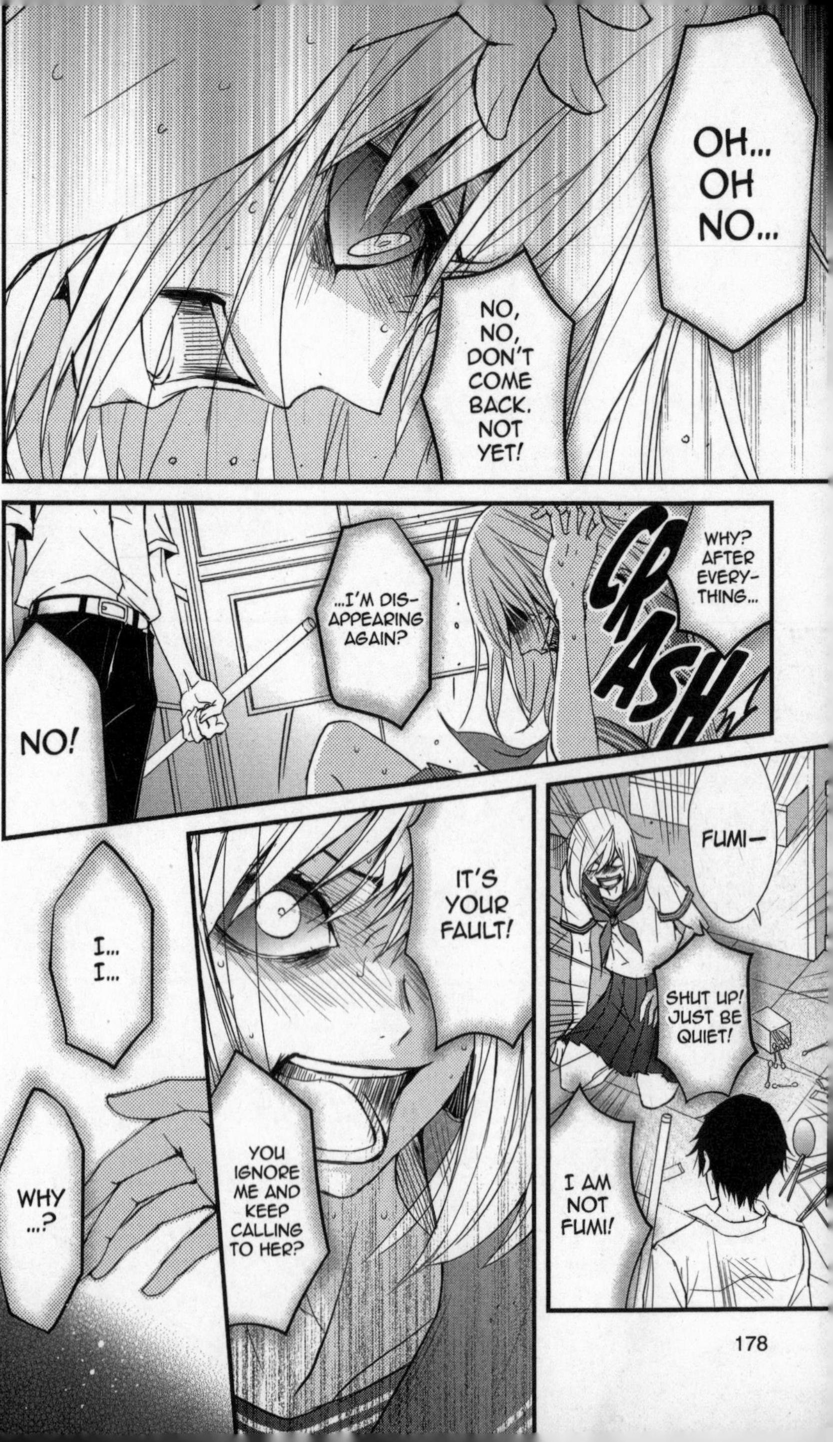
OH... OH NO...
NO, NO, DON'T COME BACK. NOT YET!
WHY? AFTER EVERYTHING...
CRASH
...I'M DISAPPEARING AGAIN?
NO!
FUMI—
SHUT UP! JUST BE QUIET!
I AM NOT FUMI!
IT'S YOUR FAULT!
I... I...
YOU IGNORE ME AND KEEP CALLING TO HER?
WHY ...?

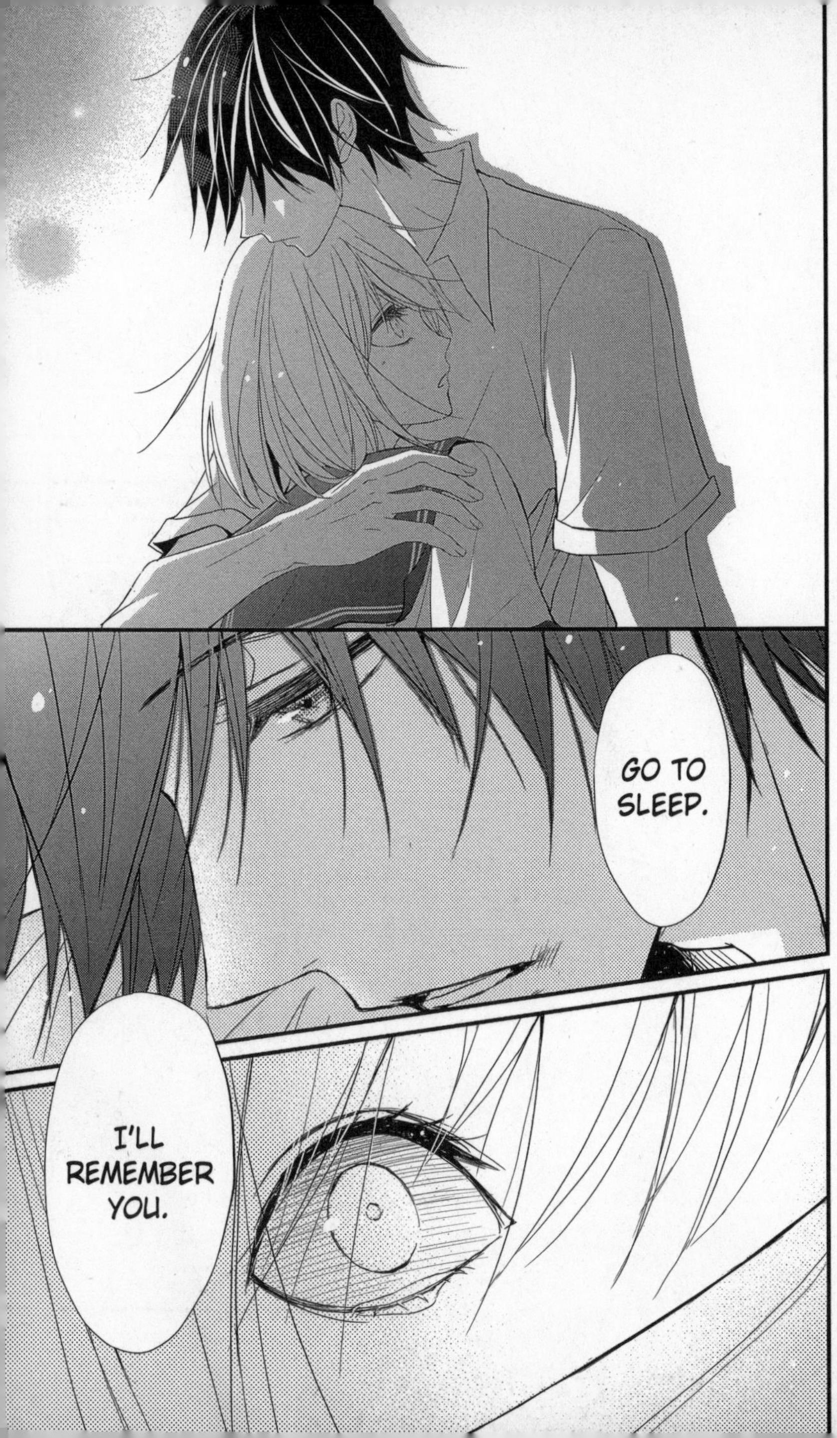
GO TO SLEEP.
I'LL REMEMBER YOU.

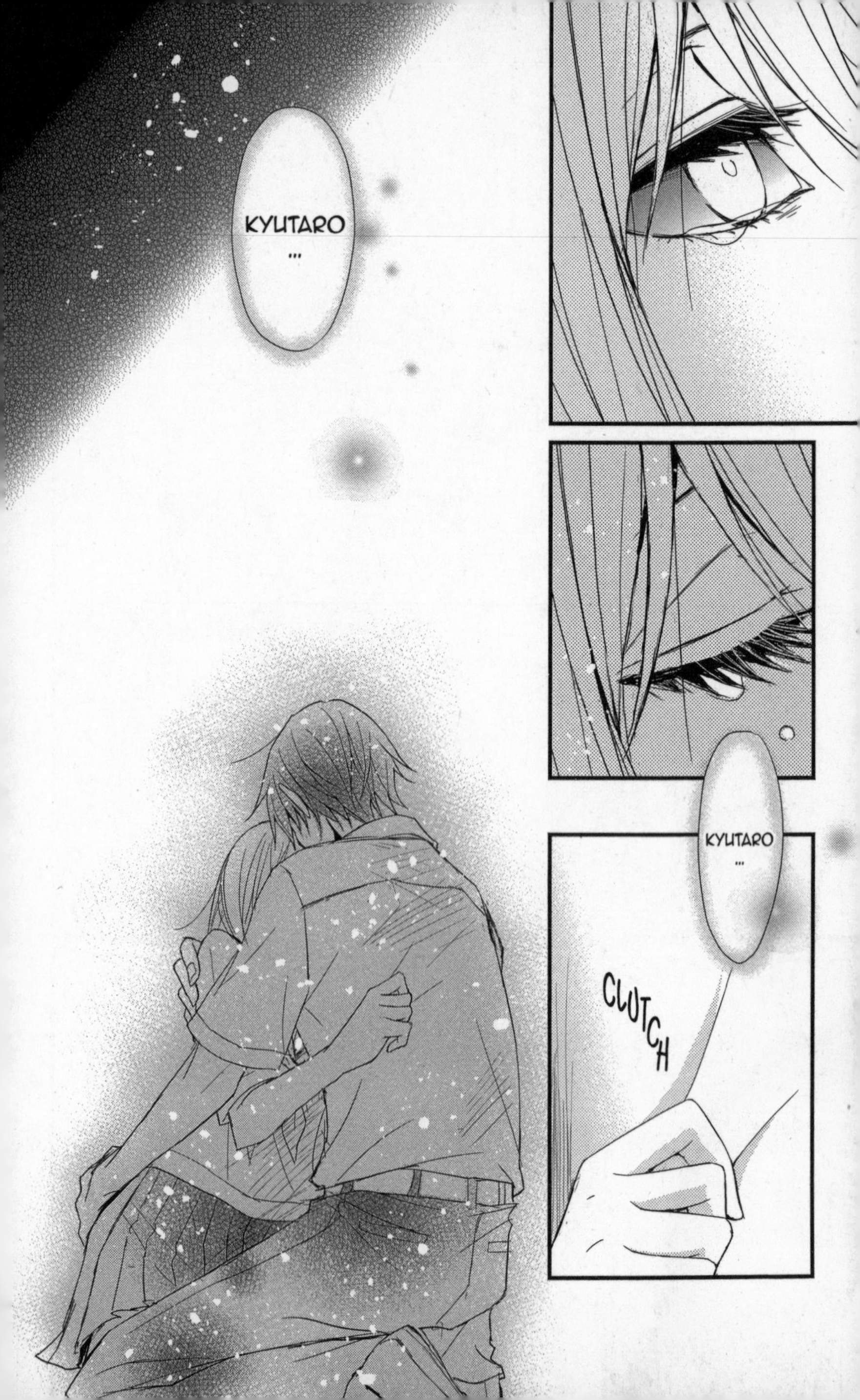
KYUTARO ...
CLUTCH
KYUTARO ...

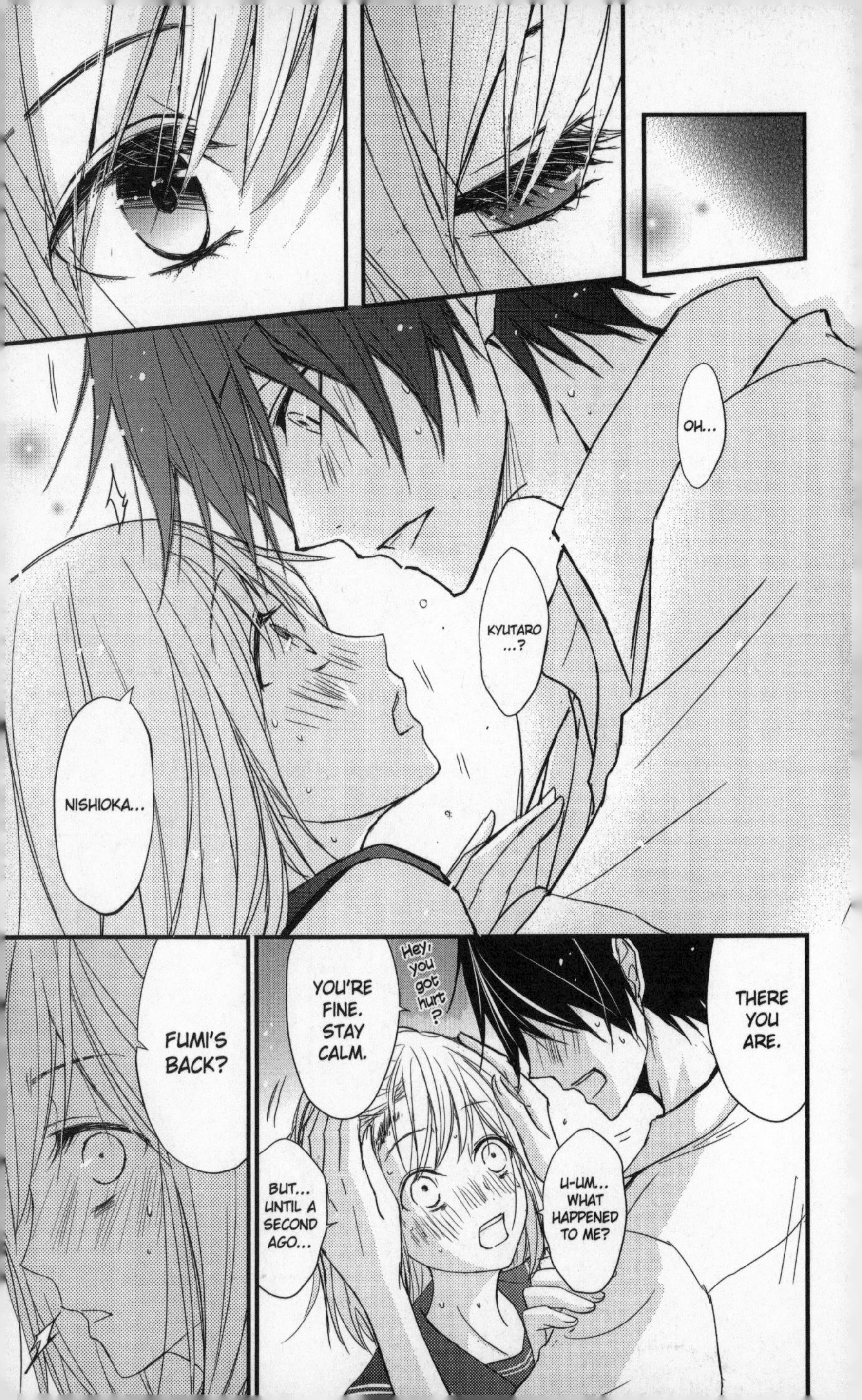
OH...
KYUTARO ...?
NISHIOKA...
THERE YOU ARE.
Hey, you got hurt?
YOU'RE FINE. STAY CALM.
U-UM... WHAT HAPPENED TO ME?
BUT... UNTIL A SECOND AGO...
FUMI'S BACK?

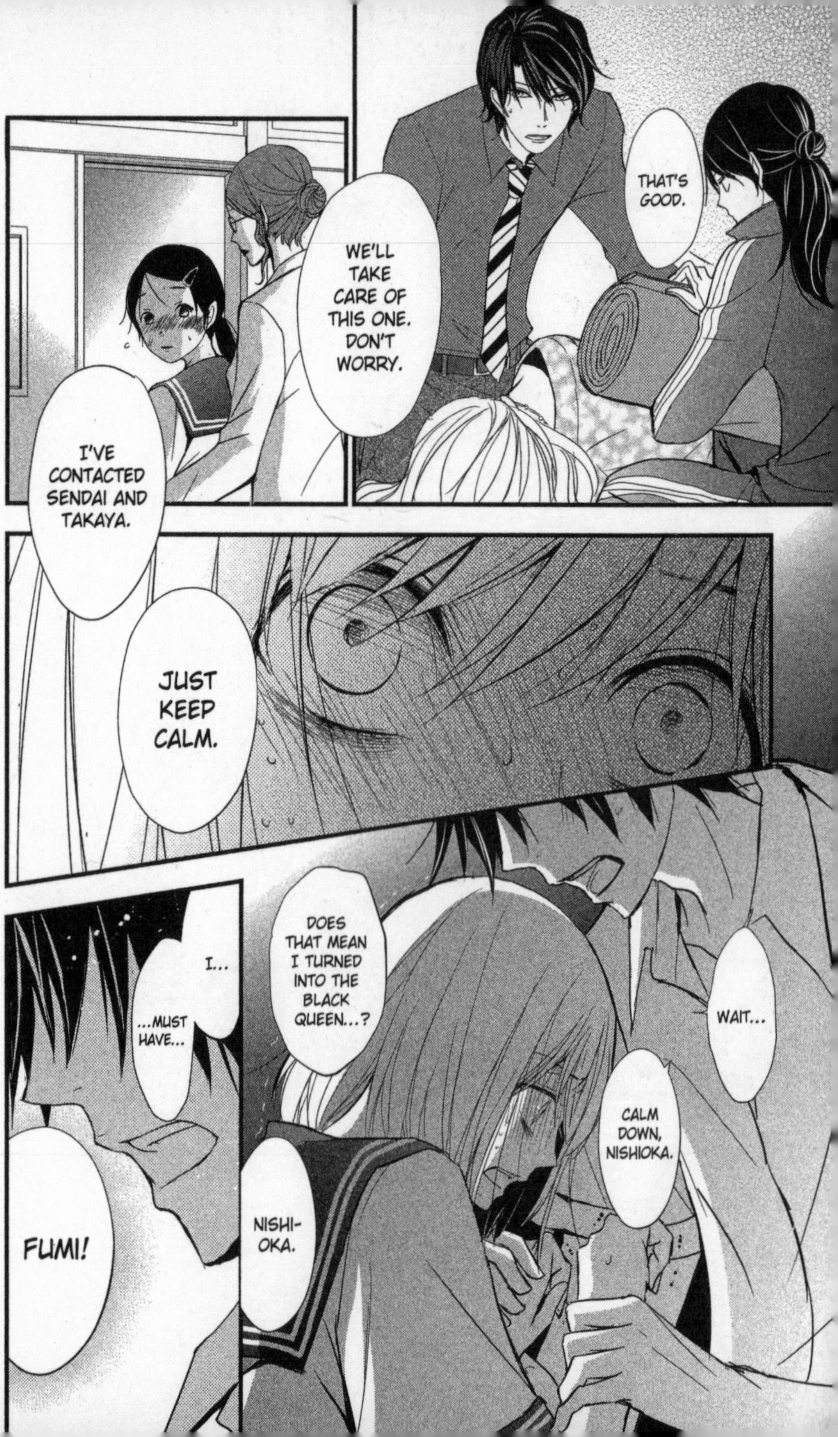
THAT'S GOOD.
WE'LL TAKE CARE OF THIS ONE. DON'T WORRY.
I'VE CONTACTED SENDAI AND TAKAYA.
JUST KEEP CALM.
WAIT...
CALM DOWN, NISHIOKA.
DOES THAT MEAN I TURNED INTO THE BLACK QUEEN...?
NISHI-OKA.
I...
...MUST HAVE...
FUMI!

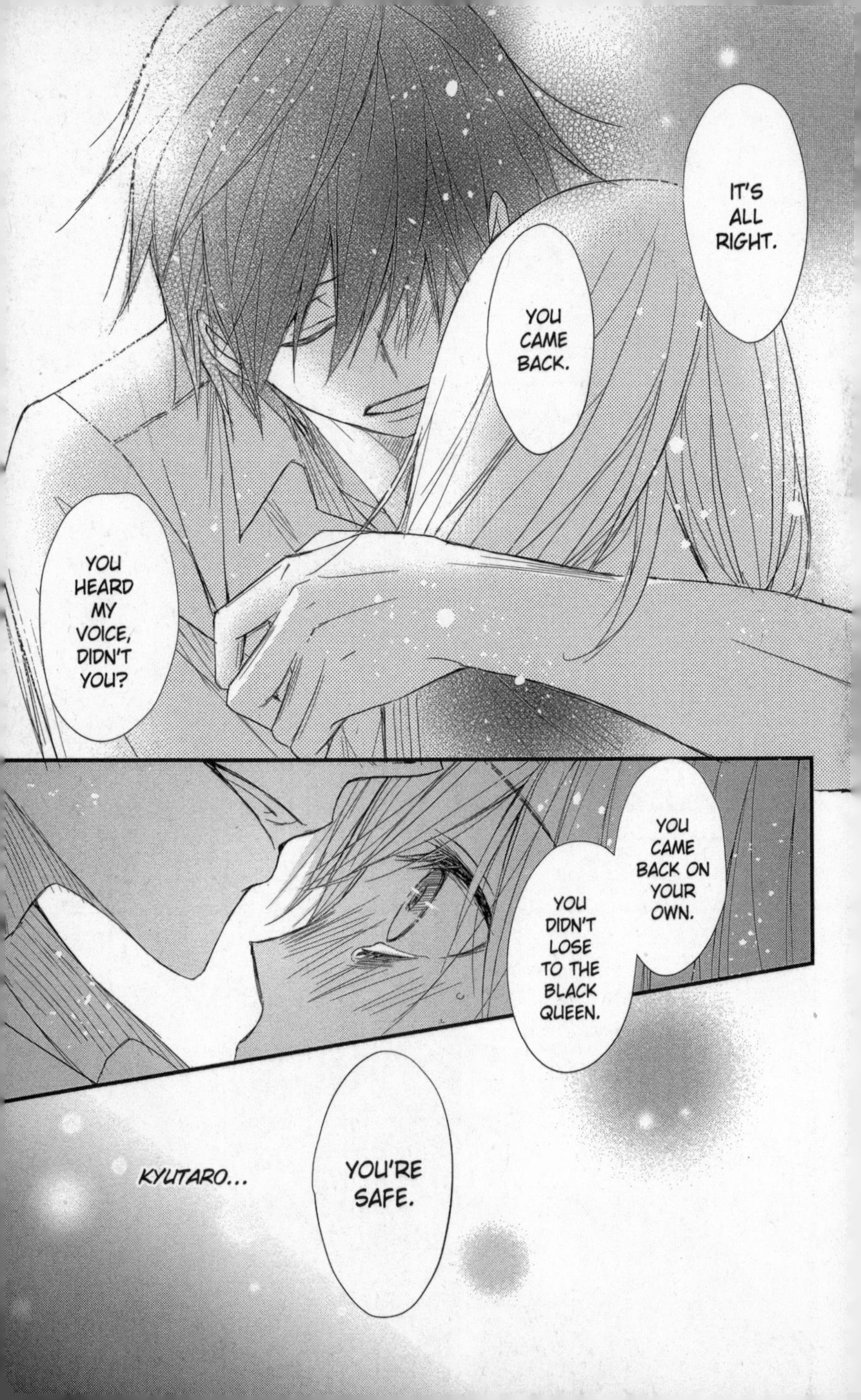
IT'S ALL RIGHT.
YOU CAME BACK.
YOU HEARD MY VOICE, DIDN'T YOU?
YOU CAME BACK ON YOUR OWN.
YOU DIDN'T LOSE TO THE BLACK QUEEN.
YOU'RE SAFE.
KYUTARO...

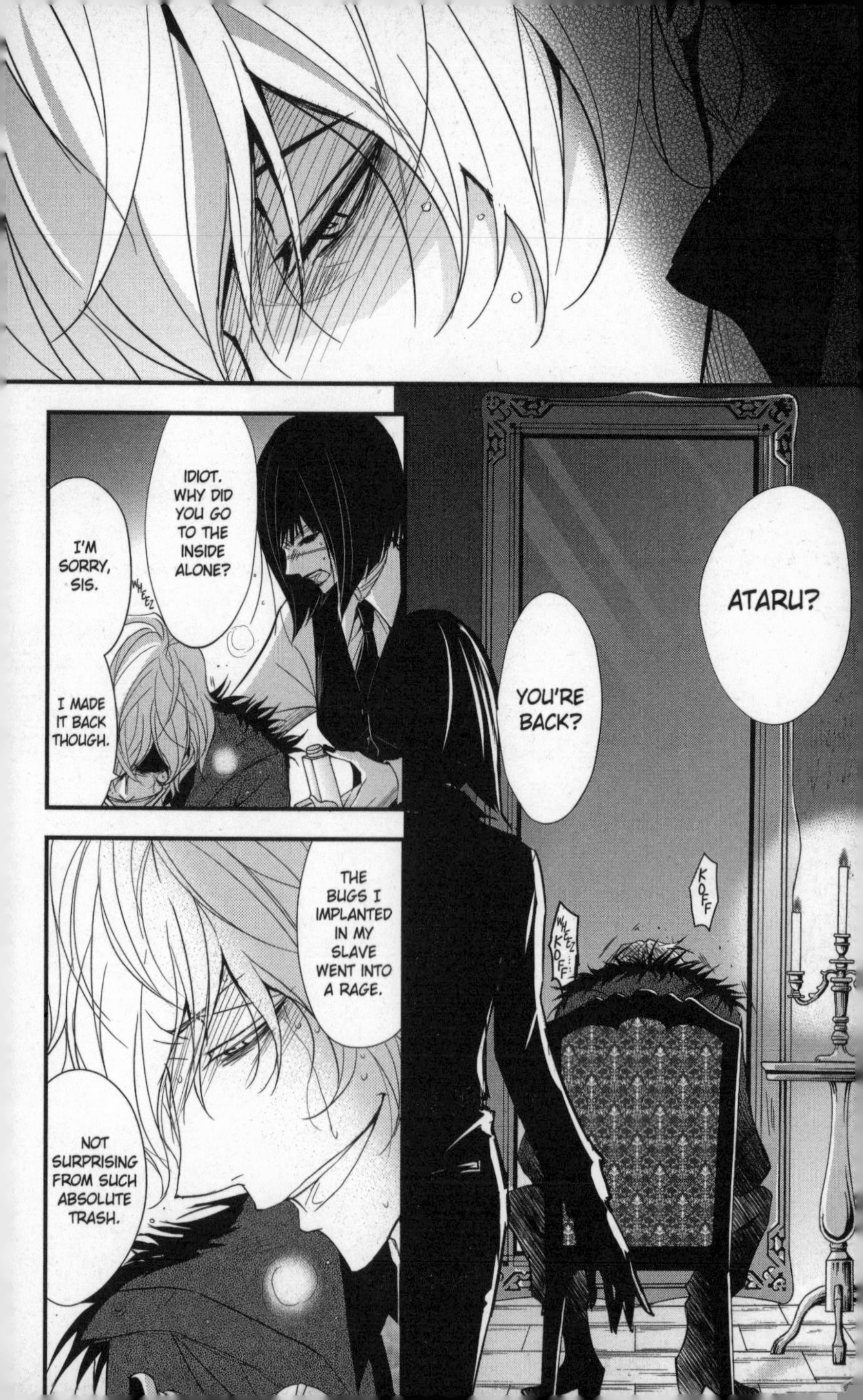
ATARU?
YOU'RE BACK?
KOFF
WHEEZ KOFF KOFF
IDIOT. WHY DID YOU GO TO THE INSIDE ALONE?
I'M SORRY, SIS.
WHEEZ
I MADE IT BACK THOUGH.
THE BUGS I IMPLANTED IN MY SLAVE WENT INTO A RAGE.
NOT SURPRISING FROM SUCH ABSOLUTE TRASH.

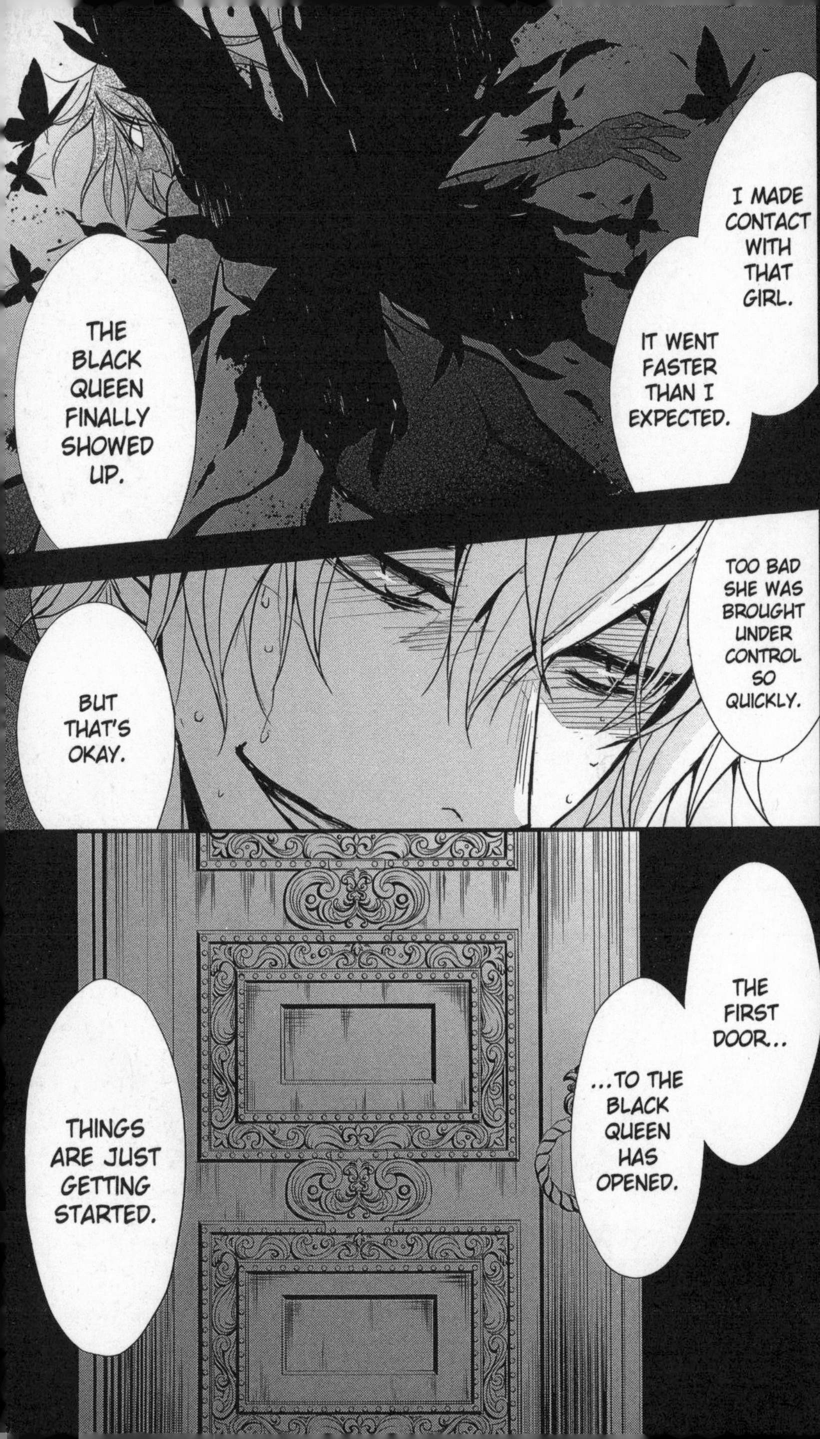
I MADE CONTACT WITH THAT GIRL.
IT WENT FASTER THAN I EXPECTED.
THE BLACK QUEEN FINALLY SHOWED UP.
TOO BAD SHE WAS BROUGHT UNDER CONTROL SO QUICKLY.
BUT THAT'S OKAY.
THE FIRST DOOR...
...TO THE BLACK QUEEN HAS OPENED.
THINGS ARE JUST GETTING STARTED.

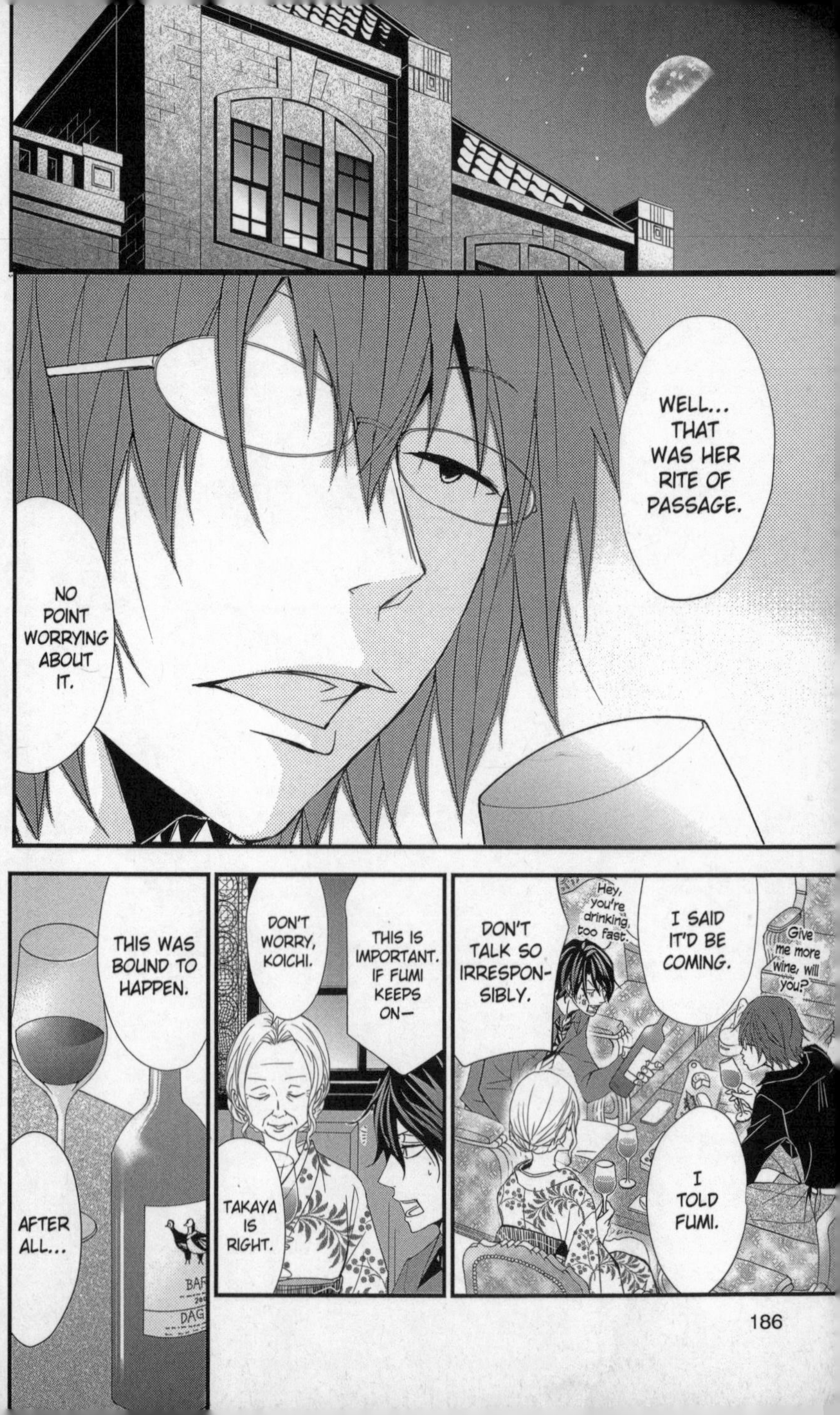
WELL... THAT WAS HER RITE OF PASSAGE.
NO POINT WORRYING ABOUT IT.
Give me more wine, will you?
I SAID IT'D BE COMING.
Hey, you're drinking too fast.
DON'T TALK SO IRRESPONSIBLY.
I TOLD FUMI.
THIS IS IMPORTANT. IF FUMI KEEPS ON—
DON'T WORRY, KOICHI.
TAKAYA IS RIGHT.
THIS WAS BOUND TO HAPPEN.
AFTER ALL...

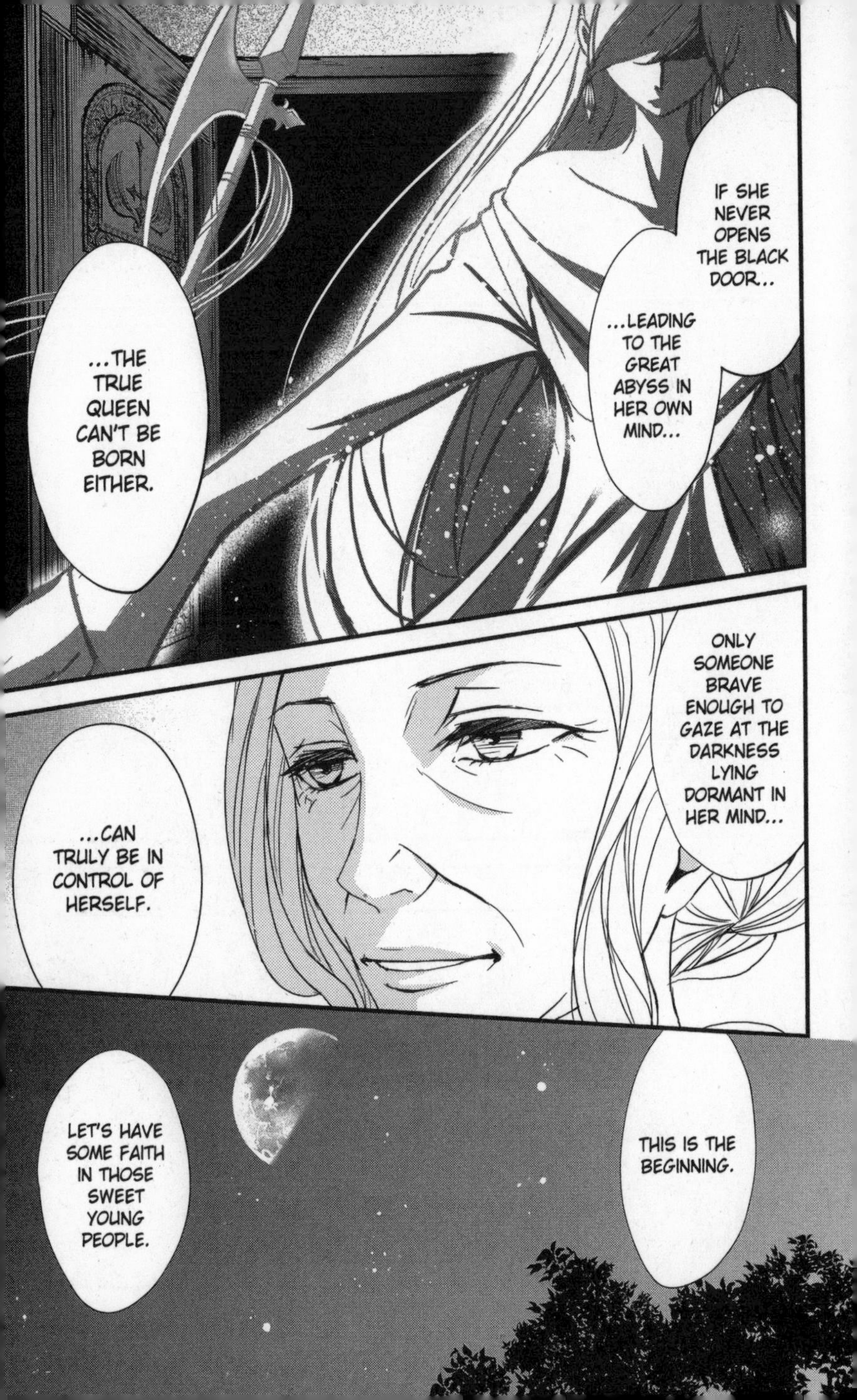
IF SHE NEVER OPENS THE BLACK DOOR...
...LEADING TO THE GREAT ABYSS IN HER OWN MIND...
...THE TRUE QUEEN CAN'T BE BORN EITHER.
ONLY SOMEONE BRAVE ENOUGH TO GAZE AT THE DARKNESS LYING DORMANT IN HER MIND...
...CAN TRULY BE IN CONTROL OF HERSELF.
THIS IS THE BEGINNING.
LET'S HAVE SOME FAITH IN THOSE SWEET YOUNG PEOPLE.

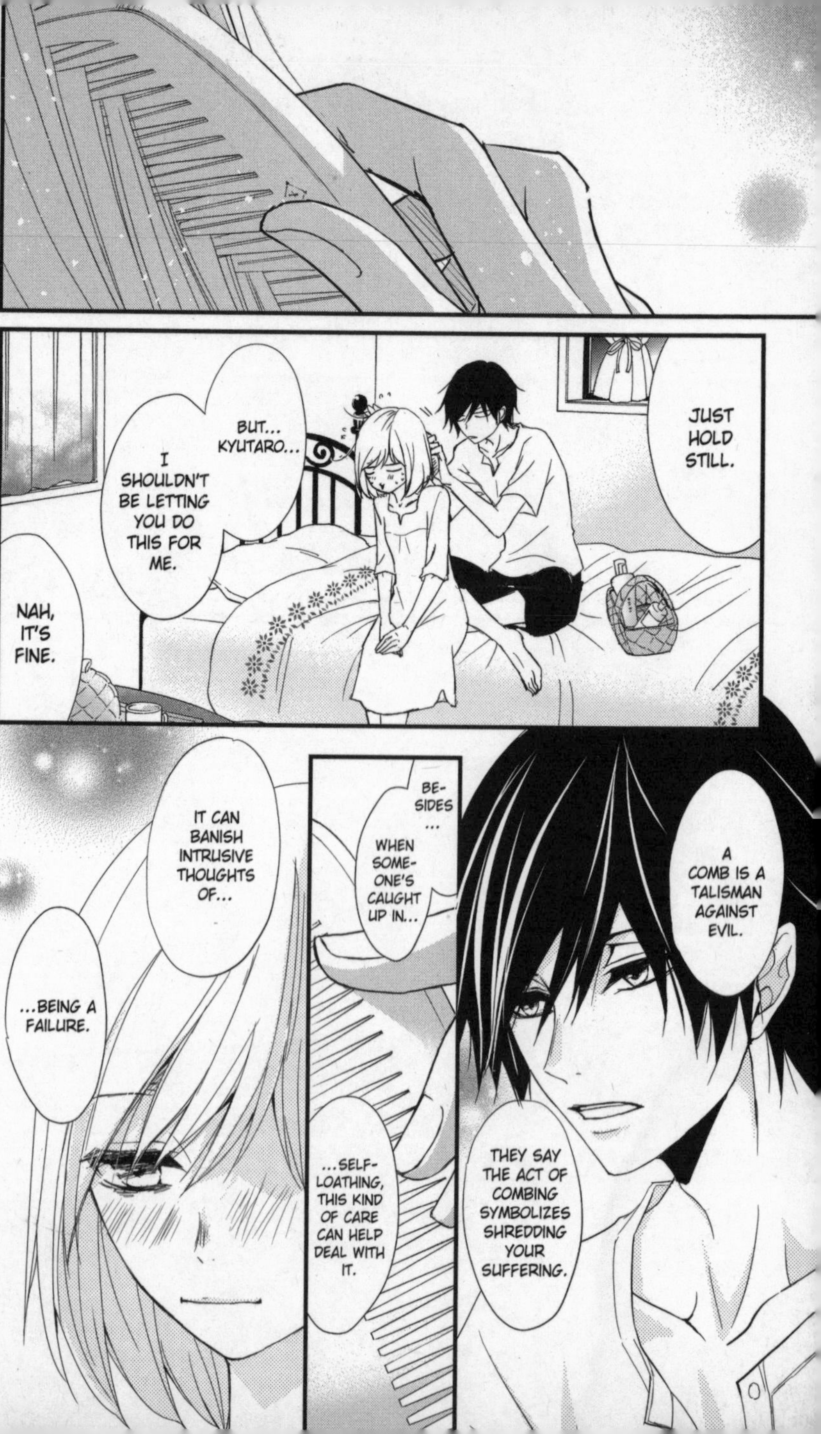
JUST HOLD STILL.
BUT... KYUTARO... I SHOULDN'T BE LETTING YOU DO THIS FOR ME.
NAH, IT'S FINE.
A COMB IS A TALISMAN AGAINST EVIL.
THEY SAY THE ACT OF COMBING SYMBOLIZES SHREDDING YOUR SUFFERING.
BE-SIDES...
WHEN SOME-ONE'S CAUGHT UP IN...
...SELF-LOATHING, THIS KIND OF CARE CAN HELP DEAL WITH IT.
IT CAN BANISH INTRUSIVE THOUGHTS OF...
...BEING A FAILURE.

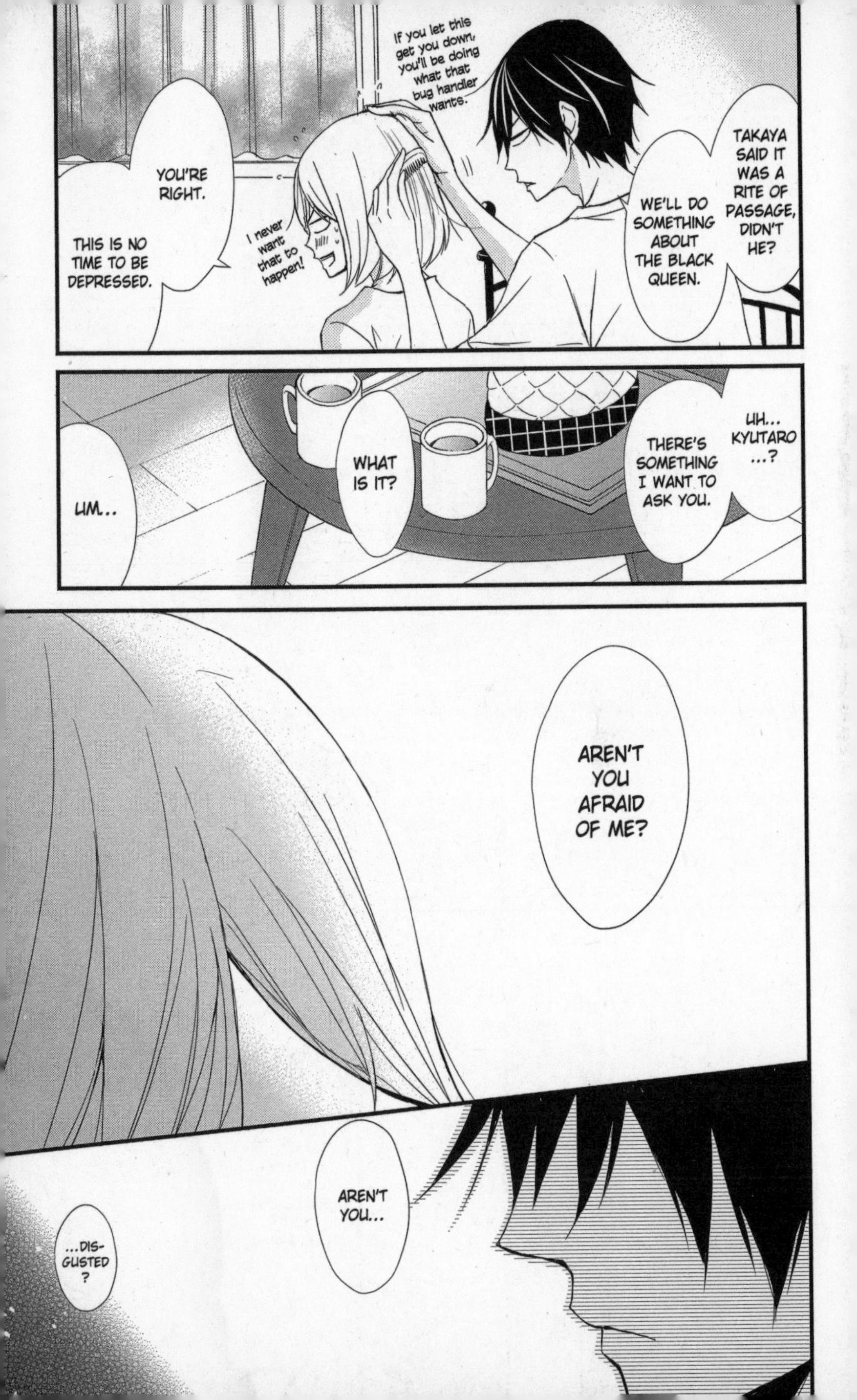
TAKAYA SAID IT WAS A RITE OF PASSAGE, DIDN'T HE?
WE'LL DO SOMETHING ABOUT THE BLACK QUEEN.
If you let this get you down, you'll be doing what that bug handler wants.
I never want that to happen!
YOU'RE RIGHT.
THIS IS NO TIME TO BE DEPRESSED.
UH... KYUTARO ...?
THERE'S SOMETHING I WANT TO ASK YOU.
WHAT IS IT?
UM...
AREN'T YOU AFRAID OF ME?
AREN'T YOU...
...DIS-GUSTED ?

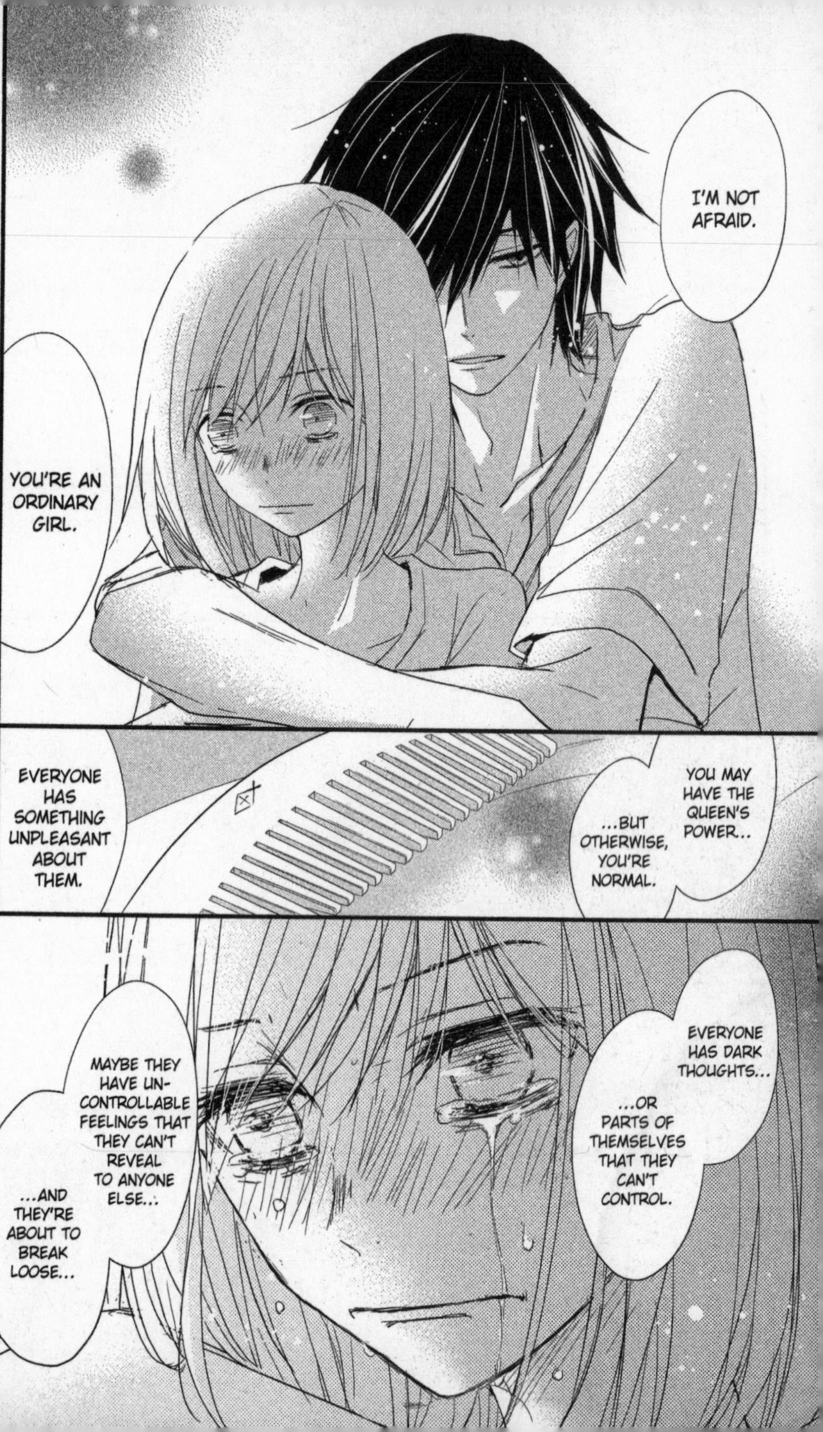
I'M NOT AFRAID.
YOU'RE AN ORDINARY GIRL.
YOU MAY HAVE THE QUEEN'S POWER...
...BUT OTHERWISE, YOU'RE NORMAL.
EVERYONE HAS SOMETHING UNPLEASANT ABOUT THEM.
EVERYONE HAS DARK THOUGHTS...
...OR PARTS OF THEMSELVES THAT THEY CAN'T CONTROL.
MAYBE THEY HAVE UN-CONTROLLABLE FEELINGS THAT THEY CAN'T REVEAL TO ANYONE ELSE...
...AND THEY'RE ABOUT TO BREAK LOOSE...

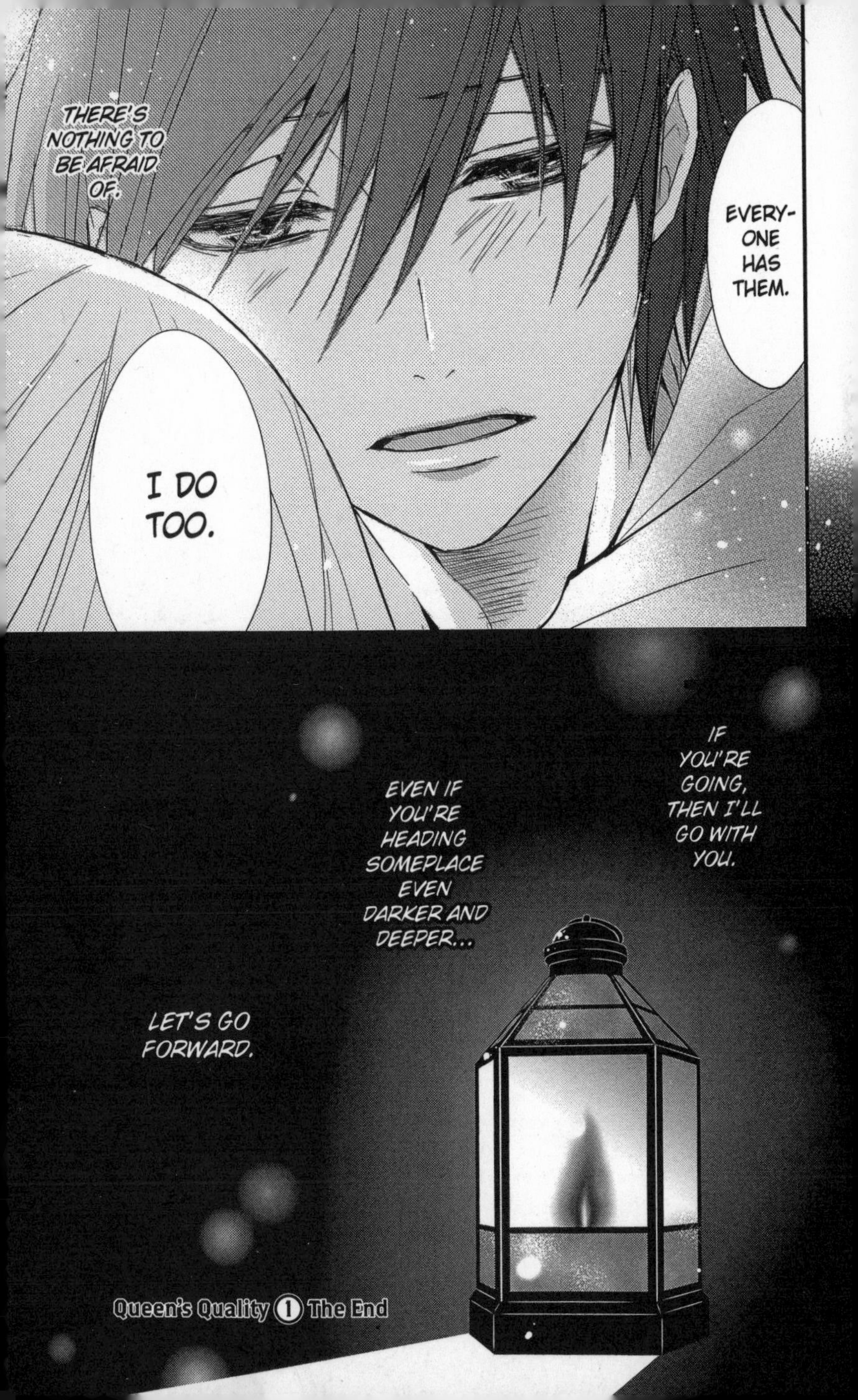
EVERY-ONE HAS THEM.
THERE'S NOTHING TO BE AFRAID OF.
I DO TOO.
IF YOU'RE GOING, THEN I'LL GO WITH YOU.
EVEN IF YOU'RE HEADING SOMEPLACE EVEN DARKER AND DEEPER...
LET'S GO FORWARD.
Queen's Quality 1 The End

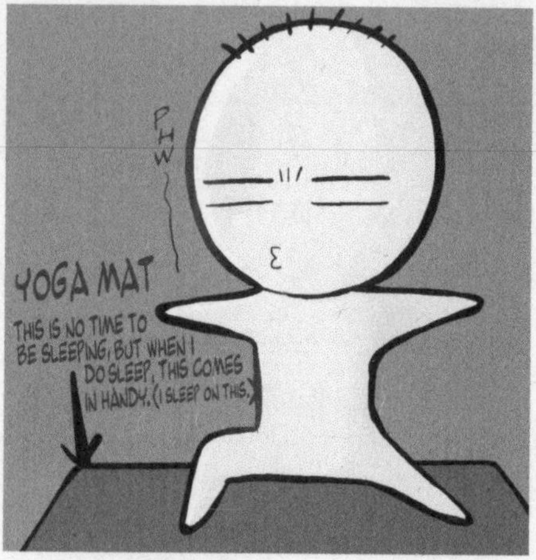
PHW~
YOGA MAT
THIS IS NO TIME TO BE SLEEPING, BUT WHEN I DO SLEEP, THIS COMES IN HANDY. (I SLEEP ON THIS.)

For some reason I often get told that I look like I do yoga. I'd like to take lessons. I wonder if there are any yoga poses that would make me draw manga faster.

—Kyousuke Motomi

Author Bio

Born on August 1, Kyousuke Motomi debuted in *Deluxe Betsucomi* with *Hetakuso Kyupiddo* (No Good Cupid) in 2002. She is the creator of *Dengeki Daisy*, *Beast Master* and *QQ Sweeper*, all available in North America from VIZ Media. Motomi enjoys sleeping, tea ceremonies and reading Haruki Murakami.

Queen's Quality

Vol. 1
Shojo Beat Edition

STORY AND ART BY
KYOUSUKE MOTOMI

QUEEN'S QUALITY Vol. 1
by Kyousuke MOTOMI
© 2016 Kyousuke MOTOMI
All rights reserved.
Original Japanese edition published by SHOGAKUKAN.
English translation rights in the United States of America, Canada, the United
Kingdom, Ireland, Australia and New Zealand arranged with SHOGAKUKAN.

ORIGINAL DESIGN/Chie SATO+Bay Bridge Studio

English Adaptation/Ysabet Reinhardt MacFarlane
Translation/JN Productions
Touch-Up Art & Lettering/Mark McMurray
Design/Julian [JR] Robinson
Editor/Amy Yu

Printed in the U.S.A.

Published by VIZ Media, LLC.
P.O. Box 77010
San Francisco, CA 94107

10 9 8 7 6 5 4 3 2 1
First printing, September 2017

viz.com   shojobeat.com

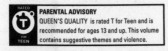

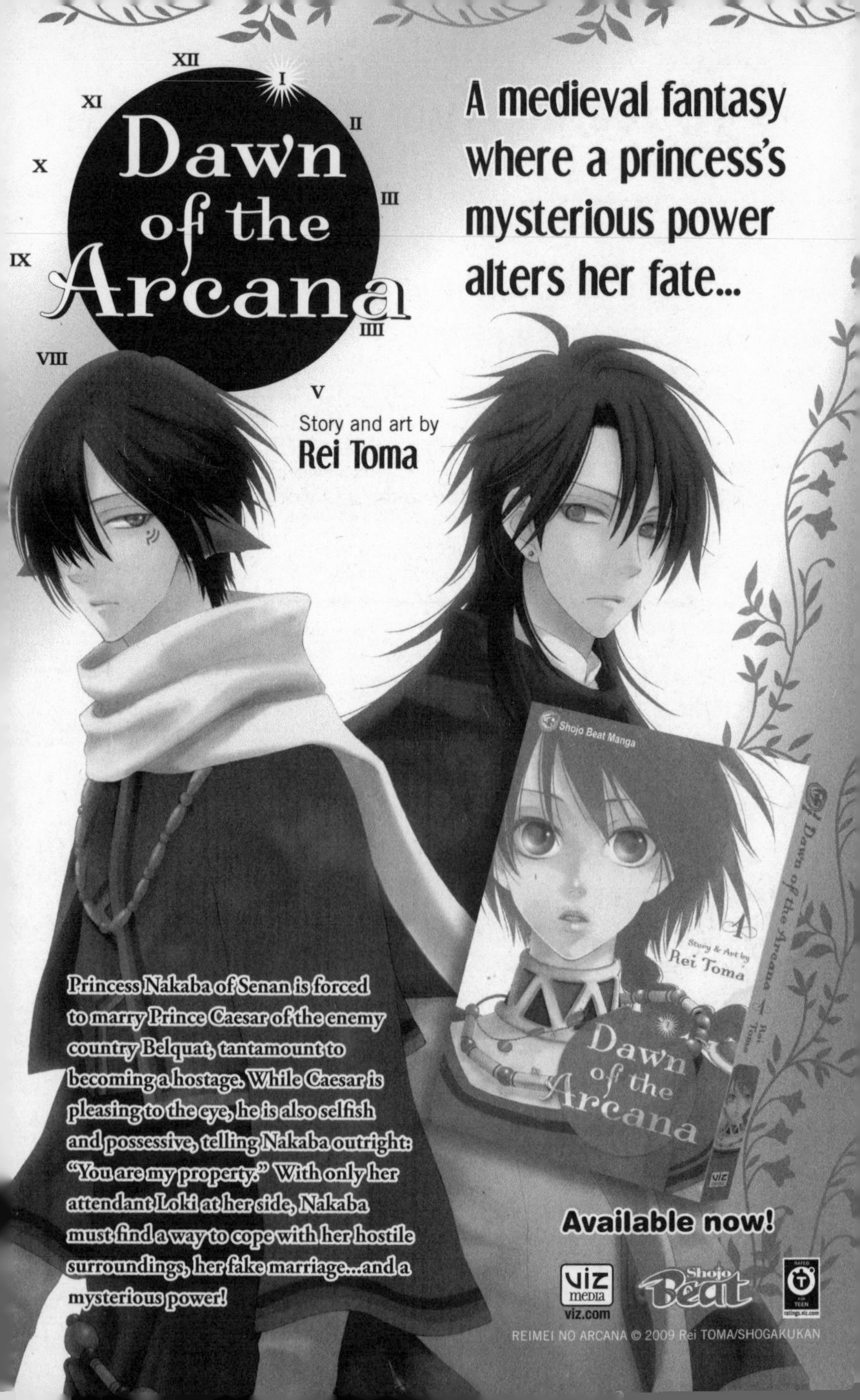
Dawn of the Arcana
A medieval fantasy where a princess's mysterious power alters her fate...
Story and art by
Rei Toma
Shojo Beat Manga
1
Story & Art by
Rei Toma
Dawn of the Arcana
Princess Nakaba of Senan is forced to marry Prince Caesar of the enemy country Belquat, tantamount to becoming a hostage. While Caesar is pleasing to the eye, he is also selfish and possessive, telling Nakaba outright: "You are my property." With only her attendant Loki at her side, Nakaba must find a way to cope with her hostile surroundings, her fake marriage...and a mysterious power!
Available now!
VIZ media
viz.com
Shojo Beat
RATED T FOR TEEN
ratings.viz.com
REIMEI NO ARCANA © 2009 Rei TOMA/SHOGAKUKAN

Honey Blood

Story & Art by Miko Mitsuki

Hinata can't help but be drawn to Junya, but could it be that he's actually a vampire?

When a girl at her school is attacked by what seems to be a vampire, high school student Hinata Sorazono refuses to believe that vampires even exist. But then she meets her new neighbor, Junya Tokinaga, the author of an incredibly popular vampire romance novel… Could it be that Junya's actually a vampire—and worse yet, the culprit?!

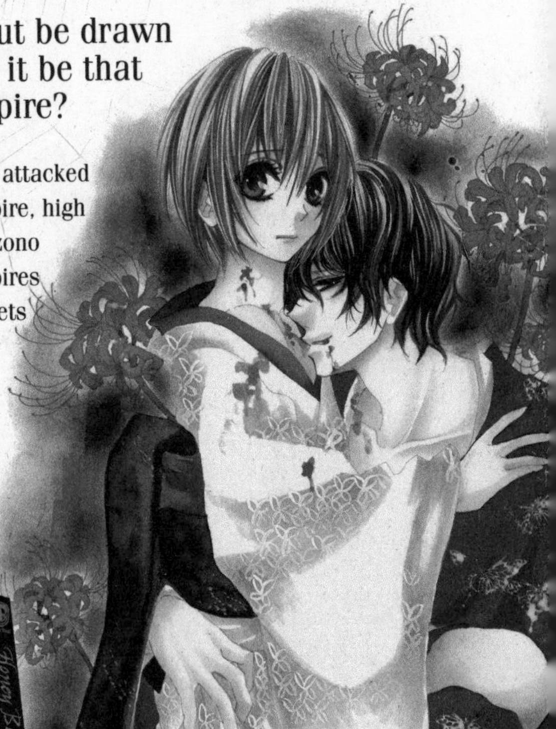

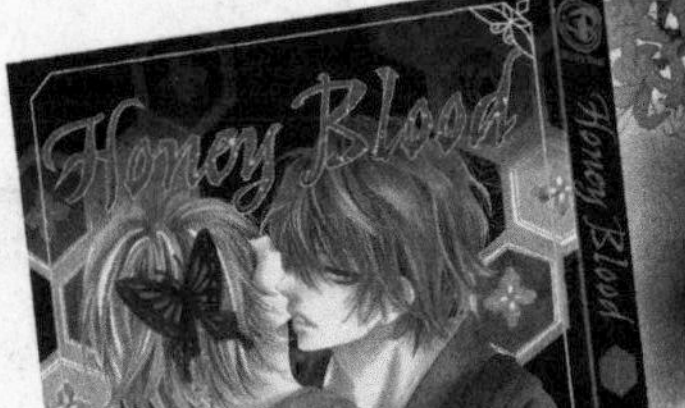
Honey Blood
Honey Blood
Miko Mitsuki
Story & Art by Miko Mitsuki

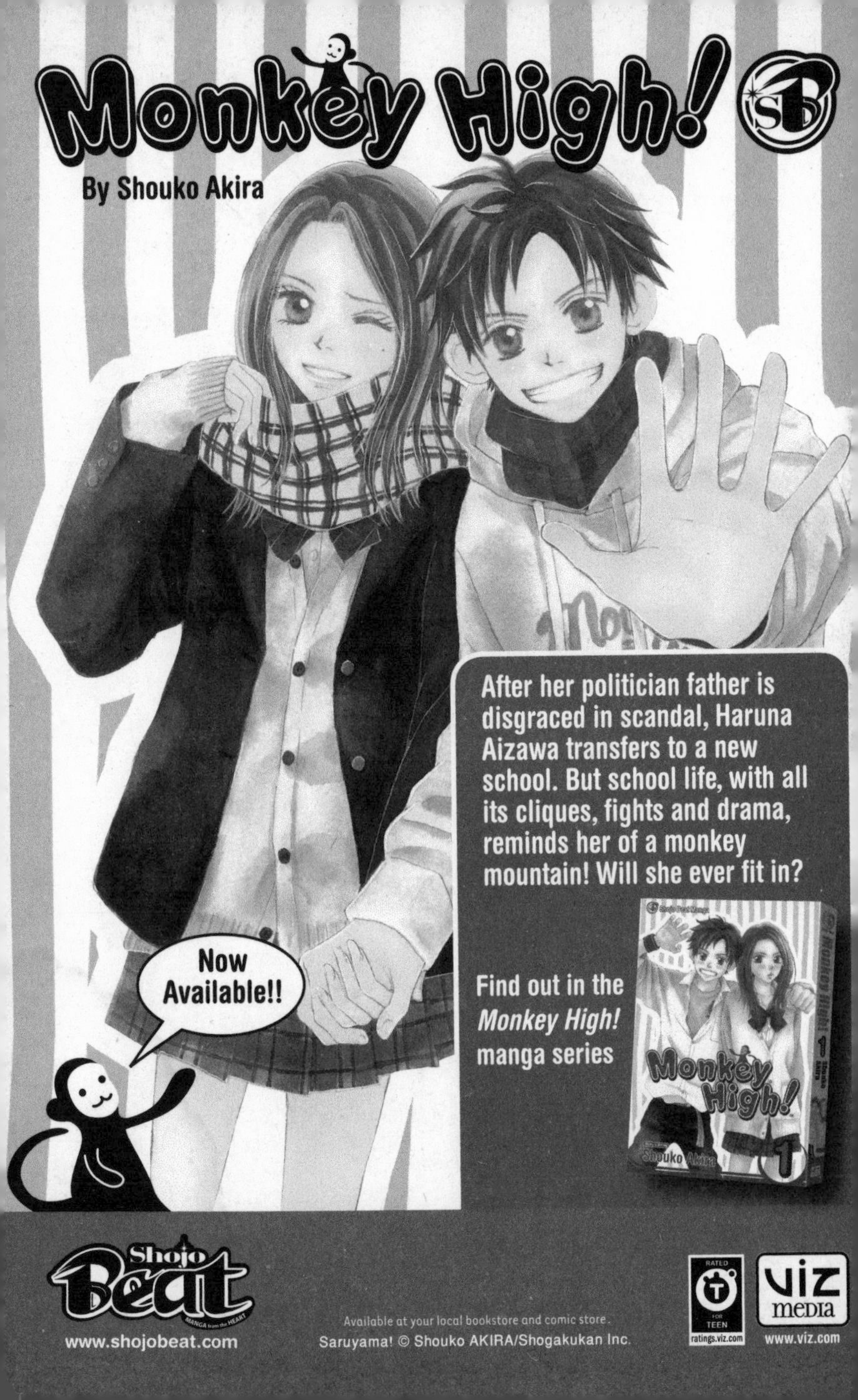

Monkey High!
By Shouko Akira
After her politician father is disgraced in scandal, Haruna Aizawa transfers to a new school. But school life, with all its cliques, fights and drama, reminds her of a monkey mountain! Will she ever fit in?
Now Available!!
Find out in the *Monkey High!* manga series
Shojo Beat
www.shojobeat.com
Available at your local bookstore and comic store.
Saruyama! © Shouko AKIRA/Shogakukan Inc.
RATED T FOR TEEN
ratings.viz.com
VIZ media
www.viz.com

Honey
So Sweet

Story and Art by Amu Meguro

Little did Nao Kogure realize back in middle school that when she left an umbrella and a box of bandages in the rain for injured delinquent Taiga Onise that she would meet him again in high school. Nao wants nothing to do with the gruff and frightening Taiga, but he suddenly presents her with a huge bouquet of flowers and asks her to date him—with marriage in mind! Is Taiga really so scary, or is he a sweetheart in disguise?

This is the Last Page!

It's true: In keeping with the original Japanese comic format, this book reads from right to left—so action, sound effects and word balloons are completely reversed. This preserves the orientation of the original artwork—plus, it's fun! Check out the diagram shown here to get the hang of things, and then turn to the other side of the book to get started!

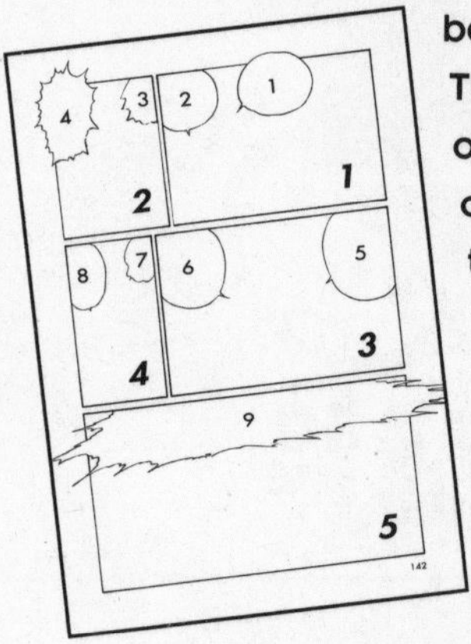
1
1
2
3
4
2
5
6
3
7
8
4
9
5
142

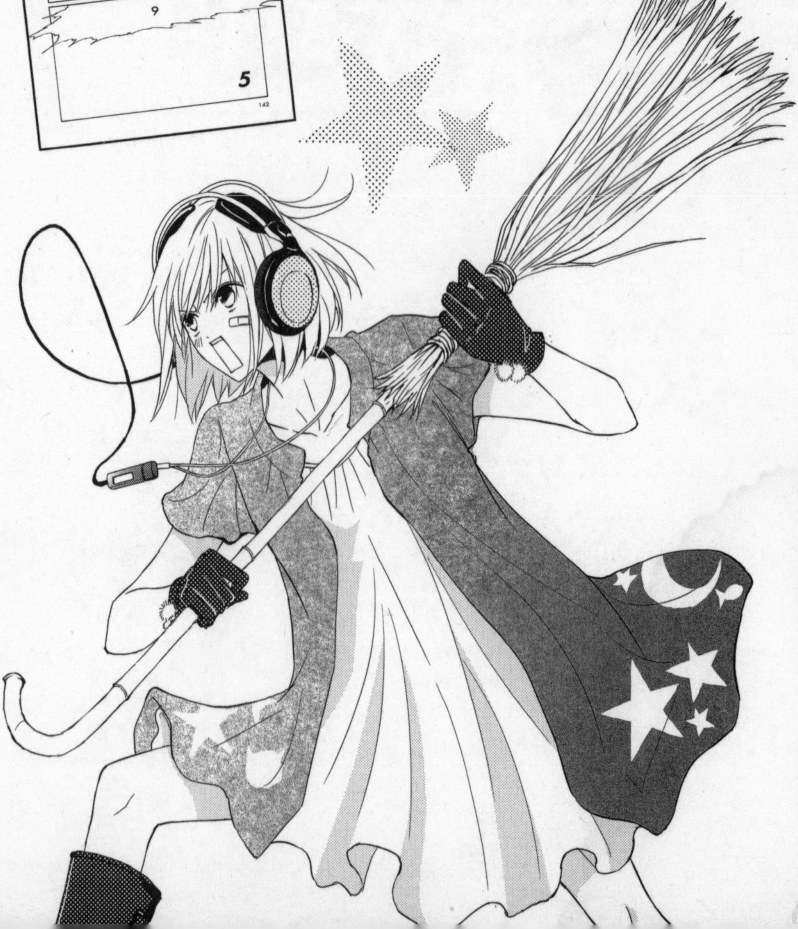